Aralsk

KAZAKHSTAN
UZBEKISTAN

Moynaq

O   MILES   100

O   KILOMETERS   100

Chasing *the* Sea

Chasing *the* Sea

BEING A NARRATIVE OF A JOURNEY THROUGH UZBEKISTAN,

Including *Descriptions* of *Life Therein,*

Culminating with an *Arrival* at the *Aral Sea,*

the World's Worst Man-Made Ecological Catastrophe

In one Volume

TOM BISSELL

Pantheon Books
New York

A version of chapter seven appeared in *Harper's Magazine* and *Best American Travel
Writing 2003*. (Boston, MA: Houghton Mifflin).

Grateful acknowledgment is made for permission to reprint lyrics from the following:
"The Real Slim Shady" (words and music by Tom Coster Jr., Eminem, Andre Young,
and Mike Elizondo) Copyright © 2000 by Ensign Music Corporation o/b/o Eight Mile
Style Music (BMI), Blotter Music (ASCAP), and Elvis Mambo Music (ASCAP) and
Strawberry Blonde Music (BMI)/Administered by BUG. All rights for Eight Mile Style
Music administered by Ensign Music Corporation. All Rights Reserved. Reprinted by
permission of Hal Leonard Corporation and Bug Music.

Library of Congress Cataloging-in-Publication Data

Bissell, Tom, 1974–
Chasing the sea / Tom Bissell.
p. cm.
Includes index.
ISBN 0-375-42130-0
1. Uzbekistan—Description and travel. 2. Bissell, Tom, 1974—
Journeys—Uzbekistan. 3. Environmental degradation—Aral Sea Region (Uzbekistan
and Kazakhstan). 4. Nature—Effect of human beings on—
Aral Sea Region (Uzbekistan and Kazakhstan). 5. Aral Sea Region (Uzbekistan and
Kazakhstan)—History. I. Title.

DK 944.B57 2003
915.8704'86—dc21   2003042032

www.pantheonbooks.com

Book design by Johanna S. Roebas

Printed in the United States of America

First Edition

9 8 7 6 5 4 3 2 1

THIS BOOK IS FOR:

Philip Caputo, Doug Fix, Larry Leffel, and Bret Lott;

and for my parents, all of them

I told the Turk he was a gentleman.
I told the Russian that his Tartar veins
Bled pure Parisian ichor; and he purred.
The Congress doesn't purr. I think it swears.
You're young—you'll swear too ere you've reached the end.
The End! God help you, if there be a God.

—RUDYARD KIPLING, "One Viceroy Resigns"

Contents

Acknowledgments

Thanks to Liz Nagle, Johno and Shelly Bissell, Les and Jeanne Rose, Leslie Rose, Dick Burroughs, Diane Wakoski, James McClintock, John Alford, Andrew Miller, Josh and Irina Kendall, Webster Younce, Erika Krouse, Gabrielle Josephson, Bea Hogan, Kent Korte, Bo King, Jeremy Wrubel, Mike Jurmu, Graham and Rima Karlin, Jeff Alexander, Rob and Sakura Keast, Noah Mass, Christina Lem, Glenn Kenny, Boris Fishman, Katy Hope, Leslie Ware, Edwin Barber, Gerald Howard, Robert Weil, Starling Lawrence, John Sterling, Jennifer Barth, Jonathan Franzen, Kathy Chetkovich, John Beckman, Robert Gatewood, Lorin Stein, Lisa Fugard, Tom Paine, Valerie Brock, Neil Gordon, Adrienne Miller, Mark Cohen, Lewis Lapham, Roger Hodge, Charis Conn, Donovan Hohn, Colin Harrison, Mary LaMotte, John Sullivan, Susan Burton, Ben Metcalf, Megan Hustad, Amber Hoover, Jennifer Jackson, Chrissy Rikkers, Fred Wiemer, Dan Frank, Heather Schroder, and Jenny Minton for faith, advice, encouragement, and, in some cases, much-needed employment.

Thanks to the staff of Peace Corps Uzbekistan. And of course thanks to Uzbekistan's Peace Corps volunteers, past and present. Private citizens are not under any obligation to talk to writers, and I am grateful to those volunteers who shared their time and thoughts with me. To preserve their privacy, I have changed many names and characteristics herein.

Bolshoye spasibo and *katta rakhmat* to my Russian, Uzbek, and Karakalpak friends, whose names and characteristics have (for more obvious reasons) also been changed. Their kindness and generosity are unforgettable.

Thanks to Ian Small and the Tashkent and Nukus staff of Médicins Sans Frontières.

Thanks to Imodium A-D.

Author's Note

I am not a scholar. My knowledge of the culture, history, and people of Central Asia in general and Uzbekistan in particular falls far short of comprehensive, and what I have learned has been thanks to the guidance of many other authorities, though any mistakes in what follows are my own. Furthermore, my working knowledge of the Russian language has faded to functional nonexistence, even if I was at one time a devoted pupil of what Vladimir Nabokov once witheringly described as the "*Kak-vy-pozhivaete-ya-pozhivayu-khorosho*" (How-are-you-I-am-fine) school of Russian speaking. My knowledge of Uzbek, a branch of the Altaic language family that includes Turkish, is stronger, though I suspect my ideal conversational partner would be an unusually bright Uzbek toddler. How and why I came to write this book deserve some explanation.

As a United States Peace Corps volunteer, I served as an English teacher in the Republic of Uzbekistan in the mid-1990s. I left after seven months, or about nineteen months short of my expected stay. This is called, rather killingly, an "early termination of service." My reasons for leaving were emotional and complicated. In other words, I lost my mind. But the strange, savage beauty of the country stayed with me, and shortly after I returned to the United States, I found myself writing short stories set in Uzbekistan. I was done with the place, but, axiomatically, it was not done with me.

I have never regretted leaving Uzbekistan. In fact, I soon profited by doing so, lucking in to a position at a New York publishing firm—a world that would, for most of my twenties, become my career. My premature departure from Uzbekistan is, nonetheless, probably the single biggest failure of my life. It is with a peculiar convergence of emotion that one looks back upon a failure that, as it turns out, had no meaningfully negative *personal* consequences at all. It leads to a heart-nibbling sort of reflection that leaves one racked with a sense of inadequacy difficult to explain to oneself, much less anyone else. This is the best explanation I have for why, no matter how many months or years I wedged between myself and my experience in Uzbekistan, my gathering obsession with this odd, fascinating, and in some ways unwelcoming section of the world soon burned beyond its sandy perimeters. Reading about Uzbekistan in the *Economist* or in one-paragraph acorns occasionally squirreled away in the *New York Times* was no longer enough. I wanted to go back. What began as a proposed magazine piece for *Harper's Magazine* about the Aral Sea, one of the largest ecological disasters in the world, soon became this book.

What follows is not history, though it makes use of history and attempts to honor it. It is not straight reportage, either. It is not a memoir, a form I am not typically inclined to admire, especially when written by people under the age of thirty. It is not a travel guide, a form to which Uzbekistan has already been excellently subject (see Calum MacLeod and Bradley Mayhew's superb *Uzbekistan: The Golden Road to Samarkand*). I did not visit nearly enough places in Uzbekistan (Khiva! How on earth did I manage to miss *Khiva*!) to write a proper travel book, nor did I journey there with that intent. This book is finally and most emphatically not "an impressionistic record" of what I encountered. Impressionism, in its literary mask, not only fails to note the emperor's nudity but quite often provides him with a blurry new set of clothes—allowing George Bernard Shaw, for instance, to tell us all what a topping chap Joseph Stalin really was. What I hope this book provides is a personal, idiosyncratic account of a place and a people and the problems and conflicts they share—problems most Americans, let us pray, will never experience firsthand. Perhaps it might also stand as a simpler story of how a faraway land once caused one young man to unravel and, years later, helped him find and reassemble a mislaid, broken part of himself.

Most of all, I hope I have written a testimony to the perils of ignoring what, as a boy, I knew as "the larger world." When I began this book, I found sad significance in the fact that only a handful of general-interest books about Central Asia and Uzbekistan were in print. Now, of course, this has changed, much as in England in the mid-1800s, when the bloody events unfolding in the region kept bookstalls packed with titles promising Central Asian intrigue and adventure. Ideally, the writing now pouring out of Central Asia will forestall future Western neglect of this perennially ignored region.

The world, finally, is no longer large, and to ignore it likely requires more effort than simply to take notice. Now that we have suffered this truth, and suffered it deeply, we might take care to remember how comparatively fortunate we are as Americans. Any attempt to recognize American "luckiness" will, I do not doubt, terrify many, anger some, and offer others mind-cleansing reassurance. Three things this recognition is not, and should never be: a call to arms, a lullaby, or a reason to stay home.

T.C.B.
New York City
October 10, 2002

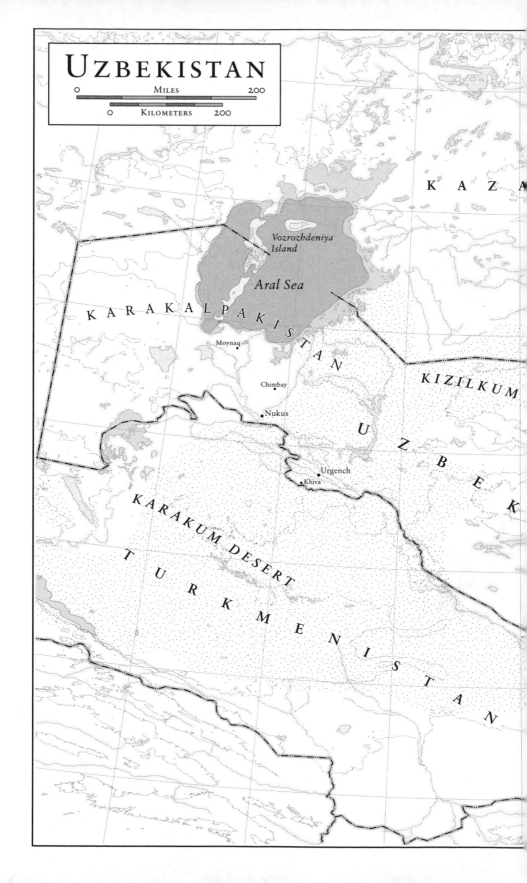

UZBEKISTAN

MILES
0   200

KILOMETERS
0   200

K A Z A

Vozrozhdeniya
Island

Aral Sea

K A R A K A L P A K I S T A N

Moynaq

KIZILKUM

Chimbay

Nukus

U Z B E K

Urgench

Khiva

K A R A K U M D E S E R T

T U R K M E N I S T A N

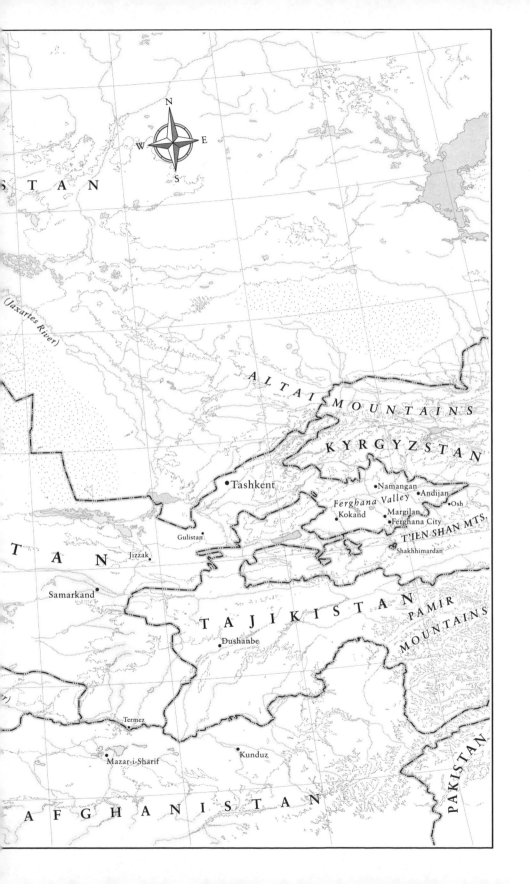

Partial Chronology

632	Mohammed dies
ca. 710	First Central Asian cities fall to Arab Muslims
751	Battle of Talas
819	Samanid rule begins
999	Karakhanids depose Samanids, rule Transoxiana
1005	Last Samanid murdered
ca. 1167	Temujin born
1206	Jenghiz Khan recognized as leader of Turko-Mongol peoples
1212	Last Karakhanid forced from power by Mongols
1219	Golden Horde's occupation of Russia begins
1220	Jenghiz Khan demolishes Samarkand, Bukhara
1227	Jenghiz Khan dies
ca. 1320	Marco Polo travels through Central Asia
1336	Timur born
1370	Timur ascendent
1405	Timur dies
ca. 1445	Uzbeks push into Central Asia
1447	Ulugbek assumes Timurid throne
1449	Ulugbek assassinated

1480	Golden Horde's occupation of Russia ends
1500	Shaybani Khan takes power in Transoxiana
1502	Last Khan of Golden Horde dies
1506	Timurid dynasty ends
1510	Shaybani Khan killed
1533	Ubaidullah Khan takes power in Bukhara
ca. 1580	Discovery of alternate trade routes to China begins to damage Central Asian trade
1599	Collapse of Shaybanid line
1717	Peter the Great's Khivan expedition slaughtered
1753	Mangits take power in Bukhara
1812	Napolean defeated; hostilities between Russia and England begin
1832	Alexander Burnes visits Bukhara
1834	Alexander Burnes's *Travels into Bokhara* published
1839	British invade Afghanistan
1841	Retreating British slaughtered in Afghanistan
1842	Stoddard and Conolly escape from Bukhara
1860	U.S. Civil War begins, cutting off Russian cotton supply
	Nasrullah Khan dies
1865	Russians capture Tashkent
1868	Russians capture Samarkand
	Bukhara made protectorate of Russia
1871	*Middlemarch* published
1873	Slavery abolished in Central Asia
	Russians capture Khiva
1876	Russians capture Kokand Khanate, rename it Ferghana
1907	Anglo-Russian Convention—the Great Game's official end
1917	Bolshevik Revolution
	Russian Civil War begins
1919	Anti-Bolshevik uprising in Tashkent
1924	Russian Civil War ends
	Central Asian Soviet republics created
	Lenin dies
1928	Ferghana Valley *basmachi* uprising finally crushed by Soviets
ca. 1930	Collectivization begins
	Central Asia sealed off by Stalin
1931	Tashkent named capital of Uzbek SSR

Partial Chronology

Chasing *the* Sea

One

No English

Anyone parted from his land will weep seven years. Whoever is parted from his tribe will weep until he dies.

—CENTRAL ASIAN PROVERB

APRIL 2001

The night was hot or cold, depending on where one stood. In this it was not unlike swimming in the ocean and feeling across one's belly an amniotic warmth followed immediately by a freezing underwater gale. I paced around on the tarmac, examining the plane that had touched us down safely in Tashkent, the capital of Uzbekistan. The flight in was much fuller than I had expected, and my fellow passengers had disembarked. Most were, like me, standing on the tarmac and looking at the plane. It was dark, and there was not much else to look at. The plane was a fine gold-and-black Lufthansa jumbo jet. Lufthansa was the least dicey airline to fly into Tashkent, though Uzbekistan Airways, the national airline, was also quite good—internationally. Uzbekistan Airways's international flights employed Boeing and British-made jets easily as splendid as Lufthansa's. Uzbekistan was the only former Soviet republic other than Russia to have ever been allowed regular direct flights into the United States, something of which it was deservedly proud. On internal flights, however, Uzbekistan Airways sealed its passengers inside shaky old Russian-made Aeroflot propjets. One rumor I hoped to confirm on this trip was that, before takeoff on these internal flights, Uzbekistan

3

Airways stewardesses poured everyone a heaping shot of vodka, including the captain. Including themselves.

Everything smelled hotly of fuel. It was as though we were downwind from a grounded F-15 with its engine at full burn. I remembered this smell. The last time I had smelled Tashkent was as a freshly arrived Peace Corps volunteer with hopes of teaching the natives English. I was not much of a traveler at the time. I used words like "natives." This was five years previous.

We had arrived in Tashkent at night. In 1996, only five years after Uzbekistan declared its independence from the Soviet Union, Tashkent's airport seemed ominously dark. When we landed and rolled toward the terminal, I saw that some of the runway lights were flickering. A few were burned out completely. Three-wheeled trucks of strange vehicular provenance sat abandoned along the runway. I remember that some of them were on fire, but this could be an enhanced memory. We deplaned and waited in clubbed silence on the tarmac. After a while a rickety metal tram arrived to haul us to the terminal. Inside the tram it was cattle-car dark and cold. It was a terrible joke—not mildly funny or even distracting—when, as the tram lurched toward the terminal, I began humming the theme to *Schindler's List*.

Now I waited for that same tram, upon that same tarmac, at that same airport. I looked around at my fellow passengers. Every pair of eyes shone with the glassy overlay of the seven-hour flight from Frankfurt. Every face was thick with sleeplessness. Many blue-jeaned and sweat-shirted Germans idled around. I leaned over and asked a British man with whom I had chatted a bit on the plane, "What's with the Germans?" and rolling his eyes he answered, "Tour groups." Three tour groups, in fact. It seemed that, for reasons unknown, Germans love Central Asia. I later learned that they are, per capita, its most frequent tourists. Lingering on the crowd's edges were several slumped Uzbek or Turkish businessmen. They seemed tired, dignified, and quietly unhappy. I looked around. No one, with the exception of the Germans, appeared very happy, not even the young Russian-speaking Uzbeks in jean jackets and stylish black shoes carrying bags of duty-free booze and cigarettes. They looked over at me with lavish pouts and fading sullen eyes, still fried from having spent their weekend discothequeing in some glamorous international capital. Not typical citizens of Uzbekistan, needless to say. I wondered if they were government ministers' kids, seedlings of the *vlasti* (the unopposable few who controlled Soviet politics, culture, and society, and who in most of the former Soviet republics survived wholly intact), or the spawn of the Uzbek mafiya. Before I left on this trip, an Uzbek friend now living in Kentucky had sprung upon me the following koan: The economy in Uzbekistan was much, much worse today than in 1996, he said, but people were living better. I spent several nights attempting to comb the logic snarls from that sentence. Now, looking at nineteen-year-olds loaded up with *importny* loot, I had an idea of what he meant.

Those who were living better today were living better than anyone here had ever lived, better even than the Soviet bosses who in the 1970s had cruised around Tashkent in black Volgas with gray-curtained windows hiding the whores in the back seat. But ten years of corrupt, hybridized capitalismoid development was slowly teaching Uzbekistan's people that such lifestyles did not exist for those who had no "in," no clan, no muscle. No matter what average citizens of Uzbekistan did, no matter how good or honest or hardworking they were, the prestige-goods economy would remain beyond reach.

Two trams pulled up, their red running lights blinking. The tram I labored aboard was no cold, dark cattle car but a brightly lit Cobus 3000 with comfortable cushioned seats. It pleased me to see that Tashkent's airport seemed less eschatological than I remembered. Some of the buildings near the main terminal still looked slightly shelled, but several new buildings were going up.

The Germans had annexed Tram One, and Tram Two seemed drab in its silence. Some Russian was spoken, quietly, behind me. I turned. A young Uzbek mother in a leather jacket crouched and played peekaboo with her daughter. Her husband, a straphanging Uzbek wearing a gold watch, looked down at them and smiled with weary contentment. A cell phone blipped Mozart. Several people reached into their pockets, but only one withdrew. He was large, thick-necked, shaven-headed, Slavic. He glanced at the number on the phone's LCD, frowned, and put the phone back into his pocket. It rang a few more times and stopped.

Next to me was a young man wearing blue jeans and a flea-market dress shirt the color and texture of a tennis ball. His birdish thinness ceded a strange prominence to his otherwise normal-sized Adam's apple. The piping of his wraparound insectoid sunglasses was a bright iguana green. His chopped hair was purposefully messy. Everything about him suggested: American. He was enjoying a pose of which traveling Americans seem fond. This pose broadcast, roughly, *I am an American, and you are an American, and we are both in a strange place. Despite that, I am not going to speak to you or make myself available in any way.* I wondered if he was a Peace Corps volunteer fresh from a reefer-fueled jaunt across Thailand. Maybe he was an employ of one of the hipper agencies like Human Rights Watch. Maybe he was the "cool" Christian in some evangelical platoon spreading the Word to Central Asians. But he was returning to what he regarded as home—that much was obvious. He had the careless look of someone comfortable enough in a foreign environment not to worry anymore about looking like he belonged.

"Hey," I said.

He looked over at me. I could see nothing behind his tinted lenses. His mouth did not move.

"Do you live in Tashkent?"

He shook his head. His Adam's apple bobbed, then sank, its transit appearing somehow painful.

"Do you work here?"

"No English," he said suddenly.

"I'm sorry?"

He unplugged from himself a small flesh-colored earpiece. For the first time I heard the tinny sound of synthesized R&B. "No English," he said again. That everything about this young man suggested American should have been the first thing to tell me he was not an American.

"Oh," I told him. "Sorry."

He replugged his earpiece. "No problem."

A few moments later the tram stopped with an angry hydraulic hiss. The doors levered open. We filed into a long gray hallway that fed into the terminal. Tram One had beaten us here and already the end of the tunnel was clogged with humanity. Customs. Uzbekistan had for a time been one of the most difficult former Soviet republics to get into. This was not xenophobia. Rather, it reflected a long, complicated ignorance of how the mechanics of international travel were handled. Stalin had from the early 1930s until his death in 1953 sealed off Central Asia not only to other nations but to the Soviet people themselves. The legendarily stalwart adventurer Gustav Krist said in the 1930s that he "would sooner pay a call on the Devil and his mother-in-law in Hell" than travel through Central Asia without the proper papers. Travel here during that time often resulted in tragedy. Post-Stalin, there were two types of visitors to Uzbekistan: young banana-republic Communists from the Afro, Arab, and Asian worlds of Successful Socialist Modernization, who were flown to Tashkent, the New Showcase City of Modern Communism, in order to witness What the Future Held; and those few tourists who decided to endure a journey in this isolated, wildly unpredictable part of the world. The latter were almost always a part of the Soviet travel agency Intourist's forced marches through what the authorities allowed to be recognized as Uzbekistan's cultural highlights (very little Islam, much anonymous peasant striving, and only the most architecturally unignorable mosques). Uzbekistan, prior to its independence, had rarely seen its consciousness touched by the notion of individual, unauthorized travel. Even Uzbektourism, the infinitely more relaxed successor to Intourist, had for a time in the early 1990s demanded that all visitors present an invitation from an Uzbek host and documented proof of one's HIV-negative status. But things had changed. Provided you were a citizen of the United States, entry into Uzbekistan now required nothing more than an easily obtainable visa.

After thirty minutes my turn came. My passport was kept in a black pouch I wore on a rope around my neck. I did this so no one would suspect that I had other, more important documents stashed upon my person, which, point of fact, I did. I approached the glass cube in which a young blond Russian customs official sat pianoing his fingers. I pushed my passport through the slot. The Russian retrieved it and cracked it open. He consulted the screen of his very, very old computer, then looked at me with coldly official eyes. That Russians have cold eyes is a cliché, but it is true. To gaze into this blond Russian's eyes was like being stabbed with an icicle. He was wearing the spruce-green fatigues of the Uzbek military, his breast stamped with Uzbekistan's tri-bar flag, a strange but not unpleasing combination of sky blue, white, and kelly green. An Islamic crescent was found in the top bar's far left corner. To see an unconditionally Slavic face in such proximity to one of Islam's most potent emblems was affecting. I smiled at him, hoping he would assume from the smile's vacuity my tranquil ignorance of the Russian language and ask me nothing.

I needed to avert the possibility of questions because I had $6,300 strapped in a money belt against my lower abdomen, only $4,000 of which was mine, only $500 of which I planned on declaring. Along with that $6,300 was a letter from a representative of the Committee to Protect Journalists (CPJ) to the wife of an Uzbek journalist I will call Omad, who was in the fourth year of his imprisonment by the Uzbek authorities for publishing a parody of the nutritionless prose style of Uzbekistan's president, Islam Abduganievich Karimov. Omad was also dying of cancer. I was to make contact with Omad's wife, give her the letter and $2,000, then quickly take my leave. We needed to meet somewhere private, as her phone and home were no doubt bugged, and we needed to meet in a way that would not tip off those monitoring her. Otherwise, minutes after I left, a "tax official" would show up. One complication: She was not expecting me. Another: I had absolutely no experience doing anything of this sort. CPJ had asked me to mule the money after learning of my trip through a friend of a friend, and I agreed mostly because of my respect for the organization. Adding to that, I had another letter stashed away in my luggage, this one from a Washington, D.C., lawyer to the daughter of an Uzbek official in the United States who was trying to defect—a difficult thing to do, it turns out, between nations with good diplomatic relations, as the United States and Uzbekistan enjoyed even in the spring of 2001. This potential defector was working stateside, on official business of the Uzbek government, and happened to be looking in to the possibility of becoming an American citizen when, two months before, his daughter, who lived in Tashkent, telephoned him in a panic. Men had just broken in to his apartment, she said hysterically, and burgled his papers and things.

He was accused, he later learned, of violating Article 159 of the Penal Code, i.e., "anticonstitutional activity," i.e., government overthrow. After a 1999 bombing in Tashkent, a miniaturized Great Terror was launched at observant Muslims and democratic reformers. Most were innocent, and many had been tortured into confessing various antigovernment plots. President Karimov had gone on a much-publicized hajj when polite Islam was fashionable in newly independent Central Asia, but a decade later he loathed and feared the faith, brutalizing even those Muslims unmoved by the idea of neo-Mohammedan rule. Democratic reformers did not fare much better, even though Karimov always cited democracy as the desired end point of Uzbekistan's development. Many others had fallen into this dragnet. When Uzbekistan's former ambassador to the United States became interested in defecting to America, for instance, his daughter, Nadira Khidoiatova, was soon arrested on drug-smuggling charges. Khidoiatova was pregnant, and under Uzbek law was therefore supposed to have been released on bond. The Uzbek authorities sidestepped this nicely by forcibly aborting her fetus. The former ambassador, for his part, now lived under protection in the United States.

This background is to provide some sense of the panic our own potential defector must have felt before going into hiding. He had made contact with a second-year law student at Georgetown, who was trying to figure out, pro bono, how his first and only client could reasonably seek political asylum here. He needed to get the man's daughter a letter, asking her to write back a detailed brief on the circumstances as she understood them. The whole situation seemed incredibly murky, to say the least, and because my involvement stemmed merely from a response to a post left on the Returned Peace Corps Volunteers Web site, I hesitated. But Mr. Georgetown lawyered me into agreeing. My task was simple. Any mail coming to the potential defector's daughter from anyplace other than Tashkent, with anything on it other than authentic Uzbek handwriting, would be opened by the authorities screening her mail. All I had to do was find someone to address the letter, come up with a convincing fake address, and pop it into a mailbox. I was not even doing anything politically untoward, when I thought about it, though my relative innocence would have been difficult to clarify with the Uzbek authorities.

It did not matter. The blond Russian customs official said nothing to me, stamped my passport, nodded curtly, and waved me through into the highly relative freedom of the Federal Republic of Uzbekistan.

Like medicine or pornography, Uzbekistan is a subject in which a person is either deeply versed or utterly ignorant. Other than the basics of the Uzbek language, I learned virtually nothing about Uzbekistan unrelated to my immediate surroundings while living there. In the fall of 1996, while my fellow volunteers and I underwent our Peace Corps training, Uzbekistan was suffering its largest agricultural shortfall in history. I knew nothing about this. Nor did I know about the potentially climacteric deals with Western companies such as McDonald's melting into air because of the Uzbek government's devotion to nativistic, strong-arm economics. I did not know much about Uzbekistan's president or, in fact, anything at all about the Uzbek government. I was especially ignorant of the strange tendency of disgraced government ministers to spectacularly defenestrate themselves.

Whatever I did come to learn about Central Asia occurred after I left. My knowledge was tumored with particular growths: the Aral Sea, the Soviet war in Afghanistan, the Great Game. This was because after I returned home I wrote short stories involving each of these topics and had done a large amount of research. When writing I tried to keep whatever I learned very light—stories less within the anthropological tradition and more within the tradition of, say, *Typee,* which was written by Melville after spending four weeks among his Polynesian subjects, though he claimed it was four months.

It is widely known that the Peace Corps attracts more larval writers than any postbaccalaureate option save for our infinite master of fine arts programs. Some of these writers go on to write professionally, and often their first books are crucially informed by their Peace Corps experience. Prominent Peace Corps writers include Paul Theroux, Bob Shacochis, Starling Lawrence, Kent Haruf, Reginald McKnight, Mark Jacobs, George Packer, Mary-Ann Tirone Smith, Jeffrey Tayler, Richard Wiley, Melanie Sumner, Norman Rush, Marnie Mueller, Bill Moyers, Moritz Thomsen . . . and these are the writers I am able to think of quickly, without consulting any of the Peace Corps's embarrassingly inspiring propaganda on the subject. ("Not born early enough to be writers in Paris during the Twenties, or old enough to write the great World War II novel . . . we are bringing the world back home with our prose and poetry." Thought I was kidding?) Why writers seem temperamentally drawn to Peace Corps service leads into caverns too numerous and complicated to spelunk here. One safe generalization about Peace Corps writers is that they are usually less committed to the organization's ideals than they are to their own experiential development. Writers are people made happiest by working at the manageable level of a sentence, after all, not rebuilding the colonial wreckage of Africa or disinfecting South America of gringo pathogens.

One of the benefits of the Peace Corps has been its indirect generation of a powerful forelimb to American literature, a literature determined to strip the exotic of its assumed exoticism. I am aware of only one Peace Corps washout who published a full memoir about the experience. The washout distinction is meaningless, though, for George

Packer's *The Village of Waiting* is as beautiful as anything published by a Peace Corps writer. But Packer served more than twice as long as I did before cracking up, and from the sound of it endured far worse privation in Togo than anything I went through in Uzbekistan. (Several people in Packer's village perished every year from walking through its perimeter of grass and stepping on green mambas, and one of his fellow volunteers was actually murdered.) Almost every year sees the publication of a new volume of Peace Corps literature. Some are brooding tales of dirty water and corrupt police and the spurting arteries of butchered barnyard animals. Others document the painful journey many Peace Corps volunteers undertake, a journey that concludes with the understanding that one kind of life is no more "genuine" than any other. Sadness sees no declensional breakdown relative to the material wealth of the sufferer. This is often followed by the appalled aftershock that this understanding has not allowed one to feel better at all. One can easily imagine, then, the hope of every Peace Corps writer: *One day, I will write and publish something about my country of service.* Of course, most do not. Those lucky enough to do so are regarded as the recipients of freakishly good fortune. Any competitive envy is usually dissolved if the work is good and true, as it is characteristic of Peace Corps volunteers to be generous to those who render the experience accurately, who get it right. Getting it right is an extremely difficult thing to do if you cut and run, as I did, after seven measly months of service. This was roughly what occupied my mind as I cleared Uzbek customs. I was, quite simply, terrified. But then I realized something, something I had over all these other Peace Corps writers:

Whatever I was going to write about had not yet even happened.

The terminal's reception and baggage-claim area had a dim, close feel. Its ceiling and hard gray rivet-patterned floor seemed too close to each other. Most of my fellow passengers were smoking and waiting around the thigh-high luggage conveyer belt that snaked through the building before vanishing at each end into a rubber-curtained portal. This was an improvement over 1996 baggage claim, which was found in a small, inhospitable enclosure, three walls of which were chain-link fence. Baggage was ostensibly to slide down a short, forty-five-degree-angled metal track and into its owner's arms. On the night we arrived, the track's metal runners had been sticky and the entrepôt quickly clogged with forty Americans' duffel bags and soft-shell luggage. Some locals quickly climbed up on the track, laughing and clearing baggage, while we all stood around and watched, stupidly grateful.

After ten minutes our flight's luggage was still not rotating on the conveyer belt. The floor had by now seen more than a few dropped cigarettes ground out against it. I walked over to where the belt vanished behind the rubber curtain, lifted it, and peered into the airport's womb. It looked like a big warehouse. Far, far away, in grainy orange light, two figures heaved large items at each other. I let the rubber curtain fall heavily back into place and turned to face the airport's front entrance. Behind its bank of windows was a thick crowd of people and a blue-black sky giving way to morning. Somewhere within this crowd were, I hoped, Natasha and Oleg, my Tashkent hosts.

Then, suddenly, standing next to me—an American. He looked straight ahead, toward the hole from which our luggage would any minute be emerging. I had not seen him on the plane or outside it. It was hard to reckon how he had escaped notice. He was an older man with thinning brown-gray hair. His face seemed heavy and burdened, an udder of flesh dangling beneath his chin. He turned to me with an unfamiliar smile. At this point I saw his nose. On the flank that had been turned away from me was a large . . . I did not know. The growth was topped with a little volcanic crater and looked twice as white as the rest of his face. A tumor, perhaps, or a benign growth, or maybe nothing more than a harmless congenital birth defect. Whatever it was, it looked like something one would need to scrape off the bottom of a sailboat with a spade.

"Hey," I said, nodding once.

"How are you?" he said, fully facing me now. I had no time to answer before he asked, "Think our luggage is ever gonna show?" His voice was adenoidal, almost a honk, a little as though it were being funneled through a large duck call. This failed to obscure his southern accent. He waved his hand at nothing in particular. "What do you suppose they're doing back there?"

"Not sure," I said. "I went and looked—"

"I saw that."

"—but I didn't see much."

He took this in, staring at the floor so hard I could nearly hear him thinking. After a long pause he looked up. "You here long?"

Six weeks, I told him, and learned that he was here for the same amount of time. Journalist, I told him, and learned he was an engineer here to supervise work at a Tashkent tractor factory. He had traveled around plenty. Japan. Saudi Arabia. Germany. Never Central Asia, though. His wife was worried! But it was fine. He was staying at the Bumi Hotel, formerly Le Meridien Tashkent, formerly the Tata. This had been one of Tashkent's premium hotels in 1996, though I understood a large shiny Inter-Continental and a new Sheraton were battling for that distinction, giving the Bumi over to a seamier reputation. Still, six weeks in the Bumi. I had stayed in the Bumi once, as a birthday treat for myself. It vacuumed out my wallet at the rate of $210 a night. Forty-two days × $210 = $8,820 for advice from a nice man with a nostril barnacle. I wondered if this factory was turning out solid-gold tractors inlaid with palladium.

"Tractors," I said.

"Well, we'll see. My company—it's a joint venture. Russian-managed. We're not certain—there are concerns, you know. I'm here to make sure we're all on the same page."

"For six weeks."

"Six weeks."

This suddenly sounded like a much longer time when I imagined spending it strolling across the same factory floor day after day, communicating through intermediaries whose interests were absolutely best served by telling you everything but the truth. We looked at each other and sighed. Then, a harsh buzz. A clacking, hesitant, metal-against-metal sound, as though a massive, ancient robot were awakening. The belt started moving. One by one, pieces of luggage appeared, only to be whisked away immediately and rushed over to the nearby row of X-ray machines. My southern friend and I hung back, watching the growing luggage scrum. We laughed, laughed some more, and then stopped laughing when all the luggage had been claimed and we were still standing there.

Everything I needed was in my luggage. I had packed two pairs of pants, one pair of shorts, six T-shirts, one dress shirt, ten pairs of socks and underwear, two guidebooks, a copy of *Middlemarch,* five research-crammed spiral notebooks, various toiletries and journalistic accouterments, a flashlight, gifts for my old host family, three boxes of Imodium, five bottles of Pepto-Bismol, an emergency medical kit, and thirty-five cans of Skoal mint smokeless tobacco. I wondered why I had not at least thought to stuff an extra pair of underwear into my carry-on.

My southern friend stormed off to confront the first Uzbek within sight, an airport employee in blue coveralls standing next to the empty, quietly rotating luggage belt, totally absorbed by his own hand. My southern friend pointed at all the passengers walking away with their luggage, then at the conveyer belt, then into the bowels of the airport, and then over at me. A few other luggageless wretches were sidling alongside the column I was leaning against. Most were German. My southern friend complained without pause while the Uzbek's head shook metronomically. Finally, I walked over. "He doesn't know English," my southern friend said, turning away. He seemed more sad than angry.

I remembered the Uzbek word for baggage: *bagaj*. "Where is our baggage?" I asked the man. He answered in Russian. This was the language of response eight times out of ten if one speaks Uzbek, even impeccable Uzbek, to an ethnic Uzbek, particularly an older ethnic Uzbek, who until ten years ago would have never before experienced a Central Asian outsider, much less an American, even attempt to speak his language. The airport worker's answer was no doubt a sensible one, but the two hours I had spent on the plane cramming over five-year-old notebooks filled with Russian vocabulary lists had not left me with the communication skills the situation demanded. The more I had looked at the notes, in fact, the stupider I felt. I had *known* these once. I knew the Russian word for "pebble"! Pronunciation was also a lost cause. Though Russian is a highly phonetic language—the words sound the way they are spelled—a word's stressed syllable is very important and often hard to discern, and Russians take unseemly delight in laughing at those who botch it up. Equally demonic are Russian verbs, as flamboyantly irregular as they are impossible to conjugate. Indeed, as I had tried on the plane to remember the proper conjugative breakdown of the Russian modal verb meaning "can," I pondered who of sound linguistic mind would devise a language riddled with such complicated tenses and irregular verbs and rules governing prepositional usage slightly less intricate than plane geometry. And then I remembered that the simple past of "to go" is "went" and the perfect tense is "has gone," and after that I tried to parse the precise differences between "through" and "into" and "throughout" and "among." This was before I had even begun to think about the crack party at which English spelling was concocted.

The rest of the baggageless now joined us. Some were muttering in displeasure, and the airport worker was growing boyish with unease. One of the four or five locals whose luggage had not yet arrived said something conciliatory to him in Russian. They did not seem particularly worried. With that the airport worker withdrew, climbing through the rubber-curtained portal and vanishing into the airport's bowels. I turned to see another Uzbek man, mustached, wearing a black suit and carrying a plastic yellow walkie-talkie, striding across the baggage-claim area.

My southern friend, recognizing authority when he saw it, intercepted him and shook his hand with incoherent need. "Where is your luggage, yes?" the Uzbek man said to him, his awkward diction neutralized by his almost complete lack of an accent. "No problem. Luggage is coming." The Uzbek's walkie-talkie chirred, and he spoke into it in brusque, frowning Russian. When the walkie-talkie dropped to his side, he shrugged. "Slow trucks."

I took a seat on the floor. Slow trucks. My southern friend, trying hard to be reasonable, looked down at me and smirked. "Efficient," he said, the word packed with ugly submeaning. One would like to think of "efficient" as a concept as normative as weather: cold was cold everywhere, rain was rain, sunlight sunlight. Efficient: slow trucks were most certainly not efficient, not anywhere. But not for nothing, it seemed to me, was efficiency, in the guise of highly punctual trains, always the caveat used to excuse totalitarian regimes. Perhaps "efficient" was what *separated* totalitarianism from its lesser, more watery sibling authoritarianism. Most authoritarian societies, like Uzbekistan's or those of Africa, were not nearly rich or organized enough to graduate into the sleek ambitions of the pitilessly totalitarian. Of course, America was the most efficient nation on earth, and only the most deluded would dare suggest it is totalitarian. But tyranny, like efficiency, does not mean just one thing. Both are a set of cultural practices, beliefs, products; like an aging patriarch, both excrete full significance only when surrounded by offspring. American tyranny—the soft, corporate tyranny of Must-See TV—was appreciable only while living within it. From without, it was too ludicrous even to waste thought upon, and, needless to say, not even in the same solar system as Sudanese tyranny or Iraqi tyranny or even Uzbek tyranny. "Efficiency" had to be similarly bracketed and nationalized. Because whatever was happening right now, it made perfect sense to the airport worker and the Uzbek man with the walkie-talkie. It was not inefficient to them.

The walkie-talkie Uzbek paced solemnly while we waited. Those who had received their luggage had mostly cleared Security, and the wall of people waiting outside had diffused considerably. I did not even bother trying to find my hosts now. It was past five o'clock in the morning. My eyes stung with exhaustion, though thanks to the odd biophysics of jet lag I was not tired. My southern friend, his accent armed, dangerous, and on the loose, was by now angry enough to seek me out for the sole purpose of exploding: "Just whut in green hail iz goin awn back thayer?"

The Uzbek airport worker appeared, unsmiling but carrying two large, touristy suitcases. A pair of Germans broke away in tandem toward him. Behind the first Uzbek came a second, smiling Uzbek, also carrying luggage. The slow truck had, evidently, arrived. I tried not to look too relieved when I hung my large black duffel across my shoulder, mostly because my southern friend was at this point upset enough to induce a stroke. His bag was still missing and he was ranting, cursing those whose luggage had arrived. When I wished him good luck, he smiled hopelessly and blew a long raspberry. Several people looked over at him, then at me. Quickly, I made some space between us. While Uzbeks were not as far removed from the surrounding world as, say, an eighteenth-century Bantu, one still felt here the responsibilities of ambassadorship. Uzbekistan was probably as isolated as was possible for an industrialized nation to be. The impressions one left still meant something. Stories of early contact between the region and the West were not always reassuring. Westerners traveling through Central Asia in the early 1800s often had to don "oriental" dress, passing themselves off as Indian holy men or horse traders from the Indus mountains. Central Asians, having no idea what such creatures might look like, accepted the disguises with shrugs. The subterfuge was necessary because of the Turkmen and Uzbek manhunters who captured and sold into slavery any European they could get their hands on. "Slave" derives from "Slav," after all, and indeed thousands of Russians were kidnapped and sold into Central Asian slavery before the vile trade's formal abolition in 1873. Isolation?

In the Uzbek city of Khiva, as late as 1840, an Englishman on a mission to free these slaves was shocked to learn that Khivans had no idea what an "Englishman" was. More incredibly, only 120 years ago, a mountain warlord in Tajikistan shared his notion with the British explorer Sir Francis Younghusband that India, Russia, and China were neighboring tribes.

I did not want to be regarded as belonging to my southern friend's tribe. As a tourist, one always wishes to be regarded as different than other tourists. A troubling paradox of travel is how consistently superior one feels toward foreigners while at the same time wishing desperately to be accepted by them as unrepresentative of the qualities that make one foreign in the first place. No wonder Americans ignore each other.

Judolike, I flipped my huge black bag off my shoulder onto the X-ray machine. Its operator, a thin Uzbek wearing a strange yacht-harborish cap, looked down at my bag and then up at me. He pushed a button and my bag disappeared into the large machine. He said something to me.

"*Shto?*" I said. ("What?" in Russian.)

He repeated himself.

"Uh. *Ozbekchi, iltimos?*" ("Uzbek, please?" in Uzbek.)

Frustration passed over his face. He repeated himself, eyes closed, in Uzbek.

"Hm."

Eyes popping open, exploding, in English: "Your baggage claim ticket! Where is your *baggage* claim ticket?"

At that moment, I looked up to see Natasha—a small, owlish woman—cresting the helm of the thinned crowd, by now mostly comprised of hopeful taxi drivers. Above her head she held with both hands a white placemat-sized sign that read TOM. She was looking at me expectantly, though not completely confidently. I waved at her once, all wrist. Natasha nodded, gave me a relieved thumbs-up, then stashed her sign behind her back.

Where *had* I put my baggage claim ticket?

The sun was coming up, a gentle pink light setting sail across the wide deserted boulevards of early-morning Tashkent. Natasha and I relaxed in the back seat, each of us using my bag as an armrest, while Oleg and Kamran, the owner of the car, argued about something in Russian in the front. Kamran was driving at a speed I would approximate at 310 miles per hour.

Kamran was very brown-skinned for an Uzbek, almost caramel-colored, farmer-colored. Upon his head was a black *doppa,* the embroidered four-cornered skullcap worn by traditional-minded Uzbek men, similar to a Turkish fez but squatter and without the tasseled pom-pom. Kamran had the uniformly thick build of a tackling dummy. Even while driving, he projected immovability. The downward chopping motion he used to stress certain key conversational points seemed potentially deadly. One word he said to Oleg as we sped down a large street was accompanied by an unusually harsh chop: *"Vazhnyi, vazhnyi."* Much later that night, in bed, peering at the atomic print of my Russian-English dictionary, I would learn this word meant *"important"* or *"significant."*

Oleg flitted away Kamran's concerns with a sneer. (Only Russians can disagree with you in such a violent manner that you feel not only disagreed with but despised—and yet you never for one moment doubt that Russian's genuine affection. How this is managed is best left to a parapsychologist.) Oleg was around forty-five, with long, stringy broom-colored hair. His features had a sharp, mantislike extremeness, and his wide lipless mouth was filled with a metallic blast of gold teeth, as is the style in Central Asia.

In response to his brush-off, Kamran said something cutting to Oleg. Oleg pushed an oily drapery of hair behind his ear and stared at Kamran for two blocks before bursting into speech in the same combustible manner in which a diva bursts into song. Natasha laughed and patted me on the leg. Her Oleg was a bit of a cutup, it seemed. My mouth pulled into a vacant, nitrous-oxided smile. Natasha wore a helmet of short blond hair and large plastic-framed glasses. Her head was slightly outsized, like a baby chick's. She was regarding me now, smirking. She turned to Kamran and Oleg and shared with them the comedy of my incomprehension. When we came to a red light, Kamran whirled around in his bucket seat. "You know Uzbek?" he asked in Uzbek.

"A little," I said.

"Peace Corps taught you Uzbek?"

I told Kamran that, yes, the Peace Corps taught me Uzbek.

His eyes narrowed, as though he already knew the answer to his next question and was seeking only to test my honesty. "No Russian?"

"Tombek!"

To respond to this in Uzbek was going to require phraseological deep drilling. Already my brain's language derricks neared collapse. A few very silent seconds later I managed, "If I wanted—no—*needed* Russian language—yes. Peace Corps said yes—study Russian please. But not serious. Uzbek language they gave us serious."

"Tombek!" Kamran said, righting himself in his seat and gunning his mufflerless Lada across the intersection. This -bek Kamran attached to my name was an Uzbek suffix of endearment, and had kingly overtones. Kamran pounded at eleven and one on his steering wheel, hooting, while Oleg and Natasha smiled the strained way one does when bored by a close friend's familiar antics. Kamran started chopping in conversational emphasis again. "Tombek is very smart! Tombek's Uzbek accent is very beautiful!"

I now understood why Oleg and Kamran were fighting. Kamran had earlier wondered why I did not speak Russian, as any sensible person who had spent time in Uzbekistan should be able to do. Oleg—whose daughter had married a Peace Corps friend of mine—had told him that we Peace Corps volunteers were taught only Uzbek. This had made Kamran, an ethnic Uzbek, very pleased, which in turn filled the Russian Oleg with low-grade antipathy. Kamran no doubt understood that Russian would have been more useful to teach a group of Americans preparing to live in his country—Russian was still Central Asia's lingua franca—but Uzbek was more (to use his word) "significant." The Peace Corps's decision to teach us Uzbek was a move to mollify Uzbek officialdom, many members of which were, in the early 1990s, still U.S. *antagonistes* who reflexively regarded Korpus Mira as one of America's most devious Cold War proxy weapons (which of course it was). But the question of what language Uzbekistan was supposed to function in was not an unemotional one, nor a frivolous one, nor even (ten years after independence) a resolved one. For seven decades the Soviet Union's officials and academicians had belittled and disparaged the Uzbek language and changed its alphabet not once but twice. At the time of Soviet collapse, only 4.5 percent of the ethnic Russians living in Uzbekistan claimed fluency in Uzbek, which many Russians caustically referred to as a "kitchen language." Upon independence, ethnic Uzbeks decisively turned the tables, quickly passing laws decreeing that official national business was to be conducted only in Uzbek, which angered and amused most Russians, since the majority of "technical" Uzbek words were loaners from Russian. (One thinks of Caliban's taunting response to Miranda: "You taught me language and my profit on't / Is I know how to curse.") The one sanctioned sop thrown to Russian was its status as the official language of "interethnic communication." But the issue went beyond mere interethnic communication into far trickier spheres of semantic nationalism.

Any great power in possession of Central Asia faced an intractable problem. The region is impossible to police and defend. The famed geopolitician Sir Halford Mackinder once wrote that Central Asia was "the greatest natural fortress in the world." Massive, sometimes flat, sometimes mountainous, sometimes terrifically hot, other times frigidly cold, plagued with thousands of miles of penetrable borders, lacking an identifiable geographic center, and home to citizens known figuratively and sometimes literally to cut the colonialist's throat, Central Asia has been the death sentence of several empires that attempted to hold on to it. The Soviet Union, the last empire to try, had some innovative ideas to obviate the concerns of previous empires. One of them was to rename everything—streets, cities, towns, roads—throughout Central Asia, to Sovietize all aspects of life and achieve lexicographical and therefore total control over its people. The decrees wended down from hastily organized Comintern subcommittees. Bishkek, the capital of Kyrgyzstan, would now be Frunze, after Mikhail Frunze, the Soviet military commander who conquered and occupied numerous cities in Central Asia previously thought unconquerable—a gambit similar to renaming Atlanta Shermantown or the Ukraine Chernobylia. Dushanbe, in Tajikistan, would a few years later be called Stalinabad, named for a man apparently unsatisfied with being known as the Benevolent Friend of All Children, the Mountain Eagle, the Leader and Teacher of the Workers of the World, and the Greatest Genius of All Time. Every large street in every large city would now be Karl Marx Avenue. Every park would now be Engels Park. Every new collective farm would now be named Lenin, or October, the month of the Bolshevik Revolution. And the Soviets did this with mind-blowing disregard for the psychological and cultural collateral damage it would cause.

How little Soviet renaming ever registered with Central Asians could be seen by how quickly they shed their Soviet integument. Moments after independence, most prominently, Frunze referendumlessly reverted to Bishkek, Stalinabad having changed back to Dushanbe in the de-

Stalinizing Khrushchev era. There were literally thousands of smaller examples, though it was hard to reckon whether anyone grasped the perfect irony of obliterating the Soviet presence by behaving like Soviets.

I looked out the window at the blurry horizontal scroll of Tashkent. This was the most populous city not only in Uzbekistan but in all of Central Asia. Almost certainly it was the worldliest, most modern-seeming metropolis in Central Asia. Unless one ventured into the Old City, one saw here very few mosques and very little architecture older than forty or fifty years. This was partly because Tashkent had been Russified since the late nineteenth century and partly because the city had been flattened by an earthquake in 1966, leaving 300,000 homeless. (The only part of Tashkent left standing was, to observant Muslims' harsh satisfaction, the mosque-peppered Old City.)

We hit Shota Rustaveli Street, a highly urbane part of Tashkent, vapor-trailing toward a middle-class neighborhood called Chilanzor on Tashkent's western edge, where Natasha and Oleg had an apartment. On the street's tree-lined side were block-long five-story apartment buildings, neutrally painted yellow or pink, with tiny gabled porches outside each window. On the other, treeless side of the street were small electronics shops, teahouses, stores selling pirated everything, and *magazins,* the Uzbek equivalent of a Quik Stop. Another Tashkent existed twenty-five feet off the ground, a spidery, threadlike world of more cables than seemed possible. Virtually every power line in the city—television, electricity, telephone—was run aboveground. Streaking down the boulevard's center, dividing Shota Rustaveli's spacious two lanes, was a track servicing Tashkent's tram system. This meant yet more cables. A tram approached us now from the opposite direction, an electric foam of white-blue sparks pouring from the contact point between the thick, uninsulated cable and the tram's switch-thin conduit pole.

Tashkent looked good. The air was humid and smelled lightly of wood smoke. Those few people walking down the sidewalk were dressed stylishly, striding purposefully. People were beginning their daily unpredictable journeys to their daily predictable destinations, meetings were solidifying, freshly washed chalkboards were drying. For one or two cool pinkish hours, every day seems fine, thinly sunlit with potential. Even the old Uzbek women thanklessly sweeping the sidewalks of dirt seemed pleased.

The neighborhood of Chilanzor was tucked back behind one of

Tashkent's larger streets, a treeish jungle of skinny broken sidewalks, gravel alleys, tiny freestanding garages only slightly larger than the cars they held, and at least a dozen featureless Soviet apartment buildings arranged to have as little relation to one another as the possibilities of community allowed. Kamran followed one of the larger alleys, nonchalantly hopped a curb, drove for thirty yards over gardens and through playgrounds, and parked millimeters away from the dark, doorless front entrance of Oleg and Natasha's building.

Oleg insisted on carrying my bag to the apartment four flights up. Kamran and I hovered behind him, talking quietly in the echoey stairwell, which stank of thick smoky urine. "What will you write about here?" Kamran asked me.

"The Aral Sea."

The change in Kamran's bearing was immediate. His face lengthened. Breath shot horsclike from his nostrils. He touched the lapels of his beaten sport coat. "Very sad story. Very bad near the Aral Sea. [Something something something]"

I recognized an imperative verb form somewhere in there but had no idea what Kamran was telling me I should do. "Yes," I chanced. "If God wills it."

Kamran smiled and gave me a grandfatherly touch on the scapula as Oleg dumped my bag on his apartment's foyer floor. What Oleg said next I understood perfectly: "Fuck! That was heavy!" If next he said, "He has more fucking shit in that bag than we have in this whole fucking apartment!" he did not need to. I was already thinking it. I had been told to expect a small apartment. What shocked me—what always shocked me about Soviet apartments—was how broken-spirited it seemed. The carpets did not cover as much as they clearly wanted to. The furniture seemed beyond the possibilities of reupholstery. The plain red wallpaper was lumpy and peeling dryly in every corner. A toaster-sized, intermittently color television convulsed in the corner of the living room. The flat's four snug rooms were arranged railroad-style, end-on-end-on-end-on-end. I had the last room. It had the only bed. I wondered where Oleg and Natasha would sleep until I saw that the living-room couch, bleeding spores of stuffing from every seam, had been turned into a cot. After dragging my bag to my room—which, I was not surprised to see, had no lock or even a catch—I returned to find that a table from the kitchen had been hauled into the living room. Oleg was sitting there now. Natasha was serving him soup and thick gray Russian bread. The other, still-empty table setting was obviously for me. It was nearly seven in the morning.

Kamran had hung around to say goodbye. He hugged me, shook my hand, and patted me on the back. "I am happy you are here, Tombek," he said. "You are a good boy. You will write many good things about my nation."

"I want that," I said.

"God willing."

"God willing."

Words were coming back now, even if my grammar remained an ebonic mangling of syntax and tense. I thanked Kamran, my hand over my heart, Central Asian–style. Kamran bowed, his hand also over his heart. He winked at me, called "Good luck!" in Russian to Oleg and Natasha, and finally ducked out.

"Sit," Natasha said in her basic English, waving her hand over the table's unoccupied chair, almost curtsying. "Please sit." *Pliz seet.* "Please eat." *Pliz eet.*

I knew better than to try to go to bed. Everyone in Central Asia—whether Russian or Uzbek or Kazakh, merely religious or fanatic or Soviet atheist, urbanite or farmer, rich or middle-class or poor—was culturally duty-bound to treat guests with as much generosity as humanly possible. Such guerrilla hospitality made Central Asia both a pleasant place and an exasperating one. Letting on that the shredded horse one has just been served is simply not one's gastronomic cup of tea can lead to hurt feelings. Turning away a shot of blindness-inducing bathtub vodka can run a punji stick through your host's overblown pride. But there was justice in the notion that hospitality should not be one-sided. If one can expect to enjoy superlative hosts, one must be a superlative guest.

Natasha set before me a plate piled with several hard shiny dumplings packed with chopped mutton and onions and smothered in sour cream. These were called manty. I liked manty, but they had once made me ill. Next came a bowl of shurpa, a tasty meat-and-vegetable soup. I leaned forward, letting its rich, greasy aerosol fill my nostrils. Swirls of oil gleamed in the broth like gasoline in water. I liked shurpa, but it had once made me ill. Next came a plate of scrambled eggs topped with coriander and onions. A tube of meat—I knew better than to inquire what kind of meat it was, as most in Uzbekistan seemed to regard this question as eccentric—lay on top of my fluffy yellow eggs. I liked meat, but it had once made me ill as well. Finally came another small plate of cold wet chopped noodles. Noodles had never made me ill. I started with them.

Natasha beamed and dithered next to me, her hands parceled tightly beneath her chin. After pushing several forkfuls of noodle and egg into his mouth, Oleg looked over at his wife and smiled. He said something and she looked down shyly. His head swiveled back toward mine, his almost invisible blond eyebrows raised significantly. I smiled.

As my mouth filled with food, my mind began to traffic in anachronistic concerns so vivid they seemed hallucinatory. Time travel through my taste buds. How overdue a letter my parents were, for instance. The molten dread with which I was anticipating teaching school tomorrow. How homesick I was. How intensely I missed L——, the woman to whom I was, in 1996, engaged. I sat there, quietly dislocated. Natasha worriedly asked me if everything was all right. Again I smiled and forced down another mant.

Oleg rapped his fork against his plate and conducted my attention to the television. Natasha wheeled it closer to the table. A music video in Russian. Oleg twisted his hand, the universal symbol for "turn it up." Natasha did, and the apartment filled with Russian pop music. Oleg's song was a catchy number called "Dumala." He began, then, to talk very loudly at me. One might think that important questions such as the duration of my trip, the places I planned on visiting, and the logistics of my home stay would have been more usefully put to me when the television was unplugged and an English speaker present. In Oleg's apparent view, this could not have been more wrong.

I was, however, pleased to see that music videos had taken the Great Leap Forward. Russian videos, such as that for "Dumala," were always fairly elaborate (most were produced in Moscow), but Uzbek-produced videos had had a distinct static nature. Most often they featured the singer in undeviating close-up as he or she lip-synched in some Tashkent park or garden. During the song's inevitable lyricless portion, the singer would simply stand before the camera, smiling beatifically. Now Uzbek videos took place in factories and forests and mansions, their cameras ripped from their anchors, their subjects joyous with perambulation. Some videos even contained a rumor of narrative. Was that a car chase?

Natasha changed over to a Russian channel showing a documentary about the social structure of a duck pond, if I was not mistaken, while a synthesizer version of "Lucy in the Sky with Diamonds" tinkled over the Russian narration. Now came Russian television commercials. The first, shilling a bottled soft drink, featured a young girl "spilling" soda all over her face, and concluded with a final image of a soda loogie hanging off the smiling girl's chin. Next was a remarkably straightforward Tampax commercial, featuring beautiful young Russian girls freely and light-heartedly bending over cars, squatting, doing splits, always camera-turned, smirking, their eyes a-sparkle, their hair as lustrous as—

"Are you tired?" Natasha asked.

Natasha's and Oleg's eyes were raw and grape-sized. They desperately needed some sleep. Natasha squired me back to my room, where I remembered another matter with which I had been entrusted. Their son-in-law, my Peace Corps friend, had given me $300 to pass on to Natasha and Natasha only. I was not allowed to let Oleg even glimpse this money. This suggested any number of unlovely social trends suffered by my adopted household. I reached into my hidden money belt and peeled off three hundreds while Natasha fluffed my pillows. When she turned back to me, I managed some incomprehensible Russian formulation such as "From son for you because I—" Natasha quickly took the money, thanked me, and gave me a quick squeeze good night. The money did not seem to make her very happy. There was nothing like coming into new money, I supposed, to remind you of your problems with old money.

And now I was in bed just before eight o'clock in the morning, awake, stomach full, luggage still packed, wearing clothes I had put on two days ago. But I had made it in. I was here, and soon, I thought, I would be a thousand miles away, walking along the former seashore of the Aral Sea.

The story of the Aral Sea is a familiar twentieth-century narrative, that of Development and Industrialization, albeit a less happy version than the one to which we are accustomed. It begins with cotton, of which Uzbekistan is the world's second-largest exporter. Cotton has for decades been Uzbekistan's national agricultural religion, mirroring a larger Russian trend to triumphalize the "heroic Soviet success of socialized agriculture," which might be funny if it were not so disgusting. Indeed, adulation of cotton extends so far into Uzbek culture that today Tashkent's soccer team is called the Cotton Pickers.

Such a huge cotton output is a strange accomplishment for a nation that is mostly desert, as cotton is a thirsty, ecologically demanding crop. For this Uzbekistan can thank the American Civil War, which cut off the cotton supply of a powerful northern neighbor, tsarist Russia, which in turn began to search for a new, easily accessible agricultural base. It found that base in Central Asia. The river that forms part of Uzbekistan's southern border and feeds into the Aral Sea, the Amu Darya, known in antiquity as the Oxus, was irrigated and bled into Uzbekistan's vast deserts, and soon "white gold" was blooming within this newly arable but fragile land. The diverting of the Amu Darya was one of the rare tsarist policies the Soviets continued. Imperialism was another.

No one knows precisely how long the Amu Darya River has flowed into the Aral Sea, the region's natural depression area. One Turkmen chieftain told agents of Peter the Great in the early 1700s that the Amu Darya's original course poured into the Caspian Sea, not the Aral. Peter the Great had, for a time, used this information to design, though never begin, an ambitious terraforming plan to restore the river to its "original" course. This would have allowed goods to travel between India and Russia without passing through the region's hazardous, bandit-plagued deserts. Whatever the case, the story illustrates how long ago Russia first set itself upon modifying the Amu Darya's course.

For 600 years the Aral Sea basin has been the traditional home of the Karakalpaks, a nomadic people who, after the Bolshevik Revolution, were first made part of the Kazakh Soviet Socialist Republic, were then briefly granted autonomy, and in 1936 were finally ceded to the Uzbek Soviet Socialist Republic. From the Karakalpaks' consistent poverty and small numbers, one can conclude that life around the Aral Sea—some scholars have suggested that "Aral" comes from an old Tatar word meaning "between"—could never have been easy. The surrounding land is not blessed with much by way of readily exploitable resources, and though irrigation-based agriculture has been practiced around the sea for hundreds if not thousands of years, its economy never much developed beyond melon growing. "The banks of the Aral," wrote the great explorer Sir Alexander Burnes in 1834, "are peopled by wandering tribes, who cultivate great quantities of wheat and other grain, which, with fish, that are caught in abundance, form their food. The neighbourhood of the Aral is not frequented by caravans." But the Aral Sea's proximity to an important center of Central Asian culture, Khiva—found in the Amu Darya's once-fertile river delta—allowed a few Western travelers some early, pristine glimpses of life in the Aral Sea basin. The Englishman Anthony Jenkinson traveled throughout the delta in 1558 and wrote that "the water that serveth all that country is drawn by ditches out of the River Oxus . . . and in a short time all that land is like to be destroyed, and to become a wilderness for want of water."

In 1960 the Aral Sea was still the fourth-largest inland body of water in the world, its volume equal to that of Lake Michigan. Jenkinson's prophecies had not been fulfilled. But an increasing hunger for cotton, which grew exponentially as the Soviet Union attempted to overtake the West, along with the strain of a population that had increased by a factor of seven and an intensifying network of irrigation, began, quite simply, to drain the Aral Sea. Moynaq, once a prosperous seaside fishing town of 40,000 inhabitants and home to a cannery that produced 12 to 20 million tins of fish a year, found itself, by the late seventies, no longer even near the Aral Sea's shore. For years dust storms had been scouring the area with hundreds of millions of tons of salt and sand from the Aral's exposed seabed, much of which was poisonous, thanks to the Soviet insecticides and toxic waste dumped into the sea over the decades. The weather turned foul as the sea shrank and shed its role as the basin's climatic regulator, affecting temperatures as far as 150 miles beyond the shore's perimeter. In its unspoiled state, the Aral Sea absorbed the solar equivalent of 7 billion tons of conventional fuel, cooling the surrounding areas during summer and feeding the stored heat back into the atmosphere during the winter. Now that the Aral Sea had lost 70 percent of its water volume, summer temperatures ruptured mercury bulbs and vaporized the soil's moisture, and months of morning frost during the increasingly harsh winters doomed the irrigation-dependent crops the sea had been drained to nourish in the first place.

Those living near the sea fell apart commensurately. A place that for so long lived off so little found itself rapidly losing everything. One by one, Karakalpakistan's industries staggered, then collapsed. Fisherman, ferry captains, canners, and shipbuilders had to reinvent their lives within a planned economy that could not afford to admit they existed. With mounting rates of infant mortality, anemia among pregnant women (which ran, and runs, at virtually 100 percent), and tuberculosis, the Karakalpaks began by the mid-1980s to question publicly what was happening to their land and themselves. "Tell me," a Karakalpak asked the Soviet Congress of People's Deputies in 1989, "is there any other state in the world which permits its own population to be poisoned?" "When God loved us, he gave us the Amu Darya," one poet wrote. "When he ceased to love us, he sent us Russian engineers."

In 1986, following the rupture of Reactor Number Four at Chernobyl, the world at last awoke to the Aral Sea's continued destruction. Meanwhile, as glasnost took hold in Soviet society, plans to save the sea were devised and revised; they accumulated upon the shelves of the Soviet government and well-meaning international agencies. None were carried through. In 1991 the Soviet Union collapsed. In Uzbekistan the cotton harvest continued, as the country's entire economy depended upon it. Moynaq sat stranded at least eighty miles from the Aral Sea, and Karakalpakistan, now a nominally autonomous republic within Uzbekistan, found its revenues shrinking and its monstrous medical-care expenditures crippling. It was one of the sickest places on earth.

Although reports of the Aral Sea's plight appeared regularly in American newspapers in the late 1980s and early 1990s, the story soon went astray in the shuffling historical cards of the Berlin Wall's breach, the Soviet Union's disintegration, and the massacre in Tiananmen Square. When the Aral Sea was mentioned, it was usually as a barely explained prime mover of numerous other ills, from Karakalpakistan's hamstrung economy to a bioweapons plant located on an island—now a peninsula—in the middle of the Aral Sea that was abandoned by Russian scientists in 1991 and left, for a decade, completely unguarded.

From the little we had attempted to talk about the Aral Sea, it was clear that Natasha and Oleg had no conception of the disaster's scope. Whether this was because the Uzbek government played down the catastrophe's irreversible aspects with Uzbekistan's citizens or because Natasha and Oleg simply did not want to know, I was not able to discern. But when the Aral Sea finally disappears, perhaps by 2010, perhaps by 2015, it will bring to a close what one Karakalpak historian has called "an unprecedented fact of anthropogenic impact on nature . . . without analogy in its scale." A huge, fascinating desert ecosystem will have been transformed into 60,000 all but lifeless square kilometers of salinized sand.

This had already begun. The Aral Sea was located where two massive deserts, namely the Kizilkum (Red Sand) and Karakum (Black Sand), met. Karakalpaks had already taken to calling the future desert Okkum (White Sand). The area was mostly desert now—the desertified former seabed was larger than Massachusetts—albeit an entirely new kind of desert, one with ruined soil and obliterated vegetation, almost incapable of supporting life. The millions of birds that each season used the Aral Sea as a mid-migration stopping point had not alighted there for years, setting off numerous interrelated chain reactions, among them a horrific mosquito problem. The two dozen species of fish native to the Aral Sea had been wiped out. The fish that Soviet scientists tried to reintroduce into the sea soon died or disappeared. Of the 178 species of animal life that have historically called the Aral Sea home, only 38 today survived. The Aral Sea's surrounding desert forests, once unique to its irreplaceably distinctive ecosystem, had been mostly chopped down.

It was tempting to regard the moral of the Aral Sea as one that urged simple human restraint. Capitalists, fascists, and Communists had for a century tried to dominate the natural world in the belief that nature was a mute, defenseless property. Despite the ideological gulfs between them, all were, in the words of conservationist Aldo Leopold, "competitive apostles of a single creed: *salvation by machinery*." Of course, our century's apostles differed little from those of previous centuries—with the crucial distinction that technology had finally proven ambition's match. Perhaps the Aral Sea told us that nothing could deny the ugly truth that human progress inevitably comes at the price of condemning obscure pockets of the world to unimaginable suffering.

I had never considered myself an environmentalist. I did not regard human beings as some sickness loose in Gaia's bloodstream. Environmentalism is a curious creed. It arose among educated nineteenth-century belletrists and was shaped by a long cold war in which neither side could offer much shelter. It is both a realist creed and an apocalyptic creed, all-American in its dissent and anti-American in its call, simply, to slow down. It was this American form of environmentalism that seemed to me stocked with individuals who appeared to have arrived at enlightenment by means of pricey juicers and hemp towels. Factories may spew sublimated coal, cause cancer, and nudge species down the plank of extinction, but industrialization brought with it Faustian comforts— jobs and development among them. People, and the economies to which they were indentured, were more important than the environment. But economics at the cost of the environment could not indefinitely secure human well-being. Faizullah Khojaev, a prominent early member of the Uzbek Communist Party, earned Stalin's wrath, a show trial beside Nikolai Bukharin, and an eventual bullet for daring to suggest, "You cannot eat cotton."

I heard Oleg pick up the phone. I did not recall hearing it ring. Then he began to shout. So did Natasha. After a few minutes I realized it was their son calling from across the country. He was serving in the Uzbek army, I remembered their son-in-law telling me. Oleg and Natasha were shouting because they could not hear him. The phones in Uzbekistan had advanced little beyond treehouse-grade technology. Let them talk. My eyes fell shut, then sprang open. Below my window, in the center of Central Asia's biggest, richest, most cosmopolitan city, a rooster was crowing.

Two

Stone City

*"Oh, so you wanted to be like the others. . . . You think you're
a growing democracy, with avant-garde painters, poets composing hard-to-read, decadent verse. Well—fuck you! None
of this is going to last!" Who is saying this? Why do I hear
this voice so clearly? And it says the same thing to every
Russian: "You want to be reasonable, predictable, you want
clearly defined powers and responsibilities? You won't get
them. Instead . . . you will love the one who drags you into
the grave."*

—VIKTOR EROFEYEV

In the receiver's transgalactic crackle, words were lost as irrevocably as
cosmonauts torn from the space-station bulkhead. I had to listen hard: "I
am very [*crackle*] to [get?] you! Today I look [forward?] to [*crackle*]!"

Rustam, my translator, was calling from less than a mile away. I
hollered into the telephone directions to Natasha and Oleg's and told
him I, too, was looking forward to meeting. I placed the flat plastic
receiver back onto its cradle. The phone, I had learned, did not ring. It
vibrated. Inside the receiver were enough broken, loose pieces to fill a
child's rattle. The small frustrated noise these pieces made were what
alerted an incoming call. (The most common cause of house fires in the
former Soviet Union? Exploding televisions.) If an inanimate object
could be said to possess a nationality, this telephone, in its broken effec-
tiveness, seemed to me extraordinarily Russian.

Thirty minutes later Rustam arrived. "Mr. Bissell?" he asked when I
opened the door—the first and last time I would hear him use my family
name. A few inches above six feet, Rustam had the default handsomeness
tall people often enjoy. His mustache was small and neatly trimmed. A
thick, gel-sculpted wave of black hair hung suspended above his forehead. At twenty-four, he was much younger than I had expected. It was

clear he had held an identical expectation about me. He wore a heavy brown-gold sport coat and a yellow tie, and his shoes were buffed to a leathery black glow. As he stepped into the apartment he began pulling loose his nicely Windsored knot.

Natasha and Oleg, relieved they could speak to me in something more complicated than kindergarten Russian, pelted Rustam with questions. Was my room all right? Did I like my food prepared in any certain way? Did I need my clothes washed?

"*Tak*," I said, my hands popping together. *Tak*, one of the few Russian phrases I could manage with native gusto, means something analogous to "So, then." I looked to Rustam. "Shall we?"

The apartment building's stairwell had been pleasanter at night. Neatly coiled human turds lay in the stairwell's filthy corners, looking like small, headless brown snakes. Defecating in a stairwell was luxurious compared to Uzbekistan's public (and often even private) restrooms. Most of them were what was bluntly known as "pit toilets," a sad mainstay throughout the Muslim world. Neither Rustam nor I spoke till we stepped into the clean box of daylight at the stairwell's base. Outside, we quickly determined that we shared one or two friends and several more acquaintances. Rustam had, in fact, "kicked it" with dozens of Peace Corps volunteers in his home city in the Ferghana Valley over the last few years.

"We're going to kick it a lot ourselves, I hope," I said.

"Dude, I hope so, too."

We strolled through Chilanzor, the air thick with the heavy green stink of vegetation. Everywhere towered enormous, well-foliaged trees. Shafts of sunlight fell down through the canopy as straight as spears. On the apartment buildings, wash hung dripping from almost every window. Down below children played tag across dirt playgrounds. As we walked past them, many froze and stared. A little girl trailed us, selling milk and cream out of the creaky wagon she dragged behind her. As we neared the edge of quiet Chilanzor, intrusions from the larger city around it grew more overt: the dirt mashed with crooked cigarette stubs, a waterfall sound of heavy urban traffic, graffiti floating along apartment buildings' walls. On the side of one building someone had written "I love rap." But "rap" had been crossed out and replaced with "rave." "Rave," too, had been slashed and replaced with "metal." Finally, "metal" had been eliminated and replaced, mysteriously, with "scooter."

"Rustam," I said. Just ahead, next to the subway stop we were walking toward, a bright metal river of glinting traffic flowed along one of Tashkent's larger avenues. "Doesn't the name Rustam come from the story of the guy who—"

"Killed his son," Rustam said instantly. "Yeah."

I knew the story because of the Matthew Arnold poem "Suhrab and Rustum." In it a legendary Persian warrior named Rustum murders his son Suhrab on the banks of the Oxus River, "from whose floor," the poem concludes, beautifully, "the new-birthed stars / Emerge, and shine upon the Aral Sea." The basis of Arnold's poem had been provided by a well-known Central Asian legend similar to the story of Abraham and Isaac, rather significantly minus its divine intervention.

"That's not an Uzbek name, is it?"

"Nah," he said. "Tajik. Or Persian, I guess."

"Are you Tajik?"

"Half. My mom is Tajik. My dad is Uzbek."

"Can you speak Tajik?"

A shrug. "Sure."

For Rustam, speaking Tajik was not a simple matter of overcoming the pronunciation differences of another Turkic dialect, such as a native Uzbek speaker instinctively picking up Kyrgyz or Kazakh. Tajik was a Persian dialect and thus belonged to the Indo-European family, making it a closer relation of German than of Uzbek. Tajiks, an Iranian though still Sunni people, were probably Central Asia's original inhabitants. The Turko-Mongol Uzbeks, Kazakhs, and Turkmen who now outnumbered them obtained their current coordinates by invasion. Tajiks and Uzbeks had between them a long history of mutual abhorrence. Prior to the mid-1800s, the people we now call Uzbeks were often illiterate warriors; those we now call Tajiks were educated traders. The Uzbek-Tajik divide was sharpened by the fact that two of Uzbekistan's flagship cities, Bukhara and Samarkand, were historically centers of Tajik culture, a subject of considerable consternation in neighboring Tajikistan. The leadership of the Tajik Soviet Socialist Republic was, as late as 1989, petitioning Mikhail Gorbachev to "return" Bukhara and Samarkand to their rightful owners.

Rustam and I stepped down into Tashkent's subway. The Metro, as it was locally known, was one of the most efficient and beautiful systems in the world. It was built in the early 1970s, a few years after the catastrophic earthquake, around the time much of Tashkent's other giganto-futurist architecture went up. The Metro's two lines totaled seventeen miles of track and provided the city with good but not comprehensive coverage. A third, badly needed line had been "under construction" for something like eight years. Thoroughness was not its achievement. The Metro's glory were the stations themselves. As Rustam talked about my need to register with OVIR, I gazed around with a secret, satisfied awe. For half a decade I had been mocked in America for extolling the beauty of Tashkent's subways. Here, all around me, was a reminder that I had been right.

Each long, spacious, cathedral-ceilinged stop was endowed with its own theme. The subways of New York City toyed with this idea, though it usually amounted to painting each station's girders a different color. The stop in which Rustam and I were waiting, Khamza, had some sort of geometrical theme. Networked upon the ingeniously lit convex ceiling were grids of rhomboidal lights. Half were burned out, but even that failed to spoil the effect. Other stops were far more impressive. Pushkin was filled with columns and accented with mirrors and glass, producing a hard diamondiferous glow rather like, I had been told, the man's verse in Russian. Chilanzor was a bright, beautiful plain white hallway illumed by massive chandeliers. Nothing, however, came close to surpassing Kosmonavtlar, the stop dedicated to the Soviet space program. Stamped into Kosmonavtlar's rippled eerie blue-green walls were equally eerie, sometimes troubling murals that ostensibly celebrated the giants of Soviet space exploration. In most of the murals the cosmonauts appeared angelic, nonterrestrial. Some, like Yuri Gagarin, made strange Vulcan hand gestures. Running along the ceiling were layered rows of warped white-purple glass, part Frank Gehry, part *Aliens*. Then there was Pakhtakor, the Metro stop devoted to *pakhta*, or cotton. Considering the ton of ecological flesh cotton had carved from Uzbekistan's hide and the coma into which it had plunged the economy, Pakhtakor was not, to my mind, appreciable under any aesthetics. The cotton buds decorating its walls were as hideous as swastikas.

The entire Metro system was said to have been built upon a massive rubber trampoline to protect against further seismic activity. It was also said that each station was, in the event of a nuclear exchange, convertible into a bomb shelter. Consequently, no photography was allowed, depriving those who did not live in Tashkent, with true Soviet logic, of one of the few things in which it could be accurately said to lead the world.

A train pulled up, and we jumped on. Behind us the doors slammed shut with amputative force. Subway etiquette seemed the same in Tashkent as anywhere. No one looked at anyone else much, each face an igloo of metropolitan apathy. Eyes landed upon one's toes and then floated up to one's chest, at which point the gaze broke off. But a trio of Uzbek teenage girls with long black hair and bright red lipstick and tight black pants and white short-sleeve shirts looked at me and did not look away. I then realized they were not looking at me. They were looking at Rustam.

Rustam stared down at the floor. "You have some admirers," I whispered. He looked up. "Over there," I said. Rustam found them and smiled. They all turned simultaneously inward, a giggling huddle. An old babushka in a yellow hair net and dark blue stockings sitting near the girls pushed her mouth off to the side in an attempt to stifle her smirk.

"Tashkent girls," Rustam said rhapsodically. "They're the best. You can talk to the hottest ones. You can even *score* with them, dude. Unless they're, like, mafiya bitches or something like this."

"I doubt many mafiya women ride the subway, though."

"Dude, I don't know."

The subway luged along through the dark tunnel. The speed felt much faster than New York's subways, though the ride was equally rough. Posters on the walls advertised unidentifiable products with words like "Delight!" and "Mega!" written across them. One said, in English, "Dental Academy." Another, simply, "Welcome to Internet." I found only one poster whose product I could I.D. This was Barf. Barf was an Uzbek laundry detergent. It was not a joke. Surely one of the more star-crossed homonyms in all language, *barf* is the Tajik word for "snow."

The subway stopped, and we got out at Independence Square, formerly Lenin Square, when it was home to the largest Lenin statue in the world. "You know," Rustam said as we ascended the stairs back up to sunny, aboveground Tashkent, "if you want me to get some bitches later, just tell me. If so, it's no problem."

"I don't think that will be necessary." I paused. "Why do you say 'bitches'?"

Rustam drew back. "What?"

" 'Bitches.' Why not 'chicks' or something progressive like that?"

" 'Chicks,' 'bitches'—it's the same thing, right?"

"Not really."

He was quiet. Then: "Jerod used to say 'bitches' all the time. 'Dude, let's get some bitches.' "

Jerod was a guy with whom I had gone through Peace Corps training. Rustam had mentioned "kicking it" with him more than anyone else. The two still e-mailed, apparently. I did not know Jerod well, though I remembered him burning his way through a fair number of the woman volunteers during training.

I asked, " 'Bitches' are . . . what? Prostitutes?"

Rustam shrugged. "I don't know." He waved all of this away, finally recognizing that I was not Jerod. "Forget it. Just . . . keep it in mind."

We walked across a large concrete plaza next to the KGB building, conveniently located a block away from the American embassy's press office. Perhaps it was Rustam's excessive talk of "bitches," but I suddenly noticed that Tashkent actually did have a weirdly extraordinary number of unbelievably attractive women. Within one hundred feet more than a dozen gorgeous Russian and Uzbek women had passed us in the opposite direction. They all seemed Doberman-lean, their rear ends sculpted from the Olympic amount of walking everyone here did. As for the Uzbeks, Muslim piety looked to have been thrown out a very big window, and hard. These Tashkent women were wearing outfits that on an American woman would have repulsed me. Tight pink pants spangled with sequins. Feloniously short skirts ringed with black ropy tassels. Capri pants to break one's heart. Stomach-showcasing blouses knotted in medias breast. Strappy black platform shoes and giant clogs with cork heels. The barriers of language and culture shielded one from ever having to figure out the motives of the human being living behind such fluorescent sexuality. It was a remove more conceptually distant than that of pornography. Just a few weeks before I arrived, one of Tashkent's biggest universities had banned short skirts. They were "distracting," the university claimed.

I knew I needed to enjoy this pageantry now. Soon something would happen to these young women. How was it that Russian women under twenty-five were so beautiful and Russian women over twenty-five were so . . . *Russian*? And twenty-five did seem to be the age. It was as if these young women were inflatable life rafts and their twenty-fifth year viciously pulled their cord. Russians joked about this themselves. Often when a young American man expressed interest in a pretty young Russian woman, the first thing that young man would be told—often by the young woman's fat, unattractive mother—would be to make sure she did not eat. Otherwise, by the time she was twenty-five . . . and the mother would look down smilingly at herself.

"You know," I said to Rustam, "there *are* a lot of good-looking young women here."

He smiled. "I *told* you, bro."

We came to the door of the embassy's press office, a separate entity from the embassy, which was across town. The door was made of thick, indestructible-looking wood. A small plaque next to the door quietly announced what lay behind it. I stood there for a few moments, hunting for a doorbell. Nothing.

"Should I wait out here?" Rustam asked from the sidewalk.

"I think so. I'll be back down in a few minutes."

I was here to check in with the press office and drop off some passport photos, which would be used to "register" me with the Ministry of Foreign Affairs. In exchange for registering I would receive a small green accreditation card that would, theoretically, discourage the *militsiya* from hassling me during my travels by letting them know I was a ministry matter, not some tourist they could sportingly shake down. It should be said that the Karimov regime had in recent years come down hard on the police for routinely squeezing tourists. It should also be said that a presidential decree would not have been necessary had it not been such a problem. As far as the Western press was concerned, things were far better in Uzbekistan today than in the first few years following independence. In the early 1990s a *Newsweek* reporter was roused from bed by Uzbek intelligence at four in the morning, escorted to the airport, and promptly tossed out of the country after publishing a negative piece about Karimov, prompting *Newsweek,* Reuters, and Agence France-Presse to move their headquarters from Tashkent to Almaty in Kazakhstan. Since 1996, however, the BBC and Radio Liberty, among others, have been allowed to broadcast in relative freedom.

I pulled open the door, walked inside, and found myself standing in a dark, roughly coffin-sized enclosure. Another, identical door stood inches before my nose, and a small closed-circuit camera whirred overhead. I had visited the American Business Center inside this building when I was a Peace Corps volunteer. Entering at that time had been a matter of walking inside. No doubt these were security measures installed after the 1998 American embassy attacks in Kenya and Tanzania. I guessed that the restrictive doors were intended to prevent someone from rushing inside with something large, such as a bazooka. I pressed forward into a smallish room crammed with a walk-through metal detector and an X-ray machine. The Russian security guard came from behind his plate-glass cubicle and through the magnetically sealed door and searched my backpack.

The embassy's press offices were on the third floor. Portraits of George Bush and Dick Cheney greeted visitors the moment the top stair was cleared. Bush's partially openmouthed smile projected the same shaky measure of control over his facial musculature that he enjoyed on the national level. Cheney did not smile well at all. Clearly, he had tried, but it came off as a smirk. Not a wry or whimsical smirk but the smirk of a man who had just popped a child's balloon with the lit end of a cigar. Clean-shaven men whooshed through the press office's hallways, leaving a wake of Right Guard and shampoo, while the female cream of Tashkent University's School of Government clacked at computer keyboards. A low quiet filled these hallways. Everything—chairs, doors, cabinets—looked vaguely fortified. The old American Business Center no longer existed.

The embassy's press officer was a tall sad-eyed gentleman with whom I had been exchanging e-mails for the last two months. They had not been friendly e-mails. Nor had they been unfriendly. Instead, they had had the cold, somewhat spectral tone of an unusually informative fortune cookie. The press officer and I shared a handshake in the center of his office. After a sigh he said, "The Aral Sea."

"The Aral Sea," I returned gamely as we sat down on small leather couches.

He regarded me, nodding. His mouth opened, several somewhat rehearsed moments passing before he spoke. "We ask one thing of the journalists who come here."

"Okay."

He blinked. "Balance."

"Okay."

His hand lifted and moved about. It was a powerful-looking, oven-mitt-sized hand. "A lot of journalists unfamiliar with the region have come to write about Uzbekistan and because of their unfamiliarity sometimes they've written things we regard here as unfair."

"I'm not unfamiliar with the region. This shouldn't be a problem."

"We know that. And that's one of the reasons we're glad you're here." He scooted forward on his couch. I did not ask what he meant by "we." Upon the wooden end table at my knees lay a Russian dictionary. Atop it was a small notepad scribbled with vocabulary words and underlined adjective endings. Around the office were various photos of the press officer in what I assumed were his other postings. He had been to a lot of deserts. In every photo he wore a tie. "We do our best here," he continued, "to help journalists get accredited, to allow them good access, and to keep them out of trouble. We run into problems when journalists take advantage of us by going out of their way to be mean-spirited, by not taking into consideration the many positive things happening in Uzbekistan." His tremendous hand floated up, preemptively. "We're not talking about whitewash reporting here. We're talking, again, about balance."

The press officer's plea for balance was not necessarily unfair. Nor was it sinister. The turbulence he suffered was determined by how happy the Uzbek government was with him and his office. If every journalist he got accredited used that accreditation to spray mace in Uzbekistan's cyclopic federal eye, he would soon find his accreditation requests spurned and the journalists screaming Peter Zenger. As we sat there looking at each other, the press officer and I both knew that he could not, in any way, control one word of what I wrote. He was simply making a request. I was, at any rate, familiar with the kind of journalism he was talking about. I had complained about it myself. Much of what I read in the American press about Uzbekistan—the little, at least, that was written—inevitably enraged me due to the shallowness of its reporting and the perfect inadequacy of its analysis. As Uzbekistan's biggest game, the Aral Sea was especially vulnerable to vainglorious, inexpert Macombers. From that safari I did not necessarily exclude myself.

"You don't have to worry about that," I told the press officer.

His hands clamped down on his knees. Thus leveraged, he rose. He straightened his tie against his stomach and smiled. "Well, that's fine. I'll look forward to reading what you write." I smiled and we shook again. Minutes later Rustam and I were strolling along one of the open-air book-and-magazine kiosks especial to central Tashkent. I was not able to decide if I was angry. I should have been, I supposed, but I was not.

"Everything okay up there?" Rustam asked me.

"I think so."

"You look . . . weird, bro."

"No. I'm just thinking."

"You want maybe to buy a book?"

I glanced over at a block-long table fanned with magazines and stacked with books. An issue of Russian *GQ* exploded off the table. Unlike the covers of American *GQ*, a reliable provider of homoeroticism, this Russian *GQ*'s cover featured a naked woman apparently trying to make love with the doodle hanging off the Q. The proprietor, an unsmiling Russian woman with small Isaac Babel glasses, looked at me and shrugged. Rustam ferociously studied the standings of a soccer newspaper. I moved down the table a few feet. In a city blessed with streets named after Gogol, Pushkin, and Chekhov, a city in which Aleksandr Solzhenitsyn set *Cancer Ward*, arguably his finest work of fiction, I looked at hundreds of lovelessly piled novels. The fabled Russian love of literature—Tsar Nicholas I was Pushkin's personal censor; Dostoyevsky was spared from a firing squad by a last-minute tsarist reprieve—was nowhere here in evidence. I lip-read the Cyrillic for something familiar-sounding. The closest I got was *Mashina Lyubvi* (Love Machine) by someone named Djakwalin Soozan. My eyes then fell upon a particularly strange volume. Quickly, I summoned Rustam.

"That one," I said, pointing at a cover that displayed a Russian man dressed up as a ninja. "Can you translate it?"

His eyes widened and then narrowed. His lips moved. He looked over at me. "Literally?" he asked. I nodded. He returned to the book, still puzzled. "'*Techniques . . . for Drawing Your Sword from Its . . . Scabbard*'?" Rustam held the book up to the proprietor. "How much?"

I worked my way down the bookstall, coming to a set of biographies—cleverly arranged in the chronological order of their rule—of Mikhail Gorbachev, Boris Yeltsin, and Vladimir Putin. Seeing their three very different heads reminded me of a wonderfully explanatory theory of Russian progress. This was the "Bald = Reform" theory. The hairless Lenin, Khrushchev, and Gorbachev, for instance, all championed great forward movements of Soviet reform. The hirsute Stalin, Brezhnev, and Yeltsin, on the other hand, all presided over unhappy, stagnant times. It was eerie how accurate a prognosticator this system was. Under which category might Putin fall? He looked bald but in fact had a good amount of hair. Before I could decide, Rustam wandered over with his freshly purchased sword book.

"What do you think of Gorbachev?" I asked him.

Rustam's frown was instant and thoughtful. "He went too far, I think. He is more important to history than to Russia."

"How about Yeltsin?"

"An idiot," Rustam said without hesitation. "And a drunk. You have Hillary Clinton. We have something much worse and that is Boris Yeltsin's daughter."

"Putin?"

Now Rustam smiled. "I like Putin. He understands our people, bro. He understands the *responsibility* that comes with being Russian. He is KGB. Do you know that? So he's smart. Very smart. And he's strong, stronger than Karimov even."

This micropaean to Slavism was, I thought, a little curious coming from a half-Uzbek, half-Tajik young man from Namangan in the Ferghana Valley, one of the citadels of Central Asian Islam.

"Do you still wish Uzbekistan were part of the Soviet Union?"

"Very complicated question, dude. Very complicated. In some ways, no. In some ways, yes. Most ways, no. But when we were the Soviet Union, we were strong and unafraid and we knew the world looked to us, you know? Who looks to Uzbekistan?"

Uzbekistan, like all of the Central Asian republics, proved massively reluctant to break free from the USSR. In this sense, at least, the European republics, particularly the Baltic republics, were far more politically evolved. Gorbachev hailed Lithuania, for instance, as a model for the possibilities of Soviet reform. Unfortunately, in March 1989, Lithuania opted to reform its way out of the Soviet Union. (Gorbachev's response to Lithuania's declaration of independence—among other things, he cut off its oil and natural gas supply—gave the West its first glimpse of the great man's darker impulses. Another would come after the Cold War, when Gorbachev's signature was found upon a document green-lighting a frightening expansion of Soviet bioweapons research.) The Ukraine, considered by Russians such a close cultural cousin that its eventual vote to secede delivered Gorbachev one of the most unpleasant surprises of his political life, broke away with a geyser of hope few republics could match. When the USSR was officially disbanded, in Minsk, the Slavic First Secretaries did not even bother to consult their Central Asian countrymen. Hapless Turkmenistan voted overwhelmingly to remain a part of the Soviet Union in a precollapse referendum, though of all the Central Asian republics its vast untapped natural resources suggested the happiest independent future. Tajikistan, the lone Central Asian republic to demonstrate in opposition to the Soviet invasion of Afghanistan, seceded surprisingly quickly for a nation lacking almost everything a modern state needs to survive. Tiny, mountainous Kyrgyzstan was the first to announce its sovereignty, largely because its comparatively liberal president, Askar Akayev, a physicist and former university professor, denounced the August 1991 Communist coup attempt against Gorbachev as it was still under way and dissolved the Kyrgyz Communist Party. Kazakhstan, by far the most Russified Central Asian republic, was last to declare its independence, and in the mid-1990s its president, Nursultan Nazarbayev, was still floating the possibility of a single currency with Russia. The leadership of Uzbekistan kept quiet during the coup, and only after its unambiguous failure was independence declared. This timidity surprised many, as Uzbekistan, home to the most numerous and self-confident of Central Asia's peoples, had been the birthplace of the first serious non-Communist social movement Central Asia had known for sixty years. It was called Birlik.

I looked at Rustam. "What do you think of Birlik?"

Without hesitation, Rustam led me away from the bookstall, across the street, and into a park. "Bro," he said. "Let's not talk about Birlik outside, okay?"

Birlik, a fragmented, now-exiled organization formed in the late 1980s, hardly seemed worth lowering one's voice over. "No one's around now," I pointed out. "We're alone."

Rustam drew in breath, slowly filling his lungs and then just as slowly emptying them. "I don't like them. I think Birlik is responsible for many bad things here. I don't support them. They're too . . . Dude, what's that word? You know."

"What word?"

"'Patriotic.' Someone too patriotic?"

"'Nationalistic'?"

"Yeah. They're too nationalist. Nationalist Uzbeks don't look ahead; they look behind. Some of them want to change the Uzbek alphabet back to Arabic."

"Isn't that Uzbek's original alphabet?"

"Dude. What are we gonna do with *Arabic*? Karimov's changing it back to the Roman alphabet from Cyrillic. Uzbek used the Roman alphabet before, I think in the thirties. *This* is what we need. We need to connect with the world, like Turkey did, not run away from it." His head shook. "Ah. I don't wanna talk about Birlik. No politics, bro. Make money, have fun—that's all I want."

Rustam's apathy toward Birlik was not surprising. Birlik (which means in Uzbek "unity" or "oneness") first appeared in late 1988, when the bloom upon the rose of glasnost was most fragrant, a period regarded by many as the golden age of political pluralism, a veritable "Uzbek Spring." At the time of Birlik's founding, most of its roughly 1,000 members were students and professors. Its main agenda was to restore Uzbek as the Uzbek SSR's official language. Soviet society was famously top-down in its cultural trends. Therefore, much of Birlik's "dissent" was, like the growing public awareness of the Aral Sea disaster, at the tacit encouragement of Mikhail Gorbachev. But Gorbachev was no friend to Central Asia, which he considered riddled with clannish cronyism. Additionally, he felt, the Uzbek Communist Party had too many line-toers on the atheism issue, and it irritated him to hear of prominent Uzbek Communists being buried with all the Islamic trimmings. But Birlik was more nationalist than a priori anti-Communist, and the spirit of glasnost allowed the group to flourish. Indeed, when race riots broke out in Uzbekistan's Ferghana Valley in 1989, Birlik leaders were dispatched there by the authorities to pacify the people.

A society in which even dissent comes with state approval is bound to feel eventual tremors of political impatience. In the collapse year of 1991, Islam Karimov renamed the Uzbek Communist Party the Popular Democratic Party of Uzbekistan—which operates on the titular principles of the Holy Roman Empire—and stole out from under Birlik much of its platform. When Uzbek, for instance, became the official state language, feisty grassroots Birlik found itself pinched. In 1990 its leader, Abdurahim Polatov, was charged with sedition after radical Birlik members set fire to some office buildings. Birlik—whose name, again, means "unity"—split into two factions that same year. The more moderate splitters quickly formed a group called Erk (Free), which took as its stated goal the reformation of the Uzbek system from within. Karimov's opponent in the 1991 presidential election, former Birlik member and then Erk leader Mohammed Solih, a nationalist poet, was driven into exile. Erk, despite Karimov's obloquies to democracy, was never allowed to register as a recognized party. Polatov, Birlik's founder, went into exile himself after being cracked on the head with an iron bar and detained by the Uzbek police. He soon hacked the Slavic patronymic "ov" from his last name and lobbied ferociously and bravely from exile, most often to denounce Karimov as a tyrant. But some of Polat's public causes became retrospectively, massively questionable. In an open letter to Bill Clinton of January 2000, Polat urged U.S. support for the Chechen rebels in Russia, many of whom are now known to have been supported, armed, and encouraged by the Taliban and Osama bin Laden. "Undoubtedly," Polat told Clinton, "tens of thousands of Chechens and Muslims from other countries of the world will merge together in order to fight holy war against Russia." Two very different years later, however, Polat would approach George W. Bush, epistolary hat in hand, and claim that "[Karimov] tries to justify [religious and political repression] with the Islamic danger. But it is the secular opposition and human rights organizations as well as people far from any religious fanaticism who are subjugated by the repression." Maybe, Polat reasoned, if barely veiled threats of worldwide jihad did not worry one president, a broken-English threnody for Uzbek democracy would stir another? Polat's opportunism, however contextually understandable, had done neither him nor Birlik any favors.

"Okay," I told Rustam. "No politics. I agree. Politics is a total drag. What I need is a map of Tashkent. My guidebook is a few years old and I'm worried it's not accurate."

"Where do you need to go?" Rustam asked.

I needed to go to the Tashkent offices of Médicins Sans Frontières, known to English speakers as Doctors Without Borders, who would be my guides in Karakalpakistan. I showed Rustam the address. MSF was found somewhere on Konstitutsiya Street.

He spurned my piece of paper. "No. I mean, what's it close to?"

"It's on Kon—"

"I know that. But what's it *near*?"

"See, I don't know. That's why I need a map." Maps were always very difficult to come by in the secrecy-obsessed former Soviet Union.

Rustam said he thought he knew where a map might be had, and we walked back toward the press office, passing Tashkent's central opera house, the dingy and overpriced but optimally located Hotel Tashkent, and a few upper-scale cafés. Ladas and BMWs and dented gypsy taxis barreled down Tashkent's large boulevards, traffic signals often little better than suggestions. Only every seventh or eighth pedestrian gave me a second look. Five years ago that number would have been every third or fourth. A small but noisy part of me, I had to admit, missed the attention.

Rustam turned left on Ataturk Street, and between a Xerox outlet and the Mir department store we found a small bookshop. Inside, very plain shelves were stacked with plainer-looking books, completely unlike the kind of work sold outdoors. A few proper-looking Uzbek women milled around, looking at leaflet-thin books of Uzbek poetry. A lone, white-haired, sad-looking Russian man read Pushkin in the corner. As one might assume from the poet Mohammed Solih's 1991 bid for the Uzbek presidency, poetry is still a vital mode of expression in the intensely oral cultures of Central Asia. Literarily, it retains most-favored-genre status among the educated. (Only one Central Asian novelist, Kyrgyzstan's Chinghiz Aitmatov, has seen his work widely translated. His most famous book, *The Day Lasts More Than a Hundred Years,* is a strange and powerful attempt to combine Central Asian legend with anti-Stalinist critique with a glorification of the Soviet space program—making for quite possibly the oddest science fiction novel in all of literature.) Despite poetry's local popularity, I was not aware of a single modern Uzbek poet who had achieved significant recognition outside of Uzbekistan. After being handheld through a few Uzbek poems, I could say that the peculiarities of Uzbek poetic language did not translate well into English. The subject matter, too, often seemed bafflingly limited. The specter cast by Soviet ideologues—the same ghouls who forced Anna Akhmatova to write odes to tills and tractors while she was cleaning floors for a living—was certainly to blame here. During Soviet rule, any Uzbek poet who wished to address something other than the greater glory of Communism was compelled to write harmlessly about the sadness of autumn or how nice moonlight looks. Nevertheless, in the early 1980s Uzbek poetry was printed in runs—anywhere from 25,000 to 100,000 copies—that put America, whose important poets rarely move more than 5,000 copies, to deserving shame. Today the condition of the

Uzbek economy disallowed such impressive financial support for literature, ideological or otherwise, and its Moscow-underwritten publishing
apparatus, the scary-sounding State Committee for Publishing of the
Uzbekistan SSR, no longer existed.

"Do you read poetry?" I asked Rustam.

He looked at me, eyes squinched. "Suuuuuure."

My smile was such that I had to look away, and we approached the
bookstore's counter. Behind it a young Russian woman read something
in French. The typical Russian refusal to accommodate customers
ensured that she would not help us until she finished her current paragraph. This took a while. An exceedingly long while. Was she reading
Proust? Finally, she looked over at us, calm and straight-mouthed.

Rustam asked her if she had a map of Tashkent. The woman thought
about it, her eyes shifting a millimeter to gaze at the empty space above
our heads. She said *nyet* and then something else.

Rustam turned to me. "She said they don't have any maps of
Tashkent. But they do have a map of Almaty."

"We're in Tashkent. Why would I want a map of a city in Kazakhstan?"

"I don't know, bro."

"Why do they even *have* a map of Almaty?"

Rustam began to ask the woman.

"Hey," I said. "That was rhetorical."

We wandered back out into the bright Tashkent morning. It was the
mild, pleasant sort of day that made you want to do nothing but eat
fruit. I had only thirty minutes before my meeting at MSF, but the lure of
Tashkent's tantalizing and time-wasting eccentricities proved too much. I
gestured toward the Mir department store. "Can we go in?"

He shrugged. "Whatever, dude."

The Mir department store, as well as next-door Mir Burger—
Tashkent's valiant attempt at McDonald's—was owned by a Turkish
company. Turkish investment in Uzbekistan had been heavy and welcomed, as Turkey was one of Uzbekistan's economic paradigms. Imitat-
ing Turkey was what President Karimov called the "Uzbek Model": a
newly independent state's by-all-means-stable transition to a democratic
market economy, favoring a gradualist, export-led approach to economic
reform, a strict preference for collective over individual rights, and the
tiki-god worship of a strong leader. Uzbeks were also one of Turkey's

long-lost Turkic little brothers, frozen for seventy years in a Soviet ice cap. Turkey's investments were not merely about enrichment; it was often said that out of this ancient ethnic kinship Turkey looked to help Uzbekistan along the lonely path of Islamic governmental sanity.

The first time I ever entered Mir was after I had been what Peace Corps volunteers call "at site" for a while. My site was a small regional capital called Gulistan, located about seventy miles south of Tashkent. Gulistan is to Tashkent what Elmira, New York, is to New York City. Finding anything in its bazaars that merited purchase was as frustrating as a treasure hunt and ultimately of the same dubious worth. That first time Mir's automatic doors whooshed open for me, I had dandruff, swampy breath, and odiously spicy armpits. Within Mir, I found deodorant, and shampoo that did not pass through one's fingers like water, and paper towels, and Skippy, and toothpaste, and canned ravioli, and cuts of shrink-wrapped meat, and *orange* juice, and Gillette *razors,* and soap, and cotton-soft toilet paper, and tampons! Stumbling upon Mir that day saved me. I hated bazaars, one of the organizing principles of Central Asian culture. Bazaars were nothing but pickpocket-infested crowds and haggling arranged to make you feel as though you had "won" by saving 50 cents.

Mir had not changed much. Its bluish, air-conditioned interior remained the haunt of diplomats' nannies, assorted Western passers-through, and Tashkent's nouveau riche. "Mir" derives from a Turkic word with royal connotations—the source of *amir,* "king"—and its prices and imported stock abetted such etymology. Off the front entrance stood a waist-high glass booth that encased relics on loan from the Museum of International Wealth such as Swatch watches and bottles of Canoe cologne. Straight ahead a staircase led to Mir's second and third floors—clothing, housewares—while the ground floor was occupied mostly by a grocery store. I wandered through its aisles, Rustam trailing me. The prices were roughly congruent to American prices. Often a little less. A stick of Brut, for instance, cost 1,700 sums (pronounced *sooms*). This was a little under two dollars by the official exchange rate, a little over one by the black-market rate. A bottle of Turkish mousse called Big Thick Hair was 2,000 sums. A six-pack of Diet Coke ran 3,000 sums, same as a jar of Extra-Crunchy Skippy.

Suddenly, an enrobed trio of skullcapped, frizzily bearded, blindingly Caucasian gentlemen appeared in the aisles, led by a similarly garbed English-speaking Uzbek guide. They themselves were speaking American English and smiling and laughing, as though everyone else were absurd. Their pastel robes seemed evocative of airport Krishnas, though their beards and skullcaps were indisputably Islamic. One of them glanced my way. Predictably, he chose to ignore the only other American within blocks. I walked over to them.

"Excuse me," I said to the member of the group I assumed was its leader, a tall, soft-waisted, gentle-seeming man. "I'm a journalist, and I'm wondering what you all are doing here."

The leader looked at me, smirking in a kind way. His massive red beard had a thick pubic curliness. "You came to Uzbekistan to interview other Americans in Uzbekistan?"

"Most Americans don't look like you."

His smirk softened into a smile. "Where are you from?"

"New York City. You?"

"Michigan."

"Hey, I'm from Michigan. Originally."

We spoke of Michigan until their guide interrupted to say that they should really be moving on. That was when I noticed an Uzbek television crew waiting just outside Mir. I looked back at him. "Who are you guys?"

"We're Sufi Muslims," the leader said. Sufis had considerable influence in Central Asia, where, along with Persia, the faith is thought to have originated. Sufism, a reaction to early Islam's obsession with jurisprudence, is the most contemplative, even joyous expression of Islam. Its singing, dancing, and prayer-while-whirling appealed greatly to Central Asians, whose pre-Islamic religions made room for similarly shamanistic impulses. "We're here on a pilgrimage," the American Sufi went on, "at the invitation of a Sufi scholar here in Tashkent. The government has been surprisingly helpful and welcoming. They've been filming us all day. We're hoping to get to Bukhara tomorrow and Afghanistan next week. God willing."

I was envious of anyone able to slip into Afghanistan, one of Sufism's most historically important cradles and the Central Asian nation I found most fascinating. It was an innocuous envy, though. Afghanistan was simply one of those places I thought I would like to see but, thanks to the pestilential Taliban, knew I never would. "I didn't think the Taliban allowed Sufism to be practiced anymore."

"From what I understand," the American Sufi said, "the Taliban is hungry for any Western contact they can get. They think it legitimizes them."

By now his fellow American Sufis had already drifted away. "Listen," the leader said, "we're staying at the Hotel Tashkent. Why don't you come by later tonight and we can discuss Sufism?"

"Hmmyuh," I called back.

Once they were out of range, Rustam stepped close to me. "Dude, you're not really going to talk to them later, are you?"

"No. I'm not that interested. Nice of him to offer, though."

Rustam snorted. He watched the Sufis leave the store with small, hard eyes. Before the friendly Sufi vanished around the corner he turned and waved. At that moment the Uzbek camera crew's carbon-white kliegs lit him up.

Rustam shook his head. "Fanatics."

Every official structure in Uzbekistan—ministries, banks, embassies— was encircled by high spiked black gates redoubtable enough, I had been told, to withstand a direct hit from a truck traveling thirty miles an hour. This has been the case since February 1999, when parties unknown detonated truck bombs at six locations around the capital. The official number of fatalities and injuries—13 and 128, respectively—is thought to be much lower than the number of people actually killed and hurt. The bombings' putative purpose was the assassination of Karimov, and they gave the president something approaching his finest hour. Unused to finding himself in physical peril but in his anger and disbelief not particularly caring, Karimov disregarded his harried security detail and demanded to be driven around the city. Bombs were still exploding, and in some neighborhoods the attackers were exchanging gunfire with police. At several sites Karimov personally surveyed the damage and tried to comfort the wounded. Later he appeared on television. "What is happening?" Karimov, still visibly shaken, asked his nation. He then beseeched Uzbeks to think hard about their war-raped neighbors Afghanistan and Tajikistan. "Look around yourselves," he implored. His meaning was clear: Do you want that, or this? Karimov squandered much when he opportunistically and in absentia blamed the attacks upon the nationalist poet (and occasional *New York Times* editorialist) Mohammed Solih and a terrorist organization known as the Islamic Movement of Uzbekistan. Solih and the IMU's leader are known to have met once, for eleven minutes, and a much-discussed photo showing Solih with IMU agents is probably the doctored work of the SNB, the Uzbek successor of the KGB. Amalgamating Solih with the IMU into a unified anti-Karimov force is one of many ways the authorities justified the ruthlessness of their variegated crackdowns. It was, however, very likely that the IMU, which was based largely in Afghanistan and enjoyed the financial support of Osama bin Laden, had some hand in the bombings. The distinctiveness of the attack's coordination—six explosions occurring within an hour—have what one might now call the Mark of Osama. The bombing also poisoned, for a time, Uzbekistan's relations with Turkey. Turkey's ambassador to Uzbekistan was temporarily sent packing after Karimov publicly accused Turkey of granting asylum to Uzbek militants. Certainly, Turkey had many Uzbek militants living within its borders, though this was most likely engineered by Turkish radicals far below Ankara's radar.

Some Uzbeks furtively maintained the bombings were the work of a coup-seeking faction within the government, variously opposed to Karimov's moribund economic policies or his sacking of a popular official in Samarkand. Others said the KGB engineered the attacks to drive Uzbekistan back into Russia's arms. Others yet claimed that Karimov planned the attacks himself to pave the way for his assault on Uzbekistan's Muslims. Governmentally sanctioned self-sabotage was a beloved turn of America's arch conspiracymongers as well. The theory was equally stupid in its Uzbek incarnation.

Rustam and I walked past one of Tashkent's many fortified structures now, on our way to finding the headquarters of MSF. Behind the gates stalked several youthful Uzbek soldiers wearing camouflage and holding assault rifles. Their unsentimental eyes tracked us, then let us go. The building they guarded was, like most in Tashkent, low to the ground and unremarkable. A buckled sidewalk, stone stairs, a few large potted plants on either side of a smudged glass door. "What's in there?" I asked Rustam. "Commando school?"

"Nah," he said. "Military court."

"Military court? What's that?"

"It's like the serious court. The big court. I don't know the word in English."

"The Supreme Court?"

"Yeah. A supreme court." He looked back at it angrily. "They're all . . . fuckers in there. Snakes. Our courts are the worst. I hate them."

The irreducible corruption of Uzbekistan's judicial system was, indeed, one of the nation's least pleasant features. Next to tax collectors, judges and lawyers seemed to be the most hated and feared members of Uzbek society. After the 1999 bombings Tashkent's courthouses threw the book at a group of Muslims belonging to the extreme though nonviolent Hizb ut-Tahrir (Party of Islamic Liberation), a movement virtually no one believes had anything to do with the attack. Of the twenty-two men accused, six were sentenced to death. "Yes," I said. "I can imagine."

He looked at me dismissively. "I don't think you can. I think actually you can't. You see, it's so *important* that they not be corrupt. If everyone *but* them was corrupt, things would still be okay. But if you corrupt the courts, then no one is safe. You have no idea."

"Then give me an idea. Say I murdered someone, someone not that important. How much would it cost me to have the charges dropped?"

He smiled humorlessly. "How 'not important'?"

"Just a person. Some guy on the street. In a fight. Say I stabbed him."

"A fight? I think five thousand dollars would be enough to escape such charges."

"How about plain murder? Say I want someone's car, and I kill him for it."

"For that, I think ten thousand dollars would convince the prosecuting attorney to lose his files. But if you killed someone important, like a minister's cousin or uncle, then I think you would have to pay fifteen or twenty thousand. So you see—we do value human life here! Then there's the sentencing. Uzbek judges, like everyone else, earn tiny salaries. So they hand out extremely long sentences with the understanding that a year can be minused from that sentence for a few thousand dollars." He shook his head. "It's really ugly. It makes me angry to talk about. Or sad. I don't even know. Sometimes I think really hard about my life and future, and I have to tell you now that I think my future is not here. It's somewhere else. It has to be, bro. It's not in Uzbekistan."

We walked on to Shota Rustaveli Street, which Rustam aspired to believe might intersect with Konstitutsiya Street. Uzbek boys and girls gamboled along the sidewalks. Some stern-looking policemen stood guard outside the Uzbekistan Airways ticket office. The air was seasoned with the thin, peppery smell of outdoor vendors cooking shashlik, Uzbek shish kebab. A row of grizzled, underemployed men whispered "Taxi?" to Rustam and me as we walked by. A row of *magazins* and specialty shops lined the sidewalk to our left. I stopped at the window of something called the Mini Medium Mart, by all evidence one of Tashkent's foremost hubs of pirated merchandise. The piracy spanned every genre imaginable, the store's gigantic windows completely covered with the sleeves of videocassettes and videodisks and CDs and video games. In Tashkent everything remotely related to home entertainment was pirated. Legitimate outlets simply did not exist. Unless, that is, Marilyn Manson released an album called *Top Hits 2001* and I had not heard of it. Or Van Halen got back together to make *Double Album*. Or Led Zeppelin's *Houses of the Holy* actually had a photo of Jimmy Page on the cover.

The pirated movies for sale suggested a network of staggering reach. I saw the video for *Gannibal* (*Hannibal*) long before I knew it would be available stateside. (Russian and Uzbek both have an *h* sound but, for some reason, neither language uses it when transliterating. Thus a Russian can speak of Gemingway the possible gomosexual living in Gavana, Cuba, reading *Gamlet, Guckleberry Finn,* and O. Genry. This also results in the markedly less demonic Adolf Gitler.) The consumption of these pirated goods was not confined to Uzbekistan's common people. Whenever Uzbekistan's national television station decided to show an American film, some producer merely walked down to a store like the Mini Medium Mart, bought a tape, then broadcast it. Dozens of times I had watched dubbed American movies on Uzbek national television only to see, midway through the film, the following message scroll along the bottom of the screen: "If you can read this, this film has been illegally reproduced. Please contact . . ." The Uzbeks I had spoken to about piracy seemed to regard it as a victimless crime, which is to say not a crime at all. I wanted to ask Rustam about it, but he had ducked inside. I went in to find him. He had already bought Depeche Mode's *Top Hits 2001* and a compilation of Russian pop. In short order I picked up Eminem and Radiohead albums for the total equivalent cost of $5.10. The nasty thing about victimless crimes is how evenly they spread criminality around.

Rustam and I floated up one of the narrow, leafy residential streets off Shota Rustaveli and began asking strangers if they knew where Konstitutsiya Street was. No one did. "It's funny," Rustam said. "Everyone in Tashkent knows where they're going. But no one knows where anything is."

I lit off half a block on my own, eager to use my Uzbek. "Excuse me," I asked an older Uzbek man, "where's Konstitutsiya Street?"

He answered in Russian: "Konstitutsiya Street? I don't know."

Uzbek: "Where is the closest telephone?"

He shrugged.

Uzbek: "A phone you pay for? Do you understand?"

Russian: "Yes."

Uzbek: "Where is it?"

The man seemed to regard this as though it were a riddle. "Where?" he asked me, smiling. In Russian.

Rustam was having no better luck. "I think maybe I am mistaken and Konstitutsiya is not near Shota Rustaveli at all."

I saw a yellow Lada gypsy cab waiting at a corner. Rustam walked around to the driver's window while I stood outside the passenger window. Both were open. The Russian driver's eyes were closed, his arms folded across his chest. Bristly tussocks of white hair grew from his head like stubborn clumps of albino grass. Rustam and I exchanged glances over the Lada's roof. Was he dead? When we looked back into the car, the man's eyes were open and flicking from one corner to the other. I then noticed, taped to his windshield, a small, loving portrait of Stalin. More Russian Stalinists existed here than one might think. All were ancient and looked the same. Like this man. Small, shabby, rat-faced, and mean. The man was now scooching up in his seat and starting the car. "Where to?" he asked.

Rustam said we didn't need a ride and asked about Konstitutsiya Street. The Stalinist sputtered out lengthy, thorough-sounding directions. Rustam kindly thanked the man and slipped him a 200-sum note. Within minutes we were looking at the huge wooden doors outside MSF's office. We walked inside. MSF was housed in a large and airy multilocular compound. The central courtyard was roofless and tall wooden columns held up the shady breezeways that connected one office to another. A few small and lovingly attended garden plots lay here and there. In a big room off to the right, a lengthy table was scattered with crumpled napkins and silverware and teacups and pear and apple husks nibbled into hourglasses. We had just missed lunch. A few people wandered about the sunny courtyard reading files or e-mail printouts while absently eating bread or fruit. A young Russian woman welcomed us and led us into a reception office, a large echoey room heavily done up in wood. It was the least stuffy-seeming NGO office I had ever seen. While Rustam and I waited, we heard throughout the hallways snatches of Spanish, Russian, French, Uzbek, and English. Frontiers had indeed vanished here.

MSF is the world's largest humanitarian, nongovernmental medical organization. Its aim—providing medical aid for people in crisis situations—won it the Nobel Prize in 1999. MSF was founded in 1972 by French doctors frustrated by the administrative obstacles they encountered while working for the Red Cross in Africa. I would quickly learn—though it was not surprising, given MSF's French origins—that MSF workers, even native-English-speaking MSF workers, loathe the English translation "Doctors Without Borders," which they regard as lacking the conceptual largesse of the original French. It was, finally, well known that of all the international convocations to stare the basilisk of the Aral Sea disaster in the eye, only MSF had not turned to stone. The organization had been working in Uzbekistan and the Aral Sea basin since 1997.

Ian Small emerged from one of the offices off the reception area and shook my hand. Small was the head of mission for MSF's Aral Sea Area Program, which Small himself founded and trailblazed in the mid-1990s. Short, stocky, and boyishly goateed, Small carried himself with an unexpectedly cheerful demeanor. My limited experience with Westerners in difficult or administratively frustrating places had led me to expect a lava-blooded tyrant.

"How are you? Everything okay?" Small asked, the last word inflected with an odd, musical urgency. I did not have to ask to know he was Canadian. Small was a geographer, not a doctor. Most of MSF's workers were not doctors. Relatively few medical doctors worked for MSF, which often had problems attracting qualified medical personnel to its missions. For a newly degreed doctor to decide to spend a year (the typical length of an MSF mission) practicing the kinds of extemporized medicine crisis situations require amounts to professional seppuku in the eyes of many Western hospitals' hiring boards.

Small invited me back to his office. It had the spare, dark, futuristic feel of a trendy restaurant. Maps were pinned to the walls. His computer glowed in the corner. We sat at a two-man conference table. Small smiled. I noticed, then, beginning at his wrist and growing up to his elbow, a series of pale fleshy growths the size of limes. He caught me looking at them. "My party trick," he said, holding his arm out for me. "Go ahead." The largest fistula was soft, as soft as a water balloon, Small's pulse pumping within like a tiny heart. I did not ask how he got this, and he did not explain beyond admitting that "health problems" had forced him from one of his MSF missions. It seemed now we were friends.

"Why," I began, "do you suppose the world, the Western world particularly, pays so little attention to the Aral Sea?"

Small breathed in and let loose a long sigh. This question was a common one. "Because it suffers from the Where-the-hell-istan phenomenon. I will go home to Toronto, and the only people who know it will be taxi drivers, who are all immigrants from the Middle East. The majority of people will not have a clue what I'm talking about. I've given up. Now I'll just say 'Russia,' which I hate saying."

"How did you ever get interested in the Aral Sea?"

"I was working as a desk officer in MSF in Amsterdam in 1992, and there was an international film festival around the corner. So I popped in and there was this film about some sea. And up came these fantastic images of the ships stranded in the sand outside Moynaq. Those images have propelled me for the last ten years. Obsessed me for the last ten years. It's such an incredible image."

"Is the Aral Sea the world's biggest ecological catastrophe?"

Small grinned. This was the Big Question. "How," he said, leaning forward, "do you quantify or qualify the world's worst ecological disaster? What is a disaster? In MSF-speak—in CNN-speak—a disaster is something that happened last night. It comes and goes very quickly. The Aral Sea is a chronic problem. It's been going on for a generation. It's affected five million people. It's affected virtually every aspect of Uzbekistan's economy, health, culture, and community. I think it's definitely up there. Especially in terms of its irrevocability, it's one of the world's worst environmental disasters, if not number one."

"What are the biggest problems facing the Aral Sea today?"

"Well, it continues to get worse. When you're discussing the Aral Sea around here it's almost always in the past tense. But you have a population doubling time in this region of twenty-five to thirty years. That's an increase in water consumption. You have places like Tajikistan, who are upstream, entering into peace, and you can be damn sure they'll be consuming a lot more water now than they were in the last decade.

Afghanistan is never in the picture at any of the meetings people have about the Aral Sea, yet it generates around twenty percent of the water to the Aral Sea basin. If the international community gets its way and stops Afghanistan's production of opium, which doesn't require a lot of water, someone will need to replace opium with cash crops, which will require irrigation. That's a lot more water. The future is bleak."

"Could you tell me about the Uzbek government's cooperation—or lack thereof—with your work?"

"When we arrived in 1997—and I'm sure you had the same experience in 1996—the nongovernmental organization was a completely foreign notion here. NGO meant antigovernment. We were foreigners in a sensitive area. There was a lack of trust, of understanding of who we are and what we do. We were able to overcome that by coming and staying. Over time, they realized we were here for the sake of the health of the population. That we weren't trying to circumvent the government. Since then the government has been very cooperative. But it's a bit of a double-edged sword. On one hand, they appreciate what we've been able to accomplish here. On the other hand, they know that we're independent, that there is a component of advocacy to our work, that we do press work, and for the government, the Aral Sea doesn't look terribly good. But it is precisely this that scares anybody off from actually doing something. The area does suffer from a lot of 'Oh, it's a chronic problem, nothing can be done.' We say, 'Yes, these are facts, facts which need action.' The fact is, Karakalpakistan has got the worst TB rates in the world. You don't need to know anything else to go in and do something about that."

"How have the local doctors fared with the work MSF is doing?"

He nodded. "Take Moynaq. A doctor has been working there, dealing with TB for thirty years, and along comes some Western upstart who's never seen TB before in his life, and he starts telling him how to treat TB—you know, that's tough. This same doctor saw not only the sea disappear but half the population leave and a lot of sickness and misery and the economy collapse all around him, and now we're showing up. So yes, it's tough for the local medical staff. But at the same time, they see drugs on the shelf and patients getting treated. In the end, they're doctors, and they want to treat patients."

"You've been here for five years. How much longer do you plan to stay?"

"You mean personally? I'm going to leave this summer."

"How do you feel about that?"

"It's emotional. I will be able to leave and feel fully satisfied that I accomplished absolutely everything I wanted. I wanted to get the Aral Sea area on the international agenda. Within that agenda, I wanted to put the health issues up front. When we first arrived, it was all about the drying up of the sea. I think now, increasingly, the fact that millions of people live in that area is clear. But then you have to start asking the question: What about those millions of people? You can't just put a period on it. That's why I've been trying to get to Moynaq and spend more time up there, poke around and meet some people. My life is pretty much this computer and this table. So. The health of the population is on the agenda. We need to keep that on the agenda. We need to start asking questions about the long-term viability of places like Moynaq, places that existed solely on the basis of there being a sea. There's no longer a sea, but there is still a Moynaq and other communities around the former coastline. What's going to become of them? At some point, someone will have to answer that question."

"If you could do anything for the Aral Sea, in a fairy-tale world, where money didn't matter, what would you do?"

Again Small smiled. "I'd bring back the sea, of course, if it's a fairy-tale world."

In the Emir Bar, near the Tashkent opera house, four strippers sat atop cushioned stools, chatting in Russian and drinking colorless beverages. They wore tiny black dresses, big black pumps. Their black hair was tightly bound in thick ponytails, exposing large shiny foreheads. The moment Rustam and I walked through the door, they scattered, ducking into a back room behind the small stage in the room's wanly lit rear. It was late afternoon; the floor show did not begin for hours.

"Why'd they run away?"

"Such women are not allowed to mix with customers," Rustam explained.

"You mean, like, strippers?"

"Any of them. Waiters, waitresses, the . . . drink-pourer?"

"Bartender."

"Yeah. Bartender. It's not really allowed."

"That's actually why a lot of people *go* to bars in America. To talk to the bartender. It's a cliché."

"Here I think it's the opposite."

We walked across the empty room and selected stools positioned dead center along the polished thirty-foot-long oak bar, inches from the taps. If their handles could be trusted, available on draft was the Russian beer Bochka, Heineken, and Murphy's Irish Stout. A Korean bartender watched the television perched high in the room's corner—some satellite-beamed BBC fashion show featuring a lot of diaphanous slow motion—while drying a glass. Behind us, in the Emir Bar's more formal area, tables and booths were only partially set. The blinds on the big windows were open enough to allow in a brightness that, as if weakened by its passage through the slats, died halfway across the room. I looked at the stage area. A chrome stripper's pole. Small black spotlights were fixed to the ceiling. Speakers. A huge silk screen, behind which, I assumed, the strippers emerged during the show, read: TAKE YOUR TIME . . . ENJOY THE LIFE . . . OBEY YOUR FEELINGS.

We had just changed money with Rustam's cousin, who worked at a telecommunications firm. We did the deal in his office, the door closed. In exchange for a hundred-dollar bill I had received eight bricks of sums, all held together with little rubber bands. Most of it was crammed in my backpack.

The Uzbek sum was introduced in 1993, after Russia required that all former Soviet republics wishing to remain in the ruble zone turn over to Mother Russia their gold reserves. Uzbekistan contains almost one quarter of the former Soviet Union's total gold reserves, and it opted instead to issue its own currency. This sent Uzbekistan's economy into an inflationary free fall from which it had yet to recover. Inflation became such a problem—at one point it was over 400 percent—that the government was forced to print larger-denomination bills in 1997. Uzbekistan's first series of sum notes were quite beautiful, the face side featuring the country's crest (a peacock encircled by sheaves of cotton and wheat) and patterned in the style of Central Asia's justly famous tilework. Most of the money I now carried with me belonged to the newer line of two-hundred- and five-hundred-sum notes. Upon my two-hundred-sum notes prowled a lion with a human face growing out of its back. This image, taken from a madrasa in Samarkand, was one of the most famous heresies in the Islamic world, since Islam does not permit representative art of any kind.

"Dude," Rustam said, "why are you looking at your money like that?"

"It's interesting," I said, folding a wad of bills into a fat, resistant U and slipping it into my pocket. "Money provides a really revealing window into a culture, don't you think?"

"Not really."

"No?"

"What does American money reveal about America?"

I decided not to get into the Freemasonry. "Our money is very federalist. You know that word?"

"I do."

"You get a sense of that from American money. Our ideas of governance. Our civic architecture and symbolism."

Now he was smirking, unconvinced. "What does Uzbek money tell you, then?"

"Maybe that your current government is trying to find its future in the past."

A bitter chuckle. "That's because our past is better than our future. Especially when we can make our past whatever we want." Rustam looked over at the Korean bartender, who was staring at us. Rustam turned back to me, alone in his understanding that we were now expected to order. "What do you want to drink?"

"Can you ask him if they really have Murphy's Irish Stout?"

The bartender broke in to say he spoke English and, yes, they really had Murphy's Irish Stout. He wore a name tag. Sergei. Sergei possessed a gibbous moon face capable, it seemed, of only one expression: conscious.

"How much?" I asked him.

"Three thousand sums," Sergei answered.

Rustam and I, simultaneously: "Man!" / "Pretty cheap."

I turned to Rustam. Economic relativity always struck hard. This was because, as an American, one was always on the decadent side of that relativity. "That's actually really a lot," I said sheepishly, "isn't it?"

"Dude, that's . . . for a beer, yeah, it's a lot."

"I don't care," I said. "Fuck it. Give me one."

Rustam, now clearly uncomfortable, ordered an Amstel Light for 1,700 sums. We drank quietly. It was the worst stout I had ever tasted. It was as though it had been steeped in cobwebs. I tried to imagine where a bar in Tashkent would get its Murphy's Irish Stout, and how long that stout would almost have to be in transit. Weeks, I reasoned, if not months.

"What did you talk about with that guy, anyway?" Rustam asked.

"Ian? We talked about the Aral Sea a bit. I guess I'm going to meet him in Moynaq next week or the week after that." Small and I had not settled on any details. "It's too bad those strippers left," I told Rustam. "We could have talked to them."

"I told you, bro. If you want bitches—"

"I don't mean like that. I mean just talk to them. I think it would be interesting."

Sergei, his back to us as he watched television, laughed softly. On screen a BBC anchorman read the news. It seemed unlikely a papal visit to Syria was the source of Sergei's laughter.

Rustam glanced at the stripper's stage. "I don't like chicks like that. They're whores."

"Yes, well . . ."

He leaned in. "You know the bitches I like?"

"Tell me."

"Mommies."

I took a sip of stout. I gazed out the window at the bright streets of Tashkent. I looked back at Rustam. *"Mommies?"*

His eyes sparkled beneath lifting-falling eyebrows. "Yeah."

"What do you mean?"

"Mommies. Women with children. Younger ones, though. I like my mommies young."

"You're fucking kidding me."

"Dude, no way. The thing is, Uzbek guys don't sleep with their wives much, so the women get lonely. And mommies are more experienced than young girls. Mommies know what they're doing. They'll do stuff with you other women won't."

"Yeah, but . . . don't you feel bad that you're sleeping with another dude's wife?"

"Bro, it's not my fault. I always think, If he made her happy, she would not want to sleep with me."

"Do most women here cheat on their husbands?"

"No. But the ones who do let you know they do."

"And how do they do that?"

"You just watch them, and listen to them. They'll say things like 'I'm bored' or 'I'm lonely,' and then you know."

"How many of these mommies have you slept with?"

"Dude, I guess a lot."

"Is there some mommy somewhere you're particularly fond of?"

"It's not like that. I don't love mommies that way. You love your wife, not the women you sleep with. Your wife is the mother of your children, bro." With his fingers Rustam smoothed beer foam from his mustache. "There was one, though, back in Ferghana. She was only a few years older than me. We had sex all the time. 'Do you want to sleep with your mommy?' she'd ask me. It was crazy, bro. Her husband was a rich man, and he was always out of town."

"What did her husband do?"

"He was a manager somewhere. Corrupt. That's why he was rich."

"Tell me, then. Are there any *honest* rich people in Uzbekistan?"

Rustam smiled at my stupidity. "Dude, forty-five percent of our shitty salaries are taken from us by the government. How would getting rich be possible without corruption?"

"*Na levo,*" I said.

"Exactly."

Na levo was Russian for "on the left." The Soviet Union—and the republics it became—was a society of constant and universal shortages. The response to this was an "informal" or "second" economy. Calling it the black market fails to honor its real contribution to the economic welfare of the state. The great dissident and scientist Andrei Sakharov once estimated that *na levo* dealings accounted for at least 10 percent of the entire Soviet economy. A form of *na levo* economics existed in Uzbekistan long before the arrival of the Bolsheviks. This was home industry, which revolved around Islamic-centered social activity, and it was of huge practical importance in Uzbekistan, especially in the villages. Under Stalin all home industry was outlawed. Even today the penalty for home industry's "concealed income" under Uzbekistan's tax code was nightmarishly severe: a *minimum* penalty of 100 percent of said concealed income plus a 100 percent fine. Since so many people here, by awful necessity, lived off *na levo,* this was cruel and wanton.

"The rich are dishonest," Rustam said. "That does not mean they are bad people. That's simply the way it is."

It was somehow emotionally exhausting to sit here and talk about money. Especially when I knew—and knew that Rustam knew—that I was paying him several times the going rate for translators. "That reminds me," I said, reaching into my book bag, "I need you to do something for me."

"Sure," he said eagerly.

I withdrew the letter from the Georgetown lawyer intended for the defecting diplomat's daughter. Rustam looked at the envelope curiously, turning toward me on his stool and fluffing his gelled black forelock. I lowered my voice and explained the situation. Halfway into the narrative Rustam leaned back, his arms slashing back and forth. "Dude, no way. *Not* interested."

"You don't have to do anything. Neither do I. All you have to do is write this address on the envelope. I can only print in Cyrillic, and it'll look terrible."

"Uh-uh. Nope. No way." He returned to his beer.

I sat there, quietly shamed, embarrassed, irritated: I could not decide. "I'm not really sure," I said at last, "why this is upsetting you. It's not dangerous, Rustam. I don't even know who this guy's daughter is."

His chin hovered above the bar, his eyes even with the Amstel Light bottle's resinous glass aperture, glistening like a blowhole. "Exactly. You *don't* know. How do you know her father isn't a traitor? That he doesn't mean Uzbekistan harm?"

My mouth opened, though I said nothing. I decided to order another stout. While Sergei stood there pouring the drink, Rustam and I stared in opposite directions. When Sergei walked away, I turned back to Rustam. "Look. Uzbekistan has human rights problems, yes? Can we agree on that?"

"Bro, I don't know. I don't want to talk about that."

"I agreed to do this, so I have to do it. If you can't do it, fine. My feeling is that this man is completely innocent."

Rustam looked at me, teeth slightly bared. For the first time he seemed angry. "I don't believe that. I think if something like this happens to you, it means you did . . . *something*." Rustam abandoned me and peeled the wet molting sticker from his beer bottle. He shook his head. "Usually, I mean. Not always." He pinched his bridge, squeezing so hard his fingernails went white.

I went to put the letter back in my knapsack.

He swore in Russian. "Give me the fucking thing."

I did. Rustam took the envelope by its edge, flattened it out on the bar, and scrawled across it the address.

"We need a fake return address, too," I said softly.

Rustam's head lifted, frozen-eyed as he thought the situation over. Suddenly, he called in Russian across the room: "Sergei, what is the address here?" Sergei told him, and Rustam wrote it down on the envelope's upper left-hand corner. "Here," he said, and without looking at it again slid the sealed letter back toward me.

How did Russia, one might ask, ever come to entwine its fate so intimately with that of Central Asia's strange, volatile lands? How does one explain anything Russia has done? It often seems the Ultima Thule of paradox itself. Epoch after epoch, Russia has taken its enlightened place among those few, world-shaping nations—only to lapse, at the worst moment, into darkness. In 1839 a French nobleman called Russia "a nation of mutes." A century and a half later a Russian physicist would say, "Russia is not a country, not a people, it is a 1,000-year-long sickness." China, India, France—all places as vexed with interest as Russia. But could they ever be called a sickness?

Even in the early 1800s thinkers and statesmen pondered the abyss that seemed to separate Russia from normal, civilized countries. Of course, many such bastions of civilization had long embarked upon the colonization and oppression of less powerful nations. In this, Russia proved itself their equal. Without match among the Great Powers, however, was Russia's auxiliary achievement in oppressing itself. Does Russia, in its heart, really have anything in common with the West? ("Scratch a Russian," one saying goes, "and you find a Tatar.") Benjamin Disraeli cleverly turned the question upon its side. "Russia has two faces," he once said, "an Asiatic face which looks always toward Europe, and a European face which always looks toward Asia." It was this European face—huge, sweaty, chop-licking—that Russia turned toward Central Asia in the early 1700s.

Many historians have suggested that the propeller of Russia's gradual Central Asian annexation was the traumatic memory of its conquest and occupation by Mongols in the early thirteenth century. In just under twenty years all of Russia's principalities fell one by one to the Golden

Horde, as the Mongols called themselves, and from whom the Uzbeks today partially descend. This was a period of great darkness for Russia—the occupation did not end until 1480—though it does explain the occasionally oriental feel of many Russian customs. Despite these resultant common cultural traits, Russia has distrusted and feared the Islamo-Asian ways of southern neighbors ever since, which contextualizes its more recent misadventures in Afghanistan and Chechnya. Equally invincible has been Russia's determination never again to find itself threatened, invaded, or occupied.

For many years following the end of Mongol rule, Russia did its best to join and influence the affairs of greater Europe. In 1714, however, Peter the Great decided to send an expedition into Central Asia, where only a handful of Westerners had ever set foot. The expedition's destination was one of Central Asia's centers of culture: the fearsome khanate of Khiva, which lay in the delta of the Oxus River southeast of the Aral Sea. Peter's decision to dispatch Russian soldiers toward this realm of violent desert law was largely inspired by rumors of gold in Central Asia's rivers. In moving toward Khiva, however, Peter's ultimate goal was not gold but India. The more Central Asian khanates Russia gobbled up, the closer it would bring Peter to a nation of growing colonial importance.

Peter's Khivan expedition did not go well. In 1717, overbudget and far behind schedule, the expedition arrived outside Khiva to be met by its ruler, Yadigar Khan. The expedition's leader, Prince Aleksandr Bekovich-Cherkassky, a Muslim convert to Christianity who hailed from the Caucasus highlands, was convinced by the affable Khan to allow his 6,600 men to be housed in various outlying villages around Khiva. For his trust Bekovich-Cherkassky was hacked to death, his hide eventually used to skin a royal drum. His soldiers were also slaughtered. Those who survived were sold into slavery, though a handful were allowed, at the urging of Khiva's appalled spiritual leader, to return home. The Khan of Khiva, a man clearly possessed of a peculiar sense of humor, mailed Bekovich-Cherkassky's head to the nearby Amir of Bukhara, who politely but firmly disavowed the trophy and returned it. Like many Central Asians before and after him, the Khan of Khiva was primevally unaware of his kingdom's relative weakness and had no conception of the power possessed by the behemoth into whose toe he had just thrust a pin. A growing crisis in the Caucasus soon occupied the Russian tsar's attention, however, and while the massacre of the ill-starred expedition was never forgotten, it was also never avenged. A Khivan ambassador who arrived in St. Petersburg in 1721 tried to explain that, in Khivan eyes, the tsar's "expedition" seemed eerily like an invading army. Unmoved Russian officials threw the ambassador into prison, where he eventually died. Russia would not return to Khiva for more than a century. Again the Russian army would be repulsed, this time by the worst Central Asian winter in a hundred years.

Russia's empire, meanwhile, had been steadily growing elsewhere. In only a few centuries Russian holdings grew at an astonishing pace: fifty-five square miles a day, or 20,000 square miles a year. By the early 1800s Russia had absorbed the empires of Sweden and Poland, gone to war with Persia and Turkey for Georgia and Armenia, and increased its subjects from 15 million to almost 60 million. Its new borders brought garrison forces within striking distance of cities such as Tehran and Constantinople, and the tsar even landed Russian troops, briefly, in Hawaii, Alaska, and California. Scholarly debate as to why Russia, one of Europe's most backward nations, launched upon such ambitious expansionism is contentious. Fear of Muslims? Worry that stealthy foreign powers would occupy its empty steppes? Or did it simply find itself, checked only on its European flank, obeying the organics of nineteenth-century nationhood and growing in every remaining direction? As George Curzon would write, "Russia was as much compelled to go forward as the earth is to go around the sun." Russian growth throughout the period confounded the rest of Europe, leading to rumors of a secret Russian plan to rule the world. After Napoleon's defeat in the War of 1812, Russia's power was exceeded only by that of England.

England noticed. The two empires had been allies against Napoleon, but Russian aspirations were soon racking the collective nerve of the British officer class. Esteemed British Russophobes penned hundreds of pamphlets warning of a coming Russian menace. On the Russian side, Dostoyevsky wrote: "If one fears England, one should sit at home and move nowhere!" The saber-rattled result was the Great Game, a Victorian-era cold war in which Russia and England, despite their best efforts, never managed to come into direct combat. England worried most about India, rightly suspecting that Russia's gradual push into Central Asia and toward Afghanistan was intended to provide the Russian army an easy path through the Bolan Pass into northern India, a nation nearly as invasion-prone as Russia. Not that England was without its own designs on Russia's sphere of influence. A British lieutenant in Afghanistan in the 1840s wrote home that "I expect very soon to see Chinese Tartary and Siberia among Her Majesty's dominions."

"Great Game" was coined by the British officer Arthur Conolly, one of its most successful—though ultimately doomed—players, in a letter to a friend ("a great game, a *noble* game"). The military historian John Kaye first allowed the term to walk tall with its capitals, and in the novel *Kim*, Rudyard Kipling popularized it. The words *bolshaya igra* (Russian for "great game") were even found scribbled in some of Stalin's notes concerning Central Asia. The other Russian term for the imperial rivalry was the much flashier "Tournament of Shadows." For another example of superior Russian coinage look no further than "cosmonaut."

The fires of the Great Game smoldered beneath the yule log of imperial expansion, though it had other sources of energy. One English participant believed the Anglo-Russian competition was all a matter of whether the natives of Central Asia would be purchasing their "implements of iron and steel from St. Petersburg or Birmingham." Cotton was one of the biggest Russian lures. Reports from the Aral Sea and the Ferghana Valley—the latter also mostly located in what is today called Uzbekistan—suggested that each region would be suitable for large-scale cotton growth. For both Russian and English merchants, Central Asia represented anywhere from 20 million to 50 million new customers. Central Asians—who were, whatever their specific feelings toward these interlopers, traders to their core—welcomed the influx of goods. This proved one of England's most reliable aces: whether porcelain, rifles, cotton, or clothing, England's wares were vastly superior to Russia's. Khans inevitably pointed this out to the impotent fury of Russian emissaries. The one area in which the Russians far surpassed the British proved to be intelligence gathering, an ugly suggestion of what was to come.

In accounting for the Great Game one can finally not discount the simple enticement of human exploration. Two very different national temperaments can be discerned in the terminology used to disavow captured agents: Russia typically claimed its spies were on a "scientific expedition" (usually to the Aral Sea), while England maintained its spies were on "shooting leave." Western exploration of the region would be one of the Gamers' most lasting legacies. Many decades before the golden age of Himalayan mountaineering, self-taught Britons and Russians roamed the uncharted peaks of Tajikistan, Kyrgyzstan, Uzbekistan, and Afghanistan, achieving almost monthly feats of cartography and exploration hitherto unknown.

While Russia and England never managed to fight each other, each crossed swords with numerous Central Asians. The Russian army tended to strike back ruthlessly against recalcitrant Muslims. This was especially the case in Russia's campaign against the Turkmen, the loathed kidnappers of Slavs as well as some of the most ferocious objectors to colonization in all of Central Asia. (The Soviets would still be fighting isolated bands of Turkmen desert warriors in the 1930s.) But for all the bloodshed suffered and inflicted by Russian troops, very little can compare to the British troubles in Afghanistan.

Eager to secure Afghanistan and prevent its Russian infestation, England invaded the ill-fated nation in the late 1830s. (It would invade again in 1878, but by that time England's colonial mettle had been weakened and the Great Game all but decided in Russia's favor.) For strategic purposes, England decided to unite the Afghan people by imposing upon them a leader of its choosing. That ruler was rejected, a huge rebellion ensued in Kabul, the British retreated, 15,000 British and Indian men and women suffered piecemeal slaughter on the long push back to India, the British army offered a reward of 10,000 rupees for the head of each rebel chief, and following their "victory" against their invaders the Afghan tribes instantly turned on one another. While these dramas unfolded, every newspaper reader in London, including the queen, suddenly had on his and her lips the name of obscure cities such as Herat and Mazar and Kandahar. It is a frighteningly familiar story, and a sad one, for every party involved. It is also instructive. Often one comes across well-meaning but politically naïve people who believe that resistance to the postmodern Western commercial leviathan arises out of some stubborn, anciently defiant sense of ethics. But it seems many of these people were not crazy about Victorian premodernism either.

The harsh lessons of holy war, not only in Afghanistan but also in the Sudan, emptied many Britons of their globe-lording resolve. Their sizable presence and influence in Central Asia has now been completely erased, though it is said the bleached bones of the 15,000 are still deposited among the hills of eastern Afghanistan. One of England's problems in Central Asia was its consistent hesitancy to let loose the hounds of war. "They hate us too much," one British officer noted of the

Afghans, "and fear us not enough." Russian thoughts were a little less circumspect. "In Asia," one general theorized, "the harder you hit them, the longer they remain quiet." This bloody doctrine ensured that, by the late 1800s, nearly all of Central Asia would be prostrate at the feet of the tsar. This was not, as has sometimes been supposed, due to a cowardly Muslim rabble fleeing from superior Russian troops. One Uzbek historian has written: "Thousands of ordinary people, armed with axes and sticks, fought valiantly despite being surrounded from all sides by several times more powerful and better armed tsarist armies." No event in that long, awful fight was more momentous than the Russian capture of Tashkent—the beginning of the end of the Great Game and the true dawn of Russia's Central Asian domination.

Despite its stubbornly ahistorical appearance, scholars believe that Tashkent (which means "Stone City") is over two thousand years old, making it one of the oldest extant cities on earth. Throughout its history Tashkent had been a sporadically independent city-state, variously controlled by invading Arabs, the Chinese, Mongols, the Timurid dynasty, the Shaybanid dynasty, the tribes we would now call Kazakhs, and, in 1865, by the Khan of Kokand. Famously encircled by a high crenellated stone wall sixteen miles long—though not one brick of it remains— Tashkent possessed a reputation for great wealth and enterprise. It had traded with Russia far earlier than most of Central Asia's other, often fanatically isolationist cities. The Russian commander in the region, General Mikhail Grigoryevich Chernyayev, had longed to capture Tashkent, but after a failed (and unapproved) 1864 attempt to take the city, he found his adventurism stymied by his superiors in St. Petersburg. Russia worried first how England would react to such a brazen move and second how General Chernyayev's troops, only a little over 1,000 strong, could possibly manage against the rumored 30,000 defenders waiting behind Tashkent's walls. But thanks to his extensive network of spies, Chernyayev knew that the merchant families who directed Tashkent commerce would have vastly preferred Russian rule to that of the Khan of Kokand, who never met a tax he did not levy. On the other side of the cultural spectrum, Tashkent's influential mullahs looked to the Amir of Bukhara for salvation, as Bukhara was and remains the Plymouth Rock of Central Asian Islam. The Amir of Bukhara was in 1865 attempting to oblige Tashkent's clergy, going to war with Kokand over control of the great walled city.

The war gave Chernyayev the perfect excuse to seize Tashkent, and he was certain he could do so before Bukhara, which had become one of Russia's archfoes in the region. He telegraphed St. Petersburg his intentions to capture Tashkent. St. Petersburg telegraphed back an order not to attack. Here Chernyayev did something ingenious and indicative of future Russian behavior in Central Asia: He did not open or read the telegraph, and in May 1865 he set off for Tashkent across Russian-controlled Kazakh grazing lands.

The Amir of Bukhara also dispatched to Tashkent his own small force of advisors and janissaries, who managed to slip into Tashkent days before Chernyayev arrived. The Buhkarans' appearance made the native pro-Russian rebellion Chernyayev was expecting even less likely, as Central Asians, historically, turned to European redeemers only when it was clear that their own rulers had no chance against them. Chernyayev's opening move was to seize a small river fort south of Tashkent. With the fort under his control, Chernyayev diverted the river, removing the city's largest water source. Requested reinforcements soon arrived, giving Chernyayev a siege force of nearly 2,000. His problems began. First he had to beat back a force of brigands who had sneaked past his perimeter. Then his spies broke the news that the anticipated native rebellion would simply never materialize and that Chernyayev's forces were outnumbered by at least fifteen to one. If Chernyayev returned now to Orenburg, the Russian frontier garrison, he faced certain court-martial, perhaps even the frontier justice of a firing squad. This was not to mention the humiliation with which such a misadventure would cloak Russia in Central Asian eyes. So he attacked.

In attacking Tashkent, General Chernyayev counted on a few things. The first was that the defenders would be spread so thinly along Tashkent's walls that punching through and getting inside would not be difficult. The second was that his troops were far better trained, commanded, and equipped than Tashkent's irregulars. The third was that surprise, under the circumstances, ensured victory. Late one night, over a month after he had arrived at Tashkent's outskirts, Chernyayev and his primary assault party wheeled up gun carriages to the portion of Tashkent's wall his reconnaissance had suggested was most vulnerable, the carriages' wheels wrapped in felt to guarantee silence. Meanwhile, miles away, a smaller diversionary party feigned attack on one of the city's twelve gates. The plan worked perfectly. Chernyayev and his men made it inside and kicked open a gate without losing a soul. An understandably legendary Russian chaplain named Malov—who would tend to Tashkent's Christians for the rest of his life—ran screaming through the gates and into the morass before all others, his only weapon a large cross. Tashkent's soft, citified defenders were simply not the same species as the fierce Muslims Russia had grown accustomed to fighting in the Caucasus Mountains and Turkmenistan's Karakum Desert, and within hours more than half of Tashkent was under Chernyayev's control. For the remaining pockets of resistance the fighting grew grisly. Five thousand fleeing Tashkent horsemen were slain outside the city walls in one skirmish alone. At one point Chernyayev was forced to shell Tashkent—something he wanted very much to avoid—leaving a large part of the city aflame. Abandoned by their Bukharan advisors and with the occupying Kokand garrison routed, Tashkent's citizens soon realized they had no choice but to submit. The city elders, astonished by Chernyayev's *dadillik* (bravery), proclaimed him "the Lion of Tashkent." Chernyayev, for his part, accepted their surrender on behalf of the tsar (something that, like everything up to this point, he had no authority to do), and promised Tashkent's Muslims that Russia would never interfere in its religious life (in which, despite subsequent history, he appears to have been sincere). Chernyayev even absolved the city of paying taxes for a year. He then awaited word from the tsar.

It soon came. Alexander II was beside himself, calling Tashkent's seizure "a glorious affair" and awarding Chernyayev the Cross of St. Anne. Chernyayev, a man of considerable honor, recommended to the tsar that Tashkent be restored to its status as an independent khanate, though one under Russian protection. The tsar and his battery of princes agreed—that is, they agreed this was what they would tell the British. Chernyayev's recommendation was never carried out, and after a few more conquests he was recalled. Russia would not leave Tashkent for another 130 years, and within a decade most of the great cities of Central Asia would be Russian protectorates. This, at the cost to Russia of twenty-five of General Chernyayev's men—a rate of exchange that must very nearly make up for selling Alaska at two cents an acre.

Russian involvement in Central Asia was not always of ill consequence. With them the Russians brought goods, medicines, railways, roads, electricity. For many years under tsarist rule Central Asia's courts were allowed to operate under the Sharia (Islamic law). Central Asia's tsarist governors-general, who took an oath that promised "to show fairness to the needs and interests of the Muslims," discouraged the efforts of Mother Russia's more zealous Christian missionaries. (The total number of Central Asian Muslim converts to Christianity during the tsarist period was exactly fourteen. The number of Central Asian Russian converts to Islam was ten.) The irrigation and diversion of the Aral Sea's feeder rivers was ecologically damaging but not insanely so, as it would be under the Soviets. Less defensible was Russia's thorough importation of alcoholism, the ruthlessness of tsarist storm troopers in putting down revolt, and its rule through native surrogates. Throughout Central Asia—and no more so than in Uzbekistan—this system spawned a hated indigenous elite the power of which came only through Russian conduits. Use of elites would spread in the Soviet era. They still existed, but now the elites answered to no one.

Russian involvement in Central Asia was rather akin to that of an irresponsible bankrupt maxing out a stack of credit cards in order to date women who do not love him and whom he cannot actually afford. Russia wanted to be a great power and could not pretend Great Power status without its captured khanates and miles of deserts and remote mosque-centered cities. And though Russia may have ruled Central Asia, Central Asia worked its own influence upon Russia. One does not merely "rule" a place of such apocalyptic possibility. How else to explain the varied roles Central Asia has played in Russia's great drama? Hope, savior, future, lifeblood, bane, and, to Solzhenitsyn, a "soft underbelly" that needed to be mercifully shed. In the last two centuries Russia has twice occupied vast territories it fought and connived for, filled the remaining world with awe and fear, and then, quite suddenly, collapsed from within. How did this happen? Any Central Asian will tell you: "That was us. We did that. We've been doing it for a thousand years."

The damnable matter of the letter was forgotten: Tashkent nightlife beckoned. For a few hours Rustam and I played pool at the Salty Dog saloon in the seamy Bumi Hotel. Rustam chalked his cue while I fingered the ropy netting and faux wooden life preservers nailed to the walls. I tried to explain to him the derivation of the term "salty dog," and he tried to explain to me why a saloon in the middle of a landlocked nation surrounded entirely by other landlocked nations had decided to traffic in nautical themes. The Library, a bar found one floor up in Tashkent's Sheraton, followed. Some American businessmen and State Department types blew cigar smoke in the Library's various nooks. The Library's walls were lined with bolted-in books, the spines of which lacked any title or colophon. Next to our table two young black men—a rare sight in Central Asia—spoke fluent Russian to a trio of transfixed young Russian women. We opted next for the nightclub Aladdin, found right off Independence Square, a joyless funhouse of whores and gangsters and loud Russian gluco-pop. We decided to end our night in the Lucky Strike. A cabdriver told us that it had been closed. A new nightclub, he said, a very nice nightclub, had recently opened nearby. We decided to visit this new nightclub. It was closed. The Lucky Strike, however, was open. Tashkent.

I had been to the Lucky Strike a few times while in the Peace Corps. It was a mid-sized, cheerful place popular with Tashkent's yuppies and less fashionable expats. A muted television above the bar broadcast French music videos, the silent images as disconnected as flash cards. While Rustam ordered drinks, I made my way into a larger back room to find that the Lucky Strike's armada of pool tables was entirely in use. Two or three of the pool players looked American, including a red-cheeked overweight blond woman wearing a California Angels baseball hat and a thin white sweater. While she was waiting for her turn, I asked her if she was from California. "Yup," she said. I told her I was from New York. "Wow," she said.

I went back to sit with Rustam. We drank for a while, quite a while, for soon I was attempting to convince a Russian prostitute drinking alone at the bar to agree to let me interview her.

"Tashkent's *sex* industry?" Rustam asked me midway through my pitch.

I had no carnal feelings for the woman. I was simply interested in talking to her. "Yeah. Tell her I'm writing an exposé of Tashkent's sex industry."

He translated. Without looking at me, the woman shook her head. She wore snakeskin pants, her tight T-shirt flattening each small, appley breast. Her nose had an Ahkmatovan bump, and cheap tawny highlights streaked through her long black hair. She was pretty but in a rough whorish way; I admired her hard physical vitality the way one might admire a set of snow tires. I tried for a little longer to persuade her, having convinced myself I actually *would* write an exposé of Tashkent's sex industry, but eventually gave up and bought her a drink. "No hard feelings," I told Rustam to tell her. She smiled. She still had not looked at me. The drink arrived. She never touched it. We left.

In Chilanzor I fell out of the taxi and experimented with walking toward the interstellar darkness of the apartment building's vestibule. Rustam had also gotten out and was noisily urinating into a flower bed when a man approached him. They had words. At this I turned. Rustam was zipping up, explaining something to the man. Rustam looked over at me. "Go home!" he called. I did not move. Now Rustam was nodding. He seemed to tell the man to wait for one moment, just a moment, and walked over to the cab. He climbed in and the cab drove away. The man took a few powerless steps after the car and was turning toward me when I ducked into the building. I ran up the stairs and held down the doorbell until Natasha opened the door and pulled me inside. "Where were you?" she said in Russian, grasping me by the cheeks. "Where *were* you?" Then she smashed me to her chest. She let go when she saw the man standing in the doorjamb.

He was Uzbek, and gulping air. He had run up four flights after me. His ears were as prominent as wings, and the closeness of his ashy gray-and-black crew cut emphasized an eggish skull. His green suit was dark, his green tie darker. Finally, his lungs having raked together his breath, he smiled. *"Dobryi vecher."* Good evening.

Natasha answered, either very calm or very worried: *"Dobryi vecher."*

Oleg stepped into the apartment's narrow hallway, crush-haired and blinking, wearing an age-grayed T-shirt and ventilated boxers. He had been reaching across himself and digging around in his itchy armpit but stopped when he saw the man. His arm hung across his body as though in a sling. He looked stick-limbed and weak and confused. Surprise had slightly pried open his mouth.

Natasha welcomed the man in. Without a look, he shouldered past me into the dark living room. Natasha rushed after him and flipped a wall switch, the prehistoric ceiling fixture's trio of naked bulbs flooding the room with a shadow-expunging light as harsh as that of a surgical theater. Oleg and I were left alone in the hallway. He looked at me. I shook my head.

The man enthroned himself within a deep velvety maroon chair, the tiny living room's biggest and most comfortable piece of furniture. His legs yawned apart and his arms lay comfortably upon the chair's cushioned rests. He looked large, in bloom. From the couch Oleg gathered the twisted blankets and unbraided them. He sat down on the couch's edge, saving room for Natasha, who was now making tea in the kitchen.

I took a seat. The man, still smiling, said something to me in Russian. Oleg told him I did not speak Russian.

"I know some Uzbek," I told the man.

The man's smile grew, a delighted little pock dimpling beneath each of his eyes. "*Ajoyyib,*" he said, nodding.

It was one of my favorite Uzbek words. It meant both "wonderful" and "strange," shading each with a meaning no single English word could match. I did not like this man using the word. It was like seeing someone you despised reading a novel you loved.

The man reached into his sport coat and withdrew a thick leather booklet. He held it out to me. When I leaned forward, he removed his thumb from the top of the booklet, its weight causing it to flop open. His name was Alijonov. He was a captain with the Uzbek police. I now understood why Rustam had opted to flee. That morning I had given Rustam a week's advance pay, and Uzbekistan's police officers were notoriously sticky-fingered. I looked over Alijonov's credentials, then nodded and sat back. Natasha appeared from the kitchen, looking manic and balancing a small tray freighted with teacups. Alijonov took a cup and thanked her. Oleg plucked a cup from the tray as well. Once mine was in hand, she quickly ducked back into the kitchen.

Alijonov meditatively sipped his tea and sighed, our eyes locking. He seemed to enjoy looking at me. He said something about *aroq,* vodka.

"I don't understand."

He sniffed hard, twice. He was saying, I gathered, that I smelled of vodka.

"No," I told him. "I was drinking *piva,* beer. Only *piva.*"

"Only *piva*. And how many did you drink?"

"Two or three." Or six. Or eight.

A heavy invisible cloud of grease spread throughout the apartment, accompanied by a hot and insistent spatter. In the kitchen Natasha was frying potatoes. The smell switched on my hunger, my stomach creaking like a floorboard.

Alijonov smiled. His sharp yellowy teeth sat in his mouth like an ivory trap. "Where is your passport?"

I withdrew the pouch I wore around my neck, unzipped it, and handed over my passport. Alijonov complimented me on my passport, as Central Asia's officials often did. Such a tidy, small, attractive document! Just to cross a regional border here an Uzbek citizen needed a three-ring binder to carry all the necessary documents. As Alijonov read over my passport, he asked Oleg for his documents as well. Every Uzbek citizen is required to carry an internal passport. On this passport's *propiska,* or identity card, one's city of residence was prominently listed. Anyone stopped by the police while not in that city had some explaining to do. I already knew that Oleg's *propiska* listed his city of residence as Ferghana City. He had been living illegally in Tashkent for years.

Alijonov held Oleg's passport away from himself, stunned by its discrepancy. Sorrowfully, he clucked his tongue. Natasha appeared again with a plate of fried potatoes, which she set next to Alijonov. He ignored them. Natasha managed a fretful look at both men before exiting. Alijonov and Oleg spoke ominously in Russian about Oleg's lack of a stamp granting him permission to live in Tashkent. Alijonov affected true pain at having to confront Oleg about this, and soon Oleg was saying very little. Alijonov seemed even sadder about that. Without asking he picked up the nearby phone and dialed a number. Whoever answered was quickly supplied with Oleg and Natasha's address. Alijonov hung up and sighed again.

Oleg's and my violations seemed to provide Alijonov with an infinity of punitive possibilities to contemplate. We sat there, the only sounds coming from the kitchen. Drawers rolled along their runners. Teacups emptied into the sink. Upon Alijonov's neglected plate the edge-browned potatoes were still so hot the salt Natasha had poured all over them glistened in clumpy melted deposits. I knew that Alijonov was not interested in terrorizing us. He just wanted money. He did not even seem to be a bad man.

"What are you writing about?" Alijonov asked me suddenly.

"Uzbekistan."

"What do you think about Uzbekistan?"

"I love Uzbekistan."

"He's writing about the Aral Sea," Oleg said, tucking a stringy bolt of yellow hair behind each ear to keep it out of his eyes.

Alijonov's eyebrows popped up. "Oh, really? What about it?"

"The people," I said. "The . . . situation?"

"How much do journalists get paid in America?"

Before I could lie, Oleg told him I was paid a dollar a word. Oleg had asked about this the night before, and I had told him. I saw little point in lying. Oleg had been very impressed with a dollar a word until I shared with him what I paid in rent. Then he was quiet. Alijonov, too, was very impressed with a dollar a word. Oleg let Alijonov soak in his envy. Then, with expert timing, he informed the man what I paid in rent. Oleg and Alijonov stared at each other in some stunned new confederacy. We in the West wonder at the East's tribalism and bigamy and dog-eating peculiarities. In the East all they seem to wonder at is how much we pay for everything.

"So," Alijonov said, gathering himself, "how many words will you write?"

"A lot," I said. Laughter. Huge laughter, a sound as dense and sudden as a flock of gulls taking flight. Alijonov reached over and slapped a falsely braying Oleg on the knee.

"Why are you not married, Tombek?" Alijonov said, wiping his eyes.

The doorbell rang. Oleg exploded off the couch to answer it.

"Too young," I told Alijonov.

"How old are you?"

"Twenty-seven."

He held up three big knuckly fingers and pushed them close to my face. "That," he said, "is how many children I had at your age."

Into the room, ahead of Oleg, strode a heavy-booted policeman in the common Uzbek patrolman's dark green fatigues. A sidearm was riveted upon one hip and a truncheon dangled from the other. A pack of cigarettes bulged unashamedly in his breast pocket. Hellos traveled counterclockwise around the room. The uniformed officer removed his hat and sat down on the couch next to Oleg. Natasha appeared with tea and fried potatoes for him, too. He thanked her and began forking the oily wedges into his mouth. Alijonov meanwhile debriefed his colleague on my passport, Oleg's lack of a stamp, one dollar a word. Oleg studied his thin, hairless thigh with a poet's dreamy half-focus. Natasha stepped into the living room and then stood silently in the corner, her lips pushed into a small prudent heart.

The phone rang. Oleg answered and said a few quick, guarded things and hung up.

"Who was that?" Alijonov wanted to know.

"His friend," Oleg said, pointing at me.

"Ah," Alijonov said, "the fugitive."

The uniformed officer, his lips and chin shiny with grease, set down his scoured plate and looked at me. We reenacted Alijonov's and my earlier conversation. Not married. X kids by my age. American rent: expensive. Uzbekistan: one hell of a place. Suddenly, Oleg pulled out a copy of *Men's Journal* in which I had published an article. I had brought a few copies of it and some other things along in the likely event that my credentials ever came into doubt. Oleg had liked looking at the magazine so much I wound up giving it to him. When I left the apartment early that morning, he was still studying its bright slick pages of flat suntanned abdomens and bullet-sleek automobiles and utterly unimaginable watersport tableaux. Alijonov and his colleague liked this magazine, too. They shared the large plush chair now and stared at the pictures in wonder. I took the liberty to page back a bit in order to show the officers my photo on the contributors' page. They nodded and speedily flipped back to their earlier place. I glanced over at Oleg. Very softly he nodded at me.

The doorbell again. It was Rustam. He barged into the living room sweating, drunk, and smoking. He was so nervous the first thing he said to the officers was in English. He covered his eyes, teeth bared, and extended his hand to Alijonov.

Alijonov stood, buttoning his coat. "Why did you run?" he asked. His eyes were ablaze with what I hoped was merely mock outrage. Alijonov waved his hand over me. "You left your American friend all alone! What if I had been a thief?"

Alijonov was joking. But Rustam's eyes nearly watered. Guests here were so serious a matter that to cast even jesting aspersions on another's commitment to hospitality was a gambit of pure humiliation. Rustam looked over at me hopelessly. Oleg touched him on the shoulder and invited him to sit down on the couch. Rustam obeyed, sucking quietly on his cigarette and knocking the ash into his palm. The room's light seemed not to fall upon him as much as burden him. His sweaty forehead was all white gloss. While the second officer sat absorbed with *Men's Journal,* Alijonov went through Rustam's passport. Rustam had the proper Tashkent stamp, but Alijonov did not seem to believe Rustam had come by it legally.

"I'm a student," Rustam explained.

"Where?"

Rustam told him.

"That is a fancy school. Perhaps you are our future minister of foreign affairs?"

Rustam laughed, Oleg and Natasha too. Alijonov asked for one of Rustam's cigarettes. Natasha dashed into the kitchen and walked back into the living room very slowly, holding in one hand a single lit match and with the other providing for the match its own windshield. Alijonov leaned into tear-shaped flame and took a long drag so powerful the tobacco popped as it burned. For Alijonov it seemed the most natural thing in the world to storm into a home at two in the morning and enjoy the kind of hospitality normally shown guests of rare occasion. It was disgusting, I supposed. I had no idea how exactly Rustam or Oleg or Natasha regarded all of this. They were not good actors. Their laughter was hollow, their deference birthed of nothing but obvious, if frightened, contempt. Not even the vainest creature could have believed his presence here was welcome or liked. I wondered if Alijonov cared.

Alijonov wrote down Rustam and Oleg's passport numbers. Both of them tried not to notice this. The uniformed officer asked if he could keep my magazine. I looked quickly to Oleg, who again softly nodded. "Certainly," I told the officer. The gentlemen stood. Natasha apologized for not having had more food or tea available. Oh, Alijonov said, not to worry. He understood. He then looked indignantly at Rustam. "Why can't you be as good a boy as your friend, little brother? You see how he respects us? You see how he doesn't run from us?"

"I did run," I pointed out. "You caught me."

More laughter. At some point I had been given a cigarette. I was now smoking it. I had not smoked a cigarette in close to a decade. This seemed very funny to me, and I laughed too, though everyone else had stopped. My head was ringing.

"You're a good boy," Alijonov said to me. Again to Rustam: "But this one . . ." Oleg finally escorted them out, Rustam following. Natasha and I looked at each other. She exhaled.

Rustam stepped back into the apartment's hallway and summoned me. One landing below, Oleg and the officers were still talking.

"How much?" I asked him.

"Ten thousand sums each, I think."

"That's . . . what? Eight dollars apiece?"

"Yeah."

I reached into my money belt and pulled from my stash two tens, as crisp as wet paper that had been blow-dried. "Here."

"Bro, that's too much."

"I don't think they'll mind."

The deed consummated, Oleg and Rustam closed the door behind them and with knowing relief slapped each other on the back. "What did they say?" I asked.

Oleg smiled and said something in Russian.

Rustam nodded, then translated: "Alijonov said we are all friends now. He ripped up that piece of paper he wrote our passport numbers on."

Oleg extended his hand. In his palm was a small nest of white shreds—Alijonov's unprompted guarantee that the matter would never arise again.

This did not come even close to satisfying me. "Who was he? Why did he follow us?"

"He is the policeman for Chilanzor," Rustam explained. "He watches the neighborhood. Tonight he watched us."

I looked at all of them. "Rustam, can you tell them I'm terribly, terribly sorry about this?"

Oleg dismissed my regret. Rustam: "He tells you not to worry. We had it easy. It went well, he said." Natasha, I saw, was nodding in accord.

"What are they talking about? They had two cops in their house at two in the morning! That was terrifying!"

Rustam translated for me, and then for them. "You don't understand. Ten days before you arrived here, Oleg was stopped outside the Metro by the militsiya. They beat him so badly he pissed blood for a week."

"[T]he city spread across the flat landscape in a succession of inhumanly wide boulevards and squares. The government buildings were too big and ill-proportioned. . . . Inside these massive buildings I would later see rows of sleazy little cubbyholes. . . . The apartment houses [were] often unpainted, badly fitted. . . . [T]his was surely the most hideous and alienating example of Soviet design I had seen. . . . The shattered, ad hoc quality of the architecture intensified the sense of alienation and placelessness. I had to look hard for beauty."

I had the Tashkent morning to myself. I spent most of it drinking pomegranate juice and reading Robert D. Kaplan's *The Ends of the Earth: A Journey to the Frontiers of Anarchy* in a small café near Tashkent's quite lovely Old City. Kaplan traveled to these frontiers of reputed anarchy in 1994. One of the places he visited was Uzbekistan, which he describes in the above passage. In the book's foreword Kaplan writes, admirably, about the travel writer's need to "confront the real world, slums and all." It is therefore a little distressing that in Uzbekistan we learn that Kaplan "stayed with a friend, a Western diplomat. 'Don't drink the tap water,' he told me."

Kaplan's books are typically informed by an unimaginable lode of historical research, with bits of Conrad and Soyinka and the Qur'an paradropped into the text like little prose commandos. A partisan of the Clash of Civilizations Hypothesis, Kaplan's reporting often suggests that our future holds nothing less than some global Ragnarök. This may or may not be true, of course. But Kaplan's seeming addiction to prophecy (his book *Balkan Ghosts* is said to have "predicted" the meltdown in Yugoslavia) has given him over to an unhappy combination of gloom and credulousness. I am unable to speak to the accuracy found within his dispatches from most of the places he covers in *The Ends of the Earth,* but I can say his Uzbekistan chapters contain reporting of consistent, disconcerting inaccuracy. All travel books contain errors, and I am sure this one has more than its share. But Kaplan's hammering insistence upon figuring out What Culture Means requires an accuracy commensurate to the conclusions he draws. And yet once he is away from his books he begins to grease his analytical wheels with the highly anecdotal. This is accompanied by an almost perverse freedom to pinion entire cultures based upon how his morning has gone.

Start with Kaplan's ostensibly salutary commitment to confronting slums. As anyone who has traveled in economically stratified places knows, *one cannot avoid slums if one tries.* So one confronts this slum— yes, before me stands a slum—but to what end? This is somehow supposed to supply the key to all poverties? Additionally, Kaplan tells us that crime "is considerable in Tashkent." Kaplan was in Tashkent in 1994. According to those I know who lived there at the time, crime in 1994 Tashkent was minimal. Crime today in Tashkent is probably worse than it has ever been—and still far, far below what one can expect on a sunny summer night in Chicago or Brooklyn. The crime that does exist in Tashkent, or any of Uzbekistan's cities, is almost always of a nuisance nature. Provided one is not looking to become a smack connoisseur or engage too deeply with the mafiya-run world of prostitution, bloodless muggings and pickpocketry are about as rough as Tashkent gets. (If one is a man, that is. Women unfortunately enjoy different worries.) "I was back in a place," Kaplan writes of Uzbekistan, "where the social fabric was thin." I have been mugged in Tashkent, more than once. Never, for one moment, did I fear for my life. It is impossible for me to imagine an average Tashkent criminal willing to murder his victim, particularly his Western victim. That is because Uzbekistan's social fabric—and its attendant obsession with hospitality—is so triple-ply strong.

Kaplan writes of "hovels, battered automobiles, and people in unsightly polyester clothing." "Hovels" is a very relative term. Many of these hovels are, on the inside, splendidly turned out. The average Uzbek family's rug collection alone is enough to unhinge one's jaw. As for battered cars, well, certainly, but so what? Most people in Uzbekistan are poor. "Unsightly polyester clothing," however, is absurd. Most urban Central Asians are obsessed—to a fault—with their appearance. And while many Uzbeks wear the same garments day after day, they are always well maintained and anything but unsightly. Indeed, most times in Uzbekistan *I* have been the one wearing the unsightly clothing, my knee-thinned blue jeans, dusty shoes, and T-shirts looked upon with obvious (though very polite) disdain.

Then there are Kaplan's mistakes: "The driver charged us twenty thousand soms [sic] for the five-minute ride, about eighty cents." In 1994 twenty thousand sums, even at the highest exchange rate imaginable, would have been around $160. Either Kaplan is winging it based on incomplete notes and a shaky memory or this cab took him for a very long ride through Suckertown. Kaplan really hits his stride when he and his translator, Ulug Beg, visit Samarkand. (The great city of Samarkand is "a would-be Bangkok," Kaplan writes, with its "army of whores." Samarkand is actually a college town, about as far from Bangkok as Ann Arbor.) Samarkand, as mentioned earlier, is a Tajik-majority city. This does afford those who live there a few cultural bellyaches, but Samarkand is not the pressure cooker of ethnic tension Kaplan pretends. "I feel strange here," Ulug Beg tells Kaplan, "as if I am in Tajikistan. . . . Why aren't our own Uzbek women so pretty? . . . We must settle Uzbeks here. We must settle many, many Uzbeks in Samarkand. . . . The only thing we Uzbeks have in common with Tajiks is the sky." (I would later let Rustam, himself part Tajik, look over some of these passages. Rustam read, the troubled indentation between his brows darkening. After a while he looked up and asked, "Bro, who wrote this bullshit?") Poor Ulug Beg, Kaplan writes, "though well groomed and educated, was crude in the way he ate and narrow in his prejudices against Tajiks. . . . This coarseness might be more than just the effect of three quarters of a century of Soviet communism. I thought and thought [!]. Could these be *pre-Byzantine* Turks?" Could it be rather that one young man's eating habits have nothing to do with the current cultural state of Uzbekistan, much less its one-thousand-year-old Turkish roots? Could it be that just because someone slurps when he eats does not mean he is a ticking time bomb of inherited cultural fate?

But this is small beer. Kaplan's most onerous failing in *The Ends of the Earth* is his willingness to pardon the dictatorship of Islam Karimov because he keeps Uzbekistan's "simmering hatreds" under control. (Actually, his most onerous failing might be titling one chapter "Clean Toilets and the Legacy of Empires." Dirty loos are a Kaplan bête noire, which makes one fundamentally question his supposed willingness to get down and dirty in the developing world. Passage after passage on toilets. These not only fill the mind with unwelcome images of Robert D. Kaplan taking a dump, they make one wonder if the title of his book should have been *It Smelled: A Journey to the Frontiers of Anarchy*.) Uzbekistan does have its ethnocultural problems, as does every nation. Occasionally they have been violent. That said, Uzbekistan's culture is, in my experience, basically tolerant. This fundamental tolerance, not only to matters of ethnicity but also to gender, is one of the most benevolent legacies of the Soviet Union. And while many ethnicities—Koreans, especially, and to a lesser extent Tajiks and Russians—are glass-ceilinged from ascending too high within Uzbek officialdom or academia, people in Uzbekistan are not anywhere close to taking to the streets in search of different-colored hides. Their frustrations are almost wholly economic. Unless all of Central Asia collapses beneath some larger regional crisis—a shortage of fresh water, for instance—it is unlikely that Uzbekistan's average citizens will ever be ready to take up arms against their countrymen, Karimov or no Karimov. Indeed, the most pressing threat to Uzbekistan's stability is *Karimov* and his repressive policies.

One would never glean this from Kaplan. In his interpretation, Islam Karimov stars as Marshal Tito in The Balkans, Part II. "Might Karimov's be a tyranny of necessity?" Kaplan asks. "Might it make sense, in the short run at least, for Karimov to idolize strongmen like Lee Kuan Yew of Singapore and Alberto Fujimori of Peru rather than idealists like Vaclav Havel of the Czech Republic?" Compare this to Karimov's own statement on the matter: "A strong executive power is necessary to prevent bloodshed and confrontation and preserve interethnic and civic calm, peace, and stability." Karimov at least has the excuse of self-interested hegemony. Kaplan is merely disguising his fatalism as pragmatism—never mind that dictators are not known for their willingness to think in terms of "the short run." Kaplan fails to address the pivotal issue here: pervasive naked power worship, something one sees again and again in societies based upon certainty-peddling creeds, be they Islamic or Soviet. Forget the Pandora's box of instability. Karimov works in the idiom of power alone, and his subjects respect him because of his power. Power worship is what George Orwell, in a different context, called the worship of the "continuation of the thing that is happening." He also called it "a mental disease." Worship of the continuation of the thing that is happening is what keeps thugs like Karimov safely ensconced in their palaces. It keeps those living beneath them in obedient line. It holds up the faulty eye chart that legitimizes American foreign policy's myopia when considering such brutes. It lessens the guilt of the American diplomats who have to deal with loutish regimes on a daily basis. And it gives tea-leaf-reading journalists like Robert D. Kaplan their stony surety. Karimov does not idolize Vaclav Havel, because why on earth would he? "I favor 'anti-political politics,'" Havel once remarked. "That is, politics not as the technology of power and manipulation of cybernetic rule over humans, or as the art of the useful, but politics as practical morality, as service to the truth, as essentially human and humanly measured care for our fellow humans."

Beliefs such as Havel's are the classical domain of the intellectual, a figure who always plays a crucial role in the transformation of society. (Only the stultifying Soviet mind could imagine an intellectual as someone "engaged in mental labor," as one official bureaucratic listing defined them. Lenin publicly considered the intellectual "more conscientious . . . and more precise than all" and privately considered them "shit.") Unfortunately, Uzbekistan's intellectuals are exiled, jailed, and neutered. This has allowed unreflective zealots both secular and devout to step into their place. Karimov's repression encourages the pessimism of sympathetic outsiders like Kaplan and fuel-injects the rage of those not inclined toward democracy. The Shah of Iran suppressed Islam and democracy with American aid, and what happened? Religious maniacs and embittered intellectual reformers, disgusted with their nation's state of affairs and the United States, came together in an unholy marriage of revolt, and soon Iran degenerated into a satrapy of fanaticism united by its hatreds.

Depressingly, common Uzbeks are even less optimistic than Kaplan about their chances without Karimov at the national helm. No doubt Kaplan's published belief that Karimov is "the alternative to chaos" was informed by speaking to many such Uzbeks. *Of course* Uzbeks fear life without Karimov. *Of course* the succession crisis that will arise with Karimov's death or overthrow will be Uzbekistan's largest, most frightening challenge. Its common citizens have, for a decade, done nothing while the most moderate opposition forces have been systematically removed and smothered. How better to guarantee that only the most militant and fanatical will be left to rush into the inevitable vacuum? This is hardly a reason to shruggingly empower Karimov. The autocrat is almost always to blame for the crises he attempts to stifle. One cannot turn this relationship around, as Kaplan does, and maintain that Karimov is the antivenom to his own snakebite. Equally offensive is Kaplan's apparent view that Uzbeks are uncontrollable children waiting for the dangerous swindle of democracy to allow them to massacre one another.

"All I had learned so far was that states in . . . Central Asia were weakening," Kaplan writes at the close of his Uzbekistan chapter, "and that ethnic-religious identities appeared stronger by contrast. Beyond that, I had little proof of anything. Travel was indeed frustrating." No bloody wonder.

I decided to take a walk down a short pedestrians-only Tashkent street known locally as Sayilgoh and to everyone else as Broadway. Broadway was a street fair, and now, at noon, things were beginning to get under way. Friendly young waitresses stood outside Broadway's many raincoat-yellow food tents and promised "Cold beer . . . cold beer" to any reasonably American-seeming passerby. Five years ago I splintered a filling upon a rock while eating plov, the national dish of Uzbekistan, within one of these tents, precipitating an emergency trip to a Russian dentist, an experience I find myself unwilling to relive even through the controlled medium of descriptive prose. Broadway spelled out and italicized the inherent difficulties of young capitalism even for a land and people with strong congenital instincts toward trade. Within stall after booth after stall, confident-looking proprietors hawked Kodak film, pirated CDs, notebooks, pens, sausages, soda, and mineral water all *at exactly the same price as the kiosk next to them.* Silent Uzbek carnies waited beside games of the pop-the-balloon and toss-the-ring variety, rows of stuffed animals hanging within the booths' festive gallows. One young man ran a boldly rigged basket toss. The game's winning prize was a banana. Three shamelessly intoxicated Uzbek teenage boys sat before a karaoke machine and crooned a version of Stevie Wonder's "I Just Called to Say I Love You" best described as Interpretive Song. Next to the boys an old woman with a scale heartbreakingly offered to weigh me for ten sums. At the end of Broadway the street fair became an art fair. Paintings, including the surprisingly international *Dogs Playing Poker,* absorbed squares of spring sunshine while ambitious middlemen sat upon nearby foldout chairs in glum silence. I stumbled upon a small, beautiful brass bust of V. I. Lenin. The Uzbek gentleman selling the bust was asking for a very un-Marxist-Leninist $50. Hamlet-like, I held up Lenin's brass skull. Just as Jesus Christ looks forbidding and Teutonic in German art and dark and Moorish in Spanish art and pale and Anglo in British art, the messiah of Soviet Communism was, in Central Asia, always orientalized, his Tatar cheekbones emphasized and his eyes slitted. This bust was one of the most Asian Lenins I had ever seen. It had a heaviness that felt almost lethal.

I circled around to meet Rustam at a small restaurant called the New World Café. Close by I found a row of promotional posters featuring Islam Karimov. I remembered an earlier suite of these posters from my days as an English teacher in Uzbekistan, since every school in the country devoted at least one corridor to Karimov's greatness. The posters always depicted Karimov in a progression of roles and milieus, leading to a final poster of the man at his most dynamic. First was Karimov with World Leaders: King Faisal, Boris Yeltsin, Helmut Kohl, Bill Clinton. The Clinton photo was from a four-year-old photo op in the Oval Office. Because of Karimov's rancid human rights record Clinton had agreed to meet with him only for five minutes alongside three other CIS heads of state. The photo used here was cropped in such a way that these gentlemen had vanished, and Karimov and Clinton appeared close and familiar enough to arm-wrestle. The next poster featured Karimov the Athlete, first dribbling a basketball; then in full tennis regalia (Karimov was such an apostle of the sport he lured a major international tennis championship to Tashkent and built for it a jumbo stadium); then playing chess, seemingly against himself, on an airplane. The last poster was not of Karimov at all but showed Uzbek athletes doing judo and swimming and boxing and playing water polo and even planting an Uzbek flag atop Everest. I then realized these posters were the remnants of Tashkent's most recent campaign to host the Olympic games, something its city fathers had tried and failed to arrange for four Olympics running. Allowing the athletes themselves to be highlighted was an uncharacteristically kind concession on Karimov's part. Indeed, it was hard to imagine him granting another human being any quarter at all. He had that combustible admixture of personality traits—arrogance, meanness, pettiness, and raving insecurity—all too common among despots. This was a man who had once argued before parliament that militant Muslims "must be shot in the head. . . . If necessary, I'll shoot them myself," and proposed that fathers of militant Muslims also be arrested. "If my child chose such a path," he reasoned, "I myself would rip off his head."

Rustam was already at the New World Café, chatting with one of the young Korean women who worked there. "You like Korean girls?" I asked him as we walked away. Koreans, who were shipped from the Russian far east to Central Asia by Stalin in the 1930s as slave labor, were one of Uzbekistan's more anachronistic ethnicities. According to Solzhenitsyn, the forced emigration of Soviet Koreans was "the first experiment in mass arrests on the basis of race."

"Dude, I like all chicks."

"What would your parents say if you decided to marry a Korean girl?"

"They would say nothing because they would be dead from having killed themselves."

"Why is that?"

He frowned and, as he often did while musing, smoothed his black mustache until it looked soft and shiny, like kitten hair. "People get along here, bro. Uzbeks are a gracious people. But that does not mean they welcome outsiders into their families. They say this will be different for my generation. We are much more open. But I'm not certain. Maybe, as you get older, like your hair and weight and appearance, your openness changes, too."

We walked over to the Tashkent offices of the World Bank, the Aral Sea's main legatee after the collapse of the Soviet Union, where I hoped to arrange an appointment. The Bank had been in Uzbekistan for ten years. Nothing having to do with the Aral Sea had improved in that time, despite the organization's initial enthusiasm (WORLD BANK IMPROVES RURAL WATER SUPPLY AND HEALTH IN ARAL SEA BASIN, an early press release trumpeted). The Bank was now scaling back on its financial commitment to alleviate the disaster and was edging away from any promises of its eventual improvement.

The World Bank is nominally a development bank—its original name was the International Bank for Reconstruction and Development—founded after World War II to help secure a durable global peace. It was one of many new measures Harry S Truman hailed as "bold new programs" intended to bring growth to "underdeveloped areas" (a term Truman—and his speechwriter—probably coined). The resulting new institutions would not, Truman believed, be like "the old imperialism—exploitation for foreign profit," but rather would be based on the concepts of "democratic fair dealing." At its 1945 founding ceremony Henry Morgenthau announced that the Bank would help create a "dynamic world economy in which the peoples of every nation will be able to enjoy, increasingly, the fruits of material progress on an earth infinitely blessed with natural riches."

It would be fair to say that the World Bank is not well regarded in many of the countries in which it operates. In Russia, especially, the World Bank and its multilateral compeer, the International Monetary Fund, had been attacked as "neo-Bolsheviks . . . imposing alien rules of economic and political conduct." The World Bank was not helped, in poorer nations' eyes, by the fact that the United States consistently refused to obey many of the ecological and tariff-related measures the Bank insisted upon enforcing elsewhere. Just days after I arrived, the IMF pulled out of Uzbekistan because of the government's refusal to introduce a unified currency exchange and liberalize the Uzbek economy. This had provoked muted anger on behalf of Uzbeks, who felt the IMF was forcing them toward practices the country could not yet afford, and more vocal annoyance from anti-internationalist critics, who believed the organization was simply blackmailing Uzbekistan into opening its markets to wealthier nations, allowing "free trade" to pit yet another postcolonial export-dependent economy against other undiversified economies in some transnational revenue brawl without any guarantees as to how this would play out for Uzbekistan's average citizens. The IMF, to be fair, was simply disgusted by a decade of Uzbekistan's economic double-talk.

The Bank's misadventures in the Aral Sea basin had among NGO workers the air of legend. One of the most famous involves a Bank palatability study concerning the basin's drinking water. "Taste is an important health concern," one aid worker told me. "If you overchlorinate in a refugee camp, the population will go outside the fence and drink from the source because it tastes better. They will do that because they have the option. Palatability implies options. But in the Aral Sea area, you can't cross the road and decrease the amount of salt in the water you drink. So we started to ask, 'Is palatability something we should set our water quality standards by?' The World Bank came along in all their wisdom and did a 'consumer preference study.' The Pepsi Challenge. You like pink, I like red. I'm sorry, but you cannot ask a guy from Moynaq, who's probably never had a good glass of water in his life, 'How do you like your water?' Is this guy the most objective person to be asking? Out of this consumer preference study, the Bank came up with two grams of salt per liter of water as safely palatable. Then they publish their study and there's one paragraph dealing with salinization and human health. In this one paragraph the World Bank says: 'Salinization has no proven link to health.' Bollocks." Another aid worker would tell me: "The Bank's been ineffective, but it's hardly their fault. If you bring in a terminally ill patient with five hundred thousand different diseases and give the doctor five minutes to cure them all, you can hardly sue the doctor for malpractice if the patient dies."

None of this prepared me for the Bank's Tashkent offices: a bright pink Western-looking house surrounded by gates and tulips. I was dropping in on the Bank unannounced, after a few attempts to cold-call invariably stranded me upon an auto-forward telephonic island overseen by a recording in Russian. I carried with me a few magazines in which I had been published, which the Bank's courteous English-speaking secretary, Rada, carefully perused. After it became clear that Rustam's services would not be needed, he and I agreed to split up for the day. I sat down in the office's small, homey lobby. Many phone calls by Rada followed. She was friendly but highly protective, and before I could explain anything, I found myself being interviewed. Rada, after a series of increasingly confrontational questions, forced me to admit that I was not an employee of *Harper's Magazine* and that my article on the Aral Sea was, additionally, "freelance," a word she wrote down on a small pad of paper next to my name. While she arranged a meeting with David Pearce, the Bank's country office chief, she allowed me to spend some time in the Bank's basement library.

Upon the library's metal shelves I found dozens of plastic-spined notebooks containing proposal summaries and pilot-project reports and feasibility studies. I pulled out at random the phonebook-thick "Assessment of the Results of Previous Pilot Projects on Irrigation and Drainage in Central Asia." I plowed through pages of graphs and columns and boxes floatingly set off above fake gray shadow. Between each paragraph was a generous space, apparently to allow one's mind to regroup after the rout the previous passage had inflicted upon it: "In that Russia and especcially under Soviet Power, under irrigation and farming lands which were located in complete natural-economic conditions, that is within high, middle, and low river terraces, flooded plains, removal cones, pre-mountain plains, and inter-mountain bowls, as well as river deltas, was introduced." I read over the "Aral Sea Basin Program Water and Environmental Management Project" from May 1998, an intelligent description of the fiasco that is Central Asian water management and what could be done about it. As it happened, about $86.4 million worth of things, according to the proposal's recommendation. Whether or not its dossiers were readable or its work ultimately as effective as its enemies wished, the World Bank's position was impossible. Every World Bank operation was lashed to the practices of the Uzbek government. When the Uzbek government continued to insist on placing large state orders for water-hungry crops its indigent farmers could not hope to fill, much of the Bank's work was poleaxed.

When I surfaced I was told I had been granted an interview with

David Pearce. I then waited for close to two hours. He was not a man in whose company I would feel comfortable wasting time. Our interview, it turned out, was delayed by nearly an hour due to an emergency meeting with some of Karimov's advisors. When, at last, I walked into his office, Pearce greeted me with "I only know that your name is Tom Bissell and you're writing something about the Aral Sea."

I told Pearce he was right on both counts. He asked me if I was an economist. In answer I looked down at myself. I had not expected to secure an interview today and was wearing multiply pouched khaki pants and a PROPERTY OF MICHIGAN STATE T-shirt. Pearce then asked if I was a water expert. I broke the unsurprising news that I was not.

"What are you?" he asked. Answering took longer, both tactically and emotionally, than I would have liked. I stood there in his office, fingering my notebook. Finally I told him that I was an adventure journalist.

For some reason this satisfied him, and we sat down on opposing leather couches. I had heard around Tashkent many positive things about Pearce, which I told him, and after a few questions—he did not allow me to tape our interview—he emerged from his confrontational chrysalis. Pearce, who had a head of silvery hair and a thin strip of bone-white beard on his chin, giving him the look of a refined Kentucky bootlegger, was a fluid question-answerer, his accent either British or Wealthy North American. When I asked how much of the World Bank's involvement in Uzbekistan concerned the Aral Sea, he said, "Not that much." He then began to annotate the Bank's expenditures with the ease of a man who knew intimately the power held within a single greenlighting pen swipe. The Bank had made nine loans to Uzbekistan, totaling $453 million, the largest of which, $75 million, was intended to finance "a more rational water management project," which was "the most visible" World Bank undertaking in Uzbekistan.

When I asked what Uzbekistan should be doing differently, Pearce immediately said, "Stop growing rice." His point was that at least with cotton one received a reasonable return for ruining the environment. Rice, on the other hand, was nearly as thirsty as cotton but a comparatively low revenue-earner. Pearce also stressed the rigidity of the Uzbek economic system as a huge stumbling block for its water-management woes. In this caveat I sensed some residual frustration doggy-bagged from his recent emergency meeting.

Why, I asked Pearce, doesn't the situation in Karakalpakistan get any better when so many organizations are working in the area? "There are a number of answers to the question," he responded. "The nature of the problem is not amenable to a quick solution. It's a forty-year-old problem." He went on, hard-heartedly but factually, to say that "you can improve the conditions of life for the people of Moynaq, but the problem is larger than that."

"But what about the people of Moynaq?" I pressed Pearce. "Are you for resettlement, or what?"

"My personal view," he said, "is that it should be considered."

I was quickly shuffled to meet Ton Lennaerts, the Bank's water-resources consultant, in a large conference room. He sat opposite from me and looked impassively across the table's acreage. Originally from the Netherlands, Lennaerts was a large, fit man, rather like a junior varsity football coach. He admitted that foreign advisors "are not very popular" within the Uzbek government, but pointed out that his long involvement with the project had earned him the ministries' respect. He was a water expert, he told me several times, and steered away any questions that were not directly related to water issues. He also quickly dismissed any notion of the Aral Sea as the world's largest ecological catastrophe. "Lakes disappear all the time," he said bluntly, bringing up the increasingly ominous water problems the United States was seeing in its western states. (Yes, I would later think in a fit of *esprit de l'escalier*, lakes do disappear, but not the fourth-biggest lake in the world, and not in a single lifetime, and not when millions of people depend on it for their very lives.) He also maintained that there are many "myths" surrounding the Aral Sea problem, one of which was dust-storm frequency, which he said was exaggerated, though he did not say how, telling me only that his paper on the topic was available on the Internet. Another myth was the common belief that Central Asia was running out of water.

"Water allocation," he said, "is simple. It's a matter of gravity." The Soviets, he told me, knew what they were doing, at least as far as irrigation's brute mechanics went. There was as much water coming from the Aral Sea's headwaters as there ever was. The problem was water management. Lennaerts came around to my side of the table and spread before me a map of Uzbekistan and dragged a thick finger along the Amu Darya, stopping when he reached Karakalpakistan. "River deltas," he explained, "are normally the most fertile places in the world. But you have exactly the opposite situation in Karakalpakistan." Karakalpak-istan's canals differed little from those dug a millennia ago. Virtually no money had been spent to preserve its 4 million hectares of irrigated land over the last ten years. The entire region was entirely without any mean-ingful infrastructure. The money allocated for better water management had been mostly used to pay ministry salaries. Along the Amu Darya were numerous green clusters. These were oases, which meant cities. Near each city dozens of obsolete pumping stations sucked up the river and spat it out onto outlying, fundless, and deteriorating collective farms, where up to 40 percent of that water was lost and squandered. What of privatizing them? Kazakhstan, in fact, did just that, and the results were disastrous. Half of all the privatized Kazakh land was quickly ruined, something of which its neighbors in Uzbekistan took careful notice. What of charging for water usage? This, too, Lennaerts said, was pointless. Water usage was already a part of the land tax. And the farmers could not afford to pay for the water anyway. The few places where water meters were installed very quickly saw them uninstalled by angry farmers.

I stared at this map, Lennaerts exhaling warm coffee-scented breath beside me. No wonder the man seemed grouchy. His job was to think daily about a problem that had no solution. I looked at bordering Afghanistan—destroyer of Buddhist idols, burner of musical instru-ments, enslaver of young women—which had been otherwise engaged for the last two and a half decades, and warlord-infested drug-running Tajikistan, only now pulling itself out of chaos, and remembered what Ian Small had said to me: More water was going to be needed through-out the region, and soon. Meanwhile, Uzbekistan's economy continued to plummet, and more cotton was the only answer Uzbekistan had. It had been an unpleasant fact of irrigated life since Babylon that down-stream communities always suffered at the expense of upstream commu-nities, especially when the population of one outnumbered the other by millions. To bring a spring tide of water back to Karakalpakistan would only mean transporting disaster somewhere else. Whether by design or necessity, value had been assigned here, and Karakalpakistan had fallen beneath the hammer of this calculus. "A cow is being milked," Lennaerts concluded sadly. "But the cow has died."

Before leaving I stopped by Pearce's office to thank him for his time. He wished me well, adding that he looked forward to my piece. I told him that, eventually, it would become a book. He sat up. How interesting. He, too, wanted to write a book about Uzbekistan. What specifically? I asked.

Pearce smiled. He wanted to address the most fascinating thing about Uzbekistan.

"What's that?"

"Why it hasn't self-destructed."

Three

Hunger Steppe

Lord my God, judge of my conscience, is my memory correct? Before you I lay my heart and my memory. At that time you were dealing with me in your hidden secret providence, and you were putting my shameful errors before my face so that I would see and hate them.

—AUGUSTINE, *CONFESSIONS*

Ten miles outside Tashkent, the oasis that made Central Asia's biggest city possible visibly, quietly died. The terrain grew so yellowy and sterile it looked cursed. Nevertheless, our bus floated past a small cotton field growing heroically in the sunlight, each bush covered by a clear plastic bag to keep off the fatal morning frost. "New technology," Rustam noted wryly.

We were on our way to Gulistan, my former Peace Corps site, to see my host family. They did not know I was coming; I had long misplaced their phone number. I was very fond of my host family but revisiting a part of my life threaded with so many tiny miseries was, even now, emotion-mangling. Part of the reason I had bought so many gifts for my host family before I left for Uzbekistan was because I knew it would force me to go through with seeing them.

I looked past the window's Rorschach-smudged glass. Other than a large complex of some sort—the sign read THE SINGAPORE TASHKENT ICE CREAM FACTORY—the landscape offered nothing. A few cars. Some old men walking donkeys beside the road. Long vistas of short brittle grass struggling atop dry flaky soil, an endless wilderness of nothing. Central Asia's ancient explorers knew this area as the Hunger Steppe. Much of it

94

had not been developed and ruined by the Soviets because the Hunger Steppe had almost nothing to develop. Gulistan was the capital of one of Uzbekistan's smallest regions, Sir Darya, named for the Sir Darya River, which looped south of Tashkent, arced up over Uzbekistan, wended through Kazakhstan, and ultimately drained into a northern part of the Aral Sea. Unlike its fellow feeder river, the Amu Darya, along which tigers and boars and panthers had long ago stalked, the Sir Darya, known in antiquity as the Jaxartes, possessed a less legendary reputation. Today the Sir Darya looked weakened and sad, despite the fact that most of the damage done to it had been concentrated in Kazakhstan. Yet, oddly, the empty plains of the Sir Darya region soon became almost pleasing. It was useful to remember that, with all of the ecological damage centralized Soviet planning had inflicted upon its colonized lands, Eastern Europe possessed three times the wolves of Western Europe and Romania alone had a larger bear population than all of Western Europe combined. When looking upon landscape the Soviet destruction had not reached, one's relief aestheticized the emptiness.

We had met some problems leaving the bus station in Tashkent. Two leaden-eyed policemen pulled Rustam and me upstairs and, despite the fact that our passports and registration were in order, threatened us with "a big fine, a very big fine." I followed Rustam's lead and affected a kind of mulish stupidity. After forty minutes they released us. "Fucking militsiya!" Rustam had growled outside the bus station. "I'm not a terrorist! Fuck this despotism! Every militsiya guy is a little fucking despot!" He soon calmed, though, and now, on the bus, I told him I was sorry he had to go through yet another criminological hazing with me.

"Aw, dude. Don't worry about it. I'm relaxed now. I was just temporarily mad. Actually, it's good you were with me. No matter how hungry the wolf, he will not steal a sheep if a shepherd's nearby."

"Yeah, but if you weren't with me in the first place, you never would have been stopped."

He thought about this. Before he could draw any conclusions I jumped in to say, "I think it's shitty you have to carry a passport in your own country."

He looked at me. "Why?"

"Because it's not free."

"We have problems here with terrorists, bro. Real problems. So at the end of the day I don't mind. You are free in America because America is stable. That was the greatest thing about America for me when I was there. How stable everything was. Canada is, like, never going to invade you."

"Rustam, when were you in America?"

"In 1998 and 1999. I lived in California on an exchange program."

I was stunned. "You never told me that."

He smiled softly and looked past me out the bus's curtained window. Of course. He had never told me because I had never asked.

A Russian girl in the seat ahead of us had turned around. She was young, her short red bob the color of autumn. Her arm was up on the divider, a dense galaxy of freckles visible through her sun-bleached arm hair. Red hair and freckles were unusual for Russians. Perhaps she was not Russian and descended instead from parents belonging to one of the nationalities Stalinism had left marooned throughout Central Asia: Ukrainians, Poles, Crimean Tatars, Caucasus Ingushes, Kurds, Armenians, Azerbaijanis, Greeks. Even Germans. Some mixture of bravery and shyness stole across the girl's wide, pale face. "Excuse me?" she asked in English.

"Yes?"

"You are American?"

"I am."

"You enjoy yourself in Uzbekistan?"

"Very much."

"Good," she said.

Rustam spoke to her in Russian. When she answered, her small, hesitant English-speaking voice transformed into a fat, forceful Russian one. Rustam turned to me. "Her name is Svetlana. Sveta's English is not so good, but she has some questions she wants to ask you."

"Great. Shoot."

Rustam's eyes narrowed. "Shoot . . . ?"

"Shoot. Go ahead. Tell her to ask."

While Sveta spoke, Rustam whipped out a small spiral notepad and quickly jotted down "shoot" and something in Russian after it. Rustam drove home the cap of his pen against his palm and turned to me. "First question, bro: How old are you?"

I told him, and he transmitted my age to Sveta. She smiled and said—this I understood—that she was seventeen. But, she added, apropos of, I hoped, nothing, she would be eighteen soon.

It turned out Sveta was Russian. When I asked where the freckles came from, she just laughed and pointed to the sky. We traded questions for a while longer, but Sveta eventually bored of us and turned back around. She was the only ethnic Russian on board the bus. Most of the Russians with the means to do so had long ago fled Uzbekistan. Not a few, however, were forced to return, startled by the bigotry of their fellow Russians, who sneered at their hayseed "Uzbek" accents and demanded they "go home." The condition faced by Russians stuck living in Central Asia was another global situation in which two equally intricate and compelling arguments collided. In the Uzbek mind, Russians never bothered to learn the Uzbek language or appreciate Uzbek culture and mistook Uzbek hospitality for Uncle Tom subservience. In the Russian mind, Russians are citizens of Uzbekistan to the same lawful extent as any Uzbek—in fact there *would* be no Uzbekistan without Russians—and, not incidentally, Russians were hardly immune to suffering under the Soviet regime. Thoughtful Uzbeks, such as Rustam, took care to recognize the differences between *priezzhye,* nonindigenous and often-arrogant ethnic Russian outsiders, and *mestnye,* ethnic Russians born in Central Asia usually given to a live-and-let-live decency. Some Uzbeks, of course, rejected the lot, and there were Russians who would pull one aside to whisper that, of course, as fellow Europeans we all understood that Uzbeks were little better than animals, *da?* In the end, one could only feel bad for Russians like Sveta, just as one felt bad for those few white Americans who suffered professionally at the hand of affirmative action. But there was no denying that a measure of historical justice, however harsh, was in both cases being served.

The rocking bus smelled of kerosene, and in the aisles it was hot and getting hotter. Most of the windows, covered with thin blue curtains, were closed. Only 10 A.M., and comets of sweat were already streaking along my jawline. Yet not a few passengers on this bus were wearing heavy cardigan sweaters or thick padded coats called *chapons.* One of many curious Uzbek health beliefs holds that certain death follows if a breeze happens to blow on one's bare skin. This widely shared conviction made for miserable public-transport experiences. In *Cancer Ward,* Solzhenitsyn addresses this: "[I]n the south people have different ideas of hot and cold. They wear woolen suits in the heat and like to put on their overcoats at the first possible moment and take them off at the last." The accumulated odor of dozens of distinct personal chemistries became eye-blurring as the ride went on. Halfway into the trip I would have been willing to believe that somewhere upon this bus a platter of tacos was baking. When I was in the Peace Corps, one of my least favorite things was when my fellow volunteers complained about Central Asian body odor, even though most people in Central Asia did indeed smell fairly bad. But Gandhi probably smelled bad. Surely Abraham Lincoln smelled, as did Betsy Ross, Tom Paine, King George, and Henry IV. William Shakespeare was, in all likelihood, rank. Ben Jonson. Most certainly Jesus and Julius Caesar and the Buddha all smelled terrible. People have been smelly for the vast majority of human history. By gooping up our pheromonal reactors with dyed laboratory gels, could it be that we in the West are to blame for our peculiar alienation? Might not the waft from another's armpit contain crucial bioerotic code? Could it be that by obscuring such code we have confused otherwise very simple matters of attraction? Did, say, Uygurs even *have* midlife crises? Did the trophy wife exist in Nepal? Was this not relevant? Was that crazy? Rustam, for some reason, did not at all care to discuss the matter and returned to one of his soccer magazines.

The bus rolled through a series of small towns. The Slavic faces one often saw in Tashkent were now gone. While Gulistan, as a regional capital, retained a small number of Russians, few if any lived in smaller Uzbek cities and virtually none lived in towns and villages. Rather amazingly, of the Soviet Union's more than one hundred recognized ethnicities, Uzbeks were the third most populous. Only Russians and Ukrainians outnumbered them. Such prominence made Uzbek regional dominance inevitable and, to Uzbeks, inarguable. In 1925 the Comintern cabled the Uzbek Communist Party that it hoped Uzbekistan would "relate to the neighboring republics as Moscow relates to you."

But Uzbek as an agreed-upon ethnicity is conceptually less than a century old. The word "Uzbek" is thought to come from the reflexive Turkic pronoun öz (self) and the noble suffix -*bek:* "the king himself." However, well into the twentieth century, "Uzbek"—still a *cultural* rather than *ethnic* signifier—had "a hint of uncouthness," in the words of the great Uzbek scholar Edward A. Allworth. In 1902, fifteen years before the Bolshevik Revolution would forever change Central Asia's understanding of itself, a Russian ethnographer noted that the tribes known as Uzbeks had no fewer than eighty clan names. Those clans would not have understood themselves as Uzbeks but rather as members of their respective clans. They would have known their language not as Uzbek but as a relation of Chighatay, a supraethnic dialect of Turkish sometimes called Turki. What, then, *is* an Uzbek, and why are 18–20 million human beings currently living under the demonstrable delusion that they *are* Uzbek?

Verifiable Uzbek history reaches back only as far as the mists of the late fourteenth century. Soviet and, consequently, Uzbek arguments that root Uzbek culture within the lush cultural soil of ancient Bactria, Sogdia, and the Seleucid empire are, according to nearly every Western scholar, false. The tribes we now understand as Uzbeks are a people of uncertain nomadic origins who pushed south from the plains of southern Siberia into Central Asia in the mid-1400s. Uzbeks enter written history as invaders so terrifying that opposing armies are said to have dropped their swords and scattered at the sight of them. Mahmoud ibn Wali, a seventeenth-century chronicler, said of the Uzbeks: "This group is famed for bad nature, swiftness, audacity, and boldness." What these Uzbeks thought of themselves we will never know, as they lacked their own literate historians until the 1500s. But as Allworth astutely imagines, early Uzbeks in all likelihood gloried in their outlaw image. Theirs was not a time that much valued restraint.

These first Uzbeks were the army of Ghiyath ad-Din Muhammad Uzbek Khan, a Golden Horde descendant of Jenghiz through one of his great-grandsons, who ruled a swath of lower Siberia from 1312 until 1341. After Uzbek Khan's death a quarter century passed before anyone claiming to be Uzbek again appeared. The group that finally did, emerging not far from Uzbek Khan's kingdom, was most likely not Uzbek but rather had suffered defeat at Uzbek hands. By co-opting such a fearsome name they probably hoped to achieve instant tribal legitimacy. These new Uzbeks in the 1430s began to conquer an area roughly congruent to the current boundaries of modern-day Uzbekistan, eventually dividing into three suborder tribes: Siberian Uzbeks, Uzbek-Shaybanids, and Uzbek-Kazakhs. This spread Uzbek identity thin, and "Sart" became the preferred sweeping term for the people living in Uzbek-controlled regions. Sart eventually grew to have bumpkinish overtones that displeased its bearers. One reason for this could be Sart's likely etymology: *sarriq* (yellow) and *it* (dog). These Uzbeks/Sarts/yellow dogs ruled their ur-Uzbekistan, with few interruptions, until the 1850s, when Russian troops began to strip away authority from the region's local rulers.

When the Russians arrived in Central Asia, they found seemingly disunified city-states and khanates. In fact, they were unified, only on a diffuse macro scale. While Uzbekistan did not yet exist, Turkistan did. For Central Asians of the nineteenth century, Turkistan provided the dim mental harmonies of place, history, statehood, and people. ("Central Asian" is a relatively recent Western invention, and even today few Central Asians use it to describe themselves.) "Uzbek," "Turkmen," "Kazakh," "Tajik," "Karakalpak": All referred to small language differences and literary traditions, and none attached to any national or political consciousness. Many "Uzbeks," for instance, spoke Tajik, whereas many "Kazakhs" spoke Uzbek. (The exception to this is the Kyrgyz, one of Asia's oldest recorded ethnicities, with traditions traceable to the second century B.C.E.) "Turkistan" may have unified, but it did not unite. It provided no stable concept of homeland among Central Asians, and internecine warfare and near-universal illiteracy (96 percent in 1926) were the rule.

During the Bolshevik Revolution and its ensuing civil war, which left an estimated 10 million to 23 million dead, the Communist Reds and tsarist Whites exchanged seeming death blows on a weekly basis. Among the decisions faced by the Revolution's leader, V. I. Lenin, was the fate of Central Asia. In addition to the Whites, a few stubborn British agents were still sticking around the region, arming Muslim rebels, exchanging invisible-ink communiqués, and gathering intelligence. Lenin, in his search for allies, bargained for the support of the Russian empire's minorities by promising self-determination once the tsar was overthrown. He even went so far as to write a widely distributed, completely insincere tract called *The Right of Nations to Self-Determination*. Lenin could afford the deception, he believed. The widely held view among the Bolos, as those few Brits skulking around Central Asia called the Bolsheviks, was that nothing less than a worldwide Communist revolution was in the offing. The Bolos believed it would start in Germany, Marx's homeland, and spread from there. Instead it would spread exactly as far as Mongolia, the lone state to turn Red that was not previously Russian-controlled. The tactics used by Lenin's Bolos were inventive, effective, shortsighted, and stupendously hypocritical. Grigory Zinoviev, Lenin's Comintern mastermind, held court at a rally in Baku, for instance, where 1,800 Central Asian Muslims had gathered to hear Communism's clarion call. Zinoviev (real name: Hirsch Apfelbaum) used jihad as the rallying point against the British—the real colonial oppressors, he claimed. The *Times* of London wrote of the occasion: "Of all the strange things which have happened in the last few years, none has been stranger than the spectacle of [a] Jew . . . summoning the world of Islam to a jihad." The only thing stranger than that would happen sixty years later, when an American president into Christian millenarianism and astrology would authorize an intelligence agency, which had privately taken to calling itself Christians In Action, to play with the same Islamic matchbook.

In 1920 a committee of ethnic Russians appointed by Lenin known as the Turkistan Commission set into motion a series of measures intended somehow to deal with the issue of Central Asia's people. Meanwhile, Lenin issued proclamations addressed "To All the Toiling Muslims of Russia and the East," assuring Central Asia that its day of autonomy was nigh. And while Lenin did urge against measures such as the imposition of a single state language, he realized the only way to adulterate the region's growing Islamic fervor was to divide and conquer its inhabitants.

An interesting sociological proposition: Take an aggregate, highly mixed group of people, herd them into invented territorial borders, impose upon them alien law, and then brand them with different, highly manufactured group identities. How long, the budding sociologist might wonder, would it take each group to absorb these new identities, to believe in them and act upon them with immemorial instinct?

After a stroke-weakened Lenin pondered this question, he handed, with some reservation, a red-hot ethnic brand to a Soviet colleague who had brutally incorporated his own native Georgia into a single entity of culturally unrelated regions known as the Transcaucasian Soviet Socialist Federated Republic. This man, then the Soviet commissar for nationalities, mapped out a scrupulous Central Asian jigsaw of new boundaries where before history had known only an ill-defined outback of clannic enclaves. Uzbek, Tajik, Turkmen, Karakalpak, and Kazakh were with Joseph Stalin's educated guessery brought into the world. The confusion was instant and widespread. A 1924 postpartition cartoon in the Turkistani journal *Mushtum*, reprinted in Edward A. Allworth's *Modern Uzbeks*, depicts a man in Kazakh costume describing himself as "Uzbek" on an ethnic questionnaire and a man in Tajik costume describing himself as "Kazakh." By the late twenties, however, many Central Asian intellectuals, enlivened by the possibility of a prosperous Soviet future, began to use these imposed nationalities as points of pride. Others who mustered this new sense of nationalism behind a column of Islamic revolt were crushed by Soviet forces so ferociously that even the official Soviet *History of the Civil War in the USSR* was forced to admit that "many of the local Bolsheviks distorted the policy of the Party on the national question and committed gross mistakes in their dealings with the native population," and a 1949 Soviet textbook noted that "the peoples of Central Asia offered prolonged resistance, and subordination to Russian rule was nowhere voluntary." (One wonders in which gulag these brave schoolmen perished.) Lenin's ugly hope that Central Asia's populace would be brought to heel by ethnic partition soon saw fulfillment.

Yet Lenin did not live to see it, dying after spending ten months in a near coma after a fourth and final stroke in 1924. (The worst fortune to befall the Russian people was Lenin's birth, Churchill remarked. The next worst was his death.) Ultimately this left Stalin, now writing obsessively on the topic of ethnicity, an area in which he departed from the marginally more open Lenin, in control of the new and worryingly multicultural Soviet empire.

After creating Central Asia's ethnicities, Stalin now set out to crush the debate arising from their bizarre nativity, compelling Central Asians toward an ethnogenetic fusion into a single Soviet nationality, *Homo sovieticus*—a species actually denoted in Soviet medical texts. Stalin's slogan was ill-advisedly candid: "Merging the Peoples." When the Great Terror began in the 1930s, thousands of intellectual but otherwise patriotic Soviet Uzbeks were liquidated for supposed crimes against the state. This included Akmal Ikramov, First Secretary of the Uzbek Communist Party, and Faizullah ("You cannot eat cotton") Khojaev, the Soviet Chairman of Commissars in Uzbekistan. They were officially charged with having been party to an attempt to make Uzbekistan a British protectorate, a crime that fell under Article 58 in the dreaded Soviet Criminal Code, which did not much bother to distinguish between crimes and *potential* crimes. Their actual crime was simply having believed too much in what Stalin himself had unleashed. Virtually all the government leaders of provincial Soviet republics soon met an identical fate.

As the scholar James Critchlow notes, "Uzbek nationality, however artificial its original premises, has been shaped and consolidated by the federal institutions of the Soviet system. For nearly seven decades, citizens of Uzbekistan have been carrying passports in which their identity is stamped as 'Uzbek.' They have been going to school in the 'Uzbek' language. They have been consumers of 'Uzbek' newspapers, and 'Uzbek' radio and television programs. . . . In this way, the idea of being 'Uzbek' has become internalized in the minds of those who compose the nationality." In Central Asia the Soviets created their own eventual impasse. They willed into being identities based on traditions and collective cultural memories that were Islamic to the core. In doing this, we can reasonably ask, what were the Soviets thinking? Soviet culture was, finally, a culture of suicide—politically, ethnically, ecologically, morally.

I was not sure how much Rustam knew about any of this. Many Western commentators on Central Asia write from the assumption that Uzbeks have unquestioningly swallowed their invented ethnicity as well as the history that came with it. Rustam, as always, surprised me. He knew about Sart ("Finally, we are all Sarts"), he knew about Stalin's gerrymandering ("At least he gave us Bukhara and Samarkand!"), and he knew about the 1930s purges of Uzbek intellectuals ("They are rehabilitated now, mostly, thanks to glasnost"). He even knew that, by and large, Uzbek "history," which regularly shellacked an Uzbek varnish upon people, movements, and events that were not in the least Uzbek, was nothing but wishful rubbish.

"Well, Jesus!" I said, exasperated. "Doesn't that bother you?"

He regarded me pityingly. "Bother me? Does what bother me?"

"That your 'ethnicity,' your whole culture, is basically one big Soviet invention?"

"Why would that bother me? The culture existed. The culture exists. What they call it doesn't matter." He shrugged. "I don't share your problem. People need to believe in things, bro. What our government tells us about the past is maybe not so true, but Uzbeks have still done many great things."

"I know *that*. It's that—" I shook my head. "I guess what I don't get is just accepting it all."

"Is accepting being an Uzbek any stranger than loving a group of strangers who play a sport in the city where you live? That seems to me very American and very, very strange."

"But you love soccer!"

"I do love football. I love the *sport*. It doesn't matter to me where they play."

———————

From Gulistan's bus station I rushed through the smoky open-air central bazaar. The bazaar was enclosed by tall brick walls and dissected with wide alleys along which rug merchants and eggplant moguls peddled their goods. Halfway into the bazaar my reasons for being in Gulistan molted their contextual skin. I began to molest myself in search of my Peace Corps *karotchka*. Peace Corps's staff had apparently not believed we could be trusted to hold on to our passports and not skip town. They issued us walk-around *karotchka*s in our passports' stead. *Karotchka*s hypothetically provided Uzbekistan's Peace Corps volunteers with preferable hotel and bus-fare rates along with the rights of average Uzbek citizens, such as the right to forfeit your money to the police, the right to be hassled and buffaloed, and the right to be hauled to a small room and interrogated. But I had no *karotchka* because I was no longer a Peace Corps volunteer. I had come to Gulistan willingly, under my own power, and now it was time to come to grips with that.

"Dude?" Rustam asked. "You okay?"

His concern touched me, but I waved him off. "I'm all right. I guess being here is a little harder than I thought it would be."

"Wait here, bro." He dashed off to an old woman selling *gazli suv,* "water with gas," or carbonated water. He had to wait in line behind several middle-aged Uzbek women dressed in their market best, breathing additive-laced Gulistan air through handkerchiefs. There was a rush on water today because, despite a chilly morning, it had grown quite hot. I looked up. The faraway sun was a yellow nova of roasting malevolence. The cooling associative blue all around it felt like a trick. I fell back against the bazaar's wall, the bricks streaky with the hardened gray remnants of sloppily troweled mortar. Or bird guano. Next to me a middle-aged man with a fat red windburned face sold a counterfeit Sony PlayStation called the Simba-138 and a counterfeit Nintendo 64 known as Sammy! The man looked at me intently. *"Salaam alaykum,"* I said.

"Va alaykum asalom," he returned. He wore a colorful chapon thick and cushiony enough, I imagined, to allow its wearer to survive a three-story fall. Huge clear bulbs of sweat sat inertly upon his skin. He looked as though he were being boiled but did not yet know it. *"Americanets?"*

"Yes," I said in Uzbek.

He took in this confirmation with a neutral nod. A boy, perhaps his son, appeared from behind him. "I am speaking English," the boy said.

Rustam returned and handed me a tall sun-warmed bottle of *gazli suv*. I drank. The water tasted of ferruginous underground caverns. I thanked Rustam and passed the bottle back to him.

"Americanets?" the man asked me, pointing at Rustam.

Rustam was in the middle of a pull. Water sprayed from his nostrils in a fine sneezy mist. "I'm Uzbek!" he told the man, wiping his nose. "From Namangan."

"Namangan?" the man said with surprise. While they chatted, I studied Rustam. It was not implausible, I decided, for this man to think my friend might be American. He was wearing Nike tennis shoes and knockoff Levi's and a plain blue T-shirt. He had a carefree lankiness, a freedom of movement and emotion, completely at odds with close-mouthed Uzbek manhood. (*Gap yoq*, the Uzbek equivalent of "no problem," literally means "talk not.") Several Gulistanis walked by and gazed upon Rustam with the same provincial curiosity that, seconds later, they brought to bear on me. We were the same foreign property. Gone was the seen-it-before worldliness of Tashkent's citizenry. City wonder is always one-sided. One's presence does not concern the city, or its inhabitants. But to be in the provinces was to feel and refract a vast, incoming wonder. To feel one has somehow altered an entire atmosphere of daily routine. A wonder at the wonder created by oneself.

We bid the video-game pirate a good day and emerged from the bazaar at the gates of a former Soviet military academy where, for seven hours a day, six days a week, over two very long months, my fellow volunteers and I had the Uzbek language drilled into us. The academy looked empty now. At the time of the Peace Corps's rental it had not yet been fully decommissioned. In some of the classrooms, alongside home-made posters deconstructing Uzbek grammar, huge plywood story-boards illustrated, panel by panel, how one properly pulled a grenade's pin, field-stripped a Kalashnikov, and donned a gas mask in the event of a biochemical strafe. (The illustrations were colorful, festive: The gas was a harmless green, the explosions cartoonishly saw-toothed, the soldiers seemingly traced from the pages of an old *Sgt. Rock*. Looking at them I wondered, more than once, whether the Soviet war machine regarded Armageddon as an even bigger, weirder abstraction than our own, with its "sunshine units" and tacit promises of being able to avoid thermonuclear incineration by taking shelter beneath a school desk.) Our Peace Corps training supervisor, who closely resembled *The Brady Bunch*'s Ann B. Davis, was a tough American woman whom the temptations of humor had thus far failed to penetrate. My feelings for Ann B. Davis were not warm. In turn, Ann B. Davis regarded me, admittedly not without cause, as our training's most porcelain link. Our interactions were typically, thrillingly hostile. When we arrived in Gulistan, I learned I was placed with a host family five miles away from this academy—farther than any other volunteer—which I took as incontrovertible proof that Ann B. Davis was trying to destroy me. I attempted to explain some of this to Rustam.

Rustam's head swiveled toward mine. "So we have to walk five miles?" After a moment he sighed. "I'm thinking there are many bad memories for you here."

"Well, I don't know. It doesn't even feel anymore like that was me, really. It's like it all happened to someone else. God, you know what? I was a giant pussy. I bet if I came here today as a Peace Corps volunteer, I would really like it."

Rustam glanced around. "Maybe," he said doubtfully. Rustam's first visit to Gulistan, it seemed, had done little to inspire his imagination. He was not alone. The city is barely mentioned in any of Uzbekistan's guidebooks.

We ventured through a section of Gulistan that was actually quite pleasant. Unreally tall trees towered along the streets, splattering little paws of shadow on the sidewalks below. This was Gulistan's nucleus, containing the National Bank of Uzbekistan's local bureau, the post office, the regional television station, and various other branch-office remnants of Soviet syndicalism. Near the city square proper, numerous buildings stood in various states of completion. We approached one of the less constructed sites. The building going up would be another in the line that Tashkent had been lately erecting by the dozen: five-to-ten-story boxes made of pale reddish brick and faced with panels of cheap algae-green glass. In Tashkent they came off as poorly financed attempts to look "modern." In Gulistan they simply looked silly. Rustam and I passed below a rickety scaffold from which a walrus-mustached Russian heaved chunks of lunchbox-sized masonry. Uzbekistan was the only country I had ever visited where you could walk through a hazardous construction area and no one would stop you or even look at you. While Rustam walked on, I stopped and watched for a few minutes. A man without safety goggles used a welding torch to solder together two beams, an orange-white spout of fire inches from his face. Tools rained from another scaffold's upper reaches, plunking in the sand at the feet of workers not wearing hard hats. One man, wearing a sport jacket and loafers, dangled precariously from a crane as he tried to touch up one of the building's corbels with a paintbrush.

"Amazing," I said when I caught up to Rustam.

"What's amazing?"

"This whole country."

He grinned vaguely. "Thanks, bro."

We stopped at a statue commemorating Alisher Navoi, known as the Father of Uzbek Literature and, less frequently, the Chaucer of the Turks. Navoi, clad in granite robes, wearing a pointy pharaonic beard and clutching a massive staff, stared out above us with a grim invincibility. Navoi was another creation of Uzbekistan's determined paleodemography. Not only was Navoi Persian and not Uzbek, he seems to have thought little of Uzbeks. In his poem "Alexander's Wall," Navoi clearly indicates that Uzbeks are aligned with the forces of evil, calling them "a river of the bloodthirsty." Yet one could hardly fault any veneration of him. Born in Herat, Afghanistan, in 1441, Navoi spent most of his time in Samarkand and the Khorezm region, an area adjacent to the Aral Sea, before dying in Herat in 1501. His supremely rational mind despised the Persian taste for astrology held over from Zoroastrianism, and in the Khorezm region he is said to have built 370 mosques, hospitals, libraries, and colleges. The childless lifelong bachelor's library was one of the largest in the medieval Islamic world, and along with his voluminous literary output Navoi was also a painter, politician, and critic. (A contemporary adds, "In music also he composed some good things.") In an early work entitled *Judgment of Two Languages,* the thoroughly bilingual Navoi convinced the Muslim world that Chighatay could stand alongside Persian and Arabic in its elegance and texture. This linguistic rearguard action makes him similar to Dante, who in *The Divine Comedy* abandoned Latin for the rougher, more expressive vocabulary of Italian. Navoi's promotion of Chighatay provided Uzbeks with their tenuously thin connection to him. Still, I thought, looking up at Navoi, it was not as though we in America were innocent of such bait-and-switch iconography. I wondered how Pocahontas might have felt to know that someday she would be viewed as a pinup of early-American splendor.

"Navoi," I finally said aloud.

Rustam covered his eyes. "Dude, don't even tell me. He wasn't Uzbek. I *know*."

Gulistan thinned as we walked farther toward Oktyabr, the former collective farm my host family lived nearby. The dense, house-packed streets around the city's core spread out and ruralized. Khaki fields replaced streets. Paved gutters became long muddy runnels. Endlessly masticating cows stood alongside the road. Ducks kicked along filthy, half-filled irrigation ditches, toxic rainbows playing upon the water's filmy surface. Cars whooshed by, beeping. (Seeing someone out here, it seemed, was notable enough to commemorate.) At the edge of Gulistan we turned and looked back at the city. Gulistan was less than seventy years old, a city planned and created by Soviets for Soviets. Despite its wistful name, "Place of Flowers," Gulistan's ambitions at its founding were wholly industrial. Apparently, cotton was washed here. Perhaps it was once a nice city. Now it looked gimcrack, lost, forgotten. A deeply earnest place one could only love with all one's heart or run away from as fast as one could. It reminded me a little of the smaller towns in Michigan's Upper Peninsula, where I grew up. No wonder I had gone crazy.

"Tough little town," I said, tossing a rock into a nearby irrigation ditch. The ensuing sploosh sounded thick and brief, like dropping a ball bearing into tar.

"Boys have dirty faces here," Rustam said with distaste. "And the girls aren't as pretty as Tashkent's."

"They eat eyeballs in Gulistan," I said. "At least my family did. Any big occasion and out came the sheep's-head stew. Big veiny eyeballs floating in broth. *Jesus* that freaked me out."

He laughed and shook his head. "They don't eat the eyeballs. They only eat the meat around the eyeball. You can't eat an *eyeball*, dude. They're too tough."

"Once my host-mother's mother was in town from Kokand, and after dinner she broke open one of the bones from the lamb we'd just eaten. Then, with her finger, she dug out the bone marrow and rubbed it onto her eyelids. I almost threw up. She explained that this made her eyes stronger."

"It does. I don't do it, but that works, actually."

"My host-mother used to hang up whatever meat she was cooking later that day on a rusty metal prong outside the house. For hours flies would crawl all over it. Then she'd cook it. Whenever I tried to explain that this was what was probably making me so sick, my host-family didn't believe it. I told them about microbes. You know, germs? They said, 'How can germs make you sick? They're so small!'"

Rustam studied Gulistan's rooftops, his head tipped back. He was flaring his nostrils, which seemed as far apart as eyes. "Hmm."

"They told me that if you drank something cold when it was hot outside you'd catch a bad cold."

A nod. "Of course you do."

"And that if a woman sits on a marble surface, even through her clothes, she'll become sterile."

"Well, not always."

I saw planted along Gulistan's lonely edge a bright new Coca-Cola billboard. Translated from the Uzbek, it read COCA-COLA, THE TASTE OF LIFE. Near the Coke sign, painted on the side of an empty building, loomed a mammoth mural upon which the wisdom of "I. Karimov" was inscribed. "What's that say?" I asked Rustam.

"'Taste of life,'" Rustam translated, with barely a look.

"Not the Coke sign. The Karimov thing."

"Oh. I didn't even notice that." He looked at the mural for several moments, his facial features, slit or pursed with absorption, inching closer and closer together. "I can't really figure it out. It's just . . . *words.*" His face relaxed. He looked tired.

"The beginning says 'Truth' something 'people' something 'homeland are better than' something, right?"

"That's only the first sentence, though. 'Truth, Unity of People, and Motherland are greater than anything else.' Then I don't know what it says. Soviet Uzbek is very complicated, bro, even worse than Soviet Russian. It's like another language to me."

I looked at him. "What language do you think in?"

He shrugged. "I don't know. Russian mostly. Sometimes English. Uzbek, occasionally, but only if I am around other Uzbeks."

We walked on toward Oktyabr. A Russian man who looked eerily like Ray Bradbury bicycled past and wished us *dobryi dyen.* The next two miles we passed in perspiring silence, walking along the occasional sidewalk, opting for a hard dirt path whenever the sidewalks inexplicably terminated, hopping across deep trenches of determined if mysterious intention, and climbing over pointless concrete partitions. Sometimes it seemed as though Uzbekistan had been civic-engineered for a race of serenely legless hovering beings. When all else failed, we drifted to the road's berm and risked being killed by the trucks, buses, and Ladas bulleting past us, shielding our eyes in their dusty, gravel-flying wake. Every few hundred yards we came across small tin meat shacks in which Uzbek gentlemen with bloodied hands and drawn faces sold ragged tuna-colored cuts from cows and sheep and goats whose throats they had most likely slit that morning. Many families here did not own refrigerators, and the meat had to be vended quickly and eaten even more quickly. A few times I stopped and looked at the glistening cuts. A dense wet stench, something like soggy rust, fogged within my skull. The Uzbek word for meat was gruesomely onomatopoeic: *gusht*. After I returned home from the Peace Corps, I lapsed into a bout of vegetarianism that lasted several months.

Now the houses became farms. Nearly every gated compound contained a goodly plot of neat, well-tended dirt mounds, each row stabbed with a wooden marker. Some of the more prosperous-looking houses had large trellises propped up near their sheep stables, many covered with the crawling green circuitry of grapevines or bean sprouts. Nothing had had much of a chance to grow yet; it was still early in the season. It was strange to see so many farms and hear so many bleating sheep and groaning cows and hear and smell nothing, nothing at all, even remotely porcine. While Central Asia's Muslims drank and smoked and slept with prostitutes like it was going out of style, Soviet ideology had failed to eradicate the inborn Muslim aversion to swine. Pig-breeding in Central Asia remained negligible, even if pig-eating occurred often enough.

These small, quiet farms were a reminder of what was one of the frailer ventricles within the Soviet heart. When it comes to the Soviet Union, American conservatives cherish many articles of faith. Few are as know-nothing as the belief that Ronald Reagan's buildup of the military during the 1980s handed the Politburo the tombstone upon which it chiseled its own busted-budget epitaph. Reagan's talk of evil empires, this view holds, along with his refusal to quail before the doddering faces of Leonid Brezhnev, Yuri Andropov, and Konstantin Chernenko, the first three elderly Soviet leaders he faced, forced Moscow to pass on the Soviet premiership to the youthful dynamo Mikhail Gorbachev, whom Reagan then cannily outmaneuvered. Like much American conservative thought, this belief fails to take into consideration anything not directly related to American conservative thought.

Gorbachev, like his eventual humiliator Boris Yeltsin, was a member of the Khrushchev Generation, also known as "the Children of the Twentieth Party Congress," so named for the secret tribunal Khrushchev used to denounce Stalin's "excesses." Gorbachev and other middle-class members of his generation's intelligentsia came of political age with great hope in the perfectibility of the Soviet system. More than anything, Gorbachev loathed what he once acidly called the "freeloading" mindset of too many Soviet citizens. The gross venality of the Brezhnev era stunted and delayed his and his fellow reformers' hopes. While climbing the ladder of the Soviet party system, Gorbachev walked a problematic line, one part of him given to toadying (fulsomely praising Brezhnev, for instance), another, more concealed part of him interested in iconoclastic ideas such as competitive pricing and allowing into Soviet economic life greater measures of self-management. Perestroika was largely the product of men in their fifties and sixties, hardly the usual age of reformers, and explicable only by the time-released post-Brezhnev thaw.

One of Gorbachev's biggest motivators—other than looking at the Soviet balance sheet every month and not being able to deceive himself, as Brezhnev had—was the controversial 1983 publication of the Novosibirsk Report, written by a brilliant, courageous sociologist named Tatyana Zaslavskaya (who, among other accomplishments, first used the term *perestroika*). The report's main thesis was that the Soviet economy was crippled by *human* factors: laziness, incompetence, apathy, and alienation. Soviet jobs, Zaslavskaya concluded, offered no meaningful connection to those who did them, and the negligible quality of their work reflected this. Gorbachev, who grew up in farming territory in the northern Caucasus, where workers felt a deep and automatic connection to their jobs, was stirred by Zaslavskaya's analysis. He had, after all, lost family members to the mass starvation that descended upon his native soil following the spectacular failure of Stalinist collectivization. Gorbachev was also mindful of the example of Lenin, who seemed to have glimpsed the bankrupt writing upon the bloodied Soviet wall well before anyone else. In his late New Economic Policy stage, cooked up to address why the world's first socialist state was starving to death, Lenin put forth a tinkered-with vision of socialism as a society of "civilized cooperators." These barely implemented Leninist innovations—an infant Stalin throttled in its crib—resembled a greatly moderated form of capitalism, which Gorbachev looked to emulate in taking further than ever before previous timid Soviet experiments with liberalization.

What did this have to do with Uzbek farms? Quite a bit. In the 1980s a Soviet farmer, on average, produced enough food to feed five people for a year. A single American farmer in that same time produced enough food to feed fifty. The Soviet shortfall was not due to agricultural cutbacks made while Moscow raced Ronald Reagan to an appointment in some atomic Samarra. The 1980s were one of the more successful Soviet decades, agriculturally. The shortfall existed because Soviet means of production were primitive and did not reach the hundreds of thousands of small homestead farms, such as those now all around me, speckled throughout the Soviet empire. The huge state farms that existed were corrupt and inefficient. Gorbachev realized this in the early 1980s, when he journeyed to Canada. Traveling throughout green, spacious North American farm country, the journalist Hedrick Smith reports, blew the tubes of Gorbachev's Soviet brain. "Who makes you get up in the morning?" Gorbachev asked one Canadian farmer. The man shrugged and said, you know, he just kinda did on his own. Another farmer showed Gorbachev his $100,000 array of farm machinery. "Do they trust you with all this?" Gorbachev asked. The man replied, "I *own* all this." Gorbachev realized that reforming the Soviet system as soon as possible was the only answer to his country's intensifying problems. When he was finally given his chance, Gorbachev started the Soviet Union down a path that opened up huge social and political fissures, spawned unimaginable optimism, and changed an entire culture. The moment came when Gorbachev could have turned back or resorted to mass state violence, Tiananmen-style, but, after a few brief scares, he stayed his hand. In doing so he obliterated the system he had tried only to save. As Hedrick Smith reminds us, there is "no precedent for a single leader attempting the peaceful transition from a dictatorship to democracy." To have the narrative any other way is to inordinately honor Ronald Reagan, a deeply average man unoriginally waging economic warfare against a failing leviathan, at the cost of a legitimately great man, whatever his flaws, truly interested in change.

But American conservatives need to have the narrative this way. The Soviet Union, with its backward farms and wheat-scything cross-eyed peasantry, was a tyrannosaur of state power, as evil as it was massive. The Central Incompetence Agency did little to dissuade such thinking, predicting in the late 1950s that the Soviet economy would triple that of America by 2000. Around this time the CIA was still using Nazi maps to determine likely Soviet nuclear launch pads and confidently predicted a Soviet moon sortie by 1967. Throughout the 1950s and '60s, the CIA consistently overestimated the number and destructive capacity of Soviet warheads, leading to famous worries about the U.S.-Soviet "missile gap." When, in 1975, Soviet engineers began screwing nose cones onto new and unimaginably powerful lines of nuclear missiles—the SS-17, SS-18, and SS-19—the CIA, as though on cue, began to report that the expansion of Soviet nuclear capabilities was finally "coming to an end." One might think that by the 1980s the CIA would have calibrated its thinking on the issue of Soviet economic might, which, as anyone who lived in Moscow or Kiev or Tashkent or Minsk could see, did not merit even polite comparison with our own. They did not. As far as "evil empires" go, the age of widespread Soviet terror had, by Reagan's time, mostly passed. The regime had relaxed into a posture of farting corruption and petty cruelty, it is true. It is also true, Cold War scholars now recognize, that Soviet leaders did believe they could fight and win a nuclear war, and drew up several first-strike scenarios to achieve that end. But a nation that only a decade before was dropping napalm on children in a war it already knew was unwinnable could hardly lob "evil-empire" opprobrium without provoking cynical Soviet chuckles. Let us say, however, that Ronald Reagan, wearing a loincloth of American righteousness, did indeed throw the spear that brought down the prehistoric Soviet lizard. What still needs explaining is why this mighty empire, when it finally did fall apart, suddenly found itself waiting in a breadline behind international starvelings such as Somalia, Nicaragua, and Bhutan. And what did the USSR get to alleviate its seven decades of mass hypnosis and disaster? Among other things, one plane after another of smiling Peace Corps ingenues not unlike myself.

Let no one lament the outcome of the Cold War. The bad guys, to resort to Reaganish crudities, did, in fact, lose. But it should be pointed out that the enemy we spent trillions of dollars not fighting turned out to have huge irreparable interior problems of which we did little to enlighten ourselves. Those who could have known chose not to. Those who knew chose not to tell. And so we Peace Corps volunteers journeyed to the former Soviet empire and met the enemy. He was not us. Nor was he them. He was not anyone. He was mist and particles. He was legend, necessity, self-justification. A rung in a cheap ladder of American rebirth.

"So, dude. Which one is it?"

"Be quiet. I'm thinking."

"You have been thinking for a long time. You have been thinking almost as long as we walked."

"*That's* not true. We walked a real long time."

"My feet hurt."

"Hey, be a man."

He lapsed into some quasi-Transylvanian accent. "But my Ameddican fdend, yoo doo nut understend. I em veddy heppy to be here vith yoo, but I em also veddy tired and slippy."

"Is that the voice you use to charm all the American girls?"

"Nah. All these houses look the same to me."

"That's kind of the problem I'm having."

"Why don't you start yelling or something?"

"Why don't *you*?"

"We need to go somewhere soon, bro, because my pee bubble is full."

"Your *pee bubble*?"

"This is the bubble which holds my pee."

"Your *bladder*, you mean. Bladder. B-l-a-d-d-e-r."

"In English you don't call it the pee bubble?"

"I will from now on, probably."

"Man, bro. I can't believe you lived out here. It seems . . . sad. This landscape has seen many tears, I think."

"It wasn't that bad."

"Then why did you quit?"

"I don't know. Reasons."

"Like which reasons?"

"Because of reasons. Jesus! What's up with you this afternoon?"

"Tell me the reasons. Was it a girl?"

"Some of them were about a girl, yeah. So what?"

"So what nothing. I admire and respect any reasons concerning girls. No kidding, bro. I mean that."

"I think it's got to be that house right there. It just doesn't look right."

"What looks unright about it?"

"For one thing I don't remember that big weird building out in front of any of these houses. But I know I lived near here because this bus stop was right across the street."

"Do they have a son?"

"Yeah."

"How old was he when you were here?"

"I don't know. Seventeen."

"I am thinking, my Ameddican fdend, zat zis son has been meddied and zat zey hev beelt for heem zis beeg new hauz."

"I forgot about that patriarchal, appallingly glad-handed aspect of Uzbek culture."

"When I am married, my father will build me a great house, I think."

"What's your father do, anyway?"

Rustam looked startled. Quickly he flashed his teeth at me. "You know, bro. He works. He just works."

We walked across the highway to the house I may or may not have lived in five years ago. Heat mirages sizzled at either end of the road. It was quiet out here. Rural Gulistan's silence was well suited, as I learned, to the incubation of despair existentialism. When we came to the gate, I looked back at Rustam. He shrugged. This gate, built into the foundation of the unfamiliar new building, was not at all how I remembered my old host-family's compound. An ancient Cerberus named Ulkhan (Uzbek for "great" or "massive") used to be chained up out front. Each morning I had to walk past Ulkhan with my back pressed up against the fence opposite his ramshackle doghouse. After always allowing me a few uneventful steps, and their attendant illusion of safety, the half-blind beast would lunge, jaws snapping, froth gobs flying, its one good eye crazed, while I prayed that the rotting baseboard to which it was chained would hold. The first time I arrived in these parts, my host-father had picked me up at the military academy. During the ride to Oktyabr he kindly pointed out things and told me the Uzbek word for them. "*Kuchasi,*" he said, motioning toward the street. "*Avtomaschina,*" he said, indicating his car. "*Darrakht.*" Tree. In this spirit of quid pro quo I began to parrot back the English word. "Child," I said, pointing at a girl playing along the road. "Sun," I said, looking up. "Sun," he agreed. "*Ha. Bilaman*" (Yes. I know). He had studied English thirty years ago in Moscow, when he was attending law school, but retained nothing but a few stray words. When we got out of the car at the house, he pointed at Ulkhan and said, "Eat!" "Eat?" I gasped in return. "No! No eat! No thank you!" "Eat," my host-father had said, more sternly. "Eat!" "No! No eat!" It was not until later that I realized he was not saying "eat" but *it*, the Uzbek word for dog. Possibly Ulkhan had held this misunderstanding against me.

I rapped the gate's metal door, covered with dozens of nummular rust patches. Nothing. This was not surprising. The main house was found at the end of a long path thirty yards away from this entrance. There was, of course, no doorbell. "What do you think?" I asked Rustam. "Should we just go in?"

"That depends," Rustam said. "Did they like you?"

"Of course they liked me!"

"Maybe at this time they are not home."

In Uzbek households someone was always home, especially in middle-class families. These people were most certainly middle-class. Haiyidar, my host-father, was a former Communist Party big wheel and cruised around Gulistan in a chauffeured BMW. Mavluda, my host-mother, was also a lawyer, though she no longer practiced. Their eighteen-year-old daughter Arkinoy was already engaged to be married when I lived here, and often I would sit and watch television with her and her quiet fiancé while they remained at decorously opposite ends of the room. Haiyidar and Mavluda's surly, jug-eared, seventeen-year-old son, Altabek, loved (1) soccer, (2) using my deodorant, and (3) making fun of Jean-Claude Van Damme. Their other daughter, Narghiza, a ten-year-old, had Down's syndrome. The disease had extracted from poor Narghiza a grievous neurological lien. She occasionally walked around the house naked and often screamed during the night. Many times, after being jolted awake, I would hear through the walls Mavluda gently singing Narghiza back to sleep.

Despite my host-family's enviable status, their one-story house lacked indoor plumbing. Heat was unreliable in the winter. Their pit toilet, sensibly located out behind the house, was not kept very clean, unless sprinkling it with ash every other week had purification properties of which I was unaware. I spent a lot of time at that pit toilet. It was while living in Gulistan that I first wondered if the most useful service I could have performed as a Peace Corps volunteer might not have been translating Upton Sinclair's *The Jungle* into Uzbek. Eventually, I came to love Mavluda too much to hector her about how she prepared my meals. I did what I could to keep my constant diarrhea from her, but I was shedding the dorm-wrought poundage I had gained during my undergraduate career at the visible rate of ten pounds a month. Mavluda's not illogical solution to this problem was to feed me more.

"I guess we should go in," I said, and pushed through the gate. Some goats in a path-side stable hissed at us. The goats were new, but other actualities were aligning with the few clear visual memories I had managed to hold on to. From here I could make out the familiar outdoor kitchen facilities and recognize the sporadic wire fence that girdled Mavluda's flower garden. This was it. When we were halfway to the main house Arkinoy came out of a smaller adjacent building with an armful of folded towels. Her long black hair dangled out the back of a complicated red kerchief and stopped mid-spine. She wore a thin purple bathrobe and slippers that shushed against the dusty concrete. She looked over at me, waved, and for one clearly confused moment kept going toward the house. Then she dropped the towels and with a burst of laughter came running toward me down the path.

I wrapped her up in an embrace of decidedly American magnitude. She hugged back but then, tensing, gently pushed me away and touched her kerchief back into place. Such hugs were not the Uzbek way, certainly not if you were a young married woman. But she was still laughing.

"When did you come? Why are you here?"

"A few days ago. I'm a writer now. I came back to write about Uzbekistan."

She said something else, and I looked to Rustam. "Help, please."

Rustam stepped forward, now enough schooled in my particulars to be able to answer most questions himself.

"*Zoor,*" Arkinoy said finally, looking at me and grinning. (*Zoor,* another terrific Uzbek word, means "great" or "awesome.") Her smile was no longer white. Three-quarters of her teeth were now shiny gold. Many people in Uzbekistan had gold teeth, but women's mouths were the principal showcase of this initially disconcerting dental enhancement. Widespread though usually mild malnutrition and a lack of regular calcium intake meant that, during pregnancy, women's teeth dropped sacrificially from their sockets. Uzbek water additionally lacked the fluoride from which we in America benefited so invisibly. This is strange if only because Uzbek water is laced with so many other periodic-table mainstays.

"You had kids," I said to Arkinoy.

"Three!" she answered proudly. One of them, a small lemur whose face seemed all eyes, peeked at us around the doorway from which Arkinoy had appeared. "Aziz," she said, turning to him. "Come here. Come see Tombek from America!" With a sudden, stubborn grimace the boy withdrew.

The door to the main house opened. Mavluda stood there in the jamb, gasping, her hands slapped upon her cheeks. She was a large, beautiful matronly woman before and remained so. I rushed over to her, stunned by the boil of feeling within me. Mavluda gathered me close. She smelled of burlap, cottonseed oil, warm skin. Beneath her colorful housedress her heart was one soft plosive boom after another. She rocked me motheringly, whispering something in Uzbek. Rustam and Arkinoy walked over. "She's saying she knew you'd come back," I heard Rustam explain. Mavluda pulled my face from her breast and held it in her hands, looking at me. Her hair was lead-colored, still streaked with a few rich veins of black. Her nose and lips were sharp, even hawkish, yet fixed above them were two large, kind eyes. They were moist. Now they were dripping. She touched her dry lips to my forehead.

"Wow," Rustam said. "You weren't joking me. They did like you!"

Mavluda ventured that, surely, we were hungry.

"We're okay," I told her. "Rustam, could you explain to her that we—" Before I could finish, Mavluda pulled me inside. Most Uzbek houses have a room with one low table where people eat traditionally, cross-legged, on the floor, and another, more European room where people sit at a tall polished dining-room table. This latter, special-occasion room, no doubt one of many Soviet attempts to erase Uzbek culture of its lingering nomadisms, was the one to which Mavluda and Arkinoy led us. While Arkinoy vanished to prepare an elaborate four-course lunch, Mavluda busied herself in the room's tall wooden cabinets. Shortly, she began to set the table with small crystal bowls of candy and sugar.

As we took our seats, I turned helplessly to Rustam. "Can you *please* tell her that we don't need anything? This is exactly what I *didn't* want to happen. These poor women are run ragged by their husbands all day long. I don't want them to do that for me. Can you tell her that?"

Rustam sighed. "Dude, you know I can't tell her that. She's not going to listen. Look at her. She's thrilled."

"That's not the point."

"I think kinda it is, though. Just relax."

Arkinoy returned with a basket of non, a tasty discus of bread of huge cultural and dietary importance in Uzbekistan, and a pot of Uzbek green tea. Behind her came Ulugbek, her husband, a young man who had the thin, serious air of a struggling mortician. We shook hands, and Ulugbek unbuttoned his black sport coat and sat down with us. Of course. The one adult I knew least well in this house would eat with us because he was a man. The women I had actually traveled here to see would remain rooms away, sweating over pots of boiling water and dicing up leek stalks. Mavluda, still tidying up the room's nonexistent messes, squeezed my shoulder as she walked by.

More children entered the room. All three of Arkinoy's kids and two others, who I now learned were Altabek's. The new house outside indeed belonged to Altabek and his wife, whom I glimpsed as she passed by the dining room, having been mustered into preparing our feast.

This menagerie of children must have pleased Mavluda, I thought. One night, when Mavluda and I had stayed up talking, she had told me, with the honesty that late hours demand, her biggest regret. She and Haiyidar had only three children. The complications of raising a Down's syndrome daughter, in a culture not known for its accommodation of retarded children, had wasted away her willingness—though not, in a cruel trick, her desire—to have more. Uzbek culture values children to an almost imprudent degree. Many rural families regularly have as many as ten children. In 1988 the Uzbek SSR's first secretary was ridden out on a rail for daring to suggest that Uzbek families limit their children to "five or six" per household. This first secretary's successor, Islam Karimov, pointedly refused to address the matter, despite Uzbekistan's dangerous, resource-draining population growth.

"Haiyidar is at work," Mavluda explained, ripping the circular bread into fragments and setting them before Rustam and me, "and so is Altabek, but I will call them now and in a few moments they will be here with us." Exeunt Mavluda.

Ulugbek pushed toward me one of the candy bowls. *"Oling,"* he said. (Please take.)

I looked at the bowl. It held a mound of small wrapped nuggets of knockoff chocolates. I opened one, the wrapper of which read TWITS. It tasted like chocolate sand. I then tried a Happy bar. It made me anything but.

Ulugbek's son climbed up into his lap and stared at me while his father and Rustam chatted. After a moment Rustam laughed. "He's telling me funny stories about you, bro."

"Oh? Like what?"

"Like how frightened you were of Ulkhan the dog."

"Yeah. That was hilarious."

Another child, a little girl, had sneaked up on me under the table and tugged on my shirtsleeve, leaving a chocolaty fingerprint. She looked up at me and grinned. "Hello," I said.

"Say hello to your uncle Tom," Ulugbek said to her.

I looked into the girl's eyes, a pair of tiny brown universes. "Uncle Tom," I said in English.

"Uncle Tom," Rustam echoed, with a chuckle.

I was again amazed by his command of English idiom. "You know what an Uncle Tom is?"

"Sure, dude. It's a Negro who loves white people, yes?"

Mavluda strolled back into the room, carrying several photo albums and three old letters it took a moment to recognize as ones I had sent her. She said something as she handed them over to me. Rustam smiled. "She says that you wrote such good Uzbek letters and wonders why you stopped writing."

"Because I forgot all my Uzbek," I told her in Uzbek. I opened one of the letters. It was haunting to hold in my hand this piece of paper I thought I would never again handle, a meager thing I had set sail across the planet to try to explain myself. I never managed to learn how to write Cyrillic script. My huge, childishly block letters looked like the work of some deranged Uzbek extortionist.

Mavluda thumped upon the table one of the photo albums and with rips of plasticized static peeled apart the pages. "These are photos from Altabek and Arkinoy's weddings," Rustam translated. Each clear-plastic page had four images. I saw Tashkent parks. Squash-faced Uzbek babies swaddlingly mummified. Huge wedding parties. Uzbek faces split open by gold-toothed smiles. A time-lapse photodocumentary of modern middle-class Uzbek life. Then I came to a photo of a lovely young woman sitting in a park. This was not Tashkent. This was not even Uzbekistan. And the lovely young woman was, I realized, L——, my former fiancée. This photo was one of the many keepsakes I had given Mavluda as I left. I flipped again. L—— standing before a rhinoceros at Potter Park Zoo in East Lansing, Michigan. I no longer remembered the day this photo was taken. That memory had been overrun by those of simply staring at this photo, here in my small Gulistan bedroom, wanting only to be with her again, wishing I had never come here. Gently, I flipped the page. L—— again. I flipped the page. L—— and me at my college graduation. We were smiling. We knew, at the time this photo was taken, that we had only a few more months to be together before the Peace Corps sent me wherever it was the Peace Corps was going to send me. We were holding on to each other. We looked terrified.

Rustam peered over my shoulder. "Man, bro. You were fat! Hey, who's the chick?"

"L——," I said.

"L——," Mavluda agreed, smiling. Mavluda had often suggested that, after we were married, L—— and I come to Uzbekistan, where Mavluda and Haiyidar would make sure we enjoyed a proper Uzbek wedding.

"Who's L——?" Rustam asked.

"My reason."

"For leaving?"

"Yeah," I said, but maybe I no longer knew. In 1996 I was a senior at Michigan State University, studying English and the other unemployment arts, while L—— prepared to follow the occupational footprints left by her physician father. We were from the same town in Upper Michigan and had been dating since our teens. We had a plan. We shared a Soviet devotion to plans. The plan we charted in college had a beautiful simplicity, painlessly designed to end our childhoods and begin, with equal succor, the adult lives that would follow: L—— would go to medical school, while I would "write." But L—— was a year behind me and by the middle of my senior year the terror of filling those catch-up months with purposeful activity began to feel less like the end of youth than like the beginning of something for which I was entirely unprepared. After talking it over with L——, I filled out applications to half a dozen MFA programs, making sure each had a reputable medical school that would allow her to follow me. Our plan suffered a point mutation the day my professor of modern American poetry canceled her lecture on Kenneth Rexroth and invited a former Peace Corps volunteer to speak to the class. This solemn PCV was probably in her twenties but looked forty. She wore no makeup. Her dress was ankle-length and vaguely African. She spoke with no discernible excitement concerning her two years of Peace Corps service, and I remember nothing of what she said. Which makes it difficult to explain why, a few days later, I decided to write to the Peace Corps for an application. The short stories I was writing at the time were counterfeits of the quietly inconclusive domestic tales that govern anthologies of postwar American fiction. Yet this was not the subject matter I wanted. What I wanted, foolishly, was to write about The World. Given my unremarkable credentials, only the Peace Corps could give me that chance. When I finally showed L—— my completed Peace Corps application, she could not speak. Perhaps she doubted my willingness to go through with it and resented this wholly unnecessary wound. I tried to explain. I could not explain. The Peace Corps granted me an interview. Afterward, L—— was asked to write a one-page letter about the state of our relationship, perhaps to provide for the Peace Corps a blueprint of its tensile strength. (I later learned that prospective volunteers embroiled in "serious relationships"—that college-age solemnity!—are for obvious reasons one of the Peace Corps's biggest applicant nightmares.) I was, in turn, asked to write a letter explaining my refusal to go to Africa, which I did, producing a lyrical, completely insane screed on my pathological fear of snakes. I asked for an assignment in Eastern Europe, perhaps Russia. Then L—— and I waited. I will never know how prepared I really was to join the Peace Corps because every MFA program I applied to turned me away. When the Peace Corps came back with an offer of Uzbekistan, a country about which I had only the slenderest notion, I was not only out of options but heartsick by the pain my indecision had inflicted upon L——. I did not know much about altruism, but I imagined that, without real pain, no decision to devote oneself to it could mean very much. I went to Uzbekistan.

Seven months later, blown apart by grief and failure, I landed in Frankfurt, Germany, at noon. My connecting flight back to the States left the next morning. I beelined for the Sheraton housed within Frankfurt's überterminal. At the check-in desk a beautiful German girl whirled crisply around from a computer screen. "Can I help you?" she asked in English. My first taste of a functioning service industry in over half a year. I stared at her, my heart in free fall. When I did not answer she asked again, in French. On the plane the next morning I sat down next to an American woman. She was an army wife, returning to Michigan for a wedding. While gliding over Greenland, I told long, elaborate lies about my Peace Corps service: I'd taken an extra year because I liked it so much. I was a little hesitant to return to America. There was so much, you know, consumerism. I had a girl back home, but I was not sure if the relationship was something I was anymore capable of sustaining. I had changed so much. She nodded, attempting to read her Maeve Binchy novel. Finally, she switched off her overhead light and closed her eyes as I was in mid-sentence. The woman who in Detroit stamped my passport looked at my Uzbek visa and Peace Corps certification and smiled. "Welcome home," she said. I stepped through double swing doors into a daylit, glass-paneled hangar. Couples reconnected, some joylessly, some ecstatically. High school students recited for their parents various exchange-program odysseys. Men in suits charged toward the Hertz phone bank. I scanned the crowd. L—— appeared between two Arabs, looked right at me, and continued her optical trawl. I stood there, too numb to move. Slowly, she worked her way back to me, her eyes suddenly stunned wide. I was skinnier by fifty pounds. My shoulder-length hair was gone. We rushed toward each other. I whispered into her shampooed hair that I would never, ever leave her again. I told her I was sorry. "Shut up," she said. "Just shut up." Three years later L—— would tell me that this moment, here, in Detroit, was when her love for me first began to fade. A crack formed upon the impact of reunion. I would not have believed her, then, had she told me. Her arms were too tight, her face too sodden. Maybe I still did not believe her. As I held L——'s head in my hands in the Detroit airport, I had a thought so crystalline it filled my mind with a relieved, limitless light: *At least I'll never have to go back there again.*

"How is L——?" Mavluda asked me now, touching my back. "Is she well? Are you married? Where is your ring?"

I stared at the photo and did not answer.

"Oh, dude," Rustam said, his voice deepening with recognition. "I'm sorry. You still love her, don't you?"

Yes. Never. Sometimes. Ask me tomorrow. Ask me in five seconds. I reached into some dark, hemorrhaging place and pulled out the first answer I could find: "Not anymore, no." I closed the album. None of this was special. It was simply life, and now it was time to eat.

Haiyidar and Altabek could not be immediately reached, and Rustam and I reclined in a guest room to digest our lunch while we waited for them to come home. Rustam catnapped on top of one of the thick blankets Mavluda had unfurled for us, his hands X'd atop his chest. Blades of amber sunlight beamed in through the window's perforated curtains. I lay on my side, slosh-stomached, paging through Mavluda's Qur'an. She was the only overtly religious member of the family, though it was unclear how devout she was. She never prayed, for instance, but she could read Arabic, the language in which this Qur'an was written. I studied the pages. To my infidel eye the letters ran ceaselessly together as though the readout of some spiritual Geiger counter, page after page of large, thick black swoops, each as beautifully pleased with itself as a skid mark left by a sports car. That Mavluda knew Arabic was fairly remarkable. Central Asians, like most Muslims upon whom Islam had been imposed, knew Arabic as "the holy language." Stalin did his best to wipe out Central Asia's educated Arabic speakers—merely possessing something written in the language was a firing-squad RSVP—though he did not get them all. One of the Arabic speakers he missed was Mavluda's father, who passed down his secret knowledge of the holy language to her and her brother.

Rustam, his eyes still closed, muttered, "Man, why are you looking at that thing?"

"I find it interesting."

"Religion is a distraction from the revolutionary cause of world socialism." I looked over at him. He held on to his expressionlessness for a few worrisome moments. Then, a smile. "Just kidding."

"You're not religious," I said.

"All these dudes my age now say that Islam is the answer. Especially in Namangan. I say Islam is the answer only if the question is 'What does the inside of prison look like?'"

"What do you think of that? When Karimov throws Muslims in jail just for being Muslims?"

His suddenly opened eyes scanned the ceiling. "I don't know, bro. I think it is sad for them. But I also don't want to be made to pray five times a day. What I truly think is that God is dead. That's what Nietzsche says, and I believe him."

I spent a few disquieting moments imagining Nietzsche in Russian. "I'm a little surprised Nietzsche's been translated into Russian."

Rustam looked around for something. Since the room was mostly empty, the fact that he set upon a pillow did not surprise me. I expected him to place it beneath his head. Instead, the large pillow came flying at me end over end. Mavluda's thick leatherbound Qur'an saw quick conversion into a shield. "What was that for?"

With a frustrated snort Rustam again closed his eyes. "I read him in *English,* dude. One of the PCVs left me some of his books."

"Oh."

"You know what else Nietzsche says? He says, 'It is terrible to die of thirst in the ocean.' When I read that I thought of all my friends and their Islam. They're dying of thirst, and they think Islam is going to save them. But it's poison, like the sea."

I smiled at Rustam. "I had no idea you were such a philosopher."

"Philosophy is life, bro. Check it. You know what other philosopher I like? Ayn Rand. I read her book *Atlas Shrugs.* It took me . . . well, it took me a long time, but I read it. Most of it. I like her a lot. She was a very smart woman, I think."

It had been a very long while since I had heard anyone refer to Rand as a "philosopher." Probably not since the beginning of college. But then Rand wrote in English, a language not well known for providing philosophers with wings. No, what we had in English was not philosophy but social criticism. This English did very well. If Orwell had written in, say, French, he would no doubt be recognized as a great philosopher, like Camus. Was it a coincidence that German gave us so many philosophers—and demagogues, the philosopher's dark half? Russian, on the other hand, provided us with many profound thinkers but not many philosophers. Dostoyevsky, one of Russia's weightiest thinkers, is regarded by Russians as rather cracked. He does not receive anywhere near the respect in Russia that he enjoys in England and America. There was, I had been told, a reason for this lack of Russian philosophers. Russian was a glorious language emotionally, but it was not an especially rigorous language. Like English—though for different reasons—Russian was poorly suited to the bellow blasts of German thought or the beret imponderables of French thought. Perhaps this was why Soviet-infected forms of Russian were so chilling. Soviet language is absolutely unexpressive. Even in translation one could see this: the harsh evasions, the sinister euphemisms. Sovietese, with its clichés, slogans, and appalling emptiness, is in direct opposition to the average Russian's huge, emotive understanding of the world. For what it was worth, I had been told on good authority that Shakespeare was fantastic in Russian.

Outside, we heard Mavluda and Arkinoy playing with the kids. High frantic child laughter, Mavluda's pretend gruffness, Arkinoy happily shrieking in A-sharp. "You know," Rustam said, "before, I was thinking how boring Gulistan must be. But they really have their own little world, don't they? I'm thinking it must be nice. I like it here."

I smiled. "I'm thinking that too." I chose not to tell him about Narghiza (I dared not ask where she was, fearing the worst), or that Haiyidar, very occasionally, when he was drunk, had been known to get rough with Altabek. But Haiyidar was a good man, much better than most of the dinner-table despots I had encountered in Uzbekistan. Spousal and child abuse, never officially measured, was thought to occur in Uzbek homes with an ugly regularity. Uzbekistan celebrated 1998 as "The Year of the Family," the notion being that strong families equal a strong society, and Uzbek courts did everything possible to prevent battered wives from attaining a divorce. Amidst these social realities, a "good man" was one of many concepts I had been forced drastically to adjust. I did not much like such adjustments, but it was either that or surrender to a naked emotionality useless to me and everyone else.

I got to my feet and walked over to the other end of the room to replace Mavluda's Qur'an in a small bookcase. Plastered all over the bookcase were stickers promoting American action films. This graffito was the work of movie-crazy Altabek, no doubt. A lot of Rambo, a lot of Jackie Chan, a few X-Men stickers. Here were the gunboats of modern imperialism, our swords rendered not into ploughshares but into decals. Such tiny cultural scuds may have not been how we won the Cold War, but they certainly did not hurt our effort. It was also highly preferable to the alternative. In a centralized, totalitarian regime, cultural imperialism can be achieved only through force. Soviet ideology came first by artless propaganda and then, if you were unlucky, by bayonet and tank. It had no other method of transference. American imperialism was a virus; Soviet imperialism was an entry wound.

Rustam sat up, his slack face sharpened by some sudden new motivation. "You know what I'm thinking? I'm thinking that from here we should visit Samarkand and Bukhara. A . . . road trip?"

"Road trip, sure. I have only two changes of clothes, though."

"So? I have only one."

I thought about it. I had been to Samarkand before, but I had to return at some point to give the imprisoned Omad's wife her $2,000. I had always wanted to see Bukhara. Of course, I also had to make it to the Aral Sea. But I did not imagine that Rustam received many chances to travel throughout his own country. "I think we could do that," I allowed.

Rustam grinned. "Cool."

"But you should know that in Samarkand I have another . . . duty I need to perform. Sort of like the letter."

Rustam fell back onto his blanket, arms outflung, as though I had shot a bolt into his heart. "Oh, duuude." He shot back up, resurrected by anger. "Why?"

"I said I would do something. For a friend."

"A friend? *Bozhe moi!* You will get us both arrested!"

"We won't be arrested. You don't even have to do anything. I'll take care of it."

He waved his arms. "Just—don't tell me anything else. I don't want to know."

From the other side of the house: "Ho, Tombek!" Haiyidar, finally, was home. Rustam and I journeyed across two rooms to meet him. Haiyidar, which means "strong lion," was the namesake of Mohammed's son-in-law Ali, the Fourth Caliph. "Strong Lion" was a little less suited to the short, squat man in an expensive taupe suit and a mismatched fedora before me. Haiyidar's facial features looked flattened, as though they had been mashed onto his skull by an unskilled potter. His round nostrils were divided by an unusually thick septum and his mouth was wide and blunt. When Haiyidar embraced me, he hoisted me off my feet. It was four in the afternoon, and he smelled as though he had been hosed down with cognac. On touchdown my soles hit the floorboards with a foundation-shaking boom.

Altabek, wearing a black leather trench coat, lurked behind his father. His long horselike face had the smooth boyishness I recalled, and he was still comically jug-eared, still slouchy and hood-eyed and sullen, still the sufferer of some deeply felt inadequacy. I wondered how prodigiously Haiyidar had been forced to bribe his son's way into Uzbek law school, as my memories of Altabek's stupidity were manifold and clear. Trying to teach him English basics as elementary as "My name is Altabek" had made drawing water from stones seem sound hydrological practice. The boy was not even half as intelligent as his sister Arkinoy and yet she was now a housewife and he was a young Gulistan *advokat*. This would not have been troubling if Arkinoy had not shared with me countless whispered agonies concerning the restricted avenues of her future. When Altabek reached out to shake my hand, I felt an obscure impulse to punch him.

"Do you still remember your Uzbek?" Haiyidar asked me in a chanting voice. He used the form of "you" usually reserved for speaking to one's social inferiors, such as children.

"A little," I said. "But my friend Rustam is here to help me."

Haiyidar looked at Rustam imperiously. "You. Where are you from?"

"Namangan."

"Namangan? There are many bad boys in Namangan. Are you friends with those crazy Muslims there?"

Rustam laughed and shook his head. "No. I hate those guys."

"Good," Haiyidar said, giving Rustam some tenderizing swats on the back. Haiyidar's brave old faith in Communism had seen enough reconstruction to allow him the luxury of a BMW but not enough to alter his thoughts concerning religious claptrap. But somehow he still seemed to think of himself as a Muslim. Shortly after I first arrived in Gulistan, Haiyidar poured me a massive finger of vodka. I claimed that drinking was against my religion and made a reverent sign of the cross. "So?" Haiyidar had said. "It's against my religion too. Now drink." God and Mammon, setting aside their differences, establishing cooperatives—the Soviet way.

"Are you hungry?" Haiyidar asked me now.

"Actually, we just—"

"Good. Tonight the *Malhallya* is having a party, and you two clowns will be my guests." The *Malhallya* was one of several pre-Soviet Uzbek institutions that worked along curiously Soviet coordinates. A *soviet*, technically, was an early workers' council that oversaw the organization and development of a small, mandated area. The formally similar *Mal-*

hallya was typically overseen by a group of old Uzbek men respectfully known as "whitebeards." It differed from the *soviet* in that it was largely a neighborhood tribunal. If one wished to buy a house, divorce one's wife, open a business, or borrow money, one had to go through the local *Malhallya*. It did not require a lot of imagination to envision what went on at a *Malhallya* gathering. Drinking, followed by prayer, followed by drinking, followed by drinking.

"Well," I told Haiyidar, "we have to leave early tomorrow and—"

Haiyidar held up his hand, frowning with such vigor that his lips vanished. "We will be leaving in ten minutes."

While Haiyidar changed clothes and Altabek and Rustam talked soccer, I pulled Mavluda aside to present her with some of the things I had brought. She obviously did not need the money I had earmarked for her, though I tried to give it to her anyway. Without a word, she closed my hand around the two hundreds I held out and again kissed me on the forehead. I removed from my backpack a small stuffed talking Elmo doll for Narghiza. I pulled the string on its back, and together we listened to one of the four things this boneless red felt creature had to say. Elmo, we learned, loved us both very much. She thanked me and said she would be sure that Narghiza received it.

Haiyidar emerged from his bedroom stripped of his tie and topped off with a jaunty new fedora, a peacock feather stuffed in its band. "*Ketdik*," he said. This meant "Let's go," or, literally, "We left," one of several peculiar Uzbekisms that use the past tense to express future activity. We marched single file out to the driveway. There Haiyidar's BMW waited, a grayish tiger tail of exhaust flickering behind it. Haiyidar's driver, Maruf, remembered me on sight and struggled out of the car in the manner of a gut-shot grizzly. His apparent reason for doing so was the ceremonial rupture of my rib cage. During his embrace he, too, lifted me up, providing me with an interesting aerial view of his massive face. It was covered with a disturbingly varied number of scars. When he set me back down, he smiled and lit up a cigarette. After a drag he said he was glad I came back, and smiled. His teeth were small and brown, like the kernels of hard Halloween corn. The gravel spray with which Maruf now left Haiyidar's driveway had the force and trajectory of a pump-action-shotgun blast, and soon we were driving back toward Gulistan at Yeager-ish speeds. To write that foreigners drive like sixteen-year-olds on mescaline is of course the literary equivalent of stock footage. It has, however, the unhappy virtue of being true. In Uzbek taxis I had been driven the wrong way down countless one-way streets. I had been threaded through the human woof of crowded city sidewalks. I had been piloted along (not across: *along*) railroad tracks and plowed over highway dividers and achieved momentary flight off the lip of steep hills. I had been helplessly party to blind turns into narrow alleys at forty miles an hour. I had flown down black roads at night alongside a drunk driver who claimed headlights made it harder for him to see. I had sincerely believed I had only moments left to live. And I had been told not to wear my seat belt.

My current attempt to buckle my seat belt was aborted when I realized there was no seat belt to buckle. It was entombed somewhere beneath the BMW's leopard-print back-seat cover. Haiyidar pulled from his pocket a wallet-sized cell phone. He shouted into the little plastic wafer, sometimes in Uzbek but more often in Russian. Maruf and Rustam laughed knowingly. "I like this dude," Rustam said. "He's one cool bro. Altabek told me that last year your host-father was made chief prosecutor of the whole Sir Darya region. I think he's a very powerful man." As some underling wheedled and apologized to Haiyidar over his cell, he turned toward me and dramatically rolled his eyes.

Soon we were back near Gulistan's city square. Maruf coasted presidentially through red lights while nearby police officers saluted Haiyidar's car. With pride Haiyidar pointed out all the new buildings going up. He said this was the work of Gulistan's youthful former mayor, who a few months ago had been appointed one of Karimov's top advisors. Rustam mentioned that this man was rumored to be one of Karimov's likely successors. "Like *when?*" I burst out. "In 2023?" Rustam chose not to translate this. Maruf steered us across an empty parking lot and pulled up beside Gulistan's new courthouse, where Haiyidar worked. Its sandstone gleamed in the sun like a rind of Caribbean beach. "Come on," Haiyidar said, once the emphysemic Maruf had lumbered out of the car and dutifully popped open all of our doors. We climbed out. "Leave it," Haiyidar ordered when I began to close my door. He motioned obliquely toward Maruf, who was still wheezing. "It gives him something to do."

In his office Haiyidar opened one of the room's many cabinets to reveal a black-shelled Daewoo color television with a built-in VCR. The window-installed air conditioner emitted a low, diligent hum. I walked over to it. It, too, bore the brand of Daewoo, a South Korean manufac-

turer of cars, appliances, and high technology that had arguably trans-
fused more blood into the necrotic Uzbek economy than any other foreign firm. I enjoyed the view from Haiyidar's office window, gazing down
upon Gulistan's main square. When I had lived here, this was a wasteland
of cracked concrete and tough weedy grass. Now the whole area had a
parade-ready majesty about it. Yet other than two or three people making their solitary way across the square, the heart of Gulistan was empty.

I turned from the window to see Haiyidar sending a shiny piece of
oblong paper through his Daewoo fax machine, which sat upon his desk
with the prominence of a fortress. Alongside the fax machine were two
phones, a plaque, and a fancy obsidian pen holster. Haiyidar had no
computer, though, and at first glance his typewriter seemed as kitschy as
a bamboo fishing rod lovingly mounted upon the office wall of a Wall
Street banker who had once been outdoors. But the typewriter was still
operational. A half-typed memo lolled over the carriage like a wide white
tongue.

"I don't know about you," Rustam quietly said while Haiyidar
guided his fax through, "but I was a lot more impressed by all the saluting cops."

I looked at the large portrait of Islam Karimov hung directly behind
Haiyidar. Only a few official portraits of Karimov were in general circulation, and most I recognized. There was Karimov the Caring, Karimov
the Mighty, Karimov the Regal. I had never seen this one before. The
president wore a huge gold pinkie ring. His hand was affixed to his chin
in an improbable pose intended, perhaps, to suggest suaveness. Karimov
the Pimp? Karimov's tie was tomato-red, his suit the color of a starless
night sky, his eyes as small and black as a mako's.

Haiyidar and Maruf took us for a ride through a completely new
section of Gulistan that Rustam and I had not seen on the bus ride into
town. We drove past a new Western-style supermarket, a new bazaar, a
large new conchiform stadium. "Nice, isn't it?" Haiyidar asked as the
stadium became a memory.

We hit the highway and drove in silence for a while. Upon this huge
flat plain towns appeared, then vanished. Fly swarms hovered above dog
carcasses bashed into intestinal red ribbons alongside the road. I tried
and failed to imagine living out here again. Everything felt unimaginably
far from everything else. Many of the homes we passed were concentrated along the highway, all connected by a long shared whitewashed

clay wall, and I jumped hungrily upon the flashes of Uzbek life occasionally provided by an opened gate. Laundry, children, cows, women doing chores, men burning trash. So normal, so utterly strange. I knew the rural mind, its maddening miscegenation of gentleness and cruelty. But this was rural on a near-intergalactic scale. To see Haiyidar's BMW coast past their tiny homes must have been quietly shattering for these people. Or maybe they did not care. Not their business, not their concern. And all around them a solid ocean of land.

At the forked entrance to some small Sir Darya town, Maruf navigated through a few narrow anonymous side streets and pulled into a junkyard. Scorched, windshieldless car husks were piled one atop the other. Spare tires, hubcaps, steering wheels, shock springs, and engine remnants were strewn like shrapnel about the sandy yard. Large cranes and wrecking machines loomed idly among the carnage. Crammed between the formidable metal teeth of one wrecking machine were the masticated remains of an old Datsun pickup, one of its headlights dangling out of its frame as though it were a popped retina. Two filthy, shirtless Uzbek men appeared like trolls from behind some debris and scrambled over to the car. Upon seeing Haiyidar, both smiled nervously. Haiyidar left the car and quietly began to upbraid them, stabbing a finger into his palm. One of the men said something. Haiyidar's shouted response boomed throughout the surrounding wreck of steel. The talk stopped. They all stood there, the sun sinking behind a crane and leaving behind sad purplish shadows. With one last glare Haiyidar froze the filthy, shirtless men in place and walked back over to our car. "Take them for a ride," he told Maruf.

"What was *that* all about?" I asked Maruf once we were a few blocks away.

"Business," he said with a shrug.

"What kind of business?"

"Business." Maruf, wanting no more discussion, fiddled with the radio. Suddenly, Elvis Presley's "Return to Sender" filled the BMW. At the song's "address unknown" line, I could only curl up on the leopard-print seat cover and laugh. Above us the sky was an immense velvety oblivion. "I think this has been the strangest day of my life."

Rustam looked at me. "I know what you mean. I felt that way when I went to Disneyland."

We soon stopped again at what appeared to be not much of a roadside restaurant. A garage-sized cube of white plaster, its windows shuttered, a few tables and chairs scattered along the portico, a lone Uzbek waitress pouring tea for an old whitebeard, spinning dust devils. Maruf told us to wait and went to have a word with the restaurant's owner. The aggrieved man, wiping his hands upon a bloodied apron, came out to greet Maruf with the same queasy smile the shirtless junk hands had worked up for Haiyidar. Maruf smoked as he lit in to the restaurateur, blowing clouds of indignation directly into the man's sputtering face.

I felt dirty watching all this. "What the fuck is going on?" I asked Rustam.

Rustam was not even watching. "You heard him. Business."

"It's totally creepy."

"Bro, check out that bitch over there."

"They're like gangsters, for Christ's sake. And do you realize they're doing this to *impress* us?"

"The bitch, though. Check her out."

He meant the waitress. She wore a short red shirt, a white blouse. Her hair blew about her head in sweat-fused tendrils. Her attractiveness was as beside the point as attractiveness could possibly be. To me she merely looked young, and tired.

"Rustam, she's probably sixteen years old."

"No, dude. She's older than that. I bet she's a mommy."

"Let's just . . . *cool* it on the mommies, all right?" This came out much sharper than I had intended.

Rustam's face hardened into smooth, indignant granite. Beneath his mustache his mouth tamped into a humorless line. Every part of him folded, tightened, bored up for assault. "What's your malfunction, bro?"

"The truth?"

His hand flipped up. "Shoot."

"'Bitches.' It kind of bothers me."

"Why?"

"Because. It does. That's not how you should refer to women."

He laughed as though relieved. "Dude. *Dude.* Come on, bro. You know I don't mean it like that. It's just fun."

"Well imagine if someone said something like that about your sister."

His face looked somehow distorted, groggy with anger. "This has *nothing* to do with my sister."

"You see? You're mad."

"My sister would never *permit* herself to be looked at this way. She is a . . . *good* girl."

"You see, this is my point. And I—"

"My sister," he went on, pointing at me. "My *sister*—" He stopped suddenly and gazed out the window. "I don't want to talk about this. My duty as a brother is to protect my sister's honor. If any guy ever called her a bitch I would kill him. All right?"

"But what if *she* has a brother, Rustam?"

Rustam did not look at me. Beyond his window Maruf was receiving something from the restaurateur. Something in an envelope. The Uzbek waitress was looking suspiciously over at our car, a flat hand shielding her eyes from the last effortful burst of light from the setting sun, which now looked as cool as a yolk. I took off my glasses and rubbed my eyes. Without my glasses, I was blind. All around the car nothing existed but blur. Everything lost its edge, went watercolor, melted.

At last Rustam spoke: "I like you a lot, Tom. You're my bro. I'm having a good time with you. I'm grateful. But if you say anything else, I'm going to grow very angry."

I allowed Rustam the violence of his thoughts.

The Peace Corps was conceived in October 1960 by John F. Kennedy on the steps of the Student Union at the University of Michigan. Kennedy arrived in Ann Arbor only hours after his final televised debate with fellow candidate Richard Nixon. His mood, reportedly, was not good. Although it was two in the morning and freezing, 10,000 students turned up to greet him. He was under no pressing obligation to speak to these students, as most of them were under twenty-one and lacked the power to vote. But candidate Kennedy, who had prepared no remarks for the occasion, spontaneously challenged his spellbound audience: "How many of you are willing to spend ten years in Africa or Latin America or Asia working for the United States and working for freedom?" This notion of a "Peace Corps," as it quickly became known, was the lone new proposal to emerge from the Nixon-Kennedy race. More people wrote to the president-elect's office offering to work for the nonexistent outfit than all other existing government agencies put together. On March 1, 1961, three months into his presidency, Kennedy signed Executive Order 10924 and created the United States Peace Corps, ignoring State Department warnings that "Peace" sounded too Soviet and "Corps" too militaristic. Kennedy's brother-in-law Sargent Shriver was appointed director, his salary of $1 a year intended to deflect already rampant charges of executive nepotism. The Peace Corps's first Advisory Board included Eleanor Roosevelt and Harry Belafonte and was chaired by Lyndon Johnson, who warned Shriver about keeping "the three Cs"—"the communists, the consumptives, and the cocksuckers"—out of the organization.

Early response to the Peace Corps was unpredictable. Barry Goldwater backed it. William F. Buckley did not, wondering what possible good it would do an average African family to host some Harvard boy speaking pidgin Swahili. The *Saturday Review,* that stronghold of middle-class horse sense, ecstatically wrote: "Instead of dreary conversation about the meaninglessness of existence, students are now earnestly exchanging ideas about the different needs of communities in Asia and Africa." But what, in 1961, was the Peace Corps supposed to do? Some have suggested that Kennedy's creation of the Peace Corps had its roots in his wider—and ultimately disastrous—fascination with the world of paramilitary elitism. Secret operations and crack squads of highly trained rangers snapping necks by moonlight thrilled Kennedy. Oftentimes, a few handsome Green Berets, another Kennedy creation, were invited to Hyannisport for weekends of touch football with the family. One argument runs that Kennedy intended the Peace Corps to function as a kind of spy school, but nowhere has this charge ever been borne out. Sargent Shriver, for his part, quickly devised protocol to block CIA infiltration of the organization, and most of the background checks the Peace Corps performed were more concerned with uncovering domestic rather than foreign spies. In addition, Peace Corps volunteers were frozen out of any intelligence work for five years following the end of their service (a hindrance George W. Bush quietly tried and failed to overturn), and were across-the-board forbidden from having anything to do with the region in which they served. The CIA, however, despite claiming it "has nothing to do and wants nothing whatsoever to do with the Peace Corps," reputedly flouted these restrictions in the Peace Corps's uncertain early days. An annoyed Shriver called Kennedy in April 1963 to say that "our friends over in the Central Intelligence Agency might think that they're smarter than anybody else." Kennedy sent a message to Richard Helms, the CIA's deputy director, that he did not "want anybody in there. . . . And if they are there, let's get them out now." None of this prevented a representative of the Soviet Union, at the 32nd Session of the United Nations Economic and Social Council, from taking the floor and for over an hour denouncing the Peace Corps as a cover for the CIA. And yet, amazingly, in a world in which the KGB and the CIA were seemingly penetrated as regularly as the Detroit Lions' offensive line, never has the Peace Corps uncovered any definitive proof that it once harbored spies. (When I was in the Peace Corps, jocular if discomforting accusations of my assumed double life in espionage routinely came up with Uzbeks. I often wondered why this was until I learned that a popular series of Russian spy novels features a particularly sordid recurring character: a Peace Corps volunteer-cum-CIA operative in Nicaragua who serves as a double agent for the KGB.)

The early Peace Corps was conceived and overseen by men not known for shirking Cold War brinksmanship, yet they never rewarded allies with Peace Corps volunteers or withdrew volunteers from nations hostile to the United States unless formally asked to do so. This is remarkable. Less remarkable was the number of fiascoes the nascent Peace Corps faced. When 40,000 applications were sent to Michigan autoworkers in an attempt to recruit skilled mechanics, the harvest was 25 volunteers. When Micronesia requested volunteers, the Peace Corps sent 700—one for every 130 Micronesians. The Peace Corps approached Japan, a nation the United States had routinely failed to take seriously as an economic power, and asked if it would like volunteers. The offer was politely declined. While just over half of the early Peace Corps's volunteers were teachers, a good portion of the remainder was sent under the cloudy mandate of "community development" (now known as the equally nebulous "business development"). Until the late 1960s, Peace Corps volunteers received virtually no guidance from Peace Corps staff, and while some volunteers relished their freedom, many others descended into alcoholism and depression. (Revealingly, the term "culture shock" was put into wide cultural circulation by returned Peace Corps volunteers.) Throughout this period volunteers chose "early termination of service" at a shocking rate. None of this was helped by the purportedly tormenting boot camp preservice volunteers had to endure, nor the childish loyalty oath each volunteer was forced to mouth before being shipped out. Early volunteers also had to carry with them a batty little treatise entitled *What You Must Know About Communism*.

Following Kennedy's martyrdom, Peace Corps applications boomed. In the mid-1960s, 42,000 people applied for 10,000 available spots. Jack Vaughn, Shriver's successor, went on the record to say, in a statement fairly shrouded with bong smoke, "The Peace Corps is about love." When other government agencies were wiretapping and arresting campus protestors, the Peace Corps was actually wooing these "high risk, high gain" prospects. One Peace Corps recruiter explained, "They'll either blow the place up or they'll get something done." When Malcolm X visited Nigeria in the mid 1960s, he spoke out against the neo-imperialist Peace Corps—only to be shouted down by the nation's biggest newspaper, which claimed Nigeria had "benefited immensely" from its Peace Corps volunteers. All of this, like so much else, began to change with Richard Nixon, who in 1970 found a memo on his desk from future Watergate felon H. R. Haldeman. "Bust the Peace Corps," it read. Nixon decided not to kill the Peace Corps—a young speechwriter named Patrick Buchanan, among others, advised against it—but he did severely cut its funding. Some of these Nixonian measures were inadvertently positive. Abolished were the boot camps and pretraining psychological tests. More average Americans were encouraged to apply. Yet Nixon also put a stop to the recruitment of "BA generalists," who were considered "troublemakers." By 1972 the Peace Corps had shrunk 56 percent; only 6,900 volunteers were in the field. After several years of catching such rightist flak, the Peace Corps began to be bombarded by the Molotov cocktails of the Left. During the Carter years, a demagogue named Sam Brown did everything to ensure the Peace Corps's burial short of seeding its grave's topsoil with grass. He discouraged the Peace Corps from sending abroad English teachers, preferring instead volunteers who would focus on "basic human needs," though many nations, especially those in Africa, still begged for teachers. He also announced that only countries that met harshly low GNP requirements would be allowed to host volunteers, suggesting Brown's profound ignorance of how undeveloped economies actually function. By 1987 the Peace Corps whimpered at its nadir:

Only 5,200 volunteers were stationed throughout the world. When, nine years later, I applied for Peace Corps service, 9,200 people applied for 7,000 spots—the fewest applicants in the organization's history.

The former Soviet Union was one of the many places the Peace Corps's founding fathers could have hardly imagined welcoming volunteers. The idea to send volunteers to the Soviet Union was first floated during U.S. Secretary of State James Baker's summit with Boris Yeltsin in 1990. When the Soviet Union fell apart the following year, the plan was fast-tracked, despite the fact that many of the former Soviet republics' presidents, including Islam Karimov, were reportedly resistant to hosting the Peace Corps. During the 1992 training of Uzbekistan's first group of volunteers, a standoff between Karimov and the American ambassador to Uzbekistan resulted in the hostile encirclement of the Peace Corps's dormitory by armed Uzbek police officers. The impasse was settled, but many of the program's primary staff, including its director, soon resigned. One of these staff members was Jeffrey Tayler, now a fine travel writer, who writes in the prologue to his *Siberian Dawn: A Journey Across the New Russia:* "I took a job of starting up a Peace Corps post in newly independent Uzbekistan. . . . The experience in Tashkent, for reasons too complicated to warrant explanation here, proved disappointing professionally and devastating personally." The complicated reasons were these: Virtually none of the staff, excepting Tayler, had any relevant experience in the region, and the volunteer sites were not at all prepped for volunteers. Of the fifty-four volunteers in the Peace Corps's first Uzbek contingent, only seventeen served out their full term of service. The program's (American) replacement staff was soon mired in scandals so bizarre and multifaceted—embezzlement, falsified grant proposals, and something as parsimonious as hoarding food meant for volunteers— the United States's General Accounting Office stepped in to investigate, and Peace Corps Uzbekistan was nearly shut down. The program was at last functioning smoothly by the time my group (Uzbekistan's fourth) arrived in 1996, though its sordid past was prudently kept from us.

When I began my Peace Corps service, I believed I would forge morality and character through a single act of heedless idealism. What actually happened to me, what I actually *did* to help people, would not much matter, even if I secretly worried that merely being witness to the developing world's suffering might not be enough. Indeed, the crevice between identifying needs and creating solutions for them was, from the moment I arrived in Tashkent, impossible to bridge.

My fellow volunteers were lost upon similar terrain, of course, but I did not much notice them. I had begun the idle suicide of spending all my time writing to L——, rereading her most recent letter to me, and tunneling through *The Brothers Karamazov*, *The Recognitions*, and *Ulysses*. If the sea, for Melville, was "my Harvard and my Yale," I believed I could make Gulistan my Boston College and my University of Connecticut. Though training quickly lost its novelty, I studied Uzbek with deranged devotion, trying to memorize no fewer than fifty words a day. In this I had no choice. For the first time in my life I had stress-induced insomnia. I usually went to bed at 6 P.M., fell asleep around 5 A.M., and woke up fifteen minutes later. I was so visibly going to pieces that Peace Corps Uzbekistan's medical staff officer often sought me out during her visits to Gulistan to learn how I was coping. My letters to my father ("Greetings from Central Asia, or, as I like to call it, Hell") prompted his own that reminded me, with unhelpful honesty, that when he was my age he was dodging Viet Cong tracer fire.

I had been in Uzbekistan a little longer than a month when a massive storm parked itself over Gulistan. The air felt cool and immobile and bristly with ions. I noted the swollen smoke-gray thunderheads in the bright night sky as I ventured out to the pit toilet around midnight. By my fourth or fifth trip to the pit toilet, it was clear something was wrong. My forehead was as warm with unfathomable inner activity as the top of a computer monitor. When I began vomiting, I no longer had the strength to make it to the pit toilet, and instead stepped out the front door and heaved into the family garden. The storm, at this point, was a sky-filling catastrophe. Clouds churned like manipulated dry ice. Rain punched into the dirt with the propulsive impact of rounds. The thunder was not the low-booming, displeased-deity sort but eardrum-bursting thunder that sounded like lightning looks.

When morning came, Mavluda found me sprawled on my bedroom floor. I pleaded with her to call my father or my mother or L—— and explain what was happening. But a febrile haze blotted out my Uzbek. Haiyidar decided that volcanically hot tea, an Uzbek cure-all, would nurse me back to full sap, and poured down my throat several cups. Mavluda brought me some watermelon, another all-purpose Uzbek restorative, the cool pink pulp of which I mashed all over my burning face. Arkinoy, over Mavluda's horrified and embarrassed objections, finally called the Peace Corps. The medical officer was luckily visiting Gulistan that day, and within minutes she was in my bedroom, holding a cold washcloth across my face. I stared up at her, the following words forming so unexpectedly they surprised even me: "I want to go home." While I sat dazed upon the edge of my bed, the medical officer packed up my books and clothing. I tried not to look at my host family, who stood shamefaced and silent beyond my bedroom door. Two days later, in the Peace Corps's Tashkent clinic, the medical staff officer came in to check on me. I had ingested nothing but Gatorade for forty-eight hours. I could barely lift my arms. The medical officer pressed the back of her hand against my forehead and smiled. "You're not as warm," she said. "You look better." "I *feel* better," I admitted. She took my temperature. It was 102 degrees.

While my plane ticket to Michigan was being arranged, I approached the medical officer and asked if I might be able to resume my training. She looked at me, sighing. I quickly explained that the fever had cleansed my spirit of its grout. I wanted to keep going. I believed this. By this point the Peace Corps's staff had about as much faith in me as they would have had in Libyans with nerve gas. I was told that, in order to return to Gulistan, I needed to write a statement in which I declared my unqualified readiness to become a Peace Corps volunteer. I wrote two bathetic pages I sincerely hope never resurface from now until the end of all time. The country director reluctantly signed off on them, and a day later I returned to training.

The next few weeks would be my best. I would score in the low-advanced range on my Uzbek language tests and prove so assured in my first session as an actual teacher of actual children in an actual classroom that our TEFL trainer refused to believe I had never taught before. At the end of the month we were sworn in as volunteers at Gulistan's palatial town theater by the American ambassador to Uzbekistan, a splendidly odd fellow whose speech quoted J. R. R. Tolkien not once but twice, creating some truly fascinating silence while his translator stared with bug-eyed composure into a crowd of Gulistan luminaries.

We celebrated in a Tashkent hotel that seemed to have been thawed from the 1960s solely for us. We drank kerosene-warm vodka and smoked peaty Russian cigarettes and then, two by two, we vanished. Paul

Theroux once wrote that, of the platter of morsels Peace Corps places before its young charges, the tastiest were the "unlimited and guiltless sex" between volunteers. That night those hors d'oeuvres were consumed ferociously. I did nothing, of course, but long for L—— in my room, even as all along the hotel's corridors doors slammed in mid-laugh and deadbolts slid home.

The following day my fellow volunteers marched out to their sites in Samarkand, Bukhara, Ferghana, Kokand, Khiva, and Karakalpakistan. My site was sad, lonely Gulistan. I returned to my host family and within days began teaching at School Number Five in the middle of the city. Number Five was a Russian-language school, and one of Gulistan's most superior. Like every school in town, Number Five had lobbied hard for a Peace Corps volunteer. The rumor was that Number Five received me because it alone had made no attempt to bribe the Peace Corps. My teaching partner was named Irina, an eraser-wielding autocrat. For the next few weeks our students endured the mid-class switchover from Irina's brutal shouted instruction to my sheepish Montessori experiments. I gave students little note cards, for instance, identifying each of them as a "cowboy," "robot," "dinosaur," or "cosmonaut," and had other students ask them where they worked and where they lived until someone guessed correctly what they were. The students laughed a lot, and seemed to enjoy such strange new vocabularies, but Irina was unmoved. "This is all very unfamiliar to me," she would sometimes say after class.

Most of my students were Russians, better-off Uzbeks and Koreans. The Soviet educational apparatus had always provided the cities of its non-Russian republics with a "Russian" school system and a "national" school system. "Russian" schools were often loaded with non-Russian pupils, while the more poorly financed "national" schools never had Russian students. Although my students were not as elite as those in the Turkish lyceum just down the road, they were solidly middle-class, hard-headedly understanding they would have to work to achieve, and good-heartedly expecting their work to be rewarded. My Korean students taught me lessons of my own. Shipped-in Koreans had slaved upon Uzbek cotton and rice farms until the de-Stalinizing Khrushchev years. Koreans were not widely liked by Uzbeks. Nor were they highly regarded by Russians, despite the fact that they had been thoroughly Russified (my students had names like Vladimir Nam and Olga Kim) and retained virtually nothing of their Korean heritage. Uzbekistan's Koreans were disenfranchised ethnically and linguistically, as very few of them could speak Uzbek with any facility. The best universities require Uzbek fluency, which meant that Koreans were isolated academically as well. Uzbekistan's laws were actively discriminatory against Koreans. And yet, who were my best students? Of course, Koreans, despite facing more institutionalized prejudice than any American minority could possibly claim, and despite having survived a culture-stripping Middle Passage.

School Number Five's English faculty had few books, or at least few books I felt I could use. Even though, in 1988, Soviet schoolbooks were declared in the government paper *Izvestia* to be "full of lies," most provincial schools did not have the funds to replace these texts. Irina gave me a few books to look at. One claimed that Manhattan saw one murder every fifty seconds. Another talked about "great world philosophers," by which it meant Karl Marx and V. I. Lenin. Aristotle, Plato, Hobbes, Hegel, and Rousseau were all passed over in a sentence—and then merely because Marx had studied them. The erratic though colossally brilliant Marx was best understood as a contemporary of Adam Smith and Thomas Malthus, men worried over the fault lines of nascent industrial capitalism, and cannot be blamed for the bloody Soviet reaping. (Censorship, he wrote in 1842, "serves only to demoralize. That greatest of all vices, hypocrisy, is inseparable from it.") But imagine an entire educational system that had been shaped and ordained by the reading habits of a lone and rather peculiar thinker. I no longer had to imagine that system. What I had to do was teach in it.

The book I decided to work from—*English*, by A. P. Starkov and B. S. Ostrovsky (that "B. S." would prove prescient)—was filled with passages such as: "To see the effect of pollution in rivers, just have a look at the Thames. . . . Large cities on the Great Lakes of North America are letting different wastes flow into the water. . . . Nothing can live or grow in this polluted water now." While other Peace Corps volunteers were writing away for grants to purchase new books and materials, I was merely reading, in dumbfounded astonishment, the ones I had. I told myself I had nothing to give to these children. I knew of no Internet connections (though I did not look) and had no idea where one might begin to search for organizations willing to grant money to struggling foreign schools (though I did not try).

After two months I stopped preparing for my classes, preferring simply to show up. I found a very sick puppy, brought it home, improvised for it a small bed made of socks and the lid of my water distiller, fed it milk and scraps of meat, and after a week saw it die in my arms on my birthday. It may seem strange that, in a place where so much unhappiness was writ so large, the last choking breath of a black puppy slightly larger than my hand could push me over the edge. But it did. The high spirits of my training's end were now fully exorcised. Stranded in the experience's horse latitudes, I pitched overboard what was left of my goodwill in order to stay afloat. Perversely, I personified my depression, which I called Blackmind. My letters and journal entries of this period are filled with completely nutty descriptions of having tea with Blackmind, walking home with Blackmind, going on a vacation from Blackmind. I am not certain how crazy I really was, though the fact that I used an invitation to write to a good friend's mother's fifth-grade class to ponder the nature of depression and elaborately quote Kierkegaard suggests I was less than tightly caulked. Around this time I received a letter from another friend, who mentioned the Blackmind portion of my letter to him and said he found it worrying. "I'm all for sticking it out," he wrote, "but part of growing up is not giving a fuck anymore about anybody else thinking poorly of you for quitting, because frankly no one gives a shit about you that much, although when I was your age I used to think so. Masochism is not mature. It's sick."

The entrails of the cows butchered on the sides of Gulistan's towpaths glistened with unknowably sinister portent. My students' smiles seemed conspiratorial. The bubble-wrap of kindness in which my family swaddled me felt somehow accusatory and insulting. I was reading Kafka not with admiration and astonishment but with shock at the wicked congruence between his fiction and what I thought I was living. My story was not about a penal colony or a man transmuted into vermin but about a boy who grew up in Michigan and then, for some reason, went to Uzbekistan. There he began to feel that there was some overwhelmingly hostile thing in the world with him, and the simplicity and unity of his character broke, and he was not the same again.

What broke him? What broke me? It was not that bad. I know that now. The tree laid across my shoulders was a featherload compared to what most are given. "I think it is God's will that you are here," my closest Uzbek friend, Odil, said to me once. Odil had, long before I knew him, converted to Christianity and was disowned by his family. It was

Odil's twenty-second birthday, and we sat alone in his apartment drinking tea and picking at a bowl of raisins. Soon I started talking about L—— and my family and, before I could stop, broke down sobbing. Odil said nothing for a while, then told me about the first time he left home to pick cotton, as every able-bodied young person in Uzbekistan is forced to do every year. At night it was cold, and his hands bled, and he missed his mother and father so much he longed to cry. But men in Uzbekistan did not cry. Every night he held back his womanly urges. But now, he told me, he had seen far worse, more private Gethsemanes. "It feels good to cry," he admitted. "Maybe we don't cry here because we are afraid. Maybe this is a bad thing. And maybe all those times I was far away from home, I should have cried because then it all wouldn't have hurt me so much." He regarded me with a calm, sacerdotal face. "Being away from home is very hard. But you will do good work here."

A few days later I took the bus to Tashkent for my monthly meeting with the medical officer. This was one of the conditions I had agreed to in order to stay. In full command of my emotions, I told the medical officer that I had begun to think about killing myself. She looked at me, expressionless. I had given her no choice. I went back to Gulistan, packed my things, and said goodbye. Odil was there to see me off. Tears again. Again they felt good. Nothing had ever felt so good. I was not strong enough, and I knew that now. I was weak, and I could go home.

We left behind Haiyidar's world of junkyard shakedowns for the crisp air and lavender hills of the dusk-dark Uzbek countryside. Maruf, wrapped in cigarette smoke, drove while Haiyidar, an envelope of half-counted dollars in his lap, dozed beside him. Rustam stared out the rear portside window. I had starboard. The scenery kept getting prettier. I had seen Uzbekistan only in the last months of fall and beneath the lifeless slush of winter. "Wait until spring," everyone here had always told me. I had scoffed then. The road twisted through the low hills and farms and past solitary trees while all around us a strangely low sky bled a darker and more beautiful blue.

When the Kazakh border appeared, Maruf grunted Haiyidar awake to halfheartedly lift his hand at some of the saluting border guards. Along the border a half-dozen cars had been pulled over, their distressed

Uzbek drivers pleading with the not visibly sympathetic Kazakhs. "Why are we in Kazakhstan?" I asked. Maruf explained we would be in Kazakhstan for only a few miles; part of it happened to thrust down into Sir Darya between Gulistan and where we needed to go. This border was a matter of some disagreement. After the Soviet Union's collapse its various republics were left with thirty-five major territorial disputes and hundreds of smaller ones. This tiny Kazakh isthmus into Uzbekistan was part of a much larger quarrel. Uzbeks had long argued that most of southern Kazakhstan (the original Uzbek homeland) should belong to them, while Kazakhs believed that Tashkent, historically (though no longer) a Kazakh-majority city, should be part of Kazakhstan. Soon we were safely in Kazakhstan and Maruf sped up. Kazakhstan's pasture-lands looked even larger and lovelier than Uzbekistan's but, as promised, we passed back into Sir Darya.

We stopped at a *choikhana* (teahouse) a few miles past the Kazakh border. The owners knew Haiyidar well, and we were given an outdoor table right off the highway. Now it was cool. The moon was just out. Smoky flags of cloud floated across its pale yellow face as though attached to invisible masts. Haiyidar, for whom no dinner was complete without a feast before it, ordered up four kebobs of lamb shashlik. Most foreign visitors to Uzbekistan wind up rhapsodic about shashlik. It was, admittedly, one of the country's more stylish dishes. But I would have preferred to have any number of things—spider eggs, broken glass—in my mouth. The satanic amoeba that nearly knocked me off this mortal coil during Peace Corps training had entered my system on a piece of shashlik. I had not been able to eat it since. Adding to this was the fact that I was already suffering from diarrhea, a condition that swallowing a pair of Imodium A-D every four hours had for the past few days managed to contain. When the shashlik arrived, Haiyidar asked immediately why I was not digging in. To placate him I took a few small bites and when no one was looking spit them out in the dirt next to me.

Suddenly, Haiyidar asked, "Is it true that you can have sex with a woman whenever you want before you get married in America?"

I explained to Haiyidar that, if two people met and liked each other, it was not considered a big deal for most Americans if they then had sex. No, the woman's family did not usually find out. No, the woman felt no shame. I realized I had been speaking Uzbek, with no help from Rustam, for the last several minutes. It hardly mattered that mine was an ugly mutilated form of the language: I was still speaking it. By the time I quit the Peace Corps, I had just begun to have the occasional dream in Uzbek. That was five years ago. Five days ago I could barely string together six Uzbek words. This was progress. Rustam, as though reading my mind, winked at me.

It was night; buckets of stars and planets seemed spilled across the sky. After the shashlik break we came upon another small town, the BMW's high beams searchlighting across whitewash and metal gates. What would have seemed quaint during the day was now shadowy, close, sinister. Within ovals of the intensified headlight, houses looked cracked and gray. Darkness and poverty, rarely a good mix, gave the few people we saw walking about a halting, undead look. Haiyidar muttered something and Maruf parked beside a small building. Thick buttery light and voices poured from its four plain windows.

"Haiyidar wishes to challenge you in billiards," Rustam told me when we got out.

"Great. I love playing pool."

"Not pool, bro. Billiards."

"What's the difference?"

Before he could answer, we stepped inside. The maleness in this cramped space was so harsh and overpowering it was as though the air were holding me down and breathing in my face. Some men ate seeds and spit the shells. Others dipped *noss,* a foul tobacco-lime-sap-opium blend, leaving their teeth mossy and their eyes as glassy as crystal. Others yet swigged off bottles of cheap Uzbek beer. No one looked at Rustam and me. They looked at Maruf and Haiyidar, both of whom strode down separate canals between the room's four billiards tables. Haiyidar walked to the room's far side, where a dozen billiard cues were balanced against the wall. He picked one up, sighted it as though it were a rifle, and nodded. These cues were short, metal, tipless, and one gave them the little chalk they were capable of holding by stabbing them into the building's plaster wall and giving their knurled handles a few rough grinding rotations. This Haiyidar now did, adding to the tommy-gunned wall's thousands of gouges. Once finished, Haiyidar took the liberty of selecting my cue and, with great Excalibur ceremony, threw it across the room to me. I bobbled the cue and dropped it. Throughout the room money began to change hands.

The room's biggest table was set up for us and the balls were racked, the rack amounting to three splintery pieces of wood nailed into an uneven triangle. While Haiyidar prepared to break, Rustam was next to me, whispering: "Remember, this is billiards. You can hit any ball with any ball. Notice, too, that the pockets are only slightly bigger than the balls. Sinking them is not easy. Okay. The table's edges have very little . . . soft part?"

"Cushions?"

"They have almost *no* cushions whatsoever. Remember that."

"Why are all the balls white?"

"Because this is billiards. They have numbers, just like pool. But no colors. Remember also that these balls are much, much, much, much heavier than pool balls."

Haiyidar broke the arranged wedge of balls harder than I had ever seen a human being break in my life. At the balls' loud watery smack the crowd burst out in admiration. Yet Haiyidar had managed to sink nothing. He walked over to the wall and stabbed it with his cue and fumed. I decided I would play a light, patient game of placement. These balls were indeed heavier than I could have imagined. My shot pinged off its target harmlessly. Haiyidar followed with another howitzer blast. At first I had detected in the room an appreciable sympathy edge in my favor. By Haiyidar's third, astonishingly forceful shot, this one actually sinking a ball, I lost every partisan I had briefly enjoyed. Ten minutes later Haiyidar sank his last ball—I had not managed to drop one—and a cheer rose up, followed immediately by another prodigious money exchange.

I was ready to leave. From the crowd stepped a gigantic young man wearing nylon Adidas track pants, a sweat-stained tank top, and a knit winter hat that read simply BOSS. He smiled at Haiyidar, held up a V of two face-out fingers, and mischievously scissored them together. Haiyidar's response was to gash the wall with his cue again. Boss walked over and requested the use of my cue. I told him it was unlucky. He said nothing and took it. Someone replaced my cue with a shot of vodka, which I drank. Something happened inside me. I leaned over, my eyes slammed tight. It was as though someone had taken an iodine-soaked scalpel and cleaved my medulla oblongata in two. "What *was* that?" I asked Rustam, who had also knocked back a shot and was similarly leaning over and breathing.

With a slightly crazed smile he looked over at me. "I believe that we have just been given *devyanosto shest protsentov.*"

"That means 'ninety-seven percent' in Russian?"

"Ninety-*six* percent."

"Why is it called ni—" I stopped.

"Bro, what is it?"

"That was ninety-six percent *alcohol,* wasn't it?"

"Almost two hundred proof!"

Haiyidar and Boss stalked each other around the table until Boss finally decided to break. Something—I was fairly certain it was a piece of Boss's cue ball—hit me in the cheek. Haiyidar, whose method of play was to billiards what the hydrogen bomb was to warfare, responded with an equally devastating shot. Both sank a few balls early on, but those points were rescinded because they had also managed to launch balls off the table and into the surrounding crowd. One onlooker was struck upon the ulna by the 12-ball after a legendarily hard shot from Boss. The man was quickly helped from the room, I assumed to a hospital. I had another shot of 96 percent and another, and as my body chemistry altered, I remembered in a distant way that forty bottles of vodka were consumed a year for every man, woman, and child in the Soviet Union. Vodka consumption provided 13 percent of the entire state budget and the spirit was widely thought to have shaved off at least six years from the average Soviet male's life expectancy. The Russian word for "water," *voda,* was distinguished from *vodka* by one letter. What does *vodka* mean? *Vodka* means "little water."

Finally, with a loud "Ho!" Haiyidar rammed home his last ball into a narrow corner pocket, the torque of the shot leaving his cue ball spinning playfully in the middle of the table. As the room redistributed its wealth for the last time, Haiyidar walked around shaking everyone's hand. (No doubt it was the gambling surrounding billiards that moved the Uzbek government, in 2002, to ban the pastime.) When Haiyidar came to the much taller Boss, he took hold of the young man's hydrant-sized biceps and looked up at him. "The next time I bring an American here," Haiyidar said, "make sure the place is clean."

Minutes later I was removing my shoes, as demanded by Islamic etiquette, at the front door of the head of Haiyidar's *Malhallya.* Rustam and I, pickled in 96 percent, were helped by two grinning men to our places of honor in the next room. Everyone sat upon the floor in a circle. This custom is traced back to the Arabic letter *ah,* the last letter in the word *Allah,* which is round. In the middle of our human ideogram was a mat used during communal meals, called a *dastarkhan,* upon which were plates of food; bottles of vodka, carbonated water, and Coke; napkins; finger bowls; dishes of nuts. The first course had not yet been served, and most of the food on display was the Uzbek equivalent of appetizers: thin, wet cucumber coins, bowls of yogurt for dipping, tomatoes cut into red fans, platters of skewbald horse sausage. We all ate and drank to unanimous blessings upon the *Malhallya,* Sir Darya, Uzbekistan, and the United States. Then the *Malhallya's* leader, a bald, thin, goateed Uzbek, placed his hands before him as though in prayer and announced the coming of the first main course, which he especially hoped his American guest would enjoy.

I already knew it was a lamb's head before the ghastly thing had been brought out and the lid pulled off its platter. It had been that kind of day. The poor lamb's head had been boiled to the point that its skin was puckered white in some places and falling off in others. Its eyes had collapsed, though one socket was still filmy. Its tongue lolled out of its mouth in a way that would have appeared ridiculous in any other context. One look at the head tempted up a surf of vodka and stomach acid. Haiyidar announced: "You'll love the head, Tombek. The head is delicious. Americans never think they'll like the head, but they always do." I wondered what other Americans Haiyidar had been eating heads with lately. I turned to Rustam. He was all but licking his lips at the prospect of devouring this head. I pressed a napkin over my mouth and looked back at the decapitated creature. As the *Malhallya's* leader barked the skull of its flesh—it fell upon a small plate as smoothly as water—I breached etiquette and poured myself a double shot of vodka. That plate, I knew, was soon coming my way. And now it was. Rustam handed me my plate, nipping off a piece of head for himself. I picked from the plate a ragged, baitlike piece of flesh and held it before my troubled eyes. Everyone leaned forward. I pushed the meat between my lips and chewed.

Four

Lost Meridians

*In the past, people left their children things when they died—
for better or worse, there was always a legacy. How many
books have been written, how many plays performed in the-
atres about those times—how they divided up the spoils and
what happened to those who received things. And why?
Because these legacies usually consisted of things obtained
as a result of other people's sufferings.*

—CHINGHIZ AITMATOV,
THE DAY LASTS MORE THAN A HUNDRED YEARS

Our car sailed through the azure cosmos of a huge-skied Central Asian
afternoon. Miles ahead I could make out through the day's magnifying
clarity misty cirrus rings atop the horizon's low, barren mountaintops.
These were the spurs of the Pamir-Altai Range, which began truly to sky-
scrape in Tajikistan. Morning-after effluents hurtled through my bloodstream. This daylight was almost too crisp. Everything I looked at hurt
my eyes in a bright new way. Rustam and I had been in such wino fugues
this morning that we did not escape Gulistan until just after the hot, fly-
blown onset of early afternoon. But it was cooler now, the air less sub-
stantial. We were gaining altitude on the way to Samarkand.

Everything I had ever read about Samarkand at some point quoted a
chestnut called "Hassan" by an otherwise forgotten diplomat-poet
named James Elroy Flecker, who never got farther east than Syria.
Although we were still several hours away from Samarkand, Flecker's
verse looped along in my head:

*We travel not for trafficking alone:
By hotter winds our fiery hearts are fanned:*

For lust of knowing what should not be known
We make the Golden Journey to Samarkand.

Rustam, sitting in the front seat, turned down Depeche Mode's *Top Hits 2001*—which our driver was genially allowing him to blast—and looked back at me. He gave me a big thumbs-up. He liked the car's stereo system, I gathered. The notion of taking a crowded bus to Samarkand, in our condition, had not been conceivable, and at Gulistan's bus station I coughed up $15 for the four-hour ride in a Daewoo Nexia, the Lexus of Uzbekistan. Rustam flipped his head at me. "What are you reading, bro?"

"A magazine," I said.

He smiled and shook his head and once more pumped up the music. "Weird!"

My reading material, stashed behind a copy of the *New Yorker,* was actually a Human Rights Watch report titled *"And It Was Hell All Over Again . . .": Torture in Uzbekistan.* An HRW representative passed the seventy-page document to me at a restaurant in Tashkent one morning before I met up with Rustam. I did not want him to see the report because I knew we would wind up bickering about its contents. The HRW representative, a young American woman, had expressed mild disappointment that I was not here to write specifically about the Sadean depravity of Uzbekistan's criminological mechanisms. When I told her of my mission, the HRW representative warned me, quite simply, to take care. "These guys are serious," she said.

I was well aware of some of the Karimov regime's more publicized abuses of power, especially toward Muslims. One of Uzbekistan's most influential (and radical) theologians, Sheik Abdulavi Mirzoyev, was "disappeared" along with his assistant Ramazon Matkarimov at Tashkent's airport in 1995 on their way to a religious conference. Both men were still missing. The Uzbek regime claimed to have no knowledge of their whereabouts, but Mirzoyev's mosque in Andijan was currently being used as a government dumping ground for construction materials. Another prominent mullah reportedly had his genitals lit on fire by Karimov's myrmidons. These outrages occurred only four years after Karimov had taken his presidential oath by swearing upon a Qur'an.

Islam itself was not forbidden in Uzbekistan any more than it had been banned in Soviet times. Both regimes corralled the faith into the same tiny pen, overseeing a skeleton crew of muftis officially known as the Spiritual Board, created by a desperate, briefly sane Stalin during World War II as a Central Asian rallying point simultaneous with his revival of the Orthodox church in Christian republics. The Spiritual Board approved all clerics, censored all sermons, licensed all mullahs, and closely monitored the more vocal Uzbek faithful. During Soviet times this alleged religious openness allowed foreign-policy advancements in Muslim nations, but Soviet religious leaders quickly lost interest in doxastic matters. In 1989 the Soviet mufti Shamzuddin Khan Babakhanov, reputedly a famed womanizer who rinsed himself out nightly with vodka, was forced to resign after disgusted believers demonstrated in Tashkent. A deep distrust of state Islam and its "red mullahs" was thus bred in many religious Uzbeks. Numerous underground madrasas were established and often even flourished, most of them led by self-proclaimed mullahs with hazy grasps of mainstream Islam. This led to what scholars call "parallel Islam," a permutation of the faith that, because of its squelched nature, is often violent and almost always revolutionary. After independence in 1991, Turkish, Pakistani, and Saudi ideologues raced to outspend one another building mosques and madrasas for Central Asia's newly active Muslims. While these schools were closely monitored, it was not until the mid-1990s that Uzbek officials, alarmed by what many new mullahs were advocating, began to legislate stiff penalties against "illegal religious activity," canceled the morning call to prayer, and wiretapped every mosque. After the 1999 Tashkent bombings, penalties were heightened. Uzbek officials, following through on what many had hoped was merely Karimov's parliamentary bluster about tearing the heads off young revolutionary Muslims, publicly announced that families would now be held accountable for the actions of relatives suspected of illegal religious activity. The old Soviet practice of setting quotas for the number of crimes to be "solved" was reintroduced, and throughout the country police officers in general seemed to unshackle their ids. But even knowing this did not begin to prepare me for *"And It Was Hell All Over Again . . ."*

Despite the international antitorture treaty Uzbekistan signed in 1995, and Articles 7 and 26 of its Jeffersonian constitution, which explicitly forbid torture, Azim Khojaev, the father of several men hunted by Uzbek police on religious grounds, was arrested in April 1999 for "narcotics possession." Relatives would claim these narcotics were planted on Khojaev by the police, the standard Uzbek method used to haul in the innocent. Three months later the forty-eight-year-old Khojaev's beaten body was returned to his family. The cause of his death was said to be "acute failure of the left stomach."

Nematjon Karimov died in a Navoi region prison in March 1999. Police forbid Karimov's family from viewing his body. Family members finally bribed a local mortician to allow them to wash Karimov's body, as per Islamic ritual. They were supplied with an unrecognizable corpse. Half of the face had been torn off. The head was caved in and parts of the skull were missing. The upper teeth were thrust inward while the lower teeth protruded out. Only a small tattoo on the corpse's hand allowed the family members their traumatized comfort that this mutilated body was Karimov's.

After being threatened with rape while in police custody in 1999, Okoidin Khajimukhamedov attempted suicide by chewing open his wrists and pulling out his veins with his teeth.

Tashkent police detained Shirin P—— along with her sister in April 1999, hoping to coerce her fiancé, Farkhod A——, into confessing his membership in an illegal religious organization. "First," Shirin P—— remembered, "they left me in a room while they questioned my sister. Then they started to question Farkhod." The police told him, "Now we'll rape your wife-to-be in front of your eyes and you'll confess to everything." They did not have to. Farkhod A—— confessed.

"Though Uzbekistan has accepted its obligations under international human rights conventions," the report concluded, "the foreign minister, Abdulaziz Komilov, has repeatedly insisted to Human Rights Watch that those instruments represent 'European' standards not fully applicable to Uzbekistan. . . . Officials in the Uzbek National Security Council have implied that the security threats faced by the country somehow excuse or explain the failure to implement human rights standards. As one official put it, 'There is concern that human rights protection problems are closely linked to the protection of security, therefore it is important to understand the complicated situation in this country.'" (Why, I wondered, when I read this passage, did I hear Rustam's voice?) Only Uzbek parliament member and director of the National Center for Human Rights, Akmal Saidov, has admitted that torture in the Uzbek system persists. And, occasionally, as Dr. Saidov pointed out to Human

Rights Watch, the Uzbek government acted on complaints. In 1998 a police officer in Namangan was convicted for beating a detainee to death. Which of course meant nothing. I nestled back in my seat, shrunken, powerless, mute.

When visiting a United Nations session in New York City in 1996, Islam Karimov was flatly denied permission by the State Department to travel around the United States, one of several examples that attest to President Clinton's low-thermostat relations with the Karimov regime. Another, more insulting instance occurred when Vice President Al Gore snubbed Tashkent completely on an official visit to Central Asia. Like so much else under Clinton, these showy gestures of proper thinking were favored over actual diplomatic pressure. Aid guidelines and developmental assistance were never linked to human rights improvements, a double standard that Karimov, no matter his offense at Clinton's indifference, must have cynically counted upon. And although the State Department had for the last decade reportedly held annual training seminars for Uzbek judges, lawyers, and police that address the nugatory worth of torturing suspects into confessions, official State Department Country Reports prior to September 2001 made only passing reference to Uzbekistan's numerous documented human rights violations—a legalism that seemed too bloodless to describe accurately what I now read.

I reached the report's appendix to find a letter written in 1999 by a young man named Dmitri Chikunov to his mother while he awaited his fate in an Uzbek prison: "Hello dear mama! I don't know if this letter will reach you. But you must know the truth, even if you and I never see each other again. I am writing this to you because I am not guilty of this crime. They forced me under torture to sign this confessional testimony. Please don't hold me in contempt. I have sinned before you, but I could not stand it all." What Chikunov could not stand was being beaten, suffocated, threatened with rape by a stone dildo, and informed that his mother would be killed if he did not confess. This finally broke him. "I would sooner die," he explained to his mother, "than allow anyone to harm you. . . . Please always think of me." Chikunov was executed on July 10, 2000, and I was sure his mother had obeyed this last, terrible wish.

"Stop the car," I said.

"What is it?" the driver asked, alarmed. I had not spoken for miles.

Rustam looked back at me. "Yeah, dude. What's wrong?"

"Just—stop the car. I have to go to the bathroom." The car slurred to a halt beside a tobacco field. I climbed out, some middle-ear trouble making me wobble-kneed, and peed into the weedy vegetation lining the road. My mouth tasted carroty. My tongue felt foreign, my brain a gray insubstantial fog in which the ghastlier images of the report still flickered.

"Check out these tobacco fields!" Rustam called behind me. I turned. His torso was thrust out of the Nexia's opened window, his long brown dangling arms even tanner against the car's gray side panels. The driver was beside him, sucking his finger after having burned it on the dash's cigarette lighter. Rustam breathed in indulgently. "Look around, bro. See all the plants? This is all money. We don't waste our land here. We may waste our water, but not our land!"

I did look around. I saw a small struggling tobacco field. Beyond it mountains stood brutally against the sky's paint-bright blue. The landscape before the mountains looked hostile and endless. Far removed from its oases, out among Central Asia's lost meridians, one understood a single fact: This was a hard place. Uzbekistan was no green Persia with its history of scholarly warrior-kings, nor some Mediterranean paradise where the roses of Hellenism bloomed. This was desert followed by desert alongside desert surrounded by desert. By horse or on foot, one would have had to travel quite a while in ancient times to see anything but bleakness, and a lifelong diet of this terrain alone must have simply killed parts of the human spirit.

Central Asian stories of monsters cavorting in gardens of human cruelty were numerous. A Hungarian traveler in Khiva in the 1800s reported watching Khivan murderers dig out men's eyes with their knives and use the blinded men's beards to wipe the gore from their blades. In Bukhara heads were sometimes lopped off onto a heated iron plate in order to allow onlookers the treat of watching the victims' voiceless faces scream and contort against the sizzling metal. This contempt for mercy had a strange way of infecting Central Asia's European visitors as well. Early Soviets displayed the heads of slain Muslim rebels on spikes outside the gates of the insurrectionists' home villages. One of the most famous instances of a European visitor taking up Central Asian butchery can be found in the story of Baron Roman Fyodorovich von Ungern-Sternberg. The Mad Baron, as he is known, was a Hungaro-Russian who broke away from his fellow Whites during the civil war that followed the

Bolshevik Revolution, wandered into Mongolia, gathered together a bizarre mishmash army, and stepped across that small though significant threshold between madness and irretrievable insanity, eventually believing himself, as the traveler and writer Fitzroy Maclean relates, "to be Jenghiz Khan or, in his less lucid moments, the God of War in person." How mad were the baron and his men? One city, as a participant recalls, was sacked thusly: "The humiliation of the women was so awful that I saw one of the officers run inside a house with a razor and offer to let a girl commit suicide before she was attacked. With tears of gratitude she thanked him in a few simple words and then cut her throat. . . . The drunken men invented a new sport, which consisted of killing people in the streets by hitting them in the face with thick wooden bricks. One Cossack was killing his own men left and right until someone shot him. Cadet Smirnov chose to strangle old ladies, because he enjoyed seeing them wriggle as he broke their necks." This is not an atrocity pulled out of Cro-Magnon vapors. Woodrow Wilson was president as this was happening. F. Scott Fitzgerald was writing "A Diamond as Big as the Ritz."

As I stood there inhaling the bitter, faintly lemony scent of fresh tobacco and fertilizer, I realized I could think about these things only in the most gutless sidelong terms—in short, as *stories*. To confront them head-on—to ask Rustam, for instance, *What the fuck is wrong with you people?*—was as unfair as it was impossible. In the end I could not really goad myself into believing that one's surroundings possessed some override able to strip away our human layers of civility and mercy. At this moment, however, it made me feel better to think that it could. The alternative was too dispiriting.

We drove on, the flat, sun-beaten oppressiveness of the landscape unchanged. As the historian René Grousset notes, "the high plateaus of Asia bear witness to the most tremendous geological drama in the history of this planet. The upheaval and isolation of this huge continental mass were due to the converging assaults of two great chains of mountains. . . . The arc of the T'ien Shan and Altai to the northwest, and the opposing curve of the Himalayas in the south, together encircle and isolate Turkestan and Mongolia, leaving them, as it were, suspended above the surrounding plains." Out of this barren geographical cradle, few Lockes or Lincolns or even, for that matter, Lenins had risen. Central Asia's native sons were a different sort. Take, for instance, the Scythians, Aryan headhunters so savage that Herodotus made appalled note of them and Persian rulers Cyrus and Darius spent their careers trying to exterminate them. The Jewish historian Josephus linked them to the armies of Magog, the traditional invaders of the End Times. The Scythians galloped across the scarcely contested area between Afghanistan and Syria from 750 to 200 B.C.E. and are thought to have invented many things, some benign (the stirrup, the riding dress), others less so (mounted archery, the "raid" as we today understand it). The Scythians were infamous for cutting the throats of their enemies regardless of age or gender and sawing open enemies' skulls and using them as drinking cups. They dangled heads—not scalps, mind you, but *heads*—from their bridles, and mourned their dead by stabbing themselves in the face with a knife, allowing blood to flow alongside their tears, which was certainly one way to do it. It was against the Scythians, not surprisingly, that Alexander the Great met his stiffest resistance while passing through the region on his way to modern-day Kabul in 329 B.C.E.

Alexander is a figure of odd cultural importance in Central Asia, where he is known as Iskandar and revered as a demigod of might and wisdom. (Even odder, Alexander makes a brief appearance in the eighteenth sura of the Qur'an.) Alexander stopped in Samarkand, then known as Marakanda, famously proclaiming it more beautiful than he could have possibly imagined. Here Alexander married the legendarily lovely Sogdian princess Roxana after her father offered her up as a spoil of war and, in yet another instance of Central Asia's bizarre mental sorcery, inexplicably murdered his most trusted general, Cleitus, in a drunken rage. Many Uzbeks today claim descent from Iskandar, perhaps forgetting that in the fourth century B.C.E. no Turkic tribes lived in Uzbekistan. Along a road that wends through a series of steep cliff walls several miles outside of Samarkand, one can still find the odd Greek letter chiseled into the rock—ancient graffiti, it is said, left by Iskandar's garrisons.

After Alexander took his leave of the region, Huns, Chinese, Sogdians, and assorted other tribes clashed to control Central Asia's long-established trade routes—including the celebrated Silk Road (or roads), which connected China to Greece—establishing any number of "realms for a day," as Grousset nicely terms their momentary victories. Most of these tribes were eventually swallowed by the desert, leaving precious few historical traces. Central Asia gradually became an altogether new battleground, where so-called Blue Turks (with origins in Turkey proper) and Persians tore at one another's throats beneath the patient shadow of the Chinese. These long innings of suffering mark a wider, recurring struggle in the region, one that would not be completely settled until the arrival of Russian troops hundreds of years later. Namely, that of the "barbaric" nomad (the Turks, in this case) versus the "civilized" settler (the Persians). The Turks began as pagans and the Persians as fire-worshiping Zoroastrians, one of their many sources of conflict. This and all else changed in 751, when Arab conquistadors overtook what was known to Romans as Transoxiana and to Arabs as Mawara'a al-Nahr ("that which is across the river") after the Battle of Talas in modern-day Kyrgyzstan. The Battle of Talas Islamicized much of Central Asia, drove out the Blue Turks, shattered Chinese designs in the region, and established throughout the region the ruling house of the Samanids, four brothers who together forged a Persian-flavored empire, naming Bukhara as their capital. The mysterious Samanids, who pretended for the sake of their Sunni masters in Baghdad to be nothing more than a regional surrogate power, oversaw an advanced and culturally sophisticated Shia kingdom. Bukhara became a pillar of Islamic learning, while Samarkand was recognized as one of the grandest cities on earth. In literature, science, and medicine, the Samanids' unique Arabo-Persian patronage allowed some true Islamic giants to walk the earth. During this magnificent medieval epoch al-Beruni compiled his fabled encyclopedia and wrote more than 150 other works, only half of which have been studied today; a great doctor named ibn Sina, known to Westerners as Avicenna, wrote *Al-Qanun fi al-Tibb* (The Canon of Medicine), a textbook so advanced it was used in Latin translation in London, Paris, and Rome until the 1700s; and al-Khorezmi, from whose name the word "algorithm" is derived, completed the mathematical treatise *Kitab al-Jabr w'al-Muqabala* (The Book of Compulsion and Comparison) and invented *al-jabr,* or algebra. The Samanids were ousted in the tenth century by the Karakhanids, a historically migratory clan looking to settle in to the pillow of urban life. The Karakhanids were in turn displaced by another Turkic dynasty, the Seljuks, in the middle of the eleventh century. Throughout these comparatively restrained power shifts Central Asian culture continued, for the most part, to develop and often flourish.

Prosperity's countdown to doom began the day a young man named Temujin was born somewhere near the Orkhon River, where southernmost Russia leaks into Mongolia, sometime around 1167 C.E. At this time Mongolia was superintended by three groups of nomads: Mongols, Siberian Turks (not to be confused with the Blue Turks), and Tungus (a tribe more or less lost to history). All spoke different languages but shared a number of ethnic similarities. These were small, stub-limbed, black-haired, bowlegged people well conditioned to Central Asia's general inhospitableness. They were also imbued, according to nearly every ancient historian who wrote about them, with a gnarled, almost superhuman strength.

Temujin was both of this stock and unusual to it. Born into a tribe of Mongol herdsmen, the closest thing to aristocracy the steppe allowed for, Temujin was by his early teens unusually tall, his body seemingly impervious to heat, cold, even pain. The year of Temujin's birth, however, his father, Yesugei, was poisoned at a putatively friendly meal with Mongol rivals, stranding Temujin and his mother and brothers within a miserable existence of subsistence hunting and fishing. One of Temujin's earliest ventures was to fill his half brother Bekter with arrows after Bekter unwisely pilfered a fish from him. Temujin's father's herd was soon appropriated by his uncles, who rejected Temujin as being too weak to rule. Fueled by rage and a forceful, otherworldly personality, Temujin was able to rustle up a small fortune's worth of sheep and horses, graduating into the life of a steppe warlord. This was not enough. After taking advantage of his regional prominence to marry well, Temujin commandeered his resources, courted some powerful allies, and finally set out to restore the ancient royal house of the Mongols. One of the first things he did was track down and massacre the tribes who had murdered his father. By 1196 Temujin's Mongol fellows belatedly recognized him as their king (a formal declaration would follow ten years later), and at the age of twenty-nine, Temujin took the name Chingghiz Xon, or, as we know it, Jenghiz Khan, which some scholars believe means "ocean king," though the etymology is debated. Jenghiz quickly imagined for himself direct ancestry from the mythical Mongol ancestress Alangoa, who conceived the Mongol race after being impregnated either by a moonbeam or a bolt of lightning. (Other sources claim Jenghiz was the result of a dalliance—odd even by mythological standards—between a wolf and a deer.) The watchful Chinese court at Beijing was impressed by this Mongol upstart and reversed its traditional alliance with the region's other tribes, inflicting upon them a trouncing of near-genocidal proportions. But Jenghiz turned coats on his Beijing sponsors to the result of an endless Mongol-Sino war. During one of their first battles, Jenghiz's third son, Ogoday, nearly died after being shot in the neck with a Chinese arrow. Mongol history tells us that the man impervious to pain wept at the sight of his wounded son. Jenghiz withdrew with his routed troops to the remote hills of Mongolia, endured his darkest hours, and emerged in 1203 to launch a brilliant surprise attack on the Chinese.

Three years later Jenghiz called together a tribunal of all the Turko-Mongol chieftains. With them he shared his belief that his right to rule was absolute, dispensed by the Mongol sky spirit Kok (which survives as the Uzbek word for "blue"), and declared himself the supreme ruler of "all those who live in felt tents." Whether or not anyone argued is not recorded. Jenghiz then turned his gimlet eye upon the rest of the world. Between him and glory, however, lay the sedentary kingdoms of Central Asia, including the enlightened if not quite peaceable pearls of Bukhara and Samarkand.

Jenghiz, his youngest son, Tolui, and 200,000 Mongol soldiers marched on Bukhara in 1220. Imagine the Mongols: wearing leather battle helmets and carrying two bows and two quivers, a curved saber, a hatchet, an iron mace, and a hooked lance they used to unhorse enemies; their favorite tactic using prisoners as human shields, so that when they came upon the opposing army many would refuse to fight, recognizing among the Mongol captives their own wives and children; referred to as the "Anti-Christ" by Christians and "the Accursed" by Muslims; striking settlements like some sort of paleo-atom bomb; their ideology based, rather ambitiously, on conquering the entire world. The Bukharan army that rushed out to meet these fearsome marauders was slashed apart to the man. Within the city proper only those who resisted were put to death. With surprising magnanimity, Jenghiz believed in sparing those who submitted and generally instructed his officers to leave intact some working remnant of civic authority in the cities he conquered. This allowed the memory of his terrible onslaught to haunt his subjects' imaginations, which he counted on to forestall future rebellion. Legend has it that, as copies of the Qur'an were being trampled by Mongol horses in Bukhara's streets, Jenghiz gathered together the city's religious leaders in the central mosque and announced: "I am God's punishment for your sins." Some scholars reject this as overly legendary and point out that the available evidence indicates Jenghiz had a great, if puzzled, respect for Islam. The religious character of Jenghiz's empire was a primeval animism sprinkled with various Chinese elements. The Mongol manifestation of the divine was Tangri, a heavenly god enthroned upon an unknown mountain. Mongol religion thus held mountain peaks and river sources in reverent awe. One could not, as a Mongol, "profane" a stream by washing in it, which caused many misunderstandings in the ablution-obsessed Muslim societies Jenghiz eventually overtook. This also explains why the Mongols so famously stank, a fact remarked upon by several discerning ancient historians. Whatever the case, an uprising late in the Mongol siege moved Jenghiz to burn Bukhara to the ground. From its smoldering bricks the Mongols chivalrously pulled survivors— whom they used as human shields in their next assault.

Jenghiz slouched on toward Samarkand, the inhabitants of which suicidally refused to surrender. The Mongols first dammed Samarkand's canals, the strategic lodestone of Central Asian siege tactics. Mongol horseman mowed down those who left the city to fight, chopping off heads as they thundered along on their horses and blackening the sky with volley after volley of bone-tipped arrows. After five days Samarkand surrendered, but its people paid for their initial resistance. Jenghiz allowed the city to be evacuated in order to hasten its painstaking looting. Once evacuated, however, nearly everyone was put to death, even the Turks who had spontaneously switched sides in mid-siege. The rest of the 30,000-strong army of Turkic defenders was, according to one observer, "drowned in an ocean of destruction." "Useful" Samarkandis—architects, calligraphers, musicians—were deported to Mongolia, while its religious leaders, who were alone in having not resisted Jenghiz, were allowed back into the city once the Mongols had finished knocking over its minarets, setting fire to its stables, and emptying its royal vaults. So few Samarkandis survived that, as Grousset reports, "barely enough inhabitants were left to populate a single quarter." Nor did they have anywhere left to live. Today virtually no buildings exist in Samarkand that predate Jenghiz Khan's apocalyptic holiday there.

On his way to China in 1227, the nation he battled for his entire adult life, Jenghiz collapsed while encamped near modern-day Pingliang. He died soon thereafter, of unknown causes, at the age of sixty. Days later, the enemy capital of Ningsia was quickly overtaken and, in obedience to Jenghiz's last wish, the entire population—man, woman, and child— was put to the sword. The massive Mongol kingdom was soon divided among Jenghiz's sons. His second son, Chighatay, received what is now

Uzbekistan, lending his name to the language and culture that would eventually grow from its bone-scattered soil. As bad as Jenghiz Khan was (though René Grousset praises him for being "a good listener"), the worst of Central Asia's mass-murdering world conquerors was yet to come. We were, in fact, headed for his hometown.

Our driver, Dilshod, pulled into a rest stop to pee, and Rustam and I got out of the car and stretched in bright spokes of sunshine. We could see something of the nearest city, Jizzak, from this rest-stop hill. Jizzak was mid-sized, though its squat white buildings and leisurely trafficked streets made it reminiscent of a newish settlement irresponsibly encouraged to grow out of control. Jizzak's old town was mostly destroyed in 1866, when General Chernyayev, fresh from his victory in Tashkent, took the city, losing six soldiers and inflicting one thousand times that many casualties.

"Sharaf Rashidov was born here," Rustam said suddenly. "You knew that, right?"

"Nineteen seventeen."

Rustam nodded. "A great man. Definitely Uzbekistan's greatest leader."

"You think?"

"Of course. He was greater than Karimov."

"Really? You think?"

"Of course." He looked at me. "What? Are you gonna tell me bad stuff about Rashidov now?"

"Not if you don't want me to."

He chuckled, for my benefit. "Whatever, dude. Whatever."

As ever, there was little I could tell Rustam about Sharaf Rashidov, Uzbekistan's most storied twentieth-century son, of which he was not already aware. A former high-school teacher, poet, and journalist who had been grievously wounded during the first months of World War II, Rashidov saw his 1942 volume of wartime poetry, *Qarhim* (My Fury), achieve Wilfred Owen–like status in Uzbek literary circles. This eventually earned him the presidency of the Uzbekistan Writers' Union in 1949. His 1951 novel *Ghaliblar* (Victors), an ideological fiction that addressed the timeless theme of irrigation, buffed his bona fides to an even brighter polish.

Rashidov was born into orphanhood and, like Islam Karimov, grew up in a Soviet orphanage (though Karimov's official biography claims otherwise). Such modest beginnings make Rashidov's 1959 promotion to first secretary of the Uzbek Communist Party even more remarkable. One can say what one will about the Soviet political system, but it was remarkably egalitarian, provided one paddled along the correct ideological currents. Rustam and I could agree on at least this. Our detach point would concern the nature of Rashidov's extraordinarily corrupt twenty-four-year rule. Issuing orders with a famous lisp, Rashidov empowered his princeling cronies in Uzbekistan with such untouchable clout that, by the mid-1970s, Uzbekistan was commonly regarded within the Soviet Union as its flash point of illegal activity. One of Rashidov's more grotesque political pilot fish was Akhmadjon Adylov, director of the Popskii Cotton Combine, who governed his native Ferghana Valley with the evil glee of a pre-Enlightenment king. His grand estate held a storybook bestiary upon which roamed tigers, lions, peacocks, and swans, and was protected by a private army. He slapped around a large harem and, some have said, enjoyed the delights to be found in a dungeon filled with catamites abducted from nearby villages. Adylov's enemies typically wound up in his estate's torture chamber, where, among other horrors, they were anally fed hot pokers.

Leonid Brezhnev, who knew his Uzbek charge by the nickname "Sharafchik," loaded Rashidov with honors and filled his breast with medals. In Rashidov's preposterous state portrait these medals number at least thirty-eight. Throughout the Brezhnev years Rashidov's novels and poems were all issued in loving Moscow-printed editions, and he eventually had the rare honor of seeing his *Collected Works* published, a Soviet truffle fed only to a literary few. As has recently become clear, however, Rashidov did not actually write any of the work attributed to him after 1964. His ghost was Yuri Karasyev, a well-known Russian translator of Uzbek literature into Russian.

Rashidov had his positive traits. Uzbek writers, particularly, viewed him as a protector. Despite his firmly held atheism, Rashidov on several occasions stood up to Soviet censors for altering medieval Uzbek literature "merely because traces of religious motifs had a place in them."

Rashidov also did much to scaffold positive relations between Uzbeks and Tajiks, possibly because Rashidov, it is rumored, was part Tajik—a whisper that also plagues Islam Karimov, whose precise ethnic background is a closely guarded state secret. But giants stumble, and following the Brezhnev years Rashidov fell out of Moscow's favorable orbit. Yuri Andropov's fearless investigations into the mess of Rashidov's Uzbekistan led to hundreds of arrests, suicides, and jailings. Even Brezhnev's son-in-law, Yuri Churbanov, a deputy in the Soviet Ministry of Internal Affairs who got rich looking the other way during the freewheeling Rashidov years, was arrested and convicted to a long sentence. The Ferghana robber baron Akhmadjon Adylov was arrested in 1984, though charges were eventually dropped when prosecutors realized no one would testify against him. Rashidov himself died of a heart attack in 1983, some say because of the stress of Moscow's increasing pressure. Others maintain he committed suicide. Nevertheless, with streamers-and-trumpets fanfare, Rashidov was buried in Tashkent's Lenin Square, though in 1986 Gorbachev publicly condemned Rashidov and had his body removed to a lesser crypt. The term *sharafrashidovschina* even became a synonym in the Soviet press for official corruption. After the Soviet collapse, however, Rashidov's body was quietly reinstalled within his former tomb. Recently, Rashidov's daughter, Sayora Rashidova, concluded a bang-up tenure as the ombudsman for human rights issues in Uzbekistan, and in Jizzak one can gaze upon Sharaf Rashidov's bust at the center of Sharaf Rashidov Square, traipse a few blocks to the Sharaf Rashidov Garden, then walk up Sharaf Rashidov Street to the Sharaf Rashidov Memorial Museum.

After returning from the toilet, Dilshod very kindly bought for us a few meat pastries, which we ate as we entered some scorched, brown-green mountains an hour before Samarkand. We wound through these hills upon a road shaped like an infinite S, Depeche Mode once again blaring. The small cinder-block homes we saw had tools and hay scattered throughout their stony yards. A different sort of chap lived out here. One gentleman bounced along the steep edge of one mountain on a pogo stick, and we saw several groups of children throwing stones at sheep.

Little by little, Samarkand came into sight. Diesel-coughing delivery trucks, passenger vans crammed with old women and men, and gypsy taxis were soon competing with us for road space. Factories—some abandoned, others in an innominate stage of rejuvenation—stood behind their crumbling concrete walls like castles of industrialization. Ancient, mountain-ringed Samarkand lay before us, the bowl-like valley that held most of the city choking beneath bluish sky-hung smog. White flat-roofed houses were shelved along cliff edges and valley slopes, and roads unbothered by the hills plunged and soared everywhere throughout the city. The drivers here were exceptionally reckless, even by Uzbek standards. "Samarkand!" Dilshod said, laughing after a barely avoided broadside. We coasted past old hilltop cemeteries and tree-filled gorges and empty weedy lots extending for entire blocks before we finally pierced the city center. WELCOME TO SAMARKAND, the road-arching sign read. As we drifted beneath it, I turned and read its reverse side. SEE YOU BACK! We passed something called the Egoist Boutique and a billboard that heralded CENTRAL ASIA'S #1 CELLULAR PHONE LEADER!

Central Asia was perhaps unique in the world for lacking a true geographical center. "It owned no Vatican, no Acropolis," the travel writer Colin Thubron once noted with frustration, no single place to endow its people with a necessary sense of settledness, no heart from which all else radiated. Or, rather, Central Asia was its own heart—the heart, perhaps, of the world. But how did the center center itself? Samarkand came closest to providing the region with this wider if vaporous significance. Remnants of Samarkand's glorious past hung close to it. For two millennia the city had been an object of terror and love and devotion and fear and commerce and invention and art. Central Asians are famous for the epithets with which they lovingly brand their cities, and Samarkand had been called Paradisiacal Samarkand, the City of Famous Shadows, the Garden of the Soul, the Jewel of Islam, the Capital of the World, and, a little less grandly, Fat Town. (A thirteenth-century Chinese traveler warned "there is one thing very strange" about Samarkand: "Some of the women have beards and mustaches.") Goethe offered his devotions to Samarkand in poetry, Handel in opera. Marlowe and Keats, too, wrote of the existent Xanadu they would never see with something close to reverence.

Before the final triumph of Islam, Samarkand was a Christian see, its central place of worship the Church of St. John the Baptist. When jealous Muslims demanded that Samarkand's Christians give back a stone they had taken from the Muslims to use as a base for a church's central column, the Christians complied—only to find that, once its support stone was removed, the column hovered in midair. "And," added Marco Polo, who visited the church, "there it still is. And this was, and still is, accounted one of the greatest miracles that have appeared in the world." The Church of St. John and its miraculous column had long been taken up to Jehovah's bosom. The unearthly glittering domes, minarets, and mosques that replaced it rank among the world's most interesting. Islam is ineradicable from Samarkand's bloodstream, allowing its status as both the epicenter of radical medieval Islamic thought and the nursery of some of twentieth-century Islam's most reform-minded ideas. Moscow tried to dilute the potion of Samarkand's Islam by making it the first capital of the Uzbek Soviet Socialist Republic in 1925. This did not take, and by 1931 long-Russified Tashkent was given capital status.

"Isn't this fantastic?" I said to Rustam as we pulled up to the Indian-built Hotel Afrosiab, named for a mythical Central Asian king and built upon the grounds of a former royal palace. The Afrosiab was Samarkand's nicest hotel—my one venture into the jeweled ribs of luxury during this trip—and its vaulting doorways, gabled roofs, layered and overlapping floors, and white, vaguely stucco walls made it reminiscent of an old Spanish mission converted into a swish spa.

"It's cool," he allowed. "But Samarkand seemed much nicer when I visited before."

"Wait. You've been here?"

"Of course. When I was twelve."

"Why didn't you tell me that?"

"I don't know."

"Fifteen dollars," Dilshod asked gently.

"Why do you look so sad, bro?"

"I sort of thought I was showing you Samarkand."

"Fifteen dollars, please."

"Oh, dude. I thought I was showing *you* Samarkand."

"Please pay now."

I paid for our room with a credit card, a perversely satisfying transaction in a nation where the number of places that accept credit cards barely breaks into double digits. The hotel was fairly full, we had been told upon check-in. Two separate groups of tourists, German and French, were traveling along the ancient Silk Road via bus, Uzbektourism's most popular outing. Rustam and I had shared an elevator up to our floor with three older Germans. These Germans were shocked to learn that one could travel alone around Uzbekistan in relative freedom. The tour company responsible for booking these Germans into Uzbekistan's most expensive hotels had led them to believe that independent travel here was dangerous, unpredictable, and not worth the trouble. I told them that it was fairly unpredictable but hardly dangerous and eminently worth the trouble. They all sighed and looked down at the fans of sums in their hands. They had just exchanged some Deutschemarks at the official rate.

Once in the room, Rustam set aside the remote and reclined on his bed while watching BBC soccer highlights through the V of his Nikes. When a commercial blinked onto the screen, he plucked from his bedside table a tent-shaped white card and read it. After a moment he laughed. "That sounds funny in Russian."

"What sounds funny in Russian?"

" 'Please feel free to leave a tip, if you wish to do so.' " He studied me as I sat on the edge of my bed and looked through my papers. "What are you doing?"

"In Tashkent the Peace Corps was kind enough to give me the phone numbers of some volunteers around the country. I figured we could call some of them and hang out and talk and see a bit of the city."

He frowned. "Why do you think they would want to do that?"

"Because I'm new. Peace Corps volunteers get completely sick of each other. It's a well-known fact."

These phone numbers had not been easy to come by. When I met Ann Hartman, the director of Peace Corps Uzbekistan's English-teaching program, my request for volunteer contact information was received with noticeable reticence. She said that this was not normally given out to journalists. I explained that I was not looking to write about Peace Corps as such, and seeing that I was a former volunteer here myself she had nothing to worry about. She maintained she was still a little worried. The American embassy's sad-eyed press officer, I shortly learned, had called Ann that morning to inform her that I was in town. And what else, I had asked, did he say? Ann remembered it as something along the lines of *I don't want to stifle free speech here, but . . .* "In other words," I said, " 'I'm going to recommend we stifle free speech here, but I don't feel very good about it.' " To my relief, Ann had laughed and said, "The thing is, we've had some problems with journalists." The previous year a writer for a conservative magazine had been in Uzbekistan and interviewed a few PCVs for a piece that, unbeknownst to them, twirled upon the thesis that all foreign aid was futile. The piece appeared with these PCVs' quotes ripped gruesomely from context, infuriating the Uzbek government and embarrassing all involved.

Rustam, flipping through channels again, suddenly shot up off the bed. "*Whoa*. Whoa!" He started pointing at the television. "Dude. *Dude!*"

I looked. On-screen a hairless man was helping a bedewed young woman from her bothersome peach brassiere. I put down my papers. What was a top-flight hotel without a channel of hard-core pornography? Rustam, laughing with joy, dialed up the sound. Above the lovers glowed an advertisement for "Arabic Hot Chat," followed by an international phone number. The man was now easing the woman through what looked like mosquito netting onto a four-poster. With one chivalrous hand he cradled her head and with the other the small of her back. Once she was laid out before him, he opted for some retiring cunnilingus that left its recipient visibly unmoved. Rustam looked at the screen, his head tilting. "They don't look very Arabic."

"That's enough," I said, standing. "Let's go. I want to see Tamerlane's tomb."

We walked through the lobby, passing a Salon of Beauty and a pair of gold lions, into the side streets of Samarkand. A pattern soon emerged. For blocks the streets were clean. Then, a mastodonic pile of rotting communal trash clouded with wasps. Spiky weeds grew knee-high seemingly from every crack. Every fifty feet along the mud walls shared by the streets' homes stood a metal gate with a number and mail slot. From behind the walls floated household chatter and an occasional low radio. All around us children played kickball. They scattered whenever a beeping Lada or taxi came barreling through, splattering the walls with muddy water from the puddles collected within Samarkand's countless back-street potholes. The city was all charmed antiquity until I looked up at a netting of telephone wires and noted along the walls dozens of gutters rusting off their moors. Dusk had just begun to fall, the sky as colorless as snow.

Like spies, we approached Tamerlane's tomb, properly known as the Guri Amir (Tajik for "Tomb of the King"), from the rear. Nearby, police officers were investigating a disturbance of some kind, a trio of what I assumed were witnesses sitting dolefully on the curb while the officers conferred. My desultory attempt to probe further was discouraged by the lead investigator's sudden black glare. As I walked back to join Rustam, a three-legged dog ran between us, chased higgledy-piggledy by two cackling children on bicycles. The Guri Amir was six hundred years old and yet all around it, with a sad sense of having somehow been widowed, huddled bulwarks of modern life. Adjacent homes' windows were open, close enough to the tomb's grounds to allow their occupants to lean outside and pluck a leaf from the outlying hedges or fruit from its mulberry trees.

Tamerlane, or, as Uzbeks know him, Amir Timur, built the Guri Amir in the early 1400s. Timur's architects botched their first attempt at the tomb, intended for Timur's sons, and upon pain of death were given ten days to raze the miscarriage and get it right. Timur wound up being buried here because the road to his nearby hometown, the site of his intended mausoleum, was, when he died, blocked off by snow. The Guri Amir was once a much larger complex. All that was left of the original founding religious college was a huge stone arch that opened onto the empty courtyard before the tomb itself. Its four surrounding minarets were survived only by their foundations, its hospice by nothing at all. What remained was still magnificent, even allowing for Soviet efforts to "restore" Guri Amir. Soviet restoration lasted for thirty years and continued with the Uzbeks today. "Unfortunately," in the words of one authority on Islamic architecture, "the authentic, majestic ruins of this mighty building have consequently been immured within a sham brick and concrete case and therefore to all intents and purposes destroyed."

The tomb's most striking feature was its bulbous cupola, a ribbed cylindrical drum unique to Central Asia. Atop the cupola was a small onion-shaped gold tip that, like much Central Asian architecture, lacked an Islamic crescent. The cupola's sixty-four ribs, which gave the structure much of its visual audacity, were as fat as goalposts. Covering the cupola was a skin of glittering turquoise tilework common to the Timurid period, regarded by scholars as lighter and more playful than most Islamic architecture. The word "turquoise" has (rather obviously, when one thinks about it) a Turkic etymology. Indeed, turquoise is the color of Turks. Samarkand was famous for this mystically bright blue, engineered by wizardly medieval alchemists for the precise purpose of sparkling in the region's harsh desert sunshine. In bright white Arabic calligraphy ten feet high, the tautology GOD IS IMMORTAL encircled the cupola's lower reaches.

We walked through the first gate's tall bullet-shaped portal (called a *pishtaq*) and lingered in the courtyard. Suddenly, our fellow Afrosiabians descended, the French and the Germans, and began to photograph the hell out of the place. Rustam sat down to smoke, laughing with the peculiar sadness of the tourist made native by other tourists, and I crept around the building's perimeter to find Guri Amir's keeper feeding some birds. Behind him one of the tomb's low munchkin-sized iron doors stood open. The door's padlock hung from the man's cloth belt.

After mutual salaams I asked him why these doors were so small. "For Allah," he said. "One must bow to Allah to enter such a place." He smiled at me. His strangely tiny face was old but smooth, worn down to its veins. He sported a large gray beard but no mustache and looked rather Amish. A bundle of folded and tucked white cloth sat smartly upon his head. "Where are you from?"

"America."

"Samarkand is a great city," he said, then clucked his tongue at the birds stepping trustingly about his robe's hem.

"Yes," I agreed.

His courtly, unimpressed air suggested that he had been working here for some time. He would have been a boy when Stalin died and would have experienced vividly the decades of wild Soviet fluctuation on Islam and Central Asia. The great travel writer Robert Byron, while decamped in Herat, Afghanistan, in the 1930s, wrote of Samarkand as desirously as a lover: "Afghanistan, till literally the other day, has been inaccessible. Samarcand, for the last fifty years, has attracted scholars, painters, and photographers. . . . Now the position is reversed. The Russians have closed Turkestan. The Afghans have opened their country." And now the grim about-face had happened again.

"Amir Timur is buried here," the man said after a moment, still scattering his birdfeed. "I can show you his tomb. His secret tomb."

"I know. I've seen it. I've been here before."

"Then you know Amir Timur was a great man."

I looked at his birds. They were very black, even their beaks. "Hm," I said.

He smiled again, as though in recognition that Amir Timur was not a great man; as though admitting, privately, between new friends, that Amir Timur ranked among the worst mass murderers in world history. Timur may have been the greatest: no single human being, not even Jenghiz Khan, managed to amass as large an empire, which spanned from Turkey to India, allowing Timur the chance to kill an unprecedented variety and number of people.

He was born around 1336 fifty miles southeast of Samarkand in the hamlet of Shakhrisabz, then called Kesh. (It is said the infant Timur's tiny fists were prophetically filled with blood.) Timur's birth, Gibbon wrote, with uncharacteristic stupidity, "was cast on one of those periods of anarchy which . . . open a new field to adventurous ambition." Shakhrisabz, today regarded as one of Uzbekistan's nicest cities, was by most accounts a place of mild, sun-washed loveliness even in Timur's time. Slavery had always been outlawed there, and the city's traditional method of execution was hanging—as opposed to Khiva, which preferred unzipping throats, and Bukhara, which preferred decapitation. A small pile of bricks in a village outside of Shakhrisabz marks Timur's proper place of birth—perhaps an admission, however demure, of the incarnate terror gentle Shakhrisabz unwittingly unleashed upon the world.

Like Jenghiz Khan, Timur was born to a clan of minor aristocracy. In regard to his ethnicity, the only thing upon which scholars agree is that Timur, which means "iron," was not Uzbek. Most authorities maintain that his Barlas clan was Mongol; Timur, then, was only an affected Turk. Other, usually older sources state that Timur was a Turk ethnically propelled to deliver Transoxiana from Mongol plundering. But Timur's lineage does not much matter, as he butchered Mongols and Turks (and Russians, and Indians, and Georgians, and Persians, and Arabs) with the same cold disregard. At the time of Timur's birth his Barlas clan was mostly interested in freebooting its way across rival clan lines and then making dutiful offerings of peace. Timur read this perfidious land well, and, again like Jenghiz, submitted to weaker masters before turning on them and triumphing. But Jenghiz was at heart a crude shepherd catapulted into geopolitics; Timur's intelligent, fastidious Machiavellianism held that the brokered pacts of autumn were merely the overture to the following summer's routs. When he was twenty-five, his shoulder was aerated by a Mongol arrow, a wound that mirrored a congenital deformity of his right knee. Thus he was known as Timur-i-Leng, Timur the Lame, which resulted in the bowdlerized European appellation of Tamerlane (and Marlowe's Tamburlaine). For the remainder of his exploits Timur attempted to disguise his crippling by grasping his withered, clawlike hand around the hilt of his sword. Despite the handicap, he still led his troops into battle, a fact that becomes less admirable when one learns that Timur habitually claimed full credit for the independent military sallies he allowed his chief commanders, and more than once was turned back in mid-campaign by obscure dreams of bent swords that he foresaw as omens of defeat.

As Grousset notes, history has visited upon Central Asia two kinds of empire. The first is the forced empire of peripheral civilizations—China, India, Persia, and Russia—which, little by little and with incalculable bloodshed, overwhelmed one "barbarian" hectare at a time. After that came assimilation, a force more compelling than the sharpest blade held against the softest throat. The second kind of empire was a violent expansionist surge from within the continent, such as those led by Jenghiz Khan and countless lesser thugs, typically exerted due to forces as elemental, and simple, as hunger or anger or cultural stagnation. But Timur's empire was different, and it is hard to know where to begin when isolating the contradictions of his rule.

Timur identified with Jenghiz Khan, proclaiming himself, at the age of thirty-four, his spiritual heir, but he did little to preserve Jenghiz's positive bequests other than ostentatiously prop up his puppet heirs. Timur refused to abandon Jenghiz's Mongol law, the *yasa,* for Islam's Sharia, yet drew all his spiritual strength from the Qur'an, looking to it for mandates and seeking out Islamic dervishes for their divine auguries. According to a fourteenth-century Spanish diplomat, this devout Muslim encouraged women and guests alike to imbibe heavily while in his company. "The drinking was such," the diplomat reported, "that all when they left the feast were besotted drunk, His Majesty finally remaining all alone in his tent in a state of much cheerfulness." A court of royal "readers" often recited for Timur the epics of other nations, providing him with a grasp of history that often surprised his contemporaries—and masked Timur's drooling illiteracy. With the true poetaster's brashness, Timur surrounded himself with books he could not read and an art collection of which he had only the dimmest understanding. He was a firm believer in justice (he once hanged a mayor of Samarkand because the city was not safe enough), a lover of civilized urban culture, a foresworn chess fanatic, and an inveterate warrior-nomad who loved nothing more than knight-errantry bent to the most malevolent ends. He was the greatest patron of the arts of his time, a lover of Persian poetry who eventually ripped from the soil all the flowers of Persian culture, and a committed jihadist who flattened all the capitals of the Muslim world. His background was Turko-Mongol, his culture Persian, his religion Arabic, his legal system a chaotic mash of all of the above. He was, again in Grousset's words, "a superman peregrinating through several civilizations at once," and he dominated his age as resoundingly as Jenghiz Khan did his own. But while Jenghiz's empire lasted for generations after his death, Timur's disappeared within fifty years, dwindling to a tiny political potshard in Transoxiana.

Timur's capital was "the threshold of paradise," Samarkand, which he pampered as thoroughly as he did his eight wives. Under his tutelage Samarkand became the site of one of the most determined public-works efforts in human history, and the city was rewarded with ambassadors from China, Constantinople, Baghdad, and Cairo. A single public garden in Samarkand was so large that, when a diplomat's horse went lost upon its grounds, the creature was not found for six weeks. Structures both holy and secular were spared no expense, and Timur, who often threw coins and lumps of meat to his toilers, never saw his orders, however unreasonable, go neglected. Timur (yet again, like Jenghiz) usually spared the artisans of the regions he conquered so they could be put to beautifying use back home. Thus thousands of architects and painters from around the world were shuttled to Samarkand to contribute to its grandeur. In this way Samarkand's remaining Timurid architecture combines Indian motifs with Azerbaijani motifs, Persian with Caucasian, a fusion of utterly different schools of artistry to the result of a gorgeously peculiar magnificence. Timurid tilework was among the most easily appreciable of these innovations, but shield-shaped spandrels in-filled with tile and the ribbed, bulbous dome of the Guri Amir and elsewhere became equally characteristic of Timur's grandiosity.

But a few peerless buildings do not excuse barbarity, and Timur was a barbarian in the most literal sense of that discredited word. While Samarkandis exulted in the desert paradise Timur created, no other land upon which he had designs was spared. After spending a decade

(1370–80) consolidating his forces and solidifying his power base, Timur and his armies marched upon the world. His soldiers stomped without complaint through the narcotic heat of India and the freezing, finger-ridding wastes of Siberia, no doubt inspired by the sight of their crippled commander leading them on horseback. They wiped out the Persian satraps of the west, slaughtered the Gobi Desert's Mongol chieftains, left Delhi (where they even "overtook the birds") in ruin, and pursued relentlessly the Ottoman sultan, Bayazid the Thunderbolt, after he defamed Timur as a "ravening dog." Once Timur captured the Thunderbolt, he stuffed him into an iron cage—used for the remainder of the outing as a stair for Timur to mount his horse. But Timur conquered only as enemy aggression determined. A campaign in Russia was parenthesized by two in Persia, an expedition in Afghanistan was interspersed by two in the Caucasus, and there was always time for another murderous venture against the hated Tajiks. Jenghiz Khan planned carefully, and plundered to make a single point: *Do not make me come back.* Jenghiz's subjects were terrorized into compliance; Timur's were merely terrorized, and his violence only incited future revolt. Thus, Timur "conquered" Iraq seven times, Persia five times, Russia twice, and he failed completely in fully routing the Ottomans or dislodging the Khan of Mongolia and the Sultan of India.

The litterateur's savagery was without precedent. His fondness for ripping apart irrigation systems and burning crops contributed to the saharification to which Central Asia is already disastrously prone. He destroyed the complicated intercontinental trade routes enjoyed by Marco Polo—one of the most glorious fruits of Jenghiz's rule—to the extent that it crippled relations between Europe and the East for hundreds of years. (Europe, oddly, never fully realized this. Its rulers instead chose to believe Timur's messengers, who claimed that Timur's riddance of the "nightmare" of Ottoman rule would result in newly galvanized trade between the continents. This is, in part, what led to Timur's European glorifiers such as Handel and Christopher Marlowe.) Timur launched an insane reverse crusade against the ancient Christian civilization of Georgia, forcing its king, Bagrat V, to convert to Islam. He abducted the raja of the Indian city Jammu and forced him to renounce Hinduism and eat beef. A fascination with compulsory heresy infected Timur's dealings with fellow Mohammedans, once compelling him to humiliate orthodox Sunnis in Aleppo by making them add Ali to their

codex of legitimate caliphs. Occasionally, his fondness for the blasphe-
mous became cinematically satanic. After sacking the Turkish city of
Smyrna, Timur bombed the escaping Christian fleet using dead knights'
heads as cannonballs.

One estimate holds that Timur's bloodthirsty wanderlust directly
resulted in the deaths of 17 million people. How was this possible? During one of his earliest victories in Asterabad in Persia, every citizen of the
city was wiped out, "even infants at the breast." Now repeat this process
for thirty-six years. One hundred thousand Hindus in Delhi alone were
flayed alive. In Baghdad he added another hundred thousand victims.
The stench of bodies was putrid enough to drive out Timur's army from
the city, along with several dozen of Baghdad's finest men of letters, to
whom the literary-minded Timur showed mercy and offered coats of
honor. He soon moved on to Damascus, whose instant admission of
defeat Timur promised to reward with mercy. After gathering together
the city's glassblowers, weavers, armorers, craftsman, and writers, he
torched Damascus and immolated thousands of innocent people. One of
the people he spared in Damascus was the twelve-year-old Ahmed ibn
Arabshah, who would become a peerless historian of the Islamic world.
Arabshah had his revenge on Timur by writing a pitilessly accurate
account of his homicidal administration. One wonders how needed is
Arabshah's account when the *Zafername*, Timur's official apologia,
speaks approvingly of 70,000 heads "piled up in heaps outside the walls
of Isfahan and of which towers were then built in various parts of the
town." The pyramid of skulls was Timur's most horrific calling card,
and throughout his rule he left it everywhere.

Timur shares a final commonality with Jenghiz. He died not in battle
but on the way to China, then the richest country in the world. China's
"Pig Emperor," as Timur called him, was to be punished for the imperti-
nence of dispatching to Samarkand a tribute-seeking ambassador.
Timur even spoke of plans to Islamicize the whole of China. After crossing the frozen Sir Darya River with 200,000 troops in February 1405,
Timur fell ill with what some scholars believe was tuberculosis and others pneumonia. The sixty-nine-year-old had been sick for some time, so
much so that, before leaving for China, he had been finally convinced to
outline officially some basic framework for succession. While a thunder-
storm detonated the atmosphere high above Timur's tent, his royal doctors surrendered. "We know of no cure for death," they explained to

their king, whose mouth now foamed with blood. The tyrant at last gave up his devils, perhaps to the storm itself, sparing China the last murderous urge of Timur the Lame. Today the non-Uzbek was Uzbekistan's national hero, perhaps even the source of its timeless inclination to bow to the caprice of iron men. Why? "The popular lore of all nations testified that duplicity and cunning, together with bodily strength, were looked upon, even more than courage, as heroic virtues by primitive mankind. To overcome your adversity was the great affair of life. Courage was taken for granted. But the use of intelligence awakened wonder and respect." So wrote Joseph Conrad in *Nostromo,* arguably the greatest political novel ever written, in 1904. While we can lament Conrad's adjectival use of "primitive," his view that predemocratic societies "went straighter to their aim"—that, to these societies, "success" functioned "as the only standard of morality"—seems hard-minded, disheartening, and inarguable. But what if Central Asia had instead looked for inspiration among its numerous more enlightened leaders? That cannot be known, especially when Islam Karimov had taken to calling himself "Little Timur" and sponsored a bizarre genealogical scheme to trace his descent back to the hobbled psychopath. This seemed to me so doubly disheartening that I could barely move when Rustam approached me to ask if I wanted to have a look inside the tomb. What I wanted to do, at that moment, was spit on it. But I nodded, and we fell in line behind some Germans excitedly gesticulating at the tomb's—yes, I admitted it, even then—exquisitely brilliant tile.

A rough stone passageway led to the actual mausoleum. I could hear the Germans and French busily clicking away with their cameras, the occasional flashbulb filling the dim passageway with compressed bursts of light. Old Uzbek and Tajik women, silent and mendicant, wearing bright pajama-patterned housedresses, sat cross-legged along the passageway selling Timur posters, maps, and calendars. Uzbek mythologists had divined for Timur a consistent look—one of bald, scowling, black-goateed nastiness. Spandrel-shed pieces of tile could be purchased here for $3, an outrageous sum considering that very few of these tiles, however painstakingly approximated, were more than a few decades old. A French woman bought $12 worth of reputedly ancient tile, then darted off toward the inner sanctum.

Rustam and I followed her into a surprisingly small, squarish chamber lit with a blaze of perpetual sunset. My arms changed color, their faint tan suddenly butterscotch, while Rustam shone as brownly as kiln-fresh clay. Our dermal luster was due not to any outside light—the tomb's four fretted windows allowed in only the whitish nebula of a fading afternoon—but to the massive glass chandelier suspended in the middle of the cupola's recessed inner dome, every square inch of which was covered with gold reliefwork. The refurbishment of this inner dome—the Soviets spackled it with something like twenty pounds of melted-down gold in a 1970 restoration—was thought to have been much more successful than that of Guri Amir's exteriors, probably because the restorers were able to base their work upon more surviving elements.

From this enchanted belfry my overpowered eyes eventually dropped. The chamber's greenish gypsum walls were paneled with onyx hexagonal tile and Arabic inscription of Timur's deeds and genealogy. Two separately employed Uzbek guides related this information for the German and French tourists. The Germans' guide spoke German while the French guide spoke English. I walked amid this odd Babel to the marble railing that blocked off the seven cenotaphs of Timur, his sons and grandsons, and his favorite Islamic sage. As with most Muslim tombs, these were mere markers; the real tombs, which Guri Amir's keeper had offered to show me, were found in a not-so-secret secret cruciform burial chamber beneath us.

Six of the seven cenotaphs were rectangular, lightly inscribed blocks of rather plain marble. The large central cenotaph belonged to Timur, next to which some maudlin soul had placed a fresh batch of roses. Upon his cenotaph was a massive slab of cloudy, blackish jade once thought to be the largest piece of jade in the world. As Timur lay dying, he had supposedly muttered that all he desired for a grave marker was "a stone, and my name upon it." It was probably the only order he ever gave that went unheeded. Even now the cemented fracture running down the middle of Timur's jade block was visible. For this severance various explanations are given. One holds that, in 1740, three hundred years after Timur's death, a Persian invader named Nadir Shah, fresh from demolishing Khiva and still incensed by Timur's butchery of his people, split the block in two with one Herculean blow of his sword. (This is, obviously, the Persian version.) Another story claims that Nadir Shah cracked the block while in the process of stealing it away to Persia. After the slab's breakage Nadir Shah is said to have been plagued with bad luck that ended only when the chagrined plunderer respectfully returned the marker to its rightful place. For years this jade block had collected dust in a Moscow museum. The Soviets also stole from Samarkand the oldest Qur'an in existence, that of Uthman, the Third Caliph, whose blood speckled a number of its pages. But the jade marker was returned, and Uthman's Qur'an was stored safely in Tashkent.

Uzbeks claimed that Soviet historians devoted little space to Timur in their redactions of Central Asian history. What was said, they complained, usually denounced him. This is not accurate. Beginning in the 1940s, Soviet scholars sought to rehabilitate Timur's legacy and put forth the claim that he was Uzbek, despite a library's worth of documentation that verifies the Uzbeks as historical foes of the Timurid empire. "Timur's activities in Central Asia," one Soviet scholar wrote, "had no small positive aspects in the sphere of ending feudal disturbances and fragmentation, for one thing, and of massive building activity, for another." Thus the unseasonable Timur was ripped from his proper historical context as a Turko-Mongol autarch and groomed with a brush of civilizing Communism. This prevented Uzbeks from seeking out their real ancestors, among them the hated Golden Horde who enslaved Muscovites of yore.

During this era of Timur rehabilitation the Soviet anthropologist Mikhail Gerasimov obtained permission to disinter Timur's body, in spite of an engraving said to be carved on the underside of his tombstone. No one quite agrees what this untraceable engraving said. Attempts to render it range from "Whoever opens this will be defeated by an enemy more fearsome than I" to "If I am roused from my grave the earth will tremble." Nevertheless, Timur's Admonishment from Beyond the Grave was of strong enough currency to have kept anyone from defiling his tomb for half a millennium. Gerasimov, mindful of offending local sensibility, entered Timur's burial vault in secret on the night of June 21, 1941. After exhuming the remains, Gerasimov was able to confirm that Timur had been well over six feet tall, a tuberculosis sufferer, and lamed by birth defects to his right leg and what looked to be an arrow wound to his right shoulder. Bits of not black but russet beard still clung to Timur's skull, of which Gerasimov made a meticulous bronze cast. Within hours of cracking open Timur's coffin, however, one of Gerasimov's trembling factotums charged into the crypt with a telegraph in hand. Hitler had just broken the 1939 Nazi-Soviet Nonaggression Pact and begun bombing the cities of Mother Russia. After working in the tomb for nearly two years, Gerasimov obeyed proper Muslim burial etiquette and reinterred Timur's remains. Within days the Germans surrendered at Stalingrad, the turning point in Hitler's catastrophic campaign against the Soviets. After the French's Uzbek guide told the story, for obvious reasons a favorite here, two older Frenchwomen crossed themselves. It seemed too picky by half to remind the guide that Hitler's invasion occurred not on the night of Gerasimov's desecration but on the following day, and that Timur's reburial and the surrender at Stalingrad did not fall "within days" but rather were separated by a somewhat less spooky five weeks.

Rustam and I were on our way out of the tomb when a thin, short man wearing a black tie against a billowy blue shirt broke away from his party and rushed up to Rustam and embraced him. This was, I adduced, a relative of Rustam's, who seemed to be visiting Samarkand with friends. Following a formal greeting and a light simultaneous kiss on the cheek, Rustam and his relative recited their inventories of common Uzbek inquiry:

"How is your mother?"

"How is your health?"

"How is your father?"

"How are your children?"

"How is your health?"

"How is your mother?"

"How is your sister?"

"How is your wife?"

"How is your work?"

"How is your father?"

Neither Rustam nor his relative bothered to answer any of these questions. Their ceremonial declamation was simply etiquette. Although Rustam and his relative's greetings were in Uzbek, both men had, after a few sentences, switched over into Russian. I stood there waiting for Rustam to introduce me. As he talked on, I realized he was gradually moving away, a clear cue for me to get out of sight. I wandered out into the courtyard. It was almost dark, the moonlight as cold as wind. Purposelessly, I kicked around a few stones. Minutes later Rustam appeared, his eyes contritely narrowed.

"Bro, I'm sorry."

"It's okay. But what was that about?"

"That was my uncle Oybek."

"Okay."

"He should not know I'm here with you."

"Why not?"

"Because I am missing school. If he tells my father, I'll be in a lot of trouble."

"Oh. I didn't know you were missing school." But of course I did. He had mentioned school to me several times. I had simply chosen not to think about that. I looked at him. "What are you going to do?"

"Hope he doesn't mention it."

"I mean about school."

"I don't know." He shook his head and, laughing, clapped a hand on my shoulder. He jostled me lightly. "Don't look that way, dude. Somehow I'll work it out."

We walked back toward the Afrosiab, now whitely illumed in the evening's shallow darkness, where I planned to call a Peace Corps volunteer named Monica. I had been told in Tashkent that she was expecting my call. But the business with Rustam's uncle still troubled me. "Wait a second," I said, suddenly turning to him, "how did you explain being in Samarkand?"

He shrugged. "It didn't come up."

"How did that not come up?"

Rustam chuckled. Once again his arm, as long and pliant as a lasso, was flung around my back. "You gotta know Uzbeks, dude. They're too polite to ask you anything directly. Especially when they're family."

I opened the door of our hotel room to find Monica, whom I had phoned only twenty minutes before. She was either excited by the chance to set her eyes upon an unfamiliar American face or lived near the hotel. (She lived near the hotel.) She was an athletic-looking blonde wearing faded sky-blue jeans and a maroon T-shirt whose sleeves ended at her shoulders, exposing soft and sun-reddened upper arms. She smiled, managed a hard-edged "Hi," and made a gesture of uncertain, here-I-am abundance.

We opted to walk around Samarkand. A sparkling cool was in the air, as though the evening were preparing for the broiling desert front due to roll in tomorrow morning. The trees along University Boulevard, one of Samarkand's most cosmopolitan streets, hissed in the wind as we walked beneath them, their leaves as dark as bats against the purple night sky. Monica, it turned out, was from Kentucky, studied education while in college, and taught English at one of Samarkand's schools. She spoke in short, guarded sentences, each as enclosed and final as a haiku. I could not tell whether she was a private person or whether the Peace Corps had recommended that she mind her words while with me. I pressed her a little. She mentioned a boyfriend back home, the usual Peace Corps frustrations, her Samarkand apartment's dependable plumbing troubles. Rustam walked silently beside us, his hands jammed into his pockets. Along University Boulevard loomed the dark nighttime façades of any number of colleges and trade schools. Each of the corners was massed with students, male and female, chatting in the hazy orange spheres thrown down by streetlights. On not a few of the boulevard's benches, young Uzbeks nuzzled and kissed, an infrequent site in this country.

"That's nice to see," I said after passing the fourth or fifth such couple.

"Yeah," Monica said, "Samarkand is a little freer in that way. But it has a dark side. Women have a really hard time here with Uzbek men."

At this Rustam glanced up sharply but said nothing.

"Some female volunteers," Monica went on, "were attacked in Samarkand a few years ago."

"When was this exactly?" I asked.

"I'm not sure. Nineteen ninety-four?"

"I know about that, actually. They were raped. That was two years before my group."

"I heard about that, too," Rustam debuted. "I also heard those women went out drinking alone at night. Not so smart. In 1994 I think it was even less smart."

Monica said nothing. We passed through a group of young Uzbeks and left in our wake an eddy of whispers and titters. We walked through a park and emerged upon the outer edge of a well-lit commons. What looked to be a carnival was dismantling itself for the night. Young men and women strolled hand in hand across the mostly empty commons, and the several policemen present smiled and nodded at passing Uzbek and Tajik mothers pushing baby carriages. A few middle-aged layabouts amassed around a picnic table, drinking bottles of beer and playing backgammon. Xylophonic ice-cream-truck music floated from behind a dense chaparral at the common's opposite end. Through these hedges I could make out a few blinking lights and hear the rough chocking sound of metal wheels rocketing along metal runners. The carnival's midway. We decided to enjoy a Ferris wheel ride before it was shut off for the night. The great wheel turned slowly and evenly, as creaky as a porch swing, most of its decorative lightbulbs fizzled out. The wheel's operator was asleep and we hitched a ride upon one of the empty circular seats as it swung by. We lifted with kicking legs toward the wheel's apex and, beneath us, Samarkand ranged as far as we could see, vast and poorly lit, an ancient metropolis, a modern city, a backwater, a glory famous to nothing but history itself. After our third revolution Monica broke the silence. "What are you writing about anyway?"

"The Aral Sea, mostly."

She folded her arms in an attempt to stave off the high nocturnal cold. "Then why are you in Samarkand?"

I thought of the $2,000 intended for Omad's wife pressing against my abdomen and, for a long time, said nothing. Then: "I'm not exactly sure."

"You're not sure?"

Rustam spoke: "He has an errand in Samarkand. This is an important young man we're sitting with. The savior of my country."

Monica and I looked over at Rustam, who stared off toward some unreadable distance. He was smiling slightly. Suddenly, his smile vanished, and he leaned forward. "Hey. You can see our hotel from up here."

The next morning I believed I had localized the cause of the Aral Sea's drainage to our room's toilet. When I flushed, its bowl gushed with water for nearly a minute, much of it splashing out onto the floor. In the spirit of empiricism I waited for the basin to refill and then flushed it again. The surge was even greater this time. A spike of water geysered up out of the bowl then fell upon itself like a building whose cornerstone had been dynamited.

"Have you checked out our toilet?" I asked Rustam.

"Powerful!" he said approvingly.

At noon we were meeting Monica and another of Samarkand's PCVs for lunch at a canteen in the city's northeastern foothills, and decided to begin the day by walking a few blocks to the Registan, Central Asia's most famous architectural ensemble. *Registan* (pronounced with a hard g) means "place of sand," so named for the executions carried out on its grounds until the beginning of the twentieth century. The sand allowed for the tidy absorption of blood. The Registan forms what is left of Samarkand's ancient city center. Even today all the city's roads seem to lead toward it. In Timur's time the Registan was the site of Central Asia's most prodigiously stocked bazaar. One could find amid its busy stalls fine camel-hair tassels, Chinese silks, suits of Bukharan chain mail, crescent-bladed Khivan knives, Indian jade, Caucasian swords, Russian gold, Tatar trousers, and one of the hundred varieties of grapes cultivated by medieval Samarkand's inventive horticulturalists. Today the bazaar is gone, and three spectacular madrasas stand upon the Registan's foundation.

The first, that of Ulugbek, Timur's grandson, was built in 1417, twelve years after Timur's death. The second madrasa, Shir Dar, went up two hundred years later. Construction of the third, Tilla Kari, began ten years later, in 1646. Workers labored on the Tilla Kari Madrasa until 1660, though the structure was ultimately never completed. Samarkand's building frenzy had finally been exhausted, the old inspirations too cold and remote. In 1899 the intrepid traveler and future Indian viceroy George Curzon wrote, in an oft-cited encomium, that he "knew nothing in the East approaching [the Registan's] massive simplicity." Europe, Curzon argued, had nothing "which can aspire to enter the competition. No European spectacle indeed can adequately be compared to it, in our inability to point to an open space in any western city that is commanded on three of its four sides by Gothic cathedrals of the finest order." That, I thought, as Rustam and I approached the Registan from its occidental flank, was shooting a bit high, though in all likelihood my disappointment had less to do with the Registan itself than the glacially massive mound of fragrantly decomposing cloth diapers, paper, and some slimy kelplike substance piled near the southern edge of the Ulugbek Madrasa.

We rounded the corner of Ulugbek's Madrasa and sauntered out into the middle of the multilevel plaza. The Ulugbek and Shir Dar madrasas faced each other, the Tilla Kari forming the ensemble's northern border. The result was an eye-catching, rather stagelike arrangement of buildings. The Registan seemed, at the same time, both ramshackle and majestic. It was just after ten in the morning, and most of the tourists were resting upon the rows of stadium-style plastic seating some idiot had decided to erect upon the Registan's unoccupied southern boundary.

"It takes a moment for the whole effect to set in, but it's pretty impressive, isn't it?"

Rustam nodded in courteous deferral. "The Soviets saved it, you know. Uzbeks did nothing for this place. For centuries they let the Registan fall apart."

"Sure, but the Soviets decided to restore it only after forty years of really half-assed administration. I read that after the Bolshevik Revolution they used the Registan as a granary, then as stables. Stables!"

Rustam head-shakingly regarded me. "What do you have against the Soviets? Don't you realize that without the Soviets I would have never been educated? That I would have never gone to America? Everything Uzbekistan has is *because* of the Soviets, dude. Uzbeks are simple people. The Soviets made us modern. Look at Afghanistan. The Soviets lost the war, right? But maybe if they had won, it would not be so unhappy there. Maybe the Taliban would not exist, and maybe all these fucking Muslims would not feel so free to kill and destroy."

"It's complicated. I admit that."

"Actually," he said, "it's not complicated. I have just explained it to you."

I nodded and walked off to the base of the Ulugbek Madrasa, the oldest surviving religious college in all of Central Asia. Ulugbek's style of rule departed significantly from that of his grandfather, and his madrasa was built to host scholars and students devoted not only to the pursuit of pristine Islam but to the secular sciences as well: mathematics, music, medicine, astronomy. Ulugbek, honorifically known as "the learned" and the Astronomer King, delivered here numerous astronomy lectures. Arguably the greatest of the pretelescopic astronomers, Ulugbek was among the first scientists since Ptolemy to discern the thousand known stars' coordinates, discovered two hundred previously unknown astral bodies, divined the westward procession of the equinoxes, and measured

the earthly year to within sixty seconds of modern computers' estimates—achievements not widely known until the seventeenth century,
when a lost copy of the Astronomer King's *Catalog of Stars* was found in
an Oxford library, the contents of which floored the European world.

Each of the Registan's madrasas was exteriorly adorned with distinct
tile mosaics. The most forceful of these mosaics were found in the area
above the main pishtaqs' portals, known as a tympanum. Appropriately,
the tympanum of Ulugbek's madrasa was stippled with blue and red
stars and sunbursts set against a bright yellow backfield, the facade's
remaining frontage filled with panels of various swimming-pool-blue
glyphs, a good number of which somehow resembled the Enron corporate logo. The madrasa's mammoth main pishtaq was set within a great,
freestanding slab, on either side of which stood a smaller façade half the
central façade's height. I stood there scribbling impressions, but it was
impossible. Seemingly everything I looked at was frescoed with tilework
and patterns of algebraic precision, "virtually every motif permitted in
Islamic art," according to one observer. One could have stood here for
hours studying these patterns and found something newly fascinating, a
missed color (only after ten minutes did I pick out a light glaze of green
simultaneously very bright and exceedingly subtle) or a neglected pattern. On each corner of the madrasa's front façade towered a slender
minaret made of glossy brick. These minarets were never used for the
muezzin's call to prayer but were instead thought to have held up the sky,
which explained their flat, crateriform tops. The right minaret had an
inward, Pisa-like lean most convincingly attributed to earthquake damage. The Soviet restoration effort attempted to straighten Ulugbek's
crooked minaret by rotating it. This predictably succeeded in making the
problem worse. Inside Ulugbek's Madrasa was a courtyard used in early
Soviet times as the site of mass veil-burnings for Samarkand's "liberated"
women. But Ulugbek's Madrasa was closed to visitors.

I turned and walked across the plaza to the opposing Shir Dar
Madrasa, built by the Shaybanid Khan Yalangtush between the years
1619 and 1636. Yalangtush fancied himself as opulent a ruler as Ulugbek,
and commissioned a madrasa to copy his predecessor's as closely as possible. A perfect copy was not allowable, as perfection is forbidden by the
Qur'an to all but Allah, which accounted for the governmental policies
of most Muslim nations. Scholarly thoughts on the relative merits of the
Shir Dar's artistry were fairly unanimous: "Cruder craftsmanship, larger

patterns, over-accentuated lines, exalted floral ornaments and less harmony in colour," claimed one. "Like so often in the history of architecture, this attempt to outdo a predecessor, or even just to equal its achievement, was unsuccessful," felt another. Shir Dar means "lion-bearing" or "the one with lions," and here were the heretical lions now commemorated upon Uzbekistan's 200-sum banknote. The mirror-image lions were for some reason striped, and looked rather incontrovertibly like tigers. Upon the tympanum each lion chased a small white fallow deer through a complicated network of flowers and vines and small white petals. A human face grew out of the lions' backs with much dynamically rendered solar fanfare. What on earth this dose of majolica LSD was supposed to mean had been long debated. Legend held that the artist responsible for the heresy of depicting a living thing was put to death, but a few other buildings from the same seventeenth-century period, such as the Nadir Diwan Begi Madrasa in Bukhara, also depicted animals. This was to say nothing of Shir Dar's solar imagery, which could be interpreted only as a risky reference to Zoroastrianism. Perhaps, by the seventeenth century, Islam had achieved such unquestioned cultural supremecy that its artists felt freer in flouting religious convention, much as the Christian artists of the Italian Renaissance drew heavily upon their own previously forbidden traditions of polytheism.

Inside the Shir Dar Madrasa courtyard I found a multitude of friendly Uzbek and Tajik merchants making their small, respectful living off tourists. As I drank a cup of tea proffered by one old whitebeard—my reward for peeking into his carpet-laden shop and speaking with him a few words of Uzbek—I had a long look around. The courtyard had been previously bordered by a two-story honeycomb of student cells. These were now transformed into small gift shops trafficking in Central Asianish bric-a-brac.

I returned to the Registan's plaza to find Rustam sitting on the stairs of the Shir Dar, head tipped back and eyes closed as he absorbed the morning's lemonade-clear solar rays. "You ready?" I asked.

He did not open his eyes. "You don't want to see the last madrasa?"

Today, and for what looked like a long time to come, the Tilla Kari Madrasa—"the one made of gold" or "gold-gilded"—was encased in an unsightly exoskeleton of scaffolds.

"I don't think it's accepting visitors today."

Rustam stood. "Then let's go."

As we were leaving, a young police officer with a black horseshoe-shaped mustache approached us, his green uniform's red-gold epaulettes large enough to set a drink upon. Instinctively I reached for my accreditation card and passport, but the young officer waved them away.

"American?" he asked Rustam of me.

"American," I said quickly.

He nodded and furtively looked around. "Follow me," he said, starting off toward Ulugbek's madrasa. Rustam and I exchanged our suspicions with a glance but nevertheless obeyed. The police officer lit up a cigarette beneath the Ulugbek madrasa's main pishtaq and set his hand upon the metal clasp that hooked the entrance-blocking rope to a short metal stele. "Do you want to go up?"

"Go up?" I asked. "Where?"

"The minarets."

Rustam laughed. "How?"

"For two dollars, I can let you inside."

I stepped back a few feet and gazed up at the minarets. "Rustam, what's the Uzbek word for 'crooked'?"

"*Qinghir.*"

"The crooked one," I told the officer, and handed him $2.

He unhooked the rope's clasp and hurriedly waved us into the madrasa. After allowing us a glimpse of its forbidden sunlit courtyard, the officer moved down a dim side corridor, stalking past tall ornamental metal lamps and dusty wall hangings and over small brass ewers and what looked like spittoons. With another wary glance Rustam and I followed him. "It smells old in here," Rustam said, trolling a hand along each of the narrow passageway's stone walls.

"Shhh," the officer called back, a finger to his lips. He was too young, I decided, for such a large mustache. "The director will kill me if he sees you in here."

The farther we journeyed from the courtyard's entrance, the darker the corridor became. The officer finally stopped next to a huge red wall hanging. This he peeled back to reveal a concealed and even darker stone stairway. Suddenly, from around the corner, the owners of two echoey voices approached. The officer directed us in, more emphatically.

"It's dark," I hissed at him.

"No problem," he answered.

Rustam darted in, and I followed. The spiral staircase, as steep as that of a lighthouse, was best climbed on all fours. As we got higher, the dust and heat became intolerable. I was sweating so profusely that wiping the grit from my eyes resulted in what must have looked like the smeared application of some dirt-based makeup. After I had counted off seventy steps, I looked back to see the twitching orange ember of the officer's cigarette as he followed us up. "It's *dark*!" I hissed at him again.

"No problem!" he answered.

Above me somewhere Rustam yelped. Then, a troubling silence. "What is it?" I called up. "Are you okay?"

"It's nothing, bro. Just watch your hands. Some of the steps are broken and kinda sharp."

At last the stairwell discharged us into a larger, well-lit area located halfway up Ulugbek's crooked minaret. Although it was impossible to tell from the Registan's plaza, these minarets had small windows that allowed in condensed jets of dusty sunlight. The staircase had been so steep and twisty because this minaret was as hollow as a silo. But here, at its spacious midpoint, all we had to walk upon was a four-foot-wide stone ledge scattered with prehistoric lumber and nails crusted with tuberous orange growths of rust. I peered over the ledge. One hundred feet down, at the minaret's base, was a crag of jagged stone, old wire, and discarded joists. I looked at the officer. "Now what?"

He pointed to a small staircase at the far end of the ledge. Rustam and I walked over to the staircase to find that it led up to a small plain wooden door. I turned to ask the officer if we should go inside, but all I saw of him was a final green flash of his uniform before he was swallowed by the blackness of the first staircase. "That fucker just left us in here!"

"You should have waited to pay him," Rustam calmly observed. He ascended the stairs, examined the door, raised his foot, and kicked it in. A cloud of dust gushed past both of us, but the filthy air soon cleared. Again a dark abscess. Again steepness. Again cracked and pulverized stairs. Rustam slapped me on the back. "You go first this time."

I had climbed a fair number of stairs when Rustam shouted. "Dude! *Dude!* I just put my hand in something!"

"What?"

"Hold on." Rustam made soft, grunting, struggling sounds in the darkness. Suddenly, his mustached face appeared, stark and ghostly, in the small vigorous beam of a penlight.

"You have a flashlight."

"Dude, it's a dead *bird*. I just put my hand in a dead bird!"

"You have a flashlight."

"There's another one. Right by your foot! And another! Dead birds!"

"You *have* a flashlight."

"For emergencies only."

"Give me your flashlight."

A few minutes later I reached the top of Ulugbek's crooked, ever-slimming minaret. It was no longer interesting that these minarets were never used for the call to prayer. Only the most anorexic, least phobic muezzins would have been capable of getting up here five times a day. At the top of the staircase an askew metal grate let in a thin curtain of sandy light. I pushed the grate aside and muscled my way through the manhole-sized space as far as my hips. Sweat tumbled down my wind-cooled face. Samarkand's foreground convulsed with functioning civilization, its background a static vista of sky and cloud, shadow and land.

"What do you see?" Rustam called, ten steps below me.

"Everything," I said. "The whole city."

"Dude, the walls down here. Check out this graffiti. In Russian it says, 'Grisha, Registan 1909, I was here.' Here's another from 1903. Here's another from 1914." Silence. "Hey, bro. Do you have a pen?"

I tossed it down to him, and as he scratched his name against the rock, I surveyed daytime Samarkand's broad avenues, its broken grid of sidewalks, its broccoli-thick green trees and countless flat roofs, its blue domes and saltine-colored mosques and tombs that rose up from such ordinariness like extraterrestrial settlements, everything wavy in the sunlight. Along the far-off horizon, phantasmically pale through the city's benzine smog, loomed the whale-back bulges of Samarkand's surrounding mountains. Rustam, properly immortalized, handed back to me my now thoroughly ruined pen.

We arrived at the canteen early, but Monica and her fellow volunteer, Alice, were already there. The canteen's windows did not have glass and the door was left open, allowing in the sugary dust blowing off the city's desiccated foothills. The canteen's cook and waitress played cards while a pot of water bubbled over in the kitchen.

"You both look happy," Monica said after we sat down. "And dirty! What have you been doing?"

"Saw the Registan," I said. "It was great. Some militsiya guy let us climb to the top of Ulugbek's crooked minaret."

"Yeah," Alice said. "They usually let you do that. I've climbed up in there, too."

"Did you put your hand in a dead bird?" Rustam asked.

Alice smiled tentatively at Rustam. She appeared to be in her middle twenties, with short black hair and a round, intelligent face. Her eyebrows had been plucked and what remained of them had a barbed-wire severity. After deciding that Rustam's comment was not worth addressing, she turned back to me. "So tell me about the book you're writing. Everyone's talking about the former PCV back here writing a book."

"It's not really that firmed up in my—"

"Is it going to be like every book about Central Asia? They all seem like a contest to rewrite the same five stories from the same two sources in the most ostentatious way possible."

"Well, I thought that—"

"You quit, right? I mean, you quit the Peace Corps. Weren't you in Tashkent or something?"

"Gulistan."

"Right. Gulistan. So you quit after how long?"

"My reasons for leaving were emotional and complicated."

"It seems a little strange to me that someone who quit would come back to write a book."

"He quit because of a girl," Rustam said protectively.

"I'd really be interested to read something by someone who quit. I say that because it's not a perspective you often get about the Peace Corps experience. I think that's because most of the people who quit are, from what I've heard, really embarrassed about it."

The waitress floated over. Alice insisted on ordering in Tajik, which she spoke with anchorperson crispness. With pained canine eyes Rustam looked at me, his thick black eyebrows seemingly trying to burrow into his forehead.

"Alice's Tajik is really good," Monica said, a little dutifully, once the waitress had left.

Indeed, Alice's Tajik was so good that she referred to every item in sight—forks, knives, plates, the table, our chairs, the floor, the sun—by its Tajik name. When I mentioned an article I had read about the Aral Sea, she jumped in to say that she had read it. When I mentioned a travel book I admired, she had read that, too. When I described the construction work going on at the Registan's Tilla Kari Madrasa, she explained when it began, how long it would last, and what exactly the workers were doing. When the food came, Alice was alone in bowing her head, lifting her hands, and saying a quick prayer in Tajik. At this Rustam rolled his eyes. She soon began a lecture on Central Asia's geopolitical unrest.

"The Taliban did *not* promise they wouldn't destroy the Buddhist idols," I cut in. We were speaking of the enormous, several-thousand-year-old idols near the Afghan city of Bamiyan, which the Taliban had last month blown out of earthly existence. "They did no such thing. They told the world they would blow them up. They were *proud* to blow them up."

"No," Alice countered, "not all of them. Several of their officials told some British newspaper that they were working to see that the idols were spared. Just a couple years ago the Taliban's leader criticized the destruction of non-Islamic art. It's caused this big schism within the rank and file, and these guys are telling journalists that it's due to the Arabs' influence, like the guy who blew up our embassies."

"I don't think that's right," I said.

"Me neither," Rustam said.

"I read it *somewhere*," Alice maintained. (Correctly, as it turned out.) She fished around in her soup, filling her spoon's shallow basin and then dumping it back into the bowl. "I heard that now, with the threat of new sanctions, the refugee situation down in Termez is getting out of hand."

The Uzbek city of Termez was located on the Amu Darya River four hours south of Samarkand. It was the southernmost city of Uzbekistan and throughout the 1980s had been a launch site of the doomed Soviet occupation of Afghanistan, located just across the river from Termez's outskirts. Since Termez was a "forbidden city," few people had any clear idea what was happening there. What was known was that the Uzbek government's fear of terrorists and refugees had made the Friendship Bridge—the obsolescently named structure that connects Uzbekistan to Afghanistan—one of the nerviest and heavily policed border crossings in the world. Northern Afghanistan was home to many ethnic Uzbeks, and the fear of additional United Nations sanctions in the wake of the Buddhist idols' demolition had impelled many to try to flee into their titular homeland.

"Those people aren't refugees," Rustam said, his voice hinting at irritation. "They're terrorists."

"That's not true," Alice scoffed.

Rustam leaned forward. "My cousin is a sniper in Termez, okay? For a living he shoots people trying to cross the border. So perhaps you can tell me why so many of these Afghan 'refugees' are well-fed young men from Uzbekistan with faked papers?"

For a long time no one spoke. Alice stared out an open window. Monica looked, as she had for the last ten minutes, as though she were doing long division in her mind. After a while our waitress gathered the energy to take away our dishes. Once she was gone, Rustam stood. "I would like," he said evenly, "to buy us lunch." He adjusted the hang of his T-shirt upon his tall lean frame and went off to settle the bill.

We debarked to Ulugbek's observatory. Alice led, Monica tailed her, and Rustam and I drew up the rear, our feet kicking up little bursts of dust along the swaybacked road, leaving our shoes looking as though they had been dunked in loam. I went slowly, enduring another spasm of what I had begun calling "the troubles." With a grimace I gobbled down some pills, entrusting Ambassador Imodium to reason with the separatists.

We came to a busy dell of shops and trinket sellers at the base of a large sandblown hill, the steep face of which was bisected by a stone stairway. Most of the trinket sellers were old women selling multihued scarves, traditional Uzbek dresses, necklaces, and shoes. Shops such as these marked only areas of high tourist passage, and I guessed that Ulugbek's observatory, which I had never before seen, was found at the top of the hillside stairway. Alice had beaten us here by a block. By the time we arrived, she was socializing in Tajik with the old women and soon had them laughing with delight and surprise. Alice was not a bad person, I knew. She had educated herself about her host culture to an admirable degree, and took her responsibilities seriously. But I could not help but wonder whether this enthusiasm was born of desperation. I had not been completely honest back in the canteen. I knew that one did not have to quit the Peace Corps to avoid being miserable. One could instead make oneself happy, as Chekhov advises, as though one were winding a watch.

But what kind of happiness would that be? Perhaps I resented Alice for having had the courage to find out.

Viewing Ulugbek's observatory set us each back 75 cents. We reached the top of the stairway to see a large round concrete esplanade, parts of it elevated to resemble the basic foundation of the vanished cylindrical three-story architectural masterwork—complete with an astrolabe, arcades decorated with zodiacal symbols, and a planetarium-style ceiling—that stood upon this hill and overlooked Samarkand from 1425 until 1449. The observatory's ruin had gone undiscovered until 1908, when an amateur Russian archaeologist named Vladimir Viyatkin excavated its underground chamber after a decade of fruitless digs. Orientalists instantly regarded the discovery of Ulugbek's observatory as one of the landmark finds in the annals of modern archaeology. After the Bolshevik Revolution the Soviets made Viyatkin Samarkand's director of antiquities, even though the former primary-school teacher was not a Party member and probably not even a Communist. He was buried close by, near the lip of the hill, as per his last request.

Admirably little restoration had been assayed here. What had been done amounted to a small pishtaq and a concrete vault built over the underground sextant Viyatkin had uncovered. The tympanum of this purely ornamental pishtaq, which was built in the 1930s, suffered in comparison even to those afflicted by the most blundering Soviet restoration. Its bright, unimaginative mosaics saddened me. The fine artistry of ancient Central Asia had been so utterly lost. Its artisans were forgotten, the styles irrecoverable, and those who attempted to continue the tradition, however conscientious, were not artists but underfunded state dabblers committed only to workmanlike augmentations of Uzbekistan's multiplying historical obfuscations. For this, for once, the Soviets were not entirely to blame. Rustam was right: For centuries the people of Samarkand had let its magnificent ruins decay. It was not difficult to understand why. After the Timurids, a newly discovered and much safer trade route around the Cape of Good Hope was discovered, and modern shipping was born. While caravan traffic across Central Asia can hardly be said to have stopped, trade became increasingly regional and stagnant, with imperial Russia as the region's only consistent European partner. Central Asia's geopolitical influence waned and died, its wealth was squandered, its cultural pride weakened. Samarkand, once the Garden of the Soul, became by the 1650s a desert boondocks in a violent, increasingly indistinct kingdom.

Monica and Alice, having visited this observatory a dozen times, took a seat, stabbed sunglasses onto their faces, and enjoyed the sunshine. Rustam and I walked through the pishtaq's portal into an eerie, cool, narrow chamber and gazed down into the underground section of a forty-foot-long arced concrete sextant that channeled deep into the earth—to minimize, as per Ulugbek's design, any seismic upset. This was all that remained of the astrolabe, an early device used to determine the angular elevation of celestial bodies. Six hundred years ago the sextant completed its radial sweep at the top of the observatory, while researchers on each of its three floors checked and marked down data and coordinates. Now a ruin of dirty earth-damp brick, the sextant had in Ulugbek's day been lined with polished marble. Its metal rails, along which the astrolabe's wheels glided, still survived, as did many of its carefully placed degrees and zodiacal symbols. This observatory predated the work of Copernicus by a century and Galileo Galilei by nearly two. And yet who had heard of its creator outside of Central Asia? I did not know of whom Ulugbek's relative obscurity spoke more poorly: the Muslim world or my own.

After Timur's death, Ulugbek became the governor of Transoxiana, while Ulugbek's father, Shah Rukh, assumed Timur's throne after a brief period of successionist chaos—Timur had left behind him a thin but bloodthirsty field—and moved the Timurid capital to Herat in Afghanistan. Ulugbek remained in Samarkand, which he sought to make the stargazing capital of the world. Together these remarkable men rid their kingdom of their forebear's tyrannical afterglow, and the steady Timurid rubbishing of Persian culture finally came to an end. During the forty-year reign of Shah Rukh the world was gifted a full-blown renaissance of Persian literature and art. "The Timurid Renascence," Robert Byron wrote, "like ours, took place in the fifteenth century, owed its course to the patronage of princes, and preceded the emergence of nationalist states. . . . Timur's descendants, in diverting the flow of Persian culture to their own enjoyment, were concerned with the pleasures of this world, not of the next. The purpose of life they left to the saints and theologians, whom they endowed in life and commemorated in death. But the practice of it, inside the Mohammedan framework, they conducted according to their own common sense, without prejudice or sentiment except in favour of a rational intelligence." I quote at such length because the sad sting these words impart illuminates the missed opportunities and tragedy that followed the partial-birth abortion of the Islamic renaissance, torn limb from limb by religious fanatics over the next few hundred years.

"It's nice," I said to Rustam as we looked at the astrolabe's remains, "to visit a completely secular place here. To look at something built by a person I actually admire."

"Who? Ulugbek?"

"Yeah."

Rustam nodded. "I like him, too. But he was weak."

Rustam spoke of Ulugbek as though he were a go-getting hand-shaker running for a seat on Samarkand's city council. One felt this strange proximity to history in many places in Central Asia. Often only two realities existed: the Historical and the Now. The past's transformation into the present left little residue and less spoor. History instead seemed a force of harsh abruptness, a partition dropped between eras, its film as thin and permeable as a slide. And even though I knew it was folly to try to defend the fifteenth-century king of a nation I could not really begin to comprehend, I told Rustam that I did not think "weak" was the appropriate word to use in dismissing Ulugbek. He shrugged.

When Shah Rukh died in 1447, Ulugbek took up the Timurid throne. Uzbek tribes had begun an expansionist march south from the Kipchaq Plain in Siberia—near the Aral and Caspian seas—and before long were raiding along the edges of Ulugbek's Samarkand. Undoubtedly catching a whiff of weakness from the Astronomer King, a leader more inclined to study eclipses while composing verse than to fight, Uzbeks raided Samarkand in 1449, destroying Ulugbek's beloved porcelain tower and incinerating his art and book collection. Ulugbek was in Herat at the time of the ransacking, but upon his return to Samarkand his response proved so tepid that his own court, which included his thieving and conniving son, Abdul Latif, whose release from prison Ulugbek had recently secured, turned against him. Ulugbek had already earned the enmity of Samarkand's powerful clerics, as his intellectual restlessness had led him to sponsor debates on highly ill-advised topics such as the existence of Allah. United by regicide, agents of the two cabals seized the brilliant if tactically hapless Ulugbek in October 1449. Loyalists sent their king on a pilgrimage to Mecca, which they hoped would clear Ulugbek's head and restore him in the eyes of his enemies. But mercenaries dispatched by Abdul Latif met Ulugbek in a village a few miles outside of Samarkand and beheaded him. As a final insult, Ulugbek's executioner was a Persian slave. Abdul Latif was himself murdered only six months later by one of Ulugbek's faithful servants, his head exhibited upon the madrasa named for his father. Thus the Timurids' empire began its disintegrating decline, thanks in no small part to the Uzbeks who now inexplicably claim them.

Ulugbek's observatory should have been one of the world's majesties, but it was pulled down by reactionaries, cursed as "the cemetery of forty evil spirits," and lost until Viyatkin's discovery. Standing upon its resting place, I had to restrain myself from regarding Ulugbek's murder as intolerance infuriatingly specific to the Muslim world. Islam has historically stomached little thought of the angels-dancing-on-pins variety. *Zannah,* the Arabic word for the sort of theological speculation that rescued the West from its priests, is said by Qur'anic scholars to have strong pejorative implications. But it seemed worth remembering that of the fifteen Nazis who actively planned the Final Solution, seven of them held Ph.D.'s.

The day neared its hottest hours. An albedo-spattered perch high above the city was not a wise place to linger. We descended the hillside stairway to be assailed by a group of beggar children wearing filthy T-shirts stamped with pirated images of smiling pseudo-Muppets. The children's little hands, spread open and star-shaped, reached out to us. Rustam and Alice shooed the beggars away with a few Tajik hisses, and quietly I stuffed away the money I had been ready to hand over to them. Alice then announced that she had a class to teach, thanked us for the interesting afternoon, and hailed a passing car.

There were still several places I would have liked to visit: the necropolis Shah-i-Zinda ("Tomb of the Living King"), Samarkand's holiest site, a series of stunning mausoleums arranged railroad car–style and an important station of Islamic pilgrimage; the Chupan Ata Shrine, which honors the pre-Islamic patron saint of Samarkand; and the Bibi Khanum Mosque, commissioned by Timur, named for his Chinese wife, and built by an amorous architect who fell in love with Princess Bibi and fled an outraged Timur by jumping off one of the mosque's minarets shortly before growing wings and flying back to Mecca. I was about to make a case for at least having a look at these sites when I realized I would much prefer a long nap in an air-conditioned room.

The walk back to the Hotel Afrosiab brought us through an area imaginatively known as Afrosiab, a series of small neighborhoods whose multiplicity of historical curiosities had led to freshly paved paths and solid new curbstones and fancy-looking homes. Tashkent Street, the unaccountably fine road we walked along, was, Monica told us, only a few years old, as were many of the area's shops. The Afrosiab area's main crux is a hilltop citadel—a kind of Islamic Masada—whose thick, vallated walls reportedly extend two stories into the earth, a feat of engineering not often encountered in such an ancient structure. From the ramparts of this fort Samarkandis attempted to hold off every invader from Alexander the Great to the Mongols sixteen hundred years later. It was a museum piece now, though nearby were the open-air remains of Marakanda, the ancient city that had once impressed Alexander. The Soviets had excavated Marakanda's few salvageable coins and tools and left its wind-smoothed, unrestorable ruins to further erosion. As Uzbekistan rarely missed a chance for nomenclatural redundancy, a small river known as the Siab cut through Afrosiab. This river, along with an impressive bridge, steep stone walls and ravines, villagey clusters of homes and shops, and birch-lined paths, provided the area with an unreasonable loveliness. The only thing that managed to spoil the idyll was the refinery spire thrust up from behind a nearby hill. I stopped in the middle of the bridge and looked over into the Siab's spritely waters burbling past the riverside homes. Monica joined me there.

"Is it just me," I said to her, watching three short and repeatedly bowing men in black frock coats emerge from one of the riverside buildings, "or are those Orthodox Jews coming out of that shop?"

"It's not a shop. It's hard to tell from up here, but that's the portal to the Tomb of Doniyor. And yes, those are Orthodox Jews."

Doniyor was the Muslim variant for Daniel. "You mean *that's* Daniel's Tomb? Right down there?"

"The portal to Daniel's tomb. That's new, too. The path to the tomb is right on the other side."

The implications of the Uzbek government's decision to build an expensive new road and portal near a tourist site likely to receive an unusual number of shall we say cosmopolitan travelers were probably best left unexplored. Yes, this Daniel was *Daniel,* the Jew who was deported to Babylon by Nebuchadrezzar (misspelled by the Bible as Nebuchadnezzar) in the sixth century B.C.E. to survive a night sealed in a lion's den. (One of the Bible's more psychotic asides tells us that Daniel's false accusers, as well as "their children, and their wives," were tossed into the den in retribution, where "the lions . . . broke all their bones in pieces.") Legend holds that Timur hauled Daniel's body back from Baghdad, though scholars, especially Israeli scholars, tend to reject this. This was not Central Asia's only religious anachronism. In Bukhara there was a shrine in which Job supposedly struck his rod against the ground, producing a spring from which tourists—at the risk of severe abdominal stress—could now drink. St. Matthew, the apostle Jesus lured away from a promising career in tax collecting, was supposedly buried near mountain-girdled Lake Issyk-Kul in Kyrgyzstan, of all places. How his remains might have reached Kyrgyzstan is explained by the ruins of a fourth-century Armenian monastery in the Kyrgyz hamlet of Svetyy Mys.

The path to Daniel's tomb, decoratively lined with bright young birch trees, ran parallel with the Siab River, while the tomb itself was sheltered atop a hill within a rectangular, unremarkable building made of yellowy brick and crowned with five domes. It had been the evident recipient of numerous restorations, each less restorative than the last. I removed my shoes and stepped inside. The tomb of Daniel smelled overwhelmingly of sweaty feet. But it was cooler within its walls by at least ten degrees. I walked around Daniel's gigantic sarcophagus, busily inscribed with Arabic. The sarcophagus was twenty-five feet, nearly as long as the building itself. Samarkand's mullahs believed that Daniel continued to grow while dead and dutifully enlarged his coffin half an inch per annum. When Daniel did not rise from the dead, as they believed he would when he reached a certain height, the tradition was understandably abandoned.

Soon a middle-aged Uzbek man in a suit and tie walked into the tomb. He looked at me with startled eyes, then knelt to pray beside the sarcophagus. I watched from the far side of the room. Daniel had negligible significance in the world of Islam. (The six great prophets of Islam are, in descending order of importance, Mohammed, Isa [Jesus], Musa [Moses], Ibrahim [Abraham], Nawh' [Noah], and Adam, a list that can only be regarded as mystifying by anyone with more than Sunday-school

knowledge of the Jewish and Christian Bibles. Noah, a prophet? *Adam?*
This register of prophets comes to us from Mohammed, a man who, for
all his spiritual gifts, was something of a religious numbskull. Very late
in Mohammed's life, for instance, he was shocked to learn that Christians and Jews were not different sects of the same faith.) Why was this
Muslim praying to a Hebrew saint with no special place in the constella-
tion of Islam? It was, I supposed, the prerogative of more recent faiths to
absorb the mythology of those established before them. But it was hard
to know whether to regard the praying man as proof that the first and
final pillars of monotheism held up the same ceiling of divinity, or as a
reminder of the two faiths' inescapably competitive mandates. The man
then finished praying and with four swift movements made a sign of the
cross, kissed Daniel's sarcophagus, and quietly stepped outside.

The next day, Cosmonauts Day—one of the few Soviet holidays still, if
unofficially, observed in Uzbekistan—every television channel featured
the same basso profundo Russian narrator exulting Soviet space exploration over only slightly different documentary footage: flame-sprayed
launch pads, pods shedding their rockets at the sparkly shore of space,
Russian cosmonauts' potato faces encased within helmet aquariums.
Rustam settled on an engrossing feature exclusively concerned with
Laika, the Soviet space collie, who, we learned, had perished within her
space capsule upon atmospheric reentry. "Poor Laika," Rustam said,
experimenting with his hairdo in the mirror and singing Offspring songs
to himself. "Too bad for her!" I was in bed. I could not move. The night
before we had gone drinking and dancing with several of Samarkand's
Peace Corps volunteers at a nightclub called Sharq. I remembered very
little of this night. I remembered doing shots with Alice, whom I had
grown to like immensely, and dancing, spastically and alone, to Tom
Jones's "Sex Bomb." I remembered standing too close to the dance-floor
vent that discharged the dry ice. I remembered Rustam splashing cold
water in my face. Vodka was no beverage, I thought. It was memory-
erasing headache fuel. It was now ten in the morning. We had to check
out by noon and by six be in Bukhara, where we were to meet another
Peace Corps volunteer named Rick. Omad's wife lived in a village fifteen
miles outside of the city, and I had to travel there and return in two hours.

And I had to do this alone, as per my promise to Rustam that I would not involve him.

After spending the next hour fretting about wasting time, I picked up the phone and dialed the number of Omad's wife. While it rang, I watched Rustam. He was still preening in the mirror, teasing up little cowlicks and with a sour look flattening them and starting over. He had spent the last few days with a flat wedge cut but today was using the Afrosiab's complimentary hair gel to sculpt his hair into a pompadour, his extra-thick forelock as defined as a black horn. After fifteen rings a recording in Uzbek told me that the number I was calling was not currently in service. I slammed the phone back on the receiver so roughly its inner bell held a long sharp note.

Rustam looked at me in the mirror. "What's up, bro?"

"The wife's phone is broken."

With two gelled fingers he sharpened the point of his forelock. "So don't go." He did not turn from the mirror.

"I have to go."

"No, actually. You don't."

Rustam escorted me outside and helped me book a cab, explaining to the driver that it was important that he, the driver, wait for me while I conducted my business, then return me to this spot, exactly this spot. The driver agreed. Rustam asked me for the slip of paper on which Omad's wife's address was written. This he gave to the driver, a youngish Tajik man with wraparound sunglasses. He looked at the address and shook his head. "This isn't an address."

"What?" Rustam asked.

"This isn't an address. This is simply the middle of the village."

"But you know where the village is?"

He shrugged yes.

Rustam looked at me, relaying what had been said. "What do you think? Do you sit comfortably with this situation?"

I did not sit at all comfortably with this situation. I remembered, now, having been told by a Committee to Protect Journalists representative that some address confusion was a possibility. In that case, I was told, I might have to ask around the neighborhood a bit. While being briefed in CPJ's quiet Chelsea office in New York City, that had sounded excellent. Adventure! "The hell with it," I told Rustam now. "I'll see what happens."

As I was getting into the car Rustam grabbed my arm. "Dude. I can go with you. Do you want me to go with you? I'll go with you."

"No, it's all right. Don't worry."

"Bro, I'm serious. You could get in a lot of trouble."

"I'm not going to get into trouble. Everything's going to be fine."

As we pulled away, I tried to get comfortable in the car. Its interior had for some reason been stripped. The backseat door handles had been removed, leaving neat square excisions filled with short sprays of thick clipped cable. Naked screws were all that survived the mid-door levers used to roll down the windows. As we drove, I slipped into and fought my way out of a series of short hangover naps, opening my drugged eyes every few minutes to see bright desert, roadside homes, bright desert, playing children, a checkpoint. I sat up. The driver and a border guard were speaking Tajik. The guard nodded, looked at me through the dirty window, and waved us through. Ten minutes later the driver pulled alongside a small, woebegone repair shop. One of its mechanics crouched shoeless outside the front door while fixing a wheelbarrow. In our wake rolled in a thick white cloud of dust, which enveloped him. When the dust cleared, the man shook his head at us and returned to his work.

I looked around. This was less a village than a suburb. A few shops and houses, a tiny empty park and rusty playground, a government building (one could determine this by the air conditioners in its windows, as loud as helicopters), some ugly Soviet-style apartment buildings, all motionless beneath an uneasy pall of dusty sunshine. The driver handed me a spanner fit with a special head. I used the tool to roll down the window, reached outside, and opened the vehicle's back door. I walked across the street to a dilapidated three-story apartment building surrounded by piles of garbage. Some of this garbage was moving. As I got closer, the moving garbage exploded and dirty feral cats streaked across my path. But soon I walked past the cats' new hiding place and the needlessly upsetting process began anew. I crept around behind the apartment building, squeezed through two of its small rusty freestanding car garages, and stepped up a shattered flight of stairs into the building's rear foyer. The ground floor stank heavily of human feces. Finely marbled through the smell were traces of cat urine, ash, and something like spoiled food. Again I had a bitter thought about the Soviet experiment, concocted to connect Man to his Work and designed to make inalienable the basic comforts of Modern Industrial Life. Yet Soviet Communism chipped and sanded Man into man until he was *unable* to do his Work, or any work, while the basic comforts of Modern Industrial Life altered and updated too quickly for its lumbering systematics. The sole things the Soviet system did with any consistency were wreck and destroy. Now the experiment's subjects were abandoned in toppled ruins no one would ever repair, and the smell of shitty failure pressed in. Few long-term fates could be considered grimmer than life on the first floor of a Soviet apartment building, where filth of all kinds collected. What if this fate were my own? Would I, too, defecate in stairwells, join Islamist whip-rounds, drink myself rotten? Would it ever occur to me to stand up to the government, as Omad had, and paid for? I did not think so. I did not think so.

Nor did I know what to do. If I knocked on a door and asked whomever answered if he or she knew Omad's wife, it seemed unlikely that he or she would feel comfortable answering. I had ruled out completely the possibility of her apartment falling under any concentrated surveillance. If she was being watched, it was by neighbors on the dole of the SNB. Which meant that alerting the village to a foreigner looking for her was the worst option I had. I stood there in the reeking humid dark, touching the $2,000 stuffed into my money belt. Unfortunately, it was the only option I had. An old ethnic Russian woman answered the first door I knocked on. She wore a tattered white shawl and smelled of moths, cats, small meals baked for one. She was murky-eyed, her wrinkled and trembly open mouth unsure whether to smile or summon help. "Excuse me," I said in Russian, "do you speak Uzbek?" She closed the door. I walked upstairs and rang the first doorbell to present itself. It made a sound like chirping birds. Another old woman, an Uzbek as small and portly as a pigeon and wearing a green Uzbek housedress over billowy gray genie pants, opened the door and looked at me. We exchanged salaams, the woman charily stepping back, her hand, still on the door, at the ready to close it. Quickly I explained that I was an American looking for the mother of a friend, who lived in this village. I had, I said, a gift for her.

"I don't know her," she said.

"I will tell you her name."

"I don't know!" She began to close the door.

"Please, good mother, I need help."

The woman looked at me through the door's six-inch crack. Upon her head she wore a scarf decorated with red and yellow flowers. Beneath it her homely face pinched and flexed. "What is her name?"

I told her and, in her hesitation, I knew that she knew. She knew, at the least, the name of the local woman whose well-known journalist husband had been dragged off and thrown into prison.

"I don't know her," she said.

"Which building does she live in?"

"I don't know her."

"I understand. Which building?"

"Three."

"This is . . . ?"

"One."

"Thank you, good mother."

Very quietly the door closed. Building Three, which was across the street, was in no better condition than One. As I approached the building, a woman on the third floor poured a plastic washtub of hot soapy water from her window to the hissing displeasure of several deluged cats. I stepped into the building's foyer and considered the shambles of its dented, doorless, ripped-apart personal mailboxes. None had names or numbers. I was not yet afraid. I became afraid when, while walking down Building Three's garbage-strewn second-story hallway and hoping to spontaneously develop extrasensory perception, a man opened his door and asked me who I was and what I was doing here.

"Trying to find my friend's mother."

The man was heavy, tan, and slovenly, with a head of flat black hair, large dirty hands, and a T-shirt that had been prodigiously stained by his armpits. "Who are you?"

"I'm an American. I'm looking for my friend's mother." I thought it over, then told him her name.

He nodded. "She's not here. She's gone." Behind him was the dead indoor light of drawn shades, squalor, the only identifiable object a television set at a low burning volume. Russian game shows, it sounded like.

"Thank you, big brother. Goodbye."

He bid me in, his expression not changing. "Come inside. Wait for her."

To reach the stairs I had to pass him. "Thank you. Goodbye."

He touched me, as lightly as a ghost, as I passed. His voice was serene. "Wait inside, my friend. She'll be back."

"Goodbye. Thank you. Goodbye." I walked calmly down the first flight, took the second in two leaps, and sprinted across the village's central plaza. The car was still here, so dusty it looked like a large metal dessert covered in confectioners' sugar. The driver was not. Wherever he went, he had locked the vehicle's doors before going. I pressed my forehead to its sizzling roof, which popped in and out of place beneath the troubled weight of my skull, and stood there trying to decipher what had just happened while listening to my clapping heart. I wondered what was worse. Failing to give Omad's wife the money, or in the process of doing so bringing down upon her head further strife? I was not going back in there. The man's calm, even voice stayed with me. Hearing it had been like an anxiety infusion. While traveling, I trusted people. To do so was personally important to me. Travel without trust could only be fraught, painful; its dimensions were dread itself. But I was not going back in there.

I turned from the car to find the driver walking toward me, smiling. "Where were you?" I yelled. "Jesus! Leave me out here!" The driver stopped, his head drawing back turtlishly. I had been shouting at him in English. *"Ketdik,"* I said.

He unlocked the car. I was searching for the nonexistent back-seat safety belt when a police officer tapped on the driver's window with a truncheon and with his fist made a firm though polite roll-it-down gesture. The driver obliged, and the two had a conversation in Tajik. I closed my eyes. A moment later the officer rapped on my window and made an identical roll-it-down gesture. I was not able to do so without the spanner. As the driver dug for the tool in his glove compartment, the officer rapped my window again, harder. He barked something in Russian. "I can't!" I called out, also in Russian, crucially forgetting the word for "open," thus confusing the nature of my refusal. "Open!" the officer shouted. "I can't open!" I shouted back. The driver leaped from the vehicle to open my door for me. In the excitement he was restrained. While the officer had him locked in a come-along hold, the driver calmly explained why I refused to open the window. The officer chuckled. The driver, stagily rubbing his released arm, joined him and opened my door.

I looked at my watch—it was a quarter to noon—and without mirth joined the officer and driver beside the car.

The officer found it unusual that I carried with me no baggage. In Uzbek I gave him my line. He nodded and asked me the name of my friend's mother. Providing him with the real name of Omad's wife was of course not possible. That impossibility punched a hole in my mind. I stood there, all of the names of the Russian and Uzbek women and men that I had ever met and could now conceivably use sinking one by one into a mental bog. "Anna," I told him. By doing so I had locked myself into conjuring up a Russian family name; Uzbek women did not have first names such as Anna. So: Anna what? *Do not say Karenina*, I told myself. *Do not say Karenina.* But the *only* Russian surnames I was suddenly able to convene came from well-known literature: Karamazov, Svidrigailov, Zhivago, Chichikov. "Anna . . . Rusanova." This came from Pavel Rusanov, the hero of Solzhenitsyn's *Cancer Ward,* one of the few great Russian novels that lacked anything approaching a household protagonist.

He repeated her name, and I repeated it, pleased with its sound. Anna Rusanova. She was seventy. She dyed her hair red. She wore bifocals. She hated cats. She lived on the third floor, with her husband, who was free, and loved her.

"Where is your gift?" he asked.

"My gift."

"Your gift. You have no bag. Where is your gift?"

Here it took effort to keep from employing the phoneme stall of "Um," which in Uzbek unfortunately means "vagina." "My gift is . . . money," I told the officer. I always carried a few sacrificial twenties in my wallet and resigned myself to martyring them here.

"Ah," the officer said with a smile, "I think I would like such a gift myself." He then asked me where I was staying. I told him. He asked for proof of that. I gave it to him. He asked for my papers. I handed them over. He studied my accreditation card with an expression so thorough in its incomprehension it seemed profound. He read aloud its formal Uzbek phrasings, then opened my passport as though expecting to find in it some pearl of revelation. With disappointment he handed both back to me. "Are you [something]?" he asked abruptly. His nostrils were wet around the rims.

Although we were speaking Uzbek, this unfamiliar word was Russian. "I'm sorry?" I said. "I didn't understand."

"[Something]"

I realized, unhelpfully, that it was two words. "I'm sorry. I—"

"[Something something]! [Something something]!"

"[Something something]," the driver pleaded. "You understand?"

I looked to one man, then the other. The officer's wet nostril rims shone. The Russian word for "nostril" was *nasdria*. Why did I know that and not these words? What, for that matter, was I doing here? Why had I not allowed Rustam to come with me? Why was I not brave or resourceful enough to get Omad's wife her money? The questions ticked away within me while I stood there, my own silence sickening.

"[Something something]," the officer tried again. "Yes? Are you [something something]?"

"I don't know!" I snapped at him. "I don't understand! Do *you* understand I don't understand?"

After a few more purposeless questions the officer let us go. I rode shotgun back to the Hotel Afrosiab with my head between my knees, breathing. The driver kept glancing over at me, an odometer of worry. I sounded in my mind the unknown words over and over in order to keep from forgetting them. We found Rustam where he promised he would be, outside the hotel, draped with our baggage and holding a bottle of Coca-Cola for me. The flat soda tasted hot and caramelized, but I drank it down to an inch below its wraparound sticker. Rustam watched me, chewing his lip. The moment I lowered the bottle, I realized I had forgotten the words. The driver, luckily, had not. As he told the story, Rustam shook his head, covered his mouth, and began laughing. Above his fingers his eyes were as narrow and moist as those of a delighted guru. "Dude, the militsiya thought you were a Jehovah's Witness!"

I took a single step backward, then sat down on the curb. "Of course he did. Why wouldn't he? That seems like a completely reasonable conclusion. Look at me. Don't I look like a Jehovah's Witness to you?" I was shouting. "Where does this stuff come from? These people should be studied! It's uncanny! Jehovah's Witness? Why not an Egyptologist? Why not a Shriner or a Jedi fucking Knight?"

Rustam toed the sidewalk's concrete. "Sorry I laughed, bro. Getting stopped by the militsiya is no fun. I know that."

Today the sun was sparkling upon the dome of the nearby Guri Amir. I calmed myself down by watching the dome flash and wink. In a few minutes we would leave Samarkand, and I had little idea if I would ever be back. I felt a nudge of melancholy, the quiet inner recognition that the velocity of farewell had become unstoppable. Such sadness I associated with airports and hotel rooms; it was disconcerting to feel it outdoors. My head dipped forward and hung off my shoulders. "I didn't get her the money."

Rustam sat down next to me. "What happened?"

"I don't want to talk about it."

"Are you going back?"

My head hung lower. I shook it.

"You tried, bro."

The driver piloted us across a few sandy miles on Samarkand's perimeter to a train station—called in Russian and Uzbek *vokzal,* after Vauxhall in London, apparently the first train station of which any Russian speaker got wind—where he told us we could easily hire a car to Bukhara. It was not quite that simple. No one at the station wanted to go to Bukhara, a six-hour drive along the Shah Rah (Royal Road), which happened to pass through the Navoi region, one of Uzbekistan's most sensitive areas, home to numerous prisons, government facilities, and power plants. The one gentleman willing to take us to Bukhara—a world-champion smiler—wanted thirty dollars and, he said, would go for nothing less. Rustam and I conferred while the man poured *noss* from a small canvas bag into his hand. He smilingly worked the *noss* into a hard little ball that would, in moments, be tucked under his tongue.

Rustam: "Thirty dollars, bro. That's way too much."

"I understand that. But it costs me twenty-five dollars to get to Brooklyn from the Upper West Side on a Friday night."

"Okay." Pause. "So, like, what are you saying?"

"I'm saying to hell with economic relativity."

"You realize that you're going to increase the difficulty for the next American who comes to this place looking for a driver."

"I'm more interested in making life easier for the people who have to live here than the visiting Americans who get to go back home."

"But I don't think that man is experiencing much hardship in his life. Look at his shoes. Leather."

"This all . . . makes me tired. Let's just agree to thirty and get out of here."

"Would you give me ten minutes to find another, cheaper driver?"

While Rustam worked his way through the train station's crowd of multifarious chauffeurs—Russians, Uzbeks, Tajiks, Koreans, old, young, friendly, desperate—I assumed my most unapproachable expression and sat down in the dirt and pulled off my plastic Coke bottle. My most unapproachable expression proved ineffective. Three younger Uzbek drivers with a rough, chuckling aura wandered over and started asking me questions in slurred and unfriendly Russian. I told them I was from Canada, the equivalent of interest-repellent. Within minutes the young men had walked away. The smiling, tobacco-sucking driver watched me from a distance. I raised my bottle to him. He bowed fatefully, with a dainty little hand flip, and spat a rope of pea-colored saliva into the dirt.

The driver Rustam dredged up was marginally better. He was short and his staticky brown hair stuck up at illogical angles, as though he were some dazed, just-born runt whose mother did not have the chance to administer a few tidying licks. His yellow T-shirt was torn at the collar and his once-nice tan dress pants had been ruined by oil stains. He looked more than dazed. In fact, he looked drunk, possibly stoned. His wall-eyed gaze seemed fixed upon the coast of some other compelling dimension. What troubled me were his tattoos. On each hand his knuckles formed the hub within a green-spoked spiderweb, and his forearms were etched with bluish, indistinct skulls and daggers—almost certainly the work of a prison tattoo artist.

"Twenty bucks!" Rustam said. "And he has a Nexia!"

Five

Sacred Spaces

The Uzbeks are a simple people, with whom one gets most readily acquainted, though they speak in a curious tone of voice, as if they despised or were angry with you. . . . Simple people! they believe a spy must measure their forts and walls; they have no idea of the value of conversation.
—ALEXANDER BURNES, *TRAVELS INTO BOKHARA*

Our driver's name was Denis. Denis was half-Russian and half-Tajik, admirably uninterested in his American passenger, and he sped out of Samarkand via the Royal Road at 120 miles per hour blasting Rustam's Depeche Mode tape. The terrain on the way to Bukhara belonged to the sands of the Kizilkum Desert. The Zerafshan (Gold-Strewn) River was another glacier-fed watercourse that plunged out of Tajikistan's peaks to expire in Uzbekistan's deserts. It roughly followed the same winding path as the Royal Road, though only rarely close enough to see it from the highway. Like every resource here, most of them negligibly protected by the government and afforded little if any worth by market mechanisms, this river had been exploited within an inch of its life. The cotton fields we passed were choked and dry, the farmland nothing but dunes, the sand whitish with salt deposits. Along the road's edges were no American-style "beauty strips" to hide what had been done just over the hills. What was happening to this land was so obvious there seemed scarcely any need for outcry. Environmentalism suddenly struck me as the most obvious philosophy imaginable: Let us not ruin forever where we live and work and breathe and eat. Earth's future inhabitants will no doubt look upon our current environmental practices—maintained despite all manner of evidence that doing so will result in planetary ruin—roughly the way we look upon eighteenth-century surgery. And that is if we, and they, are very lucky.

Before starting off I had worried that Denis's prison tattoos might cause checkpoint delays. But Denis seemed to have some acquaintance with these border guards. At each checkpoint, after mutually familiar nods, we were waved through. Ninety minutes into our trip, I had relaxed and was reading *Middlemarch*. Denis switched off the music, and while I read, he and Rustam chatted in Russian until Denis's tattooed hand lifted off the steering wheel, his finger thrust toward a fenced encampment gathered atop one of the slopey horizon's humps. *"Tam,"* Denis said. *There.* Rustam looked and nodded, silenced.

I closed my book. "What's there?"

Rustam shrugged. "That's where Denis says he was in prison."

"I thought so. Did he tell you what he was in prison for?"

"Murder. He says the other guy started it."

A scenario: If I were a psychopath, would not the perfect cover be freelance driver? Would not the perfect place to abduct rich foreigners be a train station? Would not the perfect place to take them be the desert?

"I thought you'd be interested in Denis," Rustam was saying, "for your book. He was telling me a lot of interesting stuff about prison life, bro." To Denis: "My American writer friend wants to hear your prison stories."

Denis turned his head slightly and pulled away from his shoulder a swatch of his longish brown mullet. A jagged bolt of bright keloidal scar tissue began behind his earlobe and streaked like pink mercury into his shirt collar. It stopped, he indicated with a tap, just past his shoulder. "In prison he was cut," Rustam translated. "Stabbed. By a big Kazakh guy. But his friend Vova repaid the Kazakh guy—uh, sent him to the light? I don't know the English idiom."

"Settled his hash."

"Yeah."

Denis spoke on, a chip in his front tooth giving his Russian a fluty, fricative sound. Rustam nodded along as he listened. "Denis says that he was in prison with many of the Soviet people. He says that Georgians and Armenians are very cool. Azerbaijanis, too. But Latvians and Estonians, he says, are not like our people. They are cold, they trust no one, and they hate everyone but themselves. But the worst, he says, are guys from

Moscow. Their crimes are always . . . uh, bitches' crimes? He says they cry like women and get their asses kicked at all times."

I was writing eagerly. "*Jesus* this is good stuff."

Rustam smiled. "I told you!"

We came to another, larger checkpoint, its wide concrete apron divided into sections by whitewashed partitions. This was the entrance point to the Navoi region. A dozen listless officers of the State Motor Vehicle Inspectorate watched us maneuver the partitions' unimaginative maze, including one man sitting in a rocking chair fanning his sweaty face with a newspaper. Plunked roadside was a highway patrol substation faced with reflective glass. As Denis pulled up to the checkpoint's perfectly rendered reproduction of an American STOP sign I went back to reading, expecting to be waved through. *If we had a keen vision and feeling of all ordinary human life,* I read, *it would be like hearing the grass grow and the squirrel's heart beat, and we should die of that roar which lives on the other side of silence. As it is, the quickest among us walk about well-wadded with stupidity.* What I did not see was the officer who manned the STOP sign glance at Denis's hands and with his black truncheon instantly wave us over to the berm.

However, Dorothea was crying— I looked up. "What's going on?"

Rustam's head turned, quickly, in each direction. Half a dozen police officers were gathering around the car. "I don't know. I think it's okay."

One of the officers, a tall man with a large head and sparse curly black hair, bid Denis to open his door. Denis sat motionless. As the officer lifted his arm to knock on the window again, Denis climbed out of the car and stood sullenly before him, his forehead even with the button-flap pockets upon the officer's chest. The officer looked down at Denis's hands and arms contemptuously. "Are you a drug addict?" he asked.

"Why?" Denis responded, suddenly smiling. "Did I ever smoke pot with you?"

The truncheon caught Denis across the face. On his journey to the concrete mat Denis's eyes popped wide and his jaw swiveled, as though quickly making room for the pain stretching out in his face. I pushed up against the passenger window, regarding what I had just seen as not quite real. My queer urge to laugh was doused when the officer used his truncheon to strike Denis on the back and in the ribs before gracefully lowering his knee onto Denis's right arm while another officer wrenched Denis's left behind his back. Denis did not resist. He made no sound.

Once they had handcuffed him, Denis pressed his cheek against the concrete and closed his eyes.

"You," the truncheon-wielding officer said, turning to Rustam and me, "get out of the car."

I turned to Rustam. I could hear my heart, my tiny squirrel's heart, beating. "Rustam—"

His words came quietly: "Just get out. And don't talk."

As I climbed from the Nexia, my backpack was pulled from my hands. The officers tore it open along its black zippered seam and rifled through my effects—deodorant, toothpaste, dirty underwear, pens, notebooks, books—before dropping the bag on the ground and giving it a disdainful little kick. When I went to pick it up, I was told not to move. I put my hands up. *"Gap yoq,"* I said. Rustam was speaking Uzbek with the tall officer who had beaten Denis. The officer's stance was baronial and grand, even though his uniform was yard-work dirty and his truncheon chipped and cheap. I understood perhaps every fifth word. Samarkand. Bukhara. Journalist. American. Translator. I turned. The Nexia's trunk was being opened. I watched as one officer removed my large though mostly empty black duffel bag, unzipped it, and roughly pawed its contents. I bit my lip when the man removed my Human Rights Watch report, passed over a few of its pages, and left it exposed atop the bag. A bright red Daewoo coupe crammed with too many young Uzbek men rolled past, each occupant looking us over and shaking his head. Now the tall officer was nodding as Rustam explained that we did not know Denis. We had just met him.

Suddenly the half-dozen officers stood at attention, positioned around Denis's Nexia with the formal proximity of columns. Rustam and the tall officer, sensing the atmospheric change, looked over to their left. Striding from the substation across the highway was a furious-looking young man wearing a tight black dress shirt, black slacks, and black shoes. He walked in quick stabbing leg thrusts, as though he were repeatedly kicking something. He was short and trim, his body curbed with muscle. The officers saluted him. He chopped a return salute and after speaking briefly with the tall officer approached me and asked for my passport. One of his very brown irises floated on a reddish, unwell eyeball. Pinkeye. I handed over my passport. He was not a police officer, I knew, but an agent of the SNB. I had encountered SNB agents three times previously, and in each case they had been respectful and solicitous. I

would expect no less from this man, I decided, and hazarded that showing him my accreditation card might help things along. The agent took
the card and glanced at it before throwing it over his shoulder. A breeze
took up the small green slip of cardboard and plastered it against the
car's paneling. Rustam peeled it away from the Nexia and returned to my
side.

"Are you aware your driver is a criminal?" the SNB agent asked.

"No," I said.

"No," Rustam said.

The agent studied Rustam mildly. He looked down at my passport
and turned its pages. He said, softly, to one of the officers, "Take this
one." They led Rustam away gently. Rustam looked back at me, his eyes
filled with incredulousness, offense, fear, then nothing but fear. For a
moment I could see only two stout middle-aged officers in green uni-
forms on either side of a lanky young man in blue jeans. Then I realized
what was happening. That was my friend. My friend was being taken
away! The agent was speaking to me. I ignored him. "Hey," I said, angrily
lurching forward.

The agent's outthrust arm struck me in the throat. I did not know if
the agent had tried to hit me or merely restrain me, but the wide bony
underside of his forearm had come flush upon my Adam's apple and he
did not apologize and did not seem to care when I stepped back choking,
each of my coughs wringing stunned tears from burning eyes. The agent
returned to the matter of my passport: "Where are you going?"

"Bukhara." I did not know if I was rubbing my throat simply
because it hurt or because I wanted him to apologize.

"What are you doing there? Who are you seeing? When are you leaving?" He handed my passport to another officer, who looked it over and
himself handed it along to another officer.

"I'm a journalist," I said, watching my passport drift from green uniform to green uniform. "I'm traveling around the country. I'm not seeing
anyone. I was in the Peace Corps here. You know the Peace Corps, yes? I
was an English tea—"

"You are not a Peace Corps volunteer now."

"Now? No, I'm—"

"Do you know that your driver is a hooligan?"

"No. I told you no."

"Come." He walked over to my duffel and after prissily pulling up his pant legs squatted beside it. I followed and stood on the opposite side of the bag. We looked down at the bent black mass, its dark laboratory-slick fabric gleaming in the sun. "What's this?" he asked, holding up the Human Rights Watch report.

"Papers. Work. Nothing."

He cast the report aside and dug into the bag. That was a pocketknife. This was a mess kit. That was diarrhea medicine. This was a flashlight. That was a can of Skoal chewing tobacco. Tobacco. *Tabak.* For your mouth. Yes, I will show you, like this. Certainly the other officers can try. Please, take as many tins as you like. This? This is an Uzbek-English dictionary. No. Please. Go ahead. Read.

With a small, faint smile the agent flipped through my dictionary, clearly surprised that Uzbek was celebrated enough to merit such a book. He stopped flipping pages. His brown eyes, as outsized as a falcon's, lifted to meet mine. Without breaking eye contact he tapped one of the words. "This is you."

I looked. *Ulashmoq.* To distribute. Next to us two of the officers were looking at each other, gobs of Skoal-flecked saliva dripping off their chins.

"You," the agent pressed me. "You're a distributor?"

I stared at him, lost within a confusion as huge as the desert around me. Distributor? But then a sudden black understanding breached my earnest word-by-word unfolding of a language I did not know well. He did not mean distributor. He was accusing me of something I was not likely to cadge from a dictionary's polite imprecision. "No," I told him. "No, sir. I'm not."

"You're a drug dealer."

"No. No!"

Officers were pulling everything from Rustam's and my bags before systematically searching their threaded closures and impacted corners for hidden pouches crammed with *narkotiki*. The Nexia's trunk was searched, its seats' cushioning pulled up, its wheels inspected. Denis groaned miserably. The SNB agent personally searched my windbreaker and pulled from its pocket a small white tablet and demanded to know what it was. I explained that it was a Chiclet, and after splitting the tablet we each took half and chewed, looking at each other, until he nodded and spit it out. Denis, though still handcuffed and prone next to his taken-apart car, spoke in amiable terms with the officer who had struck him. The honesty of accusation had allowed us all a new civility, it seemed. Twice I attempted picking up our gear even after I had been told not to touch anything and twice I was angrily rebuked. I was able to relocate and capture my passport only after trading it for a can of Skoal. And then I stood there, my throat still hurting.

Soon a paled Rustam emerged from the substation, accompanied by one officer. He looked pale because minutes before he had been naked, holding his clothes in a bundle over his head and yelling at the officers that he had rights, did they not know, he had rights guaranteed by his constitution and more significantly he could recite those rights right now. Why was Rustam naked? Before the officers could frisk him Rustam had smartly emptied out his pockets and, without being asked, took off all his clothes, disallowing the officers their chance to plant evidence if they sought to do so, and Rustam was certainly prepared to believe they did. Now behind Rustam and his captor came his captor's partner, led by what I could only assume was a drug-sniffing dog. The dog was a flop-eared spanielish mongrel, brown and slightly larger than a fox, with huge eyes that seemed somehow concerned with being misunderstood. For mysterious reasons it was sopping wet. After the dog was unhooked, all of us—even the officers fingering the Nexia's hubcaps for deposits of scag—burst into laughter. With his foot the SNB agent nudged the dog toward our bags. It stuck its nose into them to no effect.

"Why do they think we're drug dealers?" I asked Rustam.

"I don't know."

"Are you worried?"

He said nothing.

"Rustam."

"Yeah, dude. I am."

I nodded, watching as the agent lifted the spare tire from the Nexia's trunk, reached into the wheel well, and with horribly slit eyes and a triumphant sneer whisked out of it a clear plastic bag filled with white powder. Rustam emitted a low, sustained groan of either misery or denial. He covered his eyes with the butts of his palms. I could not speak as the SNB agent demanded to know what was in the bag. My mind was a bicycle that had shed its chain. The pedals worked but motion was impossible. The thought I was stuck on was this: Denis was a drug trafficker. Denis was a heroin smuggler moonlighting as a chauffeur. Denis was running smack across Uzbekistan while hiring himself out as a driver. A new thought: The penalty for heroin smuggling in Uzbekistan was death. Another: We are in trouble, more trouble than seemed imaginable, more trouble than I or anyone I knew had ever been in. Another, less a thought than a realization: Prone, handcuffed Denis was crying out *"Eto mel!"* over and over. *Eto* meant, roughly, "it is." *Mel,* I thought. I taught in a Russian-language school. I knew this word, too.

"Chalk," Rustam said in English. Then, pointing, in Russian, joining Denis: *"Eto mel! Eto mel!"*

I, joining them: *"Eto mel! Eto* freaking *mel!"*

With unmistakable consternation the agent held the bag out for the little dog. The dog sniffed it and looked away, its mind, unignited by drugs, concerned with other things—for instance, its own scrotum. After a long, tense moment some of the officers began to laugh again. The agent did not. He petted the dog now with the demented tenderness of a man deciding whether or not to strangle it. The officer who had struck Denis knelt next to him and asked, not unreasonably, why he had a bag of white chalk in his trunk. Denis, Rustam translated for me, was explaining that he kept a clear bag of chalk in the trunk of his Nexia in the event that he needed to change a tire in a rainstorm. The chalk, Denis said, kept his hands dry. It was the unlikeliest, least believable excuse in the long, sad history of excuses. But it was a large messy plastic bag, not even sealed, utterly unlike the dope-crammed Ziploc some smuggler might wall up behind a fake suitcase backing or hide beneath a spare tire. The bag's label, moreover, read CHALK. Denis—it took me several moments to accept this—*was not lying.* It *was* chalk, and we were not in any trouble at all. But the SNB agent was not finished with us. He moved in on me and spoke quietly, breast to breast, his revolting pinkeye close enough to allow me to make out within it several sickly yellow swirls. "Your driver is a criminal," he said unoriginally.

Rustam interrupted, asking the agent to have a look at the copy of *Men's Journal* he was holding in his hands, freshly liberated from several tobacco-chewing officers who had been enjoying its pictures of Heidi Klum. "This is a rich and famous American magazine," Rustam said, holding the issue up with one hand and quickly whipping through its thin pages with the other. The agent managed an unimpressed sniffle. Rustam flipped back to the contributor's page and pointed to my picture. "Tom Bissell." He pointed at me. "Tom Bissell." He looked at the SNB agent. "Tom Bissell works for this rich and famous American magazine. He is writing about Uzbekistan."

"Good for him," the agent said.

Rustam persisted. "He is writing many things about Uzbekistan. He will be writing about everything that happens to him here."

The agent asked for the magazine and had a long look at its pages. He did not seem upset or intimidated or worried. His expression was hard and clean and professionally subdued. But I knew I was no longer a helpless American mark to be batted from one paw to another. Now I was a bother of considerable potential. This agent did not wish to be bothered. His job did not work that way. For him all bother was one-way. Chains of command here were tightly dammed at each link, and the custodian of each link regarded whatever flowed up to him from below as the worst sort of cess. This agent now had two choices. Process me and risk future reprimand, or abandon me. With a polite nod the agent passed the magazine back to Rustam. His chin lifted and, planing the air with his right hand, he said to the officers, *"Buldi."* In Uzbek *buldi* means something akin to "finished." Denis's handcuffs were undone and with an ornery smile he got to his feet and attempted to brush clean his hopelessly filthy pants. The SNB agent was already walking back across the highway to the gleaming substation, the dog's short legs firing to keep pace with him. A few officers helped Rustam and me pack up our bags and replace the spare tire and seat cushioning. When finished, they left us with brisk salutes. Rustam, Denis, and I now stood alone on the shoulder. We looked at one another, at the desert around us, and clambered like circus clowns into the Nexia. As we sped away, Denis cranked Depeche Mode's "Walking in My Shoes." I sat in the back seat, giddy, laughing, massaging my temples, talking to myself and to Denis, both of us gesturing and speaking our native language, neither of us caring. Rustam was next to me, uncharacteristically speechless.

"You okay?" I asked after his silence had become discomforting.

He shook his head. "I have feelings sometimes," he said. "Something awful has happened."

"I know. That was pretty bad. But we're okay. It's over."

"Not back there. I mean at home. In Ferghana. I am worried I'll have to go as soon as we reach Bukhara. Perhaps it has not happened yet."

To Rustam's beliefs about bone marrow, female sterility, and Soviet magnificence, I could now append precognition. I nodded at him credulously, but he could see the doubt in my eyes.

"I know you don't believe me, bro. But I have a weird skull. Right now it's filled by the most terrible thoughts."

"Is your friend okay?" Rick asked, squinting at me through the last pinkish flare of dusk. "What's his name again? Razzaq?"

"Rustam. I think he's all right." I shrugged. "Hard day."

Minutes ago I had recounted our highway adventure for Rick. In return, he had told me that last week two Danish tourists had been seized with several bags of heroin, which went some way in providing an explanation for that adventure. Rick looked aside and pulled down the bill of his snug tan baseball cap. "Yeah," he said, nodding. "I can imagine."

I had met Rick briefly at the Peace Corps office in Tashkent. When I mentioned that my travels might take me to Bukhara, he immediately offered me a place to stay and gave me his card. At the time of our initial meeting Rick had been wearing an immense ginger Sufi-style beard. In the intervening days he had scraped his infidel face clean, and his chin seemed vulnerable and pale, his cheeks lotion-soft. He was in his late twenties and wore small, round glasses. His fine brown hair—glimpsed when he lifted his cap to wipe his forehead of sweat—looked as though it could have begun to thin as recently as last week. Rick was a graduate of West Point. He taught business development, while his wife, Janet, taught English in one of Bukhara's universities. When I had opined that Rick must have been the first West Point alumnus in history to enroll in the United States Peace Corps, he only smiled. We stood outside a Bukharan *pochta* (post office), which like *pochta*s throughout much of the former Soviet Union handled not only mail but outgoing intra- and international phone calls, no doubt functioning for the KGB as a kind of one-stop surveillance center. Rustam was inside calling his mother.

"I'd be feeling a little rattled myself if I were him," Rick told me now. "I think as PCVs we're shielded from a lot of everyday intimidation here. You know what it's like. Most PCVs are kids just out of college. They think Uzbekistan is a big party. The repression that goes on here doesn't even penetrate except in the most academic sense. They know it exists. But they don't *know*. When the militsiya looks at your Peace Corps kar-

tochka, you feel like a diplomat. Just waved right along. I'm glad I have it. You've got . . . what? One of the little green accreditation cards from the Ministry of Foreign Affairs?"

I nodded and handed it to him. "Its efficacy has so far been underwhelming. Sometimes I feel as though I might as well be handing them a baseball card."

Rick glanced at my accreditation, then passed it back. "You'll like Bukhara. This is the only city in the country the cops don't basically hold hostage. The clergy has a lot of sway in Bukhara. More, at least, than anywhere else. Luckily, most of those guys are fairly moderate. I've met a lot of them, and I know that this could change. But for now it's pretty great."

And so it was. All around us shadows lengthened and faded and disappeared on Bukhara's distinctive buildings, none higher than two or three stories and all made of swiss-colored baked mud or stone. The alleys between them were often no wider than an arm span, the rooftops so close, it had been said, that one could sprint across the city without once dirtying one's soles on its streets. On its sunward side the Old City glowed an impossibly vivid orange, while its lee side seemed dipped in plum-colored darkness. The mulberry trees glowed so brightly their leaves seemed gilded in fresh magma. Bukhara's Old City was no less than a living, functioning sanctuary of preserved medieval architecture. Rick lived near its center, and thousands more lived all around us. Many of these buildings had been wired for electricity only since the 1960s and upwards of two hundred were protected by surprisingly tough laws. But for a few Kodak signs and parked cars, Bukhara was blessed with one of the least noticeably altered city centers of all the surviving urban pillars of the medieval Muslim world. Neither Baghdad nor Herat nor Samarkand nor Mecca itself could claim as little intrusion. Especially Mecca, so much of it ruined and kitschified, non-Arab Muslims often complained, by a tasteless well-known Saudi construction family known as bin Laden.

Bukhara played a significant role not merely in Uzbekistan but within all Central Asia. It was, perhaps, the region's finest city. Tashkent belonged to the world, Samarkand lived too complacently off its past, Khiva went to sleep at eight, Almaty was run by gangsters, Bishkek was a glorified village, Ashkabat was a political Jonestown, Dushanbe was a series of checkpoints, Kabul was a shooting gallery, and Mazar-i-Sharif was sealed. But Bukhara was a great city. It had not always been an especially kind city, and its name (alternately said to come from *vihara*, a Sanskrit word that means "monastery," or *bukhar*, a Farsi word that means "source of knowledge") was for centuries enough to cause nervous Western travelers to mess their saddles. Bukhara, along with Khiva, was the boomtown of the region's slave trade. The city was also—though not always—famous for its fanaticism. Isolation is the nursery of fanaticism, and in few places had fanaticism been suckled on such poisonous milk. There were several explanations for this. Except for the Samanid period in the tenth century (a time when Bukhara was actually more populous than today) the city had not served as capital to any significant kingdom until the sixteenth century. Until that point Bukhara had in most territorial hierarchies played the role of a remote and exotic desert mistress: admired, even loved, but grudgingly subsidized and easily ignored.

Bukhara was thought to be between two thousand and three thousand years old. When the hurricane of Islam first moved east, prompt and attentive tributes paid in Bukharan gold managed for decades to hold Arab jihadists at bay. In the early 700s the sons of Mohammed finally took the city. Bukhara's wealthiest families escaped to Afghanistan rather than stomach Arab rule, which turned out to have been a wise decision. Neighborhoods were emptied and Zoroastrian temples mercilessly Islamicized. An Arab soldier was stationed within every Bukharan household to make sure the fire-worshiping pagans were obeying proper Islamic ritual—a useful reminder of the cyclical nature of oppression. These Gestapo tactics successfully wore down the fierce mental nubs of Bukharans' resistance, and the city quickly gained a reputation as one of the Arab-ruled world's holiest cities—the Cupola of Islam itself, where, according to the angel Gibreel, the light did not shine down but up. Two hundred years later the Samanids cunningly slipped Bukhara out from under Arabia's thumb and steered the city toward its cultural and historical apogee, of which the medical texts of ibn Sina and the encyclopedia of al-Beruni are immodest relics.

After the Mongols devastated Bukhara in the thirteenth century, various Jenghiz-come-latelies arrived and attempted some semblance of revival. It says something about Bukhara's toughness that, between its annihilation by the Mongols in 1220 and the Persians in 1360, Marco

Polo and his brother passed through to find it "a great and noble city." The Timurids, Bukhara's next rulers, generally left Bukhara alone but to construct a few prototype mosques they planned to build more grandly in Samarkand. When the Uzbek Shaybani Khan, founder of the Shaybanid dynasty, strode into Bukhara in 1500 and murdered its ruler, Ali, one of Timur's final descendants to wield power in modern-day Uzbekistan, decades of municipal chaos came to end. (The literal last Timurid, Babur, fled into India to establish the Mogul dynasty.) This moment of brutal consolidation launched the golden age of the Uzbek empire.

Like Timur, Shaybani Khan fancied himself a great builder and urban sophisticate, writing poetry and "improving" various masterpieces of Arabic calligraphy in his own hand. Unlike Timur, however, he was no maniacal annihilator, and beneath his short reign Bukhara's culture regained some of its former luster. His eventual successor, Ubaidullah Khan, used Bukhara to advance further the idea of the perfect Islamic city-state, overseeing the construction of some its most lasting religious buildings. But this clannish Uzbek empire ultimately fractured into competitive princedoms no longer united by any imperial fraternity. Not a few of these clans' dynastic lines were wiped out by their own members due to fears of fratricide.

During this period Europe was seeing the last remnants of its various city-states stagger to an end; in Central Asia this nationalizing process weirdly reversed. In the early 1700s Khiva plundered Bukhara, and Bukhara and Samarkand went to devastating war. At one point Bukhara had only enough citizens left to fill two residential neighborhoods, and the Shaybanids fled to survive as the rulers of a minor oasis khanate near the Aral Sea. By the mid-1700s the Persian conqueror Nadir Shah, the reputed splitter of Timur's jade tombstone, had captured Khiva and Bukhara. Nadir Shah's marionette rulers were eventually deposed, but the violent confusion of the previous two centuries had resulted in the collapse of the system of legitimacy previously shown to descendants of Jenghiz Khan.

In 1750 Bukhara fell prey to the Mangits, an Uzbek clan who were among the first violators of the long-standing cultural bylaw that forbade the use of "Khan" for all but Jenghiz's direct heirs. With the Mangits the old chaos returned to Bukhara, though it had a different, more intimately concentrated flavor. This was chaos of the civic soul, a fanaticism gained of merely local ambition, and Bukhara shriveled into what the traveler Arminius Vambery in 1868 called "the most shameless sink of iniquity that I know in the East" and later lambasted as being "crippled by boundless hypocrisy, crass ignorance, and unscrupulous tyranny." Bukhara's Mangit masters were slavers and religious charlatans. For generations they bullied Bukhara's people into puddles of quivering superstition. A visiting Russian diplomat once cabled back to St. Petersburg that Bukhara's famed falcons "were extraordinarily well-trained, the best-educated beings in all of Bukhara, humans not excepted." When Russian surveyors laid tracks to the Trans-Caspian Railway outside the city in the 1860s, Bukharans demanded that this "devil wagon" not pass within ten miles of their city. Until well into the twentieth century the Evil Eye was considered in Bukhara a coherent pretext for personal downfall.

Today I could see little that suggested Bukhara's famed black-velvet backdrop of superstition and cruelty. The faces passing me here were darker, more dramatically Asian, but they were many of them smiling. The young people looked like young people everywhere in Uzbekistan: jeans, primped hair, polished shoes. But seemingly every old man wore traditional clothing: black skullcaps, striped robes with thick cloth belts, and knee-high rubber boots. Most of the women wore thick, makeup-enjoined black eyebrows that ran straight across their brow, one of Bukhara's signature affects of high style. (This was an improvement over previous Bukharan fads. In the 1800s women blackened their teeth.) Several men walked over and shook Rick's and my hand, speaking in loud jubilant Tajik and thanking Allah we were here, together, on this beautiful evening.

Rustam's head poked around the jamb of the *pochta*'s front door. *"Dude,"* he said, waving me in. Inside the *pochta* the wooden floor was lumpy and flood-warped. Walking upon its planks seemed to set off chain reactions in the powder-blue walls at the other side of the room. The ceiling was low, its corners grayish with thick, straggly cobwebs. A bank of primitive wooden phone booths crowded one wall. To these Rustam now ushered me. The glass-paneled door of booth twelve was open, the booth was itself lit, and the receiver had been left upon a small in-booth ledge. Rustam pulled me inside, the door's glass window rattling fragilely as its catch clicked shut.

He picked up the receiver. "Dude, this is my mom."

"Is she okay?"

"She's okay."

"What happened?"

"Nothing. But we are having some family problems now and I need to get home."

"To Namangan? Now?"

"To Ferghana City. Now."

"I thought you were from Namangan?"

"Bro, it's a long story." He closed his eyes and took a steadying breath. "I hate to ask you this. But I have to ask you now if you would buy me a plane ticket to Ferghana."

"Rustam, Jesus. Of course I will. We'll go buy tickets right away. We'll leave as soon as possible."

Rustam thanked me, shifted the receiver to his mouth, and told his mother he was on his way. He hung up and looked at me with a somehow older expression. "Thanks, bro."

"Everything's okay?"

"Everything's okay. There exist now . . . problems for me."

I considered him as he stared at the booth's cheap rubber floor. The ease with which his careworn forehead crumpled told me that this expression was for him a common one. "These aren't new problems, are they?"

He shook his head and smoothed his fingers over his mustache. He coughed a small, quick breath through his nose. "Not so much."

"Would you tell me about it?"

The booth's phone rang with alarm-clock harshness. "I booked another call," Rustam explained before snatching the heavy black receiver from its cradle. The call he had booked was to my hosts Oleg and Natasha in Tashkent, who were very upset not to have heard from us sooner. Rustam explained where we were, and that tomorrow we were flying back to Tashkent and from Tashkent to Ferghana City. At this I heard Oleg's voice undergo a kind of vocal chord change. Rustam looked at me. "Oleg needs to go to Ferghana as well."

"He does."

"His friend . . ." For some reason he covered the receiver. "Dude, Oleg is telling me that his friend *died*."

"God."

"There is a funeral, Oleg says. In Ferghana. He needs to go but he doesn't have any money."

I fell back against the booth's flimsy posterboard wall. I thought. I thought nothing in particular. I simply thought.

After five seconds Rustam prompted me, pointing at the phone. "Bro."

"I need you to tell me the truth. Is he bullshitting me?"

"I don't think so. This man who died—I know him. I knew him. He was, like, a famous mountain climber in Ferghana."

"A famous mountain climber?"

"In Ferghana. Actually, Oleg's a mountain climber, too. You didn't know that?"

My hand lifted not so much to keep him from going on but to slow my own stumbling mind. "Just tell Oleg that if he looks under my bed he'll find an envelope with five hundred dollars in it. Tell him to take whatever he needs to buy a plane ticket. Tell him we'll meet him in Ferghana."

A cab ride out of the Old City into Bukhara's Soviet suburbs was all that it took to shake one's mind free of daydreams about what Bukhara must have once been like, its packed streets of camel-riding nobles and wandering Muslim jongleurs and exhausted caravans and dignitaries arriving to the sound of royal drums. Now all that lay around us was negligible stimulation of Soviet architecture, the gray-white houses falling apart, the gates rusty, the telephone poles rotting out of their bores. "Most of Bukhara's other volunteers live out here in the 'burbs," Rick said, somberly looking around before suddenly smiling. "Poor devils."

The Uzbekistan Airways ticket office was one of several small offices housed within a long strip of outlets and businesses in one of many anonymous sections of suburban Bukhara. We managed to convince the two sweet, overweight middle-aged Uzbek women closing up shop to sell two more tickets for the next available flight out of Bukhara, which left at 8 A.M. the day after tomorrow. My ticket came to $70. This was the foreigner's rate. Rustam's came to the local rate: $12. After my most recent currency exchange all I had that could cover the tickets was a hundred-dollar bill. The only change the receptionist had was a fifty. "No problem," I told her, sliding the tickets toward myself. "Keep the change." I spoke in a thudding literalism ("Keep the remains"), as there was no Uzbek idiom I knew of that resembled our phrase. For several moments their drained brown eyes simply stared at me. They blinked, then, and laughed, and thanked me, and thanked me. As we were leaving, Rick figured that I had likely just doubled their monthly salaries.

Rick wanted to walk us through a bit more of the Old City on our way home and had the cab drop us off near a strange building dating from the early 1800s called Chor Minor ("Four Minarets"), though, as in Samarkand's Registan, its minarets were never used for the call to prayer. Chor Minor was one of the Old City's more recent constructions, the library gateway to a vanished mosque. Today it was a colorless, run-down building that strongly resembled an upside-down footstool. "Actually," Rick explained, "it's looking better than it has in about fifty years. About the only use it had during Soviet times was as a stork nest." In 1995 one of its minarets collapsed, though by that time its storks had long since absconded. Three years later the United Nations Educational, Scientific, and Cultural Organization (UNESCO) rebuilt the minaret and strengthened Chor Minor's water-damaged foundation. But the quiet rot allowed so long to afflict Chor Minor was indicative of the basic Soviet approach to Bukhara, one of the rare places in Central Asia where the harsh processes of ideological refurbishment were largely stayed. What, after all, was the more effective insult: taking a bulldozer to Bukhara's mosques and madrasas (and risking an uprising) or allowing the super-annuated Old City's holiest sites to fall disgracefully apart?

It was dark. While walking with Rick through the Old City's maze of homes and small ad hoc mosques—these had the gates with padlocks on them—I saw a few limp signs of modernization. For every fifty windows we passed beneath, we looked up to see the rumbling stern of an old air conditioner. The twisty alleys, filled with mouthy Bukharan schoolboys and deep shadows, saw an occasional car rumble through, the gravel popping beneath the tires. I walked slowly, loitering at intersections, gazing down each street and watching low-talking Tajik men make their deals in the darkness, old women coming home from the market, an occasional goat waiting for someone to lead it back to its stable. I rushed to catch up with Rick and Rustam. Bukhara, I concluded quickly, would be no place to deliver a pizza. *Take the fifth alley on the left, then walk down to the dead end and muscle through the second crack in the wall on the right. Go straight. You'll come to another crack, but don't go through it. Go up the stairs right after the mouth of the third alley, turn around, walk through the second collapsed building you see, and it's the third numberless gate on your right.*

The Old City gaped unexpectedly open when we came to one of its major arteries. This street was spacious and quiet, the surrounding homes' windows lit with a glow the same color as that of the night's small orange moon. Rick lived around the corner from Bukhara's famous *choikhana* Lyab-i-Hauz, and the air was suddenly dosed with the sharp, medicinal smell of what I guessed was overly chlorinated water. *Hauz,* in Tajik, means "pool," but the word had a much deeper denotation. In the Muslim world, so much of it desert-bracketed, the urban water pool was often given shrinelike significance. Lyab-i-Hauz's pool was, and remained, Bukhara's largest and prettiest. The city once had a hundred of these tree-lined, canal-fed pools, used by all of Bukhara, from its amir to its peasants, as reservoirs for drinking and washing. Today only two pools survived, the rest having been bricked over by the Soviets to solve one of water-poor Bukhara's most intractable problems: disease. Anthony Jenkinson, Central Asia's first English visitor, wrote in 1559 of Bukhara's "most unwholesome" water, and of a tapeworm "which commonly lieth in the legge betwixt the flesh and skinne, and is pluck out about the ancle with great art and cunning." If one did not draw out this fearsomely lengthy worm with great art and cunning, it broke into pieces, each of which would later push out of the victim's skinne amid much paine and agonee. Skin diseases of one stripe or another—"Bukharan boil," "Sartian sickness"—afflicted virtually the entire populace. Alexander Burnes's *Travels into Bokhara,* published in 1834, tells us that any Bukharan who happened upon a leper had permission to kill the unfortunate creature. These plagues were not completely contained until the late 1960s, when Sharaf Rashidov's government dammed off a part of the Amu Darya River for Bukhara's benefit, then drained and refilled its two extant pools (and reportedly found any number of dog carcasses decomposing at the bottom of both). Bukharans rejoiced, and the Aral Sea slid a little more quickly toward death.

The darkness around Lyab-i-Hauz suddenly released a nativity of Westerners—man, woman, and child—enjoying their own moonlit stroll through Bukhara. They walked directly toward us. The man's arm was draped around his wife's shoulder while their daughter skipped around them in wistful figure eights. It took me a few moments to realize that the

man was Ian Small, from the Tashkent office of Médicins Sans Frontières, with whom I was at some point supposed to rendezvous in Moynaq. As Small's and my eyes caught, he stopped. We stood looking at
each other in the middle of the street, as though frozen in some gunsling-
ing preamble.

"Hey, stranger," Small finally said, grinning. "What brings you to
lovely Bukhara? I'm on vacation, so I have an excuse. Aren't you working?"

"Only theoretically," I said.

Introductions were proffered, hands shaken. Small's wife, Michele,
was lovely and blond and somehow obviously French, while his daughter,
Lola, was a small, thin girl with suspicious, intelligent eyes and bee-stung
lips. Small's mood was high. His sleekly collared lime-green shirt was
unbuttoned to the terminus of his breastbone and his mussed brown hair
had in the streetlight a dark oaken texture.

"I'm going to Moynaq next week," he said.

"In three days," Michele corrected.

"Damn. Three days." His eyebrows popped up, lifting his whole face.
"I must be having a good time, eh?"

"I can be in Moynaq whenever," I said.

"Just call ahead to Tashkent and let them know when you're coming." He paused. "You're going to love Karakalpakistan, you know. It's a
wonderful place."

When I lived in Gulistan, Karakalpakistan and the Aral Sea were
known simply as "the West"—a place, it was understood, of mythic, limitless sorrow. Since then I had done my own reading, most of which
claimed that Karakalpakistan was one of the worst places in the world,
its death throes irreversible. Even the hardier guidebooks warned travelers off the region. "Drab, impoverished, unhealthy, and forlorn," according to one. But in the months leading up to this trip, I had heard of a very
different country, a Karakalpakistan that Peace Corps acquaintances
who were stationed there described to me as one of the greatest places—
and certainly the most astounding—they had ever seen.

"Not nicer than Bukhara," I said.

Small looked around. "No. It's just different."

We said goodbye, and Small and his family started away. After a few
steps he turned around. "Have you ever heard about the five-step Soviet
strategy for dealing with crises?"

"I'm not sure," I said. "Maybe."

"It's rather famous. Step One is to make the crisis worse. Step Two is to blame the Jews. Step Three is to punish the innocent. Stop me if you've heard this. Step Four is to hand out medals to government leaders. And Step Five is—"

"Recognize the problem," I said.

"Right. There's no Soviet Union anymore, but we're currently at Step Five. And now you're a part of helping people work toward that recognition. Don't forget that."

Rick and his wife Janet's host mother, Nadira, served us a small mountain of plov, which we ate in the lovely flowered courtyard of her small, equally lovely home. Plov was Uzbekistan's national dish, and one could expect to eat one's weight in it while traveling around the country. Plov, from which our word "pilaf" derives, is a breast-shaped pile of greasy orange rice topped with a few fatty pieces of mutton and leeks, most often served communally. The various regions of Uzbekistan all have their distinct versions of plov and all claim to make the finest, an issue of fistfighting intensity. Some regions include in their plov raisins, some carrot shavings, some pistachios, and some bits of quince; some go heavier on the mutton, some heavier on the leeks; some go for a more delicate taste, and some make sure each grain of rice is soaked through with cottonseed oil. Nadira's plov was oily no-frills plov, illogically delicious. It was pleasing, too, for once, to have the cook actually eat with us rather than remain hidden away in her kitchen. Nadira was in her late forties, with long gray-black hair and a face with features so sharply disproportionate it seemed, in the manner of Japanese animation, a caricature of a beautiful face. She was eating with us not because she had the understanding husband she deserved. She was eating with us because she no longer had a husband. A few years ago, Rick had explained, she managed the rare feat of divorcing her husband, a drunken wife-beater. To be a woman in a Muslim culture was, too often, to be a saint. Those who endured the constant oppression were saints of asceticism. Those who stood up to it were saints of courage. But there seemed only two fates available to the woman saint: death or the everlasting chastity of solitude.

While we ate, a nearby ghetto blaster belonging to Nadira's teenage son, Makhsud, played Eminem's "The Real Slim Shady":

"Will Smith don't gotta cuss in his raps to sell records."
Well I do. So fuck him and fuck you too.
You think I give a damn about a Grammy?
Half of you critics can't even stomach me,
Let alone stand me.

"Such words!" Nadira's twenty-two-year-old daughter Gulnora said. Gulnora spoke fine if slightly stiff English. Makhsud, a small, weirdly buff fifteen-year-old (I was sitting on his weight bench), spoke enough English to look down at his plate and smile impishly.

"Nadira loves Eminem," Janet said, laughing. She was a blond, studious-looking woman in her late twenties to whom the Bukharan sun had not been kind. Her face was unevenly red and her nose slightly peeling. "What can we say? She says she loves the music. The beat. Sometimes I come home from school and I find her bouncing around the house to Eminem."

Nadira, who spoke no English, somehow seemed to understand what was being said. With her fingers she pressed down a ball of plov into a tidy patty and popped it into her mouth. She shrugged.

Makhsud, his head bobbing, rapped, " 'Will the real Slim Shady please stand up, please stand up, please stand up?' " Rick lined up a piece of rice on the table and after much theatrical calibration flicked it at Makhsud. The projectile went sailing past his ear. Nadira laughed.

I was in the middle of Bukhara's Old City, listening to rap music, having dinner with the least traditional and happiest-seeming Uzbek family I had ever encountered. Even Rustam seemed cheered up by them. I reminded myself that, somewhere in this city, marriages were being arranged, dowries secured, animals ritualistically slaughtered.

"How was work today?" Janet asked Gulnora.

Gulnora rolled her eyes. She was a big, heavy-shouldered girl who in America might have been called corn-fed. She had obviously inherited her father's features. Her wide, flat face, though still quite pretty, shone in a way that was almost distracting. She smiled tightly, still pained by the memory of her day. "Work," she said, significantly. "Work was . . .

work. We had two very large tour groups come through today. From Germany and France."

"They must be following us," I said. "We saw them in Samarkand."

"I am led to believe," Gulnora said, "that our hotel disappointed them compared to their hotel in Samarkand. So work was not so well."

Rustam and I tried to help Nadira with the dishes. She would not have it and forced us to sit outside and drink tea. We watched while Rick held his palms up as targets for Makhsud's hard, quick jabs, evidently a nightly ritual. Only after Makhsud had been called inside for bed did Rick grimace fondly and cool his swollen hands by waving them as though he were drying freshly polished fingernails. "That kid is *strong*."

"You must be really happy here," I said.

"We love it," Janet said, kissing Rick good night on the cheek. She had school in the morning.

When she was gone, Rick looked up at the sky. I did, too. It was streaked with a low smoky layer of cloud, the stars burning through the gauze in pinpoints of bright white light. This was unquestionably the nicest thing about Uzbek homes. One could be home, literally *at* home, and still see the sky. "She's right," Rick said finally. "We do love it here. I could stay in Bukhara for a while, I think." Rick gave us a key to the front gate before turning in, and Rustam and I were left alone in the courtyard. I reclined on Makhsud's weight bench, briefly tempted to press the barbell left across it. I decided I did not want to humiliate myself. Rustam sat upon a wooden chair and ran his hand along the graying head of the elderly family dog, its eyes silvery with some age-borne lens disorder.

"Weird day," I said.

He laughed. "I think every day is weird with you, dude."

I sat up. "I'm sorry about that. What you had to go through today."

"Yeah. Well."

"Were you afraid?"

He laughed again. "Fuck, bro. I don't know what I was." He paused. "Are you tired?"

"Not particularly."

"You wanna maybe go for a walk?"

It was a few minutes past 10 P.M., and the streets were even emptier than they had been before. We walked mostly in a circle, not wanting to get lost among the Old City's unpredictable corners. Eventually, I asked Rustam what was going on back home.

"Oh, you know," he said. "Just problems. My mother needs some money right now. It's a hard time for her. She's sick and her medicine is expensive. So I have to help her."

"What about your dad?"

"He's . . . not able to help right now."

"Are your parents still together?"

He looked at me. "What do you mean?"

"Are they divorced?"

"No, dude. Nothing like that. My dad has some problems, too. It's just a bad time."

"You have a sister, right? What does she do?"

"She lives at home. She goes to school. She doesn't have any money."

"No brothers."

"No. No brothers. Just the four of us. Weird for an Uzbek family, huh? We were real Soviets!"

We passed a storefront, where a young boy no older than thirteen smoked a cigarette in the doorway. "Look," I said, "I don't mean to pry, but do you need me to help? I have some money I could—"

"No way, bro. Don't worry. It's under . . . my control?"

"Under control. No 'my.'"

"It's totally under control. You've already given me a lot. I feel bad enough to ask you for the plane ticket."

"I would just hate it if all the money you're making—" I stopped and shook my head. "Forget it. This is none of my business."

Two possibly drunk men walked past, muttering and throwing looks of uncertain consequence our way. I felt my psychic armor harden and fade as they passed. I was not terribly worried about crime in Bukhara, even though the city had recently suffered a murder case so bizarre it made headlines throughout the former Soviet Union. Olima Karaeva was a well-known forty-one-year-old Bukharan entrepreneur who, in August 2000, launched her own private overseas-employment service. Karaeva, not surprisingly, was bombarded with applications, receiving almost two thousand in four months. In late November the Aripov family—whose six members included three children aged two, seven, and eight—were informed by Karaeva that their application to work in Canada had been accepted. Karaeva then told the Aripovs that before they could depart they had to undergo a two-week quarantine. The grateful Aripovs agreed, even though it meant being locked up in an apartment by

Karaeva, forbidden any visitors, given numerous injections, and fed six kilos of lemons a day. Karaeva soon told the Aripovs' relatives that all six of them had reached Canada and found good jobs, though she apologized that they had been forced to leave Bukhara so quickly, without being able to say goodbye. Days later, Karaeva's twenty-three-year-old son, Jeikhun, discovered in his family's basement refrigerator what was described in the Uzbek press as "a huge amount of meat." Karaeva told him it was pork. Karaeva's thirteen-year-old daughter would later tell the police that Karaeva had been feeding her family quite a lot of pork lately. Jeikhun had reason to doubt his mother's story when he found some bloody clothing and (to quote, once more, the Uzbek press) "a large metal bowl in the basement with a male haunch in it." On December 21, Karaeva heeded her son's advice and dumped the Aripovs' skulls and limbs in two city dumpsters. Within days the police tracked the remains back to her. During her arraignment Karaeva confessed to butchering the Aripovs, whom she claimed had owed her $4,800. "I got mad," she explained, "and decided to kill them all." The police, who did not wish to harm Bukhara's tourist industry, accepted Karaeva's story. In doing so they overlooked various details—the lemon-feeding, a volume entitled *Cannibals* found among Karaeva's books, several bottles filled with pickled human flesh—that suggested something much larger and more sinister afoot. Seventeen passports were eventually recovered from Karaeva's home, though the police assured the press that the holder of each passport had been located and verified as alive. But other Bukharans came forward to say they had friends who had gone overseas to work and had never been heard from again. Others yet claimed to have bought or been given large quantities of meat by Karaeva. A few Uzbek journalists, writing anonymously for Web-based publications beyond the reach of government censors, wrote of their belief that Bukhara's police had uncovered merely one cell of a complicated organ-smuggling operation (used by Karaeva, it seemed, to indulge her taste in human flesh) with connections to Bukhara's mafiya and, naturally, various members of its city government. Rustam did not believe that, of course, though he did admit to finding the whole thing "fucked up." He also admitted to me that the story had made him inexplicably afraid of lemons. I tried not to laugh, but I did. Then he laughed as well. Lemons. Pork. Male haunches in metal bowls. It was either laugh or sit down and weep for humanity, as embodied by six honest people who were slaughtered for wanting something so unreasonable as a better life.

Our morning began as all mornings in Bukhara must, or should: drinking tea beneath the trees in the shady beauty of Lyab-i-Hauz while two ancient Uzbek raconteurs named Alisher and Alisher described life in the Old City in the 1930s and '40s and '50s and '60s and '70s and '80s and '90s. Both wore black doppa skullcaps and white open-collar dress shirts and gray slacks. They were lifelong Bukharans, they told us proudly, and had been friends for fifty years. They were retired now, living off small pensions. Alisher One had worked in construction; Alisher Two was a schoolteacher. Every morning they had tea at Lyab-i-Hauz and played backgammon until noon, at which time they would go home, have lunch, and return to Lyab-i-Hauz to play backgammon until five.

The Alishers offered opinions that stood eccentrically at odds with their own, other opinions. The Soviet Union had been great! But how glad they were the Soviets were gone. Mosques were reopening in Bukhara daily! But what trouble those Muslims caused. I wanted to hear more about Bukhara's history, I said. Their eyes came youthfully alive. History! How about the 1930s? *These* were the most exciting years to be alive, they maintained. Bukhara was the center of the world! Everything was changing, and the future of the city and the Union of Soviet Socialist Republics seemed unlimited. But did not Bukhara's population fall by half in the years following the Bolshevik Revolution? Nonsense, they said. Everyone had a job, everyone was happy. "Don't believe everything you read in books," Alisher One told me. "You weren't alive then. It was a great time."

My small but supple Uzbek vocabulary had been outstripped by our subject matter. I turned to Rustam. "What about the purges?" I asked him to ask them. Faizullah ("You cannot eat cotton") Khojaev, born and raised in Bukhara, was worth mentioning here. The highborn, matinee-idol-handsome Khojaev had for several years agitated against Bukhara's firmly lodged amir on behalf of the Soviets, whose venture socialism failed to take Bukhara in the immediate aftermath of the Bolshevik Revolution. The twenty-member Bolshevik contingent that embarked to

Bukhara in 1918 on Khojaev's invitation was wiped out on arrival by the amir's army. (The forces of Russia's tsar had never technically conquered Bukhara, the clergy of which launched a jihad against the Russian Empire. An 1868 treaty, agreed to after a series of military defeats outside the city, made Bukhara an independent khanate under Russian protection.) Khojaev's political group, the Young Bukharan Party, was a strange fusion of Communism and reform-minded Islam heavily influenced by the Jadids, a pan-Turkic movement that sought to unite the world's Turks under a system of government friendly toward Europe but proud of its Islamic heritage and, most of all, dedicated to a system of education that stressed the hard sciences and nonideological history. As intellectual pacifists, the Young Bukharans opposed the viciously arbitrary rule of Bukhara's amir. They hoped that the Soviet regime, despite its violent rootstock, would, as Lenin had promised, give them the freedom for which they had been struggling. "Here in the conditions of Turkestan," wrote Mannan Ramiz, an early Jadid and, later, a leading Uzbek Communist, "there is no need for a communism like the communism in Russia that denies religion. Instead, we must create a communism that is completely compatible with the Islamic religion." Before Bukhara finally fell, the still-unsteady Soviet regime lost more than two dozen spies to the amir's secret police while encouraging the Young Bukharans to rally the sympathies of the city faithful under the unlikely oriflamme of Islamic Communism. The Young Bukharans were consequently despised by many of their fellow Muslims as godless Russian quislings. (They were not.) After its surrender to the Soviets in 1920, Bukhara was allowed a period of semiautonomy during which a few well-placed Russian agents kept local watch and amassed thick damning files on prominent Young Bukharans, Jadids, and Muslim Communists. In 1922 the Soviet secret police, then called the Cheka, pounced. Roughly 15,000 Bukharans were tried and either executed or exiled for being "Turkish spies." (They were not.) By 1924, the year the Republic of Bukhara was formally absorbed by the Uzbek Soviet Socialist Republic, Bukhara's Communist Party had been liquidated nearly out of existence; only 1,000 remained, Khojaev among them. He was soon named commisar chairman of the Uzbek Republic and survived fourteen years of Twilight Zone Stalinism only to be executed during the Great Terror. These were the salad days my new friends had claimed as Bukhara's finest.

At Rustam's translated mention of the purges the two Alishers grew silent. Small vigorous nods lifted their lowered heads. "Yes," they agreed, "it was a terrible time."

We were interrupted by the arrival of Rick, who took us deeper into the Old City. I saw that he had not exaggerated the militsiya's relative presence in Bukhara. Tashkent is reportedly policed by a militsiya force 40,000 strong, and it sometimes felt as though I had been stopped and questioned by every one of them. In Samarkand police officers were as plentiful as street corners. But in Bukhara there seemed to be no militsiya at all. All around me the thick market crowds seemed freer and less apprehensive, the sky bluer, my mind lighter. But my breath was nearly taken away when I saw something I had never seen before in Uzbekistan: a covered woman. She walked alongside us with her daughter, also covered, their eyes visible through almond-shaped slits, their long black dresses hiding their necks and arms and legs. They turned a corner, then, and were gone. Muslim apologists claim that the covered woman is not the extension of oppressive religious policy but an individual effort toward transcendence. Men, too, they point out, must always keep their legs covered. To cover the parts of oneself most excitable to others was a plea for uniformity and decorum, an abolition of the crass individuality that separates us from the god in whose image we were created. I did not at all buy that, certainly, but I also knew that body-conscious American girls were gagging themselves and barfing over toilets from sea to shining sea. Muslim culture was not alone in having its dark edges.

We walked into a covered bazaar, called a *taq,* which seemed an elaborate hive of latticed-off rooms and turns. Inside, the spacious ceilings vaulted and arched upon thick pillars. A series of small windows allowed in a surprising amount of daylight. This taq was known as Taq-i-Telpak Furushan ("Hatsellers' Dome"), and its stone galleries once accommodated more than thirty skullcap-making workshops. Bukhara previously had five taqs, but only three remained. They were the oldest commercial structures in all of Central Asia. What they sold today was mostly junk: Russian dolls and cheap tea sets and small dull knives and "silk" scarves and piles of black and purple skullcaps. And bongs. Large gold Bukharan hookah bongs with snaky mouthpieced tubes for smoking *tabak* or whatever else. I even saw for sale a volume of Islam Karimov's *Uzbekistan on the Threshold of the Twenty-first Century,* a turgid manifesto published in a dozen languages in 1997. Written (or, more likely, ghost-written) to portray its author as an incisive political intellectual open to foreign investment, *Uzbekistan on the Threshold of the Twenty-first Century* was now selling for approximately 21 cents.

Beyond the taq the Old City no longer seemed a wormhole into a faded Islamic past. All around us loomed the architectural embodiment of Islam triumphant. The city's low skyline was crowded with numerous smooth blue domes. In Samarkand these domes tended to be separated from one another by blocks, if not miles. But in the center of Bukhara's Old City the domes and mosques seemed a diorama blown up to miraculous scale. These domes and huge pishtaqs and minaretless façades did not seem strange or out of place. What seemed strange and out of place were the scooters and cars pushing through the streets and the plane flying high overhead. Most ancient civilizations survive in large, unrepresentative fragments. The pyramids of Egypt, for instance, removed from their original context, look literally impossible today. But temples and shops and streets and homes and palaces once surrounded the pyramids. Nothing in Bukhara was as old or monolithic as the pyramids, though the principle was the same. The difference was that its context was intact. You traveled into Bukhara, but Bukhara also traveled into you.

The majority of the Old City was constructed during the Shaybanid reign of Ubaidullah Khan. In making Bukhara his capital, Ubaidullah abandoned the costly and extravagant styles of Timurid architecture. One saw here very little of Samarkand's elaborations, such as the ribbing covering many of its domes. Ubaidullah's architects and craftsmen also discarded the cut ceramics and carefully arranged tile favored during the Timurid era in favor of more modest painted tile. Bukhara's buildings were mostly brown, and held little of Samarkand's polychromatic dazzle. Functionality had been the goal, not deification. The most beneficial change came with domes' inner designs. Previously, the domes of Central Asia rested upon a complicated, collapse-prone system of squinches. The Shaybanids preferred a simpler, stronger support scheme of overlapping arches. These would soon dominate Central Asian architecture and allowed for the survival of many Shaybanid buildings into modern times.

While I stood looking at Bukhara's still-functioning public bathhouse, the waft of some pleasant spice hooked my face around. Its origin was a small pathside stall, the counter and shelves of which were amassed with curios and spices and secretive little containers. It was as though someone had hijacked a fourteenth-century caravan and decided to rummage off one of the wagon's contents. The stall's proprietor was a middle-aged man as flamboyant-looking as a circus sharpshooter. He was dressed in a black vest over a floppy-sleeved white shirt and held forth from behind his crowded counter for a few German tourists. Steam twirled up from various pots boiling behind him. Every few seconds he turned to his shelves and spun back around with a new jar of spice, which he waved like smelling salts under the Germans' noses.

"That's Mirfaiz," Rick said to me, "but we all call him the Spice Guy. He's probably the most voluble person in Bukhara, and one of its most successful small-business owners. His tea . . . well, his tea is the best tea in the world. I'd be willing to put some money on that."

Mirfaiz brightened when he saw Rick approaching. "Reek! Reek! Reek! Who have you brought me today? An American!" Mirfaiz loved Americans, he said. The best people in the world. Which was quite a coincidence, because Bukhara was the best city in the world! An even greater coincidence, I said, because I was here to sample the best tea in the world. As he set about preparing a pot, he described how his tea had nearly set off an international conflagration. So determined was Mirfaiz to give Madeleine Albright a cup of his famous tea as she passed his stall during her visit to Bukhara, the Secret Service nearly wrestled him to the ground. Only the repeated assurances of the local entourage touring with Albright convinced the Secret Service to allow her to sample Mirfaiz's tea.

"So what happened?" Rustam asked.

Mirfaiz held up a small round handleless white cup and passed it to me. "She loved it. One of her people came back later and bought some spices from me."

Before trying the tea I looked into the cup. The liquid was light yellow, some spice remains floating exotically on the surface like tiny green snowflakes. A good amount of brownish sediment sat at the cup's bottom. I sipped. The taste came in increments. First a fruity tang, then a taste with a deeper honeyed core, then something gingery and hard. I sipped again.

"What do you think?" Rick asked finally.

I was still rhapsodizing about the tea when Rick led us into the most important complex of Bukharan architecture, a plaza known as the Poi Kalon (which translated means "Foot of Sublimity" or "Pedestal of Greatness"), a name it earned thanks to its slightly elevated foundation.

With all due respect to Lord Curzon, here loomed three structures easily as commanding as Samarkand's Registan. The first was the 150-foot-high Kalon Minaret, which towered slightly off center between the Poi Kalon's two other major buildings, the Kalon Mosque and the Mir-i-Arab Madrasa. The Kalon Minaret's colorful history was best captured by its other name: the Tower of Death. The thousand-year-old minaret was one of Bukhara's oldest surviving structures. From 1127—its year of construction—until the 1300s, the Kalon Minaret is thought to have been the world's tallest building. Round and made of fourteen sections of diversely reticular gold-tinted brick—each section divided by a thin belt embroidered with "God Is Immortal"–type Arabic script—the Kalon Minaret thinned and tapered as it rose to meet its beautiful and many-windowed crown-shaped summit, called a "lantern" likely due to the minaret's peacetime function as a lighthouse for desert caravans. Beneath the lantern the minaret's one burst of color, a slender girdle of bright turquoise, burst out at the eye. Part of the minaret was destroyed in 1920 when General Mikhail Frunze, the Soviet vanquisher of much of Central Asia, rudely introduced it to modern artillery.

This was the third minaret to bless Bukhara with its majesty. The first was erected here in the early 900s and burned to the ground a century later. The second, built around 1070 during the Karakhanid era, was made of either wood or brick. It also collapsed, unfortunately onto an adjacent mosque, to a massive loss of life. (Official cause of the collapse: the Evil Eye.) Frunze's shelling was not the first time the surviving Kalon Minaret very nearly met the fate of its predecessors. When Jenghiz Khan arrived in Bukhara, he galloped right up to its octagonal base and dismounted. He is said to have stared up in wonderment at the lantern for some time, leaning back so far that his hat fell off. As Jenghiz knelt to retrieve his hat—an unfamiliar position for him—he ordered that the minaret be spared, virtually the only part of Bukhara that was. One can imagine Jenghiz's delight when he learned of one of the minaret's time-honored sideline uses. This was jaculation, or, more bluntly, sewing people in sacks and pitching them from one of the lantern's windows. This mode of punishment achieved its greatest popularity under debauched Mangit rule. Typically, jaculation was carried out on bazaar days on the order of the amir himself. The victims were most often petty criminals, religious apostates, and wives accused of adultery. A nineteenth-century French traveler reports that the bodies fell from the tower as though they were "large parcels," twisting and turning as they plummeted. The Frenchman witnessed so many jaculations during his brief visit that it became to him a "distraction." Fitzroy Maclean claims that "the repeated impact of these terrible packages produced a little hollow in the hard ground at the foot of the minaret," which I attempted and failed to confirm. Rick told us that most Bukharans, embarrassed by the stories, insist no one was ever thrown off the minaret; it was all a legend. The Soviets maintained the practice ended in the 1880s, but at least one visitor mentions seeing jaculations in the 1920s. Another use of the Kalon Minaret, according to Alexander Burnes's *Travels into Bokhara*, was as Bukhara's prime spot for peeping Mohammeds to spy on the city's women, no doubt allowing for a different sort of jaculation.

We walked thirty feet to the entrance of the Kalon Mosque, built upon the foundation of the earlier minaret-crushed mosque, and stepped through its primary pishtaq. The portal tympanum was decorated with pinwheelish designs set against a dark blue. Stairs led down into the mosque's spacious open courtyard, its paving glowing salt-white in the sun. Planted in the middle of the courtyard was a large, squat mulberry tree, its trunk coated in a whitish paint-based insecticide to keep off burrowing insects. Mulberry trees were often found around holy sites in Central Asia, an ancient pagan tradition absorbed into the nucleus of monotheism: the Islamic equivalent of Christmas trees. We had the courtyard to ourselves, and each of us walked off to a different corner. *Kalon* means "great," and this was the second-largest mosque in Central Asia, able to contain 10,000 faithful, a number said to parallel the number of Bukhara's of-age male population at the time of its reconstruction in the 1100s. Tradition holds that Bukhara's amirs all came to the Kalon Mosque to pray. From 1920 to 1989, however, worship was forbidden here. (Under Stalin alone, an astonishing 26,000 mosques were closed in Central Asia. To wrap one's mind around that number, imagine every hospital in America being closed, virtually overnight. Now multiply that by a factor of four.) Jenghiz cottoned equally little to the great mosque, mostly demolishing it after sparing the Kalon Minaret. Where the four of us now strolled idly, the Mongols had executed thousands. It is said that, when Jenghiz ascended the steps back to the Poi Kalon's foundation, the slosh of blood in this courtyard came up to one's shins. The mosque was not fully rebuilt until three hundred years later, when the Shaybanids began their revitalization of Holy Bukhara.

Rustam drifted over to me, his face awash with perspiration, looked at his watch, and sighed.

"Pretty amazing place, huh?"

He shrugged irritably and glanced about the courtyard. "I don't know, bro. It takes more than this to impress me. To be truthful, I'm getting a little sick of all these sacred spaces."

I watched a bird fly overhead, its shadow gliding across the courtyard's paving, shooting up onto a wall, and disappearing. "We're almost done, I guess. I just want to see the madrasa."

Rick joined us, sweating equally. "What's up?"

"Madrasa," I said.

"You can't go in, you know. As an unbeliever you can only go as far as ten feet inside."

"We'll see about that, Reek." I held up my accreditation card. "Just wait until the mullahs have a gander at this little baby. They're liable to kill something in our honor."

The Mir-i-Arab Madrasa faced the Kalon Mosque directly across the plaza, a placement system known as *kosh* (pair) that achieved wide use in Central Asia during the sixteenth and seventeenth centuries. A game of soccer had migrated over from the Poi Kalon's far reaches, and the children were now using a portion of Mir-i-Arab as a goal. They were quickly chased away by an old man with a stick. Once the children were gone, we walked over. This madrasa was built in 1535 by one Sheik Abdullah Mir-i-Arab (Prince of the Arabs), a Yemeni who tried to help along the Uzbek Shaybanids' not always facile interpretation of Islam. It was a massive building, reminiscent of the Tilla Kari Madrasa in Samarkand, which was likely modeled upon it. Much of the decorative mosaic found upon the large central pishtaq's tympanum and facing had been faded by time, making its gigantic stone plainness more akin to a rough, carved mountainside than to an Islamic seminary. The mosaics and stucco stalactites respectively found upon the madrasa's inner portals and domes—everything we were not allowed to see, in other words—was according to one scholar "extremely refined."

The Mir-i-Arab functioned for centuries as the Harvard of Central Asian Islam. History tells us that it was closed from the mid-1920s until the mid 1940s, and upon reopening became one of only two madrasas allowed to operate by the Soviets, the other being the Imam Bukhari

Madrasa, the resting place of Uthman's Qur'an, which despite its name is found in Tashkent. Bukharans themselves claimed it had never closed. It was a working religious seminary today, many of its 250 students living in quiet balconied quarters within the Mir-i-Arab, an overcrowded few consigned to cells in the next-door Kalon Mosque. Study was in Arabic, the holy language, and most students weathered a seven-year-long course devoted to a curriculum of the Qur'an, theology, the Qur'an, theology, theology, and the Qur'an.

As Rick predicted, ten feet into the madrasa a plaque explained that infidels were not allowed. Rick and Rustam lingered inside its dark stone-cooled foyer, watching the pitiless sun beat down on the plaza outside, the light as thick as a waterfall. I stepped a little farther than advisable into Mir-i-Arab to find myself mere inches from a lattice gate. I approached it gingerly, steeling myself for a glimpse into the secret gears of Islam. I fit my eye against one of the lattice's diamondine openings. In the courtyard of the Harvard of Central Asian Islam, a half-dozen bearded young men were playing Ping-Pong.

Rick had arranged for a local guide, a friend, to meet us at the Ark, the Old City's most fearsome and imposing structure. The guide was late. While Rick and Rustam shared a Coke beside the Ark, I walked across the street and poked around in a shady green commons formerly known as Lenin Park. Through the trees I could see the Bolo Hauz Mosque, the site of Bukhara's other remaining pool. The mosque's colorful porch, with its painted poplar- and elm-hewn columns, was even through the park's crowded foliage so hypnotically pretty it seemed as though it were covered in butterflies. When I ventured back across the street to the Ark, Rick was alone with a half-drunk Coke bottle. "Where's Rustam?"

"One of his uncles walked by. Rustam said, 'Oh, shit, there's my uncle,' and he just . . . *took off*. I think he ran back to the Kalon Mosque."

I stared down the street. "Christ. Not again."

"It's happened before?"

"In Samarkand. Probably it's the same uncle. This is ridiculous."

"Why doesn't he want to see his uncle?"

"I guess he's afraid his dad will find out he's missing school."

He nodded. "I hope you're paying him enough to cover the bribes he's going to have to pay his dean."

"What do you mean?"

"Interesting absentee policies here. You miss all the class you want, you bribe your dean, you still get an A. It's part of the reason Uzbekistan's doctors and lawyers are so awful. Hardly anyone actually goes to school except for the poorer kids and the superhumanly disciplined— who are usually one and the same. Didn't your students ever try to bribe you?"

"I mostly just taught little kids." I watched two old men walk by, their conversation consisting mostly of gestures. Then, looking back to Rick: "How much, typically, do you have to pay?"

"I don't know. It probably varies. You should ask him."

"The corruption here . . . it's—"

"I know. Sucks. You try to help someone out and you only wind up contributing to it."

We opted to park ourselves in front of the Ark. This was no sacred space. A version of this brick mountain, the castrametation out of which the city of Bukhara developed, had towered here as long as history has been reliably recorded. One could see why. The hill the Ark stood upon had obvious strategic benefits in such flat country. The Shaybanids, who supplied the castlelike structure with its surviving armature, were helped by the fact that, over the years, central Bukhara's hill had grown higher due to the amassed rubble of the (at last count) eight wrecked, burned, and otherwise obliterated fortresses that predated this Ark, itself an architectural Frankenstein's monster of additions tagged on by Bukhara's various custodians. A steep platform, much like a chainless castle drawbridge, angled up to the Ark's main entrance portal. Built in 1742 by the Persian architects of Nadir Shah, this portal was the structure's least-restored section as well as its most elaborate. On either side of the portal stood a tall pale tower with six tightly latticed windows. The towers had rounded, slightly blunt tops, each tipped with a stone nipple, betraying the towers' Persian influence. Linking the towers, several feet above the main gate, was a high, roofed patio known as the Music Pavilion, where an entourage of royal musicians once pounded on drums and fluted their reed pipes to hail the amir upon returning from Bukhara's various penumbral palaces. The fortress's most imposing feature, however, was its wraparound walls. They fanned out on either side of the main entrance, as steeply angled as cliffs, encircling the Ark at an irregular, slithering angle, the corners fortified with rounded triangular keeps. These pocked, saltine-colored walls were forty feet high, and to look up at their ramparts gave one over to a sensation of sinking, soldierly empathy with all those who arrived here to storm them.

Delimiting the Ark was a public square as large as a city block. As with Samarkand, this area was called the Registan, and it, too, had drunk the blood of numerous executions before Russian heavy machinery paved it over in the 1920s. The Soviets were less solicitous of the fort itself, blowing much of it to pieces as Frunze's forces rode into the city shortly after its last Mangit amir, Mahomet Alim Khan, made his getaway to Afghanistan after fielding a call upon Bukhara's only telephone that warned him of the Soviet advance. The Red Cavalry had arrived to find the Ark on fire, Alim Khan having opted to burn the fort down rather than see it captured. Once the fire was extinguished, Frunze defiantly ran the Soviet flag up its charred mud walls, and the Ark soon saw conversion into a museum on the horrors of preindustrialism. Four years ago, in honor of Bukhara's supposed 2,500th anniversary, the Uzbek government repaved the Ark's Registan with bright new bricks. As I ran my boot tip over the already well-gouged makeover, I mentioned to Rick that the Ark was the reason I had wanted to come to Bukhara in the first place. He looked at me. "For God's sake, why?"

"A pilgrimage, I guess."

He shook his head. But something awful had happened here, and it felt important to me that I pay my respects, however small or meaningless.

When Alexander Burnes lit out for Bukhara, overland from Delhi, in 1832, he already had behind him an enviably swashbuckling career. A Scotsman born of a literary family (the poet Robert Burns was a relative), Burnes first traveled to India at the age of sixteen. Once in Bombay, he quickly discovered that he had a gift for languages, and after only a few months he was made an interpreter of Urdu and Hindi for the Third Regiment Bombay Native Infantry. Bombay's officer class was top-heavy with Scotsmen, and Burnes used what historians Karl E. Meyer and

Shareen Blair Brysac wryly describe as "tribal links" to climb the imperial outpost's military-administrative ladder. By eighteen he was a full lieutenant and the speaker of a half-dozen tongues, including Persian, the language of Central Asian trade and diplomacy, which Burnes claimed to speak "as my own language." But the self-proclaimed "vagabond" was restless and proposed to his superiors that he put his Persian skills to use and undertake an information-gathering mission to Bukhara, then regarded as the most secretive and perilous of Central Asia's legendary caravan cities. The last Englishman to return safely from Bukhara with any useful information had been Anthony Jenkinson, and this was before the time of Shakespeare. (Burnes, not atypically for a Scottish officer, considered himself an Englishman.) India's governor-general sanctioned Burnes's mission, and he rode off for Bukhara with an equally youthful "medical gentleman" named James Gerard, a "native Surveyor" named Mohammed Ali, a "Hindoo lad" named Mohan Lal, and a few other servants. Before leaving, both Burnes and Gerard shaved their heads, blackened their beards, and adopted "purely Asiatic" dress, the particulars of which Burnes described to his parents in a winning letter obviously intended to shock them. ("You would disown your son if you saw him. . . . I now eat my meals with my hands, and greasy digits they are.") The intrepid pair's first long stopover came in Kabul, where Burnes cut such a sporting figure that he was spontaneously offered the command of its ruler Dost Mohammed's army, which he politely refused. Next was Balkh, where Burnes and Gerard looked with melancholy upon the moonlit grave of William Moorcroft, an Englishman who had attempted the same mission seven years earlier and died of fever on the return push to India. After months of posing as Afghan and Armenian travelers, and hitching along with various armed caravans to avoid the region's Turkmen and Uzbek slavers ("most fatiguing and trying"), Burnes and Gerard reached Bukhara's outskirts and dismounted their horses, as only Muslims were allowed to ride within the city proper. Once in Bukhara, Burnes did not deny being a European, and explained to its perplexed vizier (the city's prime minister and the amir's most trusted advisor) that he was on his way to England and wanted only to enlighten the world about life in what Burnes blandishingly referred to as "the Tower of Islam; the Gem of the Faith, the Star of Religion, the Dispenser of Justice, Pillar of the State, &c. &c." Burnes was allowed to roam the city more or less freely, though he did so alone, as Gerard had fallen ill and

Ali and Lal opted for their safety's sake to blend into the city. Writing was also not allowed within the city walls, and Burnes had to note secretly Bukhara's number of mosques (366, or one for each day of the year), its arcane methods of punishment (wearing dead birds around one's neck, being boxed on the head for looking at the amir's harem, a blackened face for smoking), its luxuries (chopped ice, a plethora of books), and the "miserable" lives suffered by its Russian and Persian slaves. Shockingly, during Mangit times, two-thirds of Bukhara's 150,000 citizens were of slave extraction, of one nationality or another. The slave situation ("this most odious traffic") greatly alarmed Burnes and Gerard, especially after a Russian named Gregory Pulakoff, who had been captured by Turkmen at the age of ten, threw himself at Burnes's feet and wept. "My heart burns for my native land," Pulakoff told Burnes, "where I would serve in the most despotic army with gladness." Burnes did all he could for Pulakoff, which was to take supper with him and listen. After a month of daytime wanderings and long nighttime conversations with Bukhara's now thoroughly fascinated vizier—about pork, whether Christian crosses were idols, Russia, and the function of compasses, eyeglasses, and scissors—Burnes and Gerard slipped out of the city to Persia carrying a letter from Bukhara's amir, with whom they were never offered an audience. When Burnes returned to England, he scribbled out his epic three-volume *Travels into Bokhara,* which remains as exciting and interesting today as the day it was set to type. The esteemed house John Murray had the book printed in mere weeks, and a then-inconceivable nine hundred copies were sold on its publication date. At the age of twenty-seven Burnes found himself a celebrity known as "Bukhara" Burnes. (Gerard ultimately died of the illness he contracted on the journey.) A return to Afghanistan followed, the ruler of which, Dost Mohammed, Burnes had earlier impressed in Kabul. Burnes's official mandate was to open Afghanistan to British trade in hopes of jamming various Russian designs there. In his lobbying Burnes was always respectful of Dost Mohammed and the Afghans—too respectful, some felt, and many of Burnes's reports were tampered with by his superiors. Soon it was apparent to Burnes that his presence in Afghanistan was a mere prelude to the nation's military occupation, and in 1839 the troops rolled in from India and a fort was established in Kabul. Burnes was pleased to be made a knight at the age of thirty-three but suspected it was a move of conciliatory intent, as most of his recommendations were by now being ignored. He stayed on in Kabul as a "highly paid idler," vainly hoping to influence England's Afghan strategies, which he felt were shortsighted and potentially disastrous, from within. By the autumn of 1841, Burnes found himself the enforcer of policies he neither agreed with nor believed in. Perhaps, in his increasing depression, the dashing young officer partook of too many local women and offended too many local men. Or perhaps the whirl of Kabul rumor, which held that a local army was soon arriving to oust the British, spiraled out of control. Whatever the case, on the evening of November 2, Burnes and his younger brother Charles, visiting from India, looked out from their balcony to find a mob of Kabulis crying out for the head of Sekunder, Burnes's Afghan name ("and a magnanimous name it is," he once noted, at a happier time). A burst of gunfire volleyed up at them, mortally wounding one of Burnes's secretaries. Burnes refused to allow his Indian sepoys to return fire and bravely attempted to reason with the Afghans. The Afghans responded by setting fire to Burnes's compound. At this Burnes ordered the sepoys to shoot into the mob, but their enfilade was hopeless. All of Kabul now seemed to have converged upon Sekunder, the undeserving locus of the occupied city's accumulated resentment. Several accounts exist of what happened next. One holds that a local man appeared to offer the Burnes brothers safe passage through the crowd. Nervously, they thought it over, accepting only after the man swore upon a Qur'an that he intended them no harm. Robes were thrown over the brothers' heads and the stranger led them downstairs. Once in the plaza, however, the man whisked off their disguises. "This is Sekunder Burnes!" he proclaimed. A Kabuli man of the cloth stepped forward and clubbed Burnes to his knees, and within seconds the mob had hacked both brothers to death. Another version holds that Charles, a subaltern in the Indian army, elected to fight his way out, slaying six members of the mob before vanishing beneath a bloody orgy of knives. This his elder brother watched, alone amid the growing flames. Lieutenant-Colonel Burnes then tied a bolt of black cloth around his eyes, walked downstairs, and stepped calmly into the rabble, who ripped him apart. While wild dogs tore to shreds the body of Burnes's heart-shot secretary, the brothers' cleaved bodies were paraded through Kabul's streets, a macabre fact no source denies. Meanwhile, the 4,500 British soldiers stationed a mere hour's march away did nothing but debate what to do. The Afghans, emboldened by this inaction, elected to make the British army pay. As

Kabul exploded, forts were seized and hostages taken, and the British war machine was suddenly surrounded on all sides and abandoned by its trusted local envoys. The murder of Bukhara Burnes ultimately led to a full British retreat from Kabul and, finally, to the massacre of 15,000 British soldiers, Indian sepoys, and their families in the hellish passes of eastern Afghanistan.

Yet it is possible that Burnes had been living on nine years of borrowed time. The Bukharan amir who had neglected to receive Burnes during his 1832 visit was the city's most vicious and unpredictable ruler in a despairing procession of vicious and unpredictable rulers. It may be hard to imagine, but had Burnes and Gerard been allowed entrance to this ruler's court, their fates could have been far more protracted, if not exactly worse.

The Mangit Nasrullah Khan (or, as Burnes called him, Nussier Oollah) is described by Arminius Vambery as having a "mixture of cunning and stupidity, of pride, of vain-glory and profligacy, of blind fanaticism and loathsome vices," and by the normally cool-minded Uzbek scholar Edward A. Allworth as "personally despicable, unethical, geopolitically introverted, devoid of historical understanding or human consideration, essentially uncultured, and ruthlessly ideological." History, one can say with confidence, has delivered its verdict on Nasrullah Khan.

Nasrullah's father, an early member of the Mangit dynasty, was another ethical pervert whose special weakness was organized pederasty. (This was not a problem consigned merely to Bukhara's upper echelons. Urban Tajiks throughout Central Asia were infamous for their lad buggery, a topic that today remains sensitive. The Taliban, for instance, achieved much of its early local support by standing up to Northern Alliance warlords, many of them ethnic Tajiks, who were raping Afghanistan's boys.) In this and other things Nasrullah inherited his father's taste, eventually encouraging Bukhara's poorest families to sell their children to his court for use as sexual toys. The mother of all surprises: Nasrullah was also a devout Muslim, ruthlessly enforcing the Sharia among Bukhara's populace and commanding his religious police to ask random citizens to complete suras from the Qur'an.

When Burnes arrived in Bukhara, Nasrullah Khan was twenty-seven and had been in power for just six years. This had been more than enough time for the Mangit ruffian to clear the decks of potential challengers to his throne. The only trouble was that most of these challengers were his relatives. No matter. His three younger brothers were beheaded and twenty-eight of his closest relatives were variously throat-slit, chopped up, stabbed, and strangled—murders orchestrated by the vizier who years later would treat Burnes with such kindness. Nasrullah then contented himself with terrorizing the city's unlanded Uzbeks, whom he hated, and persecuting everyone else, including his own court, a member of which, in a fit of pique, he once cut in half with an ax. His own immediate family fared little better, and several of Nasrullah's daughters were stabbed before his eyes to ensure their eternal virginity. When Nasrullah was informed that the Englishmen Burnes and Gerard had entered Bukhara, it is possible he thought it a mere curiosity. The people of Central Asia justifiably viewed the Great Game as a hostile Christian incursion into a Muslim world quite content with its faith, but in 1832 the British and Russian presence in the region had not yet graduated into the land-grab debacle it would become. In the months and years following Burnes's visit, word spread to Nasrullah that the Russians were absorbing the northern reaches of modern-day Kazakhstan and preparing for a massive assault on Khiva, and that the Afghan city of Herat had fallen to the British. Nasrullah, rightfully, began to worry. Worry can sober the savage man (one thinks of Stalin valiantly—for him, anyway—remaining in Moscow while the blitzkrieging Nazis were only miles away) or it can propel him into a new, deeper, more paranoid savagery. Nasrullah Khan chose the latter path. A Bukharan historian who lived during Nasrullah's reign wrote that, two years after Burnes's departure, "a decline began in affairs of religion and state." To this valuable eyewitness, Nasrullah's increasingly metastasizing rule signified nothing less than the fall of Holy Bukhara.

In December 1838, the year after Herat's collapse, the British Empire's East India Company sent out to Bukhara an intemperate colonel named Charles Stoddart to convince Nasrullah to free the city's Russian slaves. Doing so, Stoddart was prepared to argue, would eliminate St. Petersburg's prime justification for annexing Nasrullah's kingdom. Stoddart, one of the heroes of the Siege of Herat, was also authorized to offer Nasrullah a friendship treaty. Colonel Stoddart had likely read Burnes's *Travels into Bokhara* but had not, it seemed, heeded its most useful piece of advice—namely, to dismount one's horse while within the city's walls. Instead, Stoddart trotted up to Nasrullah's Ark in full, button-gleaming uniform. Nasrullah could only stare in hot-eyed disbelief. Stoddart, not adept in picking up on these strange oriental signals, smartly saluted the Butcher. This was bad. Stoddart had with him no gifts. This was also bad. When allowed entrance to Nasrullah's court, Stoddart refused to bow down to the amir, lashing out at the royal attendant who helpfully attempted to hasten the colonel's supplication. This was truly bad. When Stoddart handed over his letter of introduction, Nasrullah found that it was not properly signed by Queen Victoria, in Nasrullah's eyes a royal peer, but was rather a generic request for Stoddart's honorable treatment—the Victorian equivalent of letterhead. This was worse yet. Then one of Stoddart's servants passed the Butcher a missive from the Amir of Herat, who it seemed had not forgotten Stoddart's key role in the fall of his city. Nasrullah learned, on his fellow amir's honor, that Charles Stoddart was a spy who deserved nothing less than swift execution. This earned Stoddart immediate entry to the Sia Chat, or Black Well, which like the Kalon Minaret had a far more expressive nickname: the Bug Pit.

Nasrullah was a bigoted ogre stupid with narcissism, but he possessed some brutish measure of self-preserving intelligence. Just as a Neanderthal would have hesitated before single-handedly assaulting a woolly mammoth, Nasrullah now weighed his options as he held captive an officer of the most powerful country in the world. In *Tournament of Shadows*, Karl E. Meyer and Shareen Blair Brysac make an obligatory attempt at fairness in describing Nasrullah's motives: "[Nasrullah's] erratic behavior was not entirely irrational. Along with the khans of Khiva and Kokand [Nasrullah's local nemeses, the latter a breakaway kingdom from Bukhara], he closely tracked the progress of Russian and British arms in Asia. Like his fellow rulers, he was intent on discovering how to placate and outwit both imperial powers." True enough, but what Meyer and Brysac do not attempt to explain is how heaving an admittedly haughty Brit into a twenty-foot-deep feces- and bone-littered pit swarming with lice, scorpions, sheep ticks, and vermin specially bred to feast on human flesh can possibly be construed as an attempt to "outwit" an imperial empire. Beneath their evenhandedness lurk the screams of Charles Stoddart.

From India the British sent word to release Stoddart, but Nasrullah refused. When the Russian tsar diplomatically made the same request,

Nasrullah refused. He similarly refused to release Stoddart when asked to do so by the Sultan of Istanbul and his fellow amirs in Khiva and Kokand, who were worried of attracting yet more foreign attention to their region. Only word sent directly from Queen Victoria would slake Nasrullah's vanity. Stoddart, for his part, despaired. When Kabul fell to the British in July 1839, Nasrullah, newly fearful of a British column advancing upon his kingdom, gave Stoddart an opportunity to escape from the Sia Chat, where he had festered for seven months. This opportunity came under the life-or-death rubric of becoming a Muslim. Stoddart, by now bloody, chewed up, desperate, diseased, and half insane, agreed. After sending a royal surgeon to circumcise Stoddart, Nasrullah had his captive bathed and installed in the home of Bukhara's chief of police. Colonel Stoddart now had some freedom of movement and often went to "pray" at the Kalon Mosque. He also, through some still unclear but no doubt ingenious arrangement, managed to sneak several letters out of Bukhara. Heartened somewhat by the news "of the probable fall of Cabool" to his countrymen, Stoddart wrote to his family in Norwich that his "release will probably not take place until our forces have approached very near to Bokhara. This Ameer is *mad*." (Stoddart underlined that word twice.) When the fall of Kabul proved to Nasrullah to have no immediate Bukharan ramifications, and with his own message to Queen Victoria snootily unanswered, the maniac threw Stoddart back into the Bug Pit, then pulled him out, then threw him back in. A year of this torture, disguised as Nasrullah's moodiness, passed. When Stoddart's friends and family in England learned that he had been forcibly converted to Islam, they demanded that something be done. Nothing was. (At the same time in England, a hugely elaborate search was underway for the arctic explorer Sir John Franklin and his 100-plus crew of sailors, who had vanished in search of the Northwest Passage.)

Among the Englishmen most outraged by Stoddart's plight was Arthur Conolly, the very coiner of the phrase "great game." A Christian of evangelically fanatical convictions, Conolly had long envisioned shepherding the Oozbucks and Toorkmuns and Avgauns out of Moslem woggery and into the light of Chistendom, and of uniting the long-warring khanates of Bukhara, Khiva, and Kokand into a united anti-Russian front welcoming of British goods. He also deplored the region's slave trade and wished for nothing more than to abolish it off the face of the earth. But how could all of these things come to pass? Conolly, thirty-three years old, recently jilted by a lover, and doubtless suffering the queer megalomania that typically follows such heartbreak, felt quite certain that he could enter the khanates and, at the very least, convince their rulers to accept English treaties over those of the fiendish Russians. For this scheme Conolly found many London backers, especially when he decided to make a go of freeing Stoddart. Among those who found Conolly's plan roughly as practical as sailing to Byzantium was Sir Alexander Burnes. Conolly, Burnes wrote tartly, was "a very nice fellow," but even if he succeeded, "is England to become security for barbarous hordes some thousands of miles from her frontier?" The only thing that could possibly convince the khans to unite, Burnes felt, was "the wand of a Prospero." The socially adroit Conolly overcame Burnes's opposition, and final approval for the mission came from Conolly's own cousin, William Macnaghten, the British envoy in Kabul—the man who a year later would do nothing while Burnes was being slaughtered by a blood-thirsty mob. (Macnaghten would fare no better. His dismembered corpse would wind up hanging from a meat hook in a Kabul bazaar, his arms and legs and head, in the unimprovable words of historian Peter Hop-kirk, the unrivaled laureate of the Great Game, whose account of these events I have relied upon heavily, "passed round the town in triumph.")

In September 1840 Conolly set out for Khiva (*"Inshallah!"* he wrote in his journal) with eighty servants in tow. He was well received in Khiva, but no assurances were forthcoming. He was, however, told to stay away from Bukhara. Off Conolly went to Kokand. He was well received in Kokand, but no assurances were forthcoming. He was, however, told to stay away from Bukhara. Perhaps, with this warning, Conolly was pre-pared to listen. But somehow a packet of letters met him in Kokand. They were from Charles Stoddart. "The favor of the Ameer is increased in these days toward me," Stoddart wrote. "I believe you will be well treated here." Conolly reached Bukhara in November 1841, almost three years after Stoddart had first been imprisoned. What Conolly did not know was that Nasrullah's spies had been tracking his movements for weeks, all of whom found it curious that Conolly had visited the palaces of Bukhara's devoted enemies. (Some have speculated that Stoddart's enticing letters reached Conolly on the devious order of Nasrullah him-self.) A mysterious Persian mercenary named Naib Abdul Samat, brought into the fold by Nasrullah to provide him with additional paranoia, advised his master to toy with the rescuing Christian promisor as the British and Russians were toying with them. But Nasrullah was not yet sure how to regard Conolly and was, apparently, sincere in his hope that relations between Britain and Bukhara would normalize, not realizing that for most of Buckingham Palace's inhabitants a Bukharan was roughly as imaginable as a Martian.

Conolly's initial reception with the Butcher of Bukhara was polite, if brief. Where, Nasrullah asked Conolly, was his long-awaited response from the queen? Conolly had no idea, but assured Nasrullah that word would soon arrive. He was, after all, the sovereign's representative. Nasrullah hedged, and Stoddart and Conolly were placed under house arrest. Soon enough, word did arrive, not from the queen but from someone named Lord Palmerston. Yes, Palmerston's message related, the amir's letters to Queen Victoria had been received—and transmitted not to her majesty but to another mysterious personage called the governor-general of India. Nasrullah was outraged but did not act against his British guests until receiving another message, yet again from Herat, which predictably denounced Captain "Khan Ali" as a spy. This earned Conolly his first taste of the Bug Pit, Stoddart his . . . fiftieth? three hundredth? Likely even Stoddart had lost track. When India's British governor-general finally wrote to Nasrullah to demand the liberation of Stoddart and Conolly, he bizarrely referred to the men not as agents of the British Empire but as "private travellers"—a common British tactic of disavowal for captured spies but, under the present circumstances, evidence of a cold and criminally negligent heart. This something-less-than-inadvertent brush-off, combined with the news of the annihilation of the retreating British forces in Afghanistan, convinced Nasrullah that, no matter what he now did to his captives, no British army would be along to take issue.

In one of his last letters, Conolly wrote to his younger brother, John, who numbered among the few British soldiers taken alive in the aftermath of the Kabul riots: "This will probably be my last note hence, so I dedicate it to you, who now alas! stand next to me. . . . Stoddart and I will comfort each other in every way till we die." Lieutenant John Conolly succumbed to fever while being held in Kabul, never learning of his idolized sibling's fate. This is, one imagines, just as well. Fresh from his victory against the Khan of Kokand, against whom Bukhara had declared war the year before, Nasrullah returned to the Ark in May 1842 in murderously high spirits. On June 24, four years into Stoddart's captivity and eight months into Conolly's, Nasrullah's playthings were led into the Registan and made to dig their own graves. After finishing the grisly chore, the two bloody, emaciated Englishmen embraced and wept in each other's arms while a transfixed crowd of Bukharans watched in silence. No doubt it was a bright day, perhaps a day much like this one, the sun a jewel of light. Within the Ark's Music Pavilion, now filled with tourists waving to other tourists, Nasrullah's royal drummers pounded a dirge. Stoddart's and Conolly's hands were bound behind their backs. They were forced to their knees. As a Muslim, however insincere his conversion, Stoddart very likely had the luxury of having his throat cut. After watching the man he had come to rescue jerk and bleed to death beside him, Conolly was no doubt shocked to hear the executioner explain that, on command of Nasrullah Khan, the Shadow of God upon Earth, Khan Ali would be spared if he discarded his Christianity for Islam. Whether this was yet another of Nasrullah's disgusting tricks we will never know. "I am ready to die," Conolly replied, leaning forward. Moments later his headless corpse was pushed into the open grave and covered. Stoddart's followed. A year later, still reeling from its losses in Afghanistan, the British government finally acted—declaring both men dead. This was to the particular grief of the Conolly family, its sons lost in an increasingly nebulous conflict concerned with increasingly inexplicable gains. The monster Nasrullah Khan ruled for another twenty years, never punished for this or anything else, and died, to the world's disgrace, in bed.

As Rick welcomed Rustam back from his refuge in the Kalon Mosque, I knelt at the spot where I imagined Stoddart and Conolly had embraced. Nearby, some schoolchildren walked across the Registan and into the Ark, over all the other spots where Stoddart and Conolly may have embraced. I felt for the tragically arrogant Stoddart and the troublingly Christian Conolly a kinship so ghostly it may well have been imaginary. But they were travelers. They had toiled in these vicinities of suffering, bled upon this soil, been interred beneath these loose bricks, lived now amid the troubling echoes of history, and this was hallowed ground.

Scenes from a Tour of the Ark

THE PERSONS

TOM, 27, an adventure journalist
RUSTAM, 24, a dude
RICK, 29, a humanitarian
FARUZA, 45, a guide

FARUZA: Forgive me, Reek! I am late today!

RICK: Hello, Faruza. Not to worry. I don't think we're in any great rush. It's good to see you.

FARUZA: You as well, Reek.

TOM: So was it the same uncle? Oybek?

RUSTAM: Bro, it wasn't! It was my uncle Hamid. But I don't think he saw me.

TOM: So how many uncles do you have?

RUSTAM: Ten.

FARUZA: Shall we begin our tour of Ark?

RICK: Uh . . . yeah. Let me round up these guys.

TOM: You have *ten* uncles?

RUSTAM: I think ten. And four aunts. And cousins. A lot of cousins.

FARUZA: Today, I welcome you on the part of Holy Bukhara, the Religion City. So if you follow me up this platform ramp, you can see here the minarets and special enhancements which keep Fortress Ark amazing with its genius design. Behind these walls we see the actual remains of Fortress Ark's magnificent inside city. Now, in feudal times this inside city was occupied by a prison, as well as a mint for the money manufacture, and also a department of the police and mosques and a harem room and of course the amir's treasury, which as you must know held the largest gold reserves in the world. Here as well in the inside city were kept the amir's relatives and his court. Upwards there were three thousand of such people. Therefore, we call it the inside city. The working people of Bukhara

called the residents of Fortress Ark "the wealthy prisoners" for the reason being they could not leave Fortress
Ark. And now I will tell you that Ark is Persian for "place
guarded by soldiers."

TOM: What about back there? Those rooms were where the
amir's prisoners were kept in chains and tortured, right?

FARUZA: Unfortunately, many prisoners who were not so wealthy
were similarly brought into Fortress Ark. Others were
prisoners of the imperial struggle taken prior to the end
of class society beneath Soviet power. Of course you
must know that Bukhara properly known is Bukhara-i-
Sharif. This means Bukhara the Noble and only several
such cities so known exist today in the world. There is
Baghdad-i-Sharif and Mazar-i-Sharif and several others.
But Bukhara is noblest.

FARUZA: Now, if you please, it will be important for you to see the
top of Fortress Ark to manifest the full sweep of Bukhara
city's history. No, not that way. This way is better. We see
that on top of Fortress Ark much of the monumental
buildings have not survived the momentous Bukhara city
history.

TOM: Jesus. It looks like we're in a desert.

RUSTAM: I thought they restored all this.

FARUZA: Only walls and outside of Fortress Ark were restored for
Bukhara city's 1997 jubilee anniversary.

TOM: How come there are animal skulls up here?

FARUZA: Quite likely this is because of Fortress Ark's horse stables
which were situated very nearby us now.

RICK: Yeah, and when they washed the horses all the dirty
water was washed into guess where?

TOM: Where?

RICK: The torture chambers downstairs. Look here. You can
still see the drain.

TOM: Nice.

FARUZA: Here we can see all of Bukhara city's magnificent skyline
which is most photographed of any in Asia Minor.
Across the street you can see the beginning place of a new

255

hotel where Turkish investors will build a hotel of luxury. You must know that Bukhara city's *hakim* is planning to rebuild all of Fortress Ark to scale for the many visitors of Bukhara. In one hundred years Bukhara has traveled from a city which allowed no visiting tourists but those on religious pilgrimage to a city with more tourists than any in Asia Minor. Of course, this we can credit to the end of class rule and the openness of the Uzbek people.

FARUZA: Now I think it would be appropriate for you to see the Coronation Court of Bukhara city's amirs. Not that way. This way is better. Ah. Here we see the famous Coronation Court of Bukhara city's amirs. The throne that now stands in the middle of the famous Coronation Court is a meaningful reproduction of the amir's marble throne which is now situated in Tashkent as an artifact of Holy Bukhara's history. When ruling from his throne the amir used seven robes to sit upon in the order to make him appear taller to his subjects and visitors. For most amirs were short men. But now you should be aware that not all of Bukhara city's amirs enjoyed Fortress Ark. By twentieth century A.D. Bukhara city's amir had established many beautiful summer palaces outside the city for his relaxation. Khan Alim was Bukhara city's final amir and history knows him to have hated Fortress Ark.

TOM: Is that why he burned it down?

FARUZA: Unfortunately no one knows who burned down Fortress Ark.

TOM: I think it was Alim Khan.

FARUZA: Perhaps this is possible.

TOM: And what was this wall blocking the entrance for, exactly?

FARUZA: This wall allowed only those so invited to see the amir as they passed by. Also it was to protect the amir from the Evil Eye.

TOM: What I'm wondering is how many people were sentenced to death here in the Coronation Room.

RICK: Any idea, Faruza?

FARUZA: Of that . . . forgive, but I am not allowed to say.

TOM: You're not allowed to say.

FARUZA: Unfortunately, yes.

TOM: And why is that?

FARUZA: Guides are prohibited from making negative opinions in regard to Bukhara city's amirs.

FARUZA: At last here in the museum of Fortress Ark you can see the many artifacts attesting the glory and tumult of Bukhara city history.

TOM: These bows and shields are what the amir's armies used to fight the Russians, aren't they?

FARUZA: Of course this is so. Many thousands of Muslims were killed by colonial power of tsarist Russia.

RICK: Did you know that Russians claim to have lost only 400 men in Central Asia between the 1840s and 1870s? That just blows my mind.

TOM: And what's this parchment here?

FARUZA: You can read here a list written in Persian of the various slaves of Bukhara city from precolonial times. You must know that Bukhara city had very many strong slave men in these times. But of course the slave market was closed by progressive Russian peoples.

TOM: And this?

FARUZA: Here you can see the clothes of working people.

TOM: And there he is. Nasrullah Khan.

FARUZA: Yes, this portrait is of Khan Nasrullah.

TOM: A bad, bad man.

FARUZA: Some say this is so.

TOM: Is it true that the last European he killed was an Italian clockmaker?

FARUZA: I am not certain of this.

TOM: And that the clockmaker made for Nasrullah a clock, Bukhara's only clock, and when it stopped running, Nasrullah got mad and had him bludgeoned to death? Or had his head chopped off. I've read both.

FARUZA: Of this story I am not certain.

TOM: Hey. You all right?
RUSTAM: I'm all right.
  TOM: Are you having a good time, or are you ready to go home?
RUSTAM: Both, bro.

Rick had some final business to take care of in Bukhara's Jewish quarter before we decamped to his house for dinner and, then, sleep. Since Rustam and I had to be at the airport by six-thirty in the morning, our excursion to Bukhara was, in practical terms, all but over.

The Jewish quarter was found a few minutes' walk from Lyab-i-Hauz in a typically picturesque warren within the Old City, the streets as narrow as sidewalks and the sidewalks nonexistent. I loped along, hearing televisions and voices and spades thucking into dirt, mothers calling out for their children, men bellowing for their wives, until we came across a building Rick said was Bukhara's last remaining synagogue. It was tucked nondescriptly behind huge iron gates and a high white-washed wall.

For centuries Bukhara was home to a large Jewish community. Bukharan Jews controlled the city's banks and bazaars, and held the receipt upon many of the horses and wagons that caravanned along the Silk Road. Various theories exist as to how such a cohesive community of Jews wound up settling in Bukhara. Some claimed they were one of the mythological "lost tribes" of Israel, driven east millennia ago by persecution. Others claimed they were brought out of Baghdad to Bukhara and Samarkand by Timur. Still others thought that Bukhara's Jews arrived in Bukhara only in the early 1700s, via Afghanistan, but then the question is, How did *they* get to Afghanistan? ("Till a year ago the Afghans claimed that they themselves were Jews," Robert Byron wrote in the 1930s. "But nothing is too fantastic for Asian nationalism.") Whatever the case, Muslims and Jews had peacefully coexisted within the Cupola of Islam for hundreds of years, though Jews were subject to quite a few restrictions. They were not allowed to ride within the city walls, had to wear certain identifying garments, and as non-Muslims were subject to an infidel tax. But no Bukharan pogroms exist in history. No doubt it helped that Bukhara's Jews were, for the most part, physically indistinguishable from its Muslims, and spoke not Hebrew but Persian and then Tajik. Only with the arrival of the Russians did anti-Semitism, Europe's most poisonously influential import, assert itself. When the Soviet empire crumbled, many of Bukhara's Jews sold their homes and belongings and booked tickets to Brooklyn and Tel Aviv, which for a time was linked to Bukhara by several daily direct flights. Today there were anywhere from 1,000 to 4,000 Jews left living here, less than a sixth of their former number. No longer the thriving tuggers of Bukhara's fiduciary strings, its Jews had long turned to more modest pursuits such as cobbling and blacksmithing, and memorized their untranslated Hebrew Bibles, shipped in by the boxful from Israel, written in rough transliterated Cyrillic.

"Do you have a project in the Jewish quarter?" I asked Rick.

"Not anything official," Rick said. "A friend of mine named Mila has bought a few houses from some of the last of Bukhara's Jews and is trying to turn them into bed-and-breakfasts. She's really smart and decent, but real-estate laws are complicated here. Zoning doesn't really exist except when it does, if you know what I mean. It's the hangover of the Planned Economy, 'planned' being to 'economy' what 'organized' is to 'crime.' It's sort of ridiculous, actually. And it's not just the government. The animosity a lot of small-business people encounter from average Bukharans gets weird sometimes. Do you know the Russian word *spekulatsiya*?"

"What? Speculation?"

"No, bro," Rustam said. "It's, like, making money off people."

Rick sighed. "Yeah. It has exactly that connotation. Which is the problem. The catch-all phrase for any private profitable enterprise has inescapably negative overtones." We came to a plain green metal door, which Rick rapped. "But anyway, I try to help her out. It's mostly amounted to my teaching her how to use Quicken."

Mila opened the door and welcomed us into the cool, wind-trapped courtyard of one of her up-and-running bed-and-breakfasts. She was a short, overweight Russian woman wearing Western-style slacks and a tight pink blouse. Around her neck she wore a beautiful jade necklace, and her harried eyes were similar to those one often encountered among Uzbekistan's businesspeople, still parsing the joy and terror of captaining their own economic fates. She quickly took Rick aside and whispered something. Four shaggy German male budget travelers in khaki shorts and white T-shirts sat at four small separate tables drinking tea and reading John Irving and Tom Robbins paperbacks in translation. Mila's daughters floated from table to table, occasionally refilling their cups. They wore maidenly little aprons and quickly approached me, obviously eager to use their English with a native speaker rather than the grudging version spoken by these tourists. Tall, leafy plants brightened the compound's edges, and clay pots sprouting with bright yellow flowers hung on chains from the second-story balconies' eaves. Mila and Rick walked upstairs, and we followed.

"What an incredibly nice place," I told Mila as we entered her office, undecorated but for a map of Uzbekistan and a bulletin board with various papers tacked to it. Mila's laptop computer sat flipped open atop a corner-pushed wooden desk, its warped drawers sitting askew within their slots. On the laptop's screen glowed a Quicken spreadsheet.

"Thank you," Mila said, nodding to me. Her expression changed then and she stepped forward slightly. "And do you have accommodation in Bukhara?"

"They're staying with me, actually," Rick said.

"Of course," Mila said, smiling a moment too late to hide her disappointment. She turned to her desk and busied herself moving around the loose pieces of paper strewn upon it.

"How are you?" Rick asked quickly. "How is business?"

She sighed. "Business is good, but not so good it could not be better. Actually, I have called you over because I am having more computer trouble." She waved dismissively at her laptop and threw up her hands. "Oh, Rick. I am an old woman and this, this"—she searched for a word—"*device*. It is little more than magic to me. It keeps . . . crashing? Crashing, yes?"

Within minutes Rick determined that the problem was the memory-hungry Castle Wolfenstein video game Mila's son had installed on the laptop. Mila covered her eyes. "Get rid! De-lete! That awful game! The shooting and shooting! This shooting makes him crazy!"

Mila walked us down the block to another house that, as she explained, she had recently purchased. We stepped through its gate to find an equally pretty but empty compound with a staircase made of stunning dark brown wood, its varnish whitely highlighted by the sun.

We all walked into the middle of the courtyard and looked around. Mila stuffed the gate key into her pocket and shook her head. "I think I am not able to do much with this. The former occupants are in Canada. They sold it to me for not very much money, and now I understand why. Sometimes I think I am not such a smart businessman."

"You're a great businessman," Rick consoled her, moving over to the staircase and giving one of its smooth bulbous balusters a shake. It looked solid. He turned to her. "What's the problem with it?"

"Oh! What is not the problem with it? The wiring is bad, the water is bad, the rooms not big enough. A foolish purchase, made too quickly. I think I should sell this home now. I have enough worries."

"How much did you pay for it?" Not until everyone looked at me was I fully aware that I had said this. Only then did the question's rudeness occur to me. This was followed by my realization of the question's clear implication.

For several moments Mila studied me. Then she shrugged. "Two thousand dollars."

I nodded. I let my backpack's straps slip from my shoulders and drop to the ground. I took a few steps across the courtyard and peeked into the ground-floor kitchen. A steel black stove, as massive as an automobile, hulked in the corner. Opposite the stove was a sink basin large enough to wash laundry in, its faucet insistently plinking. All around the room its paint-chipped cabinet doors had been left open, some of them mouse-chewed around their edges. On the floor, between the sink and a particularly tall cabinet, was a clean square where I assumed a refrigerator had once stood. I turned around. "And how much would you want for it?"

Mila looked to Rick, then back at me. Her balance shifted from one foot to the other; she was still uncertain how seriously to take this. "Perhaps twenty-five hundred dollars? I'm not sure. I would be open for negotiations."

"What?" Rick asked me, chuckling in disbelief. "You looking to live in Bukhara?"

I tallied the bribes I would almost certainly be required to pay for a new refrigerator, a good phone connection, and consistent mail delivery. I rehearsed the explanations I would just as certainly be required to give my family and friends. I thought of the loneliness, the exhilarated transformation, of walking these streets as though they were my own. I imagined long days of waiting for plumbers and electricians to show up, long nights of reading in this courtyard as the moon surfaced in the sky, long Saturdays of setting mousetraps and painting these rooms and working in the garden, and the long weeks and months of wondering what on earth I had done, what on earth I was trying to prove, what correlative might remain after the act of moving here had lost significance to everyone but me.

There was no impulse I distrusted or admired more than that of exile. Distrust because of exile's narcissism, its modal insistence that, above all, location forged the content of one's conscience. Admired because of exile's bravery, its intransigence, the embrace hidden in its denunciation. Mila was still staring at me with much curiosity. My hand reflexively fingered the belt around my waist, tight and thick with cash. I imagined how, with everything I published from this day on, my biography could now end: *He lives in Bukhara.*

Rick laughed. "Are you serious about this?"

I glanced up at him, my thoughts reverting to a steady timid flatline. After a moment I shook my head. "It was just a thought. A romantic but . . . impossible thought. I'm sorry."

Mila was not surprised. "Well. Perhaps you know someone else who would be interested. I am inclined to sell." She sighed, then, and looked around at the house that made her so unhappy. "Aren't all the best thoughts romantic?"

Six

Mountain Funeral

*In looking back to this period, and calling to remembrance
the numberless proofs of kindness and respect which I
received from the natives of the valley, I can scarcely understand how it was that, in the midst of so many consolatory
circumstances, my mind should still have been consumed by
the most dismal forebodings, and have remained prey to the
profoundest melancholy.*

—HERMAN MELVILLE, *TYPEE*

Our flight out of Bukhara was delayed by an hour. I was annoyed until
our flight out of Tashkent was delayed by two hours. Then I gave up.
Weather. The whole nation of Uzbekistan lay trapped beneath a bucket-
ing gray ceiling of what seemed a single massive cloud. Around 1 P.M. the
sky cleared to reveal its blue backcloth, and by two we were back in the
air. Half an hour later Rustam and I looked down at the peaks that
shielded and encircled the Ferghana Valley in the easternmost reaches of
Uzbekistan. "Pretty, isn't it?" Rustam asked.

It was. The red-brown mountain faces were brushed with thin deso-
late streaks of snow, their crests frosted with caps of hard shiny ice. Farther down the slopes fuzzy green tree lines began as abruptly as pubic
hair. The few roads we could see meandered among the mountains,
white and empty, like shed snakeskin. Here and there, below us, floated
bits of cloud that looked as though they had been torn from the day's
earlier unicloud, their edges ragged and their formless cores pierced by a
few of the higher summits. A silent, windless world.

I turned away from the window and sipped my plastic cup of apple
juice. "I was under the impression that you were served vodka on these
local flights."

"Vodka?" Rustam asked. "Nah. Who told you that?"

"I don't remember. I heard it somewhere, from someone."

"The only people who would get vodka would be the pilots."

"That's comforting."

"Just enough to relax them, bro."

"I'd hate for them to be nervous."

He looked past me out the window, slapping his knees with sudden hambone flair. "You're gonna love Ferghana. It's like Russia, except prettier. And I have to say, the people in Ferghana are much cooler than in the rest of the country."

"How do you mean?"

"You know, bro. In Ferghana we're . . . mountain people? Valley people?"

"Okay."

"Everyone else in Uzbekistan is desert people. Desert people are much more, like, stressed out about everything. In the mountains you can just chill. Nothing is that big a deal. The Kyrgyz are like that. They're calm. They don't worry."

"But isn't Tajikistan eighty percent mountainous? They didn't seem to be very willing to chill during their civil war."

He shook his head. "Okay, that's true, but you see, that was all about the Wahhabis, and drug-running. People say the civil war in Tajikistan was Islam against Communism. But it wasn't, bro. All it was about was the Wahhabis controlling the mountains so they could move their heroin and guns through them. And guess where these Wahhabis come from? Fucking deserts. They're the worst, dude. The *worst*. Now they're trying to ruin Ferghana, but I can guarantee you they won't."

Wahhabi. The Soviets had kept this word at the rhetorical ready throughout the empire's life span, using it as a derogatory blanket term to smear any Central Asian Muslims who partook of even the most innocuous Islamic ritual. In the post-Soviet era, however, the Wahhabi threat had become far more literal. These Wahhabis Rustam mentioned were, indeed, Islamist automatons programmed by missionaries from the deserts of Saudi Arabia, who in the early nineties poured into newly open Central Asia, concentrating most of their efforts in the Ferghana Valley. Tajikistan was one of the first places within the former Soviet Union where Wahhabism caught on in any meaningful way. (The other places were Dagestan and Chechnya and, not coincidentally, they too

saw the outbreak of war.) The royal House of Saud uses Wahhabism—
one of Islam's most repressive (and youngest) schools of thought—to
govern the morally despicable petrocracy of Saudi Arabia, and since the
1970s the Saudis have sought to spread its doctrine around the Muslim
world. The other slur used by Soviets to describe Muslims, *basmachi*
(bandits), reflected a legacy more local to Central Asia. The Ferghana
Valley's *basmachi* guerrillas withstood the Soviet counterinsurgency
until 1928, when their last mountain commando was hunted down and
shot between the eyes. The ongoing *basmachi* resistance had been behind
Stalin's cagey 1924 division of the Ferghana Valley, for centuries a unit of
common cultural and economic concerns, among Uzbekistan, Kyrgyzstan, and Tajikistan. Uzbekistan received the largest and most arable
part of the Ferghana Valley, which the Soviets used as a cotton cradle
once the region was subdued. Called by many "the heart of Central
Asia," the Ferghana Valley had a regional importance that could not be
overstated. Although only two hundred miles across and one hundred
miles wide, the lush and picturesque valley was home to 10 million
inhabitants—20 percent of Central Asia's total population—and it
today retained the most religiously observant Muslims, especially in portions of the valley belonging to Uzbekistan. Thus it was difficult to
accept Rustam's claim that the Ferghana Valley was some laid-back
mountain paradise. Even before the Bolsheviks arrived, the tsars had
averaged in the valley about one revolt a decade.

"But the valley does have unrest problems," I said, "doesn't it?"

"Sure. But it's the Wahhabis. It's not Ferghana."

"But a lot of the Wahhabis are Uzbeks *from* Ferghana, right?"

"Yeah, but we don't like them."

I settled back into my seat, the overhead nozzle blowing a steady jet
of polar air into my face. Before I could say anything else, Rustam cut in:
"Ferghana is safe, bro. I don't want you to worry."

"I'm not worried."

"The only thing you have to worry about is the Wahhabi rebels in the
mountains. And then only during Rebel Season."

"Rebel Season."

"Yeah. When the snow melts. They move around."

"When exactly is Rebel Season?"

"Well, I guess now."

"And we're going into the mountains."

"It's going to be fine. Most of them are in Kyrgyzstan."

"What I would really like is for you to tell me about the violence in Ferghana."

"What do you mean?"

"I mean what it was like for you to see and experience it, honestly."

He folded his arms. "Like when, exactly?"

"Like Namangan in 1991, like Namangan in 1997. You lived there then, right?"

He glanced away, nodding. "Of course. I know what you're talking about." He shrugged. "It was frightening. What do you expect? I was only thirteen in 1991. My dad was manager for one of the biggest car factories in Namangan, and there were a lot of unemployed people then. Sometimes when he went to work, people would throw shit at him and call him names, then demand that he hire them. Just stupid things. A lot of my friends' dads didn't have jobs anymore, and their older brothers couldn't find jobs, and they started fights with me. It was a shitty time for our country, bro. People were angry. The Wahhabis took advantage of the anger. You know who Tohirjon Yuldashev is, right?"

"He was the leader of Adolat." Adolat, Uzbek for "justice," was one of Uzbekistan's many banned radical Islamist organizations.

"He still is the leader, I think. He's in exile. You know your Uzbek history, bro. That's cool. And of course you know Jumaboi Khojaev?"

I thought. "That *sounds* familiar."

"He has another name."

"Juma Namangani." A former Soviet sergeant who, in his late teens, served as a paratrooper in Afghanistan and three years ago had, with Yuldashev, cofounded the Islamic Movement of Uzbekistan—the likely perpetrators of Tashkent's 1999 truck-bombing.

As Rustam described it, the mood in Namangan in the months following the Soviet meltdown was high, low, happy, terrified—no one knew what to think. Goods were suddenly scarce, pensions were going unpaid, and for weeks at a time Rustam's father had to invent work for his car-parts factory, as orders had been choked off in the administrative confusion. Soon mosques in Namangan began reopening at the rate of three per week. Rustam's father, though not religious, thought this was healthy, culturally appropriate, and a potentially useful primer to local industries such as construction. Until, that is, some of the mosques began to bear signs that said things like LONG LIVE THE ISLAMIC STATE!

Others were emblazoned with the *shahad,* the first postulate of Islam: THERE IS NO GOD BUT ALLAH! MOHAMMED IS ALLAH'S MESSENGER! Rustam's father had been a prominent Communist and was therefore a potential enemy of Namangan's more religiously awakened citizens; he warned his son to be careful when outside the house. These signs, and the sentiment behind them, were, of course, directly traceable to Saudi Arabian Wahhabi missionaries, whose first incursion into the Ferghana Valley had been way back in 1912. Now the Wahhabis had returned, much richer, and charmed the Uzbek government to sleep with promises of an endless stream of Saudi money and friendly neighborhood mosque building. During Karimov's 1992 visit to Mecca, King Fahd personally escorted the lifelong Communist into the inner sanctum of the Kaaba, the single holiest site in the entire Islamic world, making Karimov one of the only world leaders to have ever stepped across its threshold. What Karimov did not know was that, at the same time, the Saudi government's well-funded Wahhabis were encouraging small cells of the Ferghana Valley's young unemployed men to militarize and throw off secularism. This was in spite of the fact that not *once* in Central Asian history has there *ever* been an Islamic state, not under Timur, nor the Shaybanids, nor Nasrullah Khan, all of whom were observant, certainly, but were also ruthless pragmatists insofar as the manner in which Islam shaped political expediency. It was also in spite of the fact that Uzbeks and Tajiks and Kyrgyz belong to one of the most tolerant and flexible subdivisions of Sunni faith, namely Hanafi Islam, known for its moderation and capacity for obliging local pre-Islamic rites, which in Central Asia are numerous and well entrenched, such as when village healers invoke Allah in one sentence and traditional mountain spirits in the next. Nonetheless, the Wahhabis managed to stir up a good deal of ill will among a few of Namangan's economically optionless young men. Two of the more inspired acolytes of Wahhabism were Tohirjon Yuldashev, a twenty-four-year-old college dropout and self-appointed mullah, and his younger associate Jumaboi Khojaev, both of whom called for the implementation of the Sharia as the basis of Uzbek law. Adolat, an outgrowth of Tajikistan's violent Islamic Resistance Party (another Wahhabi brainchild), was born. No one, Rustam told me, took the group very seriously at first, though when "deputies" belonging to Adolat's vigilante wing began policing the streets and beating up thieves, people were pleased. Namangan, everyone agreed, had grown lax and spiritless. Adolat then insisted that Uzbek women cover themselves, that its men pray five times a day, and began attacking shopkeepers for the crime of raising their prices, while, every morning, local muezzins friendly to Adolat called out promises of a coming Islamic order. Now, Rustam said, matters in Namangan grew tense. The increasingly dire economic situation had reduced much of Namangan's middle class to virtual pauperhood, attracting to Adolat a good number of followers. The city's mosques became crowded with thousands of Uzbeks eager to hear the by all accounts brilliant Islamist oratory of Yuldashev. Both Namangan's police force and its red mullahs found themselves too cowed to confront the growing movement. In April 1991, Yuldashev asked—actually, dared—President Karimov to travel to Namangan to debate the notion of establishing Islamic law in Uzbekistan.

"I remember when Karimov came," Rustam said. "No one could believe it. The whole presidential fleet drove right past my house. I was surprised by how few cars there were. Security was a lot less serious then, or maybe the government didn't have any idea how angry people were. But Karimov outsmarted Adolat, and forbade its representatives from attending his speech. He only wanted to talk to Namangan's government officials, he said. And dude, he yelled at them! My dad was there, and he said that Karimov shouted for an hour, until his face turned red. But Adolat's people went to the mosques and agitated a bunch of Muslims to surround the building Karimov was in until he agreed to talk to them. Lucky for Karimov, by the time they got there, he'd already flown back to Tashkent. But the protestors didn't leave. They stayed there all night, two thousand of them, and Karimov had to come back the next day."

Now Yuldashev received his chance to confront Karimov, and unfurled a long list of Adolat's ludicrous demands. Karimov angrily but calmly told Yuldashev he would address the matter of instantaneously transforming Uzbekistan into a theocracy before the Uzbek parliament and, again, flew back to Tashkent. A few months later Adolat stormed the former headquarters of the Uzbek Communist Party, announced that Namangan was henceforth under Islamic law, and issued a jihad against Karimov. In response, Karimov banned Adolat, sacked Namangan's administrators, and replaced its state-sanctioned mullahs with new state-sanctioned mullahs. In March 1992 seventy-one of Adolat's organizers were arrested while the rest, Yuldashev and Khojaev among them, fled into the wild south of Tajikistan (which had just begun its civil war) and Afghanistan (which had just fallen to the mujahedeen). It was amazing, given future events, that throughout these potentially explosive tremors no one had died.

After putting time in at various Tajik madrasas, Yuldashev went to Pakistan, where he found connections to Saudi Arabia's small Uzbek community, who had lived on the peninsula's immaculate Islamic soil since fleeing the Soviet *basmachi* annihilation of the 1920s. These exilic Uzbeks, now more Wahhabi than the Wahhabis, worked with the head of Saudi intelligence, Prince Turki al-Faisal, to funnel enough funds through Islamic charities to Yuldashev to allow him to spend the better part of the next decade organizing from Peshawar, Pakistan, another, bloodier Ferghana uprising. Jumaboi Khojaev, a younger and more reckless acolyte, stayed in Tajikistan to fight with the Islamic Resistance Party (IRP) against the regime of Tajik president Imamali Rakhmanov, who was holding on to power with help from 25,000 Russian troops sent by Boris Yeltsin to protect what many Russians still believed was their southern border in everything but name. Khojaev, reborn in Islamist fire as Juma Namangani, was indispensable in the fight against Rakhmanov. As the journalist Ahmed Rashid was told by a Tajik political activist, "Namangani knew the tactics of the Soviet army and special forces, which was extremely useful to the IRP." In 1992 Namangani arrived in northern Tajikistan's Tavildara Valley with no more than forty Uzbek militants. In Uzbekistan itself, the number of committed Islamists dedicated to the overthrow of the Uzbek regime between 1992 and 1995 is thought to have never been more than one or two hundred, the vast majority of whom were concentrated in the Ferghana Valley. As Karimov squeezed the vise, more and more young men who had had only a cultural (and completely understandable) interest in Islam were beaten and detained. Many of these embittered souls, and their brothers, and cousins, and friends, rushed to join Namangani in Tajikistan. By 1996 the number of his followers reportedly approached a thousand, and as an aside, one is hard-pressed to find a lesson here. Suppressing violent manifestations of Islam clearly does not work, as we can see when the Wahhabi grandchildren of *basmachi* Uzbeks in Saudi Arabia are still seeking violent redress. Ignoring militant Islam only hastens its spread. Accommodating militant Islam hardly seems an option, as hard-line Islam has, with the possible exception of Iran, proven repeatedly incapable of forming anything resembling a functional human society. The other option

269

that comes to mind—making a sign of the cross and grabbing a rifle—is precisely what the Islamists most desire. If the strange career of Juma Namangani is any indication, it seems we all have a long, long century ahead of us.

While in Tajikistan, Namangani made several forays into Afghanistan, where he liaised with the various now-familiar players within that nation's bloody Shakespearean dramas: Ahmed Shah Masood, the ethnic Tajik Northern Alliance commander eventually assassinated by al-Qaeda; Gulbuddin Hekmetyar, the chronically side-switching Pashtun warlord; Mullah Omar Mohammed, the one-eyed future leader of the Taliban's Islamic Emirate of Afghanistan; and the nowhere man himself, Osama bin Laden. The latter two Namangani was especially taken with, and they with him, despite Namangani's comprehensive lack of interest in doctrinaire Islam. "[Namangani] is essentially a guerilla leader," one IRP functionary told Ahmed Rashid, "not an Islamic scholar. . . . He is a good person but not a deep person or intellectual in any way . . . but he hates the Uzbek government—that is what motivates him above all." When the Tajik cease-fire took place in June 1997, the hateful young guerrilla, not yet thirty, found he was unwilling to stop fighting. He was also a regional celebrity, despite the fact that virtually no one knew what he looked like. Eventually, the IRP leadership convinced him to lay down his arms, and Namangani, somewhat unbelievably, became a farmer in a small town along the Tajik-Kyrgyz border. His retinue of Uzbek and Arab fighters, however, was far too large to support by cultivating northern Tajikistan's drought- and war-ruined land, and he put out his shingle as a heroin smuggler. From the Ferghana Valley, Namangani and Yuldashev's contacts and "sleepers" (men who live normal lives in wait of their Islamist "activation") visited the farm weekly, providing Namangani with ever-worsening bulletins from the front of Uzbekistan's war on terror. On December 2, 1997, it seems that some of those sleepers were, at last, activated.

"I remember that day very well," Rustam told me now, as we descended into Ferghana City. "Nothing was reported, but soon enough everyone knew. My father came home from work pale. 'What happened?' my mom asked. For a long time my dad didn't say anything. Then, finally, he told us, 'A police chief was beheaded today.' Dude, they stuck his head on a spike outside the gates of his office. His fucking *head*. It was the Wahhabis." The officer's beheaders were not captured, and the

Namangan killings did not end there. Nine days later the former chairman of a collective farm and his wife were also beheaded, and eight days after that three policemen were killed in a shootout with assailants, also never captured. No one claimed responsibility for the killings for the simple reason that these terrorists had no platform and no demands. They sought one thing: to destroy their enemies. The killings spread to the nearby valley city of Andijan. The perpetrators, this time, were arrested, and all confessed to having been trained by Juma Namangani and Tohirjon Yuldashev, though, as some have argued, this admission was likely preceded by hours of excruciating torture, making its final basis in fact difficult to evaluate. In the aftermath of the killings Karimov growled his famous proclamation before parliament that, if necessary, he would shoot in the head Uzbekistan's terrorists himself. Yuldashev's poor mother made or was forced to make the following statement in a public meeting: "What can I say if this good for nothing, unbelievable evil is my son? . . . May Tohir be swallowed up by the earth, may he and his accomplices rot in their graves. I blush before our president and all the people. May this rebellious Tohir, who made me feel like this, die." Namangani's family was also harassed and imprisoned, even after they traveled to his farm in Tajikistan to beg him to turn himself in. He did not, and Namangani's mother's face was publicly blackened with paint. When a thousand of the Ferghana Valley's inhabitants were arrested in government sweeps, Namangani's farm soon had even more asylum seekers. The Karimov regime constantly petitioned the shaky Tajik coalition government, a few of its members Namangani's erstwhile fellow fighters, to do something about their renegade adopted son. By 1998 Tajikistan was reportedly willing to act. The Taliban had by this time occupied all but a fraction of Afghanistan, and Namangani and his followers departed for safe haven in Kabul, where Yuldashev was already living. In Kabul the two Uzbek dissidents announced the creation of the Islamic Movement of Uzbekistan. "It takes only a spark to burn down a forest," Yuldashev unoriginally metaphorized in a rare interview with Voice of America, "and for that one match is sufficient. We have enough strength to settle the score with Karimov, and God willing there are many more thousands of mujahedeen who share this dream." A year later six truck bombs exploded in Tashkent.

"So maybe now," Rustam told me, "you can see why I hate Muslims."

"Wahhabis, you mean."

He looked away, and with a rumble the plane's landing gear lowered. "Yeah. Sometimes I can convince myself that they're not the same thing."

Oleg met us at Ferghana City's small, unrenovated airport. His hair had been cut since I last saw him, his dirty-blond mane survived only by a skull of butched yellow nettles. Without his hair's visual ballast Oleg seemed concentration-camp skinny, his jeans hanging off his hips' pelvic knobs and his biceps not even close to filling out the short-sleeve eyelets of his soft-collared white shirt. When he embraced me in greeting, days' worth of stubble rasped across my ear.

Outside in the circular parking lot it was cool and breezy, the sun's reflection a series of hazy orbs in the large black puddles of standing water from the day's earlier downpour. We tramped past police and jeeps and professionally intimidating military personnel, among whom my salaams went unanswered. The driver Oleg had hired was sitting on the bumper of his gem-blue Daewoo Tico, smoking. As we neared, he looked over at us, leaped up off his bumper, and flicked his cigarette into a puddle. With smoke dragoning from his smiling gold-filled mouth, he relieved us of our bags.

"Nice car," I told the driver once we were moving. I was not certain why I said this. The Daewoo Tico was made of aluminum and its wheels were slightly larger than dinner plates. When we drove over gravelly, half-finished roads, it was as if we were being hit by a hailstorm from below. But it was new, and clean, and it was clear our driver was having a ball piloting it.

"Thank you!" he said. "I just won it in the *lotereya*!"

"The what?"

"The lottery," Rustam said.

"Uzbekistan has a lottery?"

"Of course," Rustam said.

"*Lotereya!*" the driver said—seconds before a policeman appeared from behind a tree. The policeman lifted his truncheon, its plastic tip flashing red, and coolly directed us over to the side of the road. The driver complied, shaking his head with hand-in-the-cookie-jar rue. He flipped down his visor, where a thick stash of sums had been tucked beneath a clip.

"Can't someone do something about this?" I asked while the driver was paying off the officer.

Rustam looked at me with puzzlement. "About what?"

"About the cops. It's ridiculous. They don't even attempt to *pretend* that this isn't simply naked profiteering."

"What are you talking about? He was speeding."

"But *everyone* here speeds, all the time."

"Right."

"Why not give people a ticket?"

"Why give people a ticket when you can just take care of it here?"

"I think I've been in Uzbekistan too long."

Rustam laughed. "Why do you say that?"

"Because what you just said makes perfect sense."

Soon Ferghana City formed around us. Homes first, then stores, then the city center. It was a young and very Russian city, heavy on parks, statues, fountains, and intersections. The streets were arranged in the same radial manner of equally Russified Tashkent. In Tashkent the streets streaked out into surrounding neighborhoods from the city's central statue of Amir Timur. Ferghana City's locus was provided by a largely built-over Russian fortress constructed in 1874, which was also the year of the city's founding. This fort had been the base of valley operations for the regional tsarist garrisons. The Soviets had let the fort fall apart as an artifact of Old Russia's imperialism, though they rather pointedly neglected to knock it down. It was useful as a symbol of one of the few successful European interventions in such a devoted Muslim region. Ferghana City's Russian origins explained the startling number of Slavs still walking its sunny, tree-lined streets.

Rustam noticed me looking. "I told you it was like Russia, bro. Much better than Namangan. I may be from Namangan, but Ferghana City is home."

"It's nice," I said. "When did you move here?"

"In 1994. I was sixteen." He brightened. "Hey, check it out! See that house? That's where I first got laid!" He pivoted in his seat and pointed out the back window. "And that park's the first place I ever smoked pot."

Oleg grunted something. Rustam nodded and said, "Oleg is saying that tomorrow morning, early, we're leaving for Shakhimardan. That's where the funeral is. But it's not really a funeral. Oleg's friend Yuri has been dead for forty days now, and it's a tradition, a Russian tradition, that after forty days all of Yuri's friends have to go to his grave and share . . . a quiet moment?"

"Before you said that all the rebels were in Kyrgyzstan. Isn't Shakhimardan *in* Kyrgyzstan?"

"Of course. But—"

"Just making sure you knew that."

"Okay, but they're not in *that* part of Kyrgyzstan. Not anymore. After the American hostage crisis, they left."

A few minutes later we pulled up to Rustam's house. I was not able to see much of it behind the dented front gate save for the roof, a gently pitched triangle of reddish shingles, and a tall side building that had the dark, neglected look of a stable. I had begun to climb out of the car when Rustam's hand flew to my shoulder. "Whoa, dude. What are you doing?"

"Going with you."

"No. You're staying with Oleg tonight. I thought I told you this."

I looked down at Rustam's hand until he pulled it away. His eyes were wide and brown, perfect circles of worry. I asked, "I can't even say hello to your mom and dad?"

"She's sick, bro. I told you that. You can meet them later. When we get back." The old accommodating smile returned, growing beneath his mustache with the almost unnoticeable pretense of the actor I had begun to realize he was. "Okay? Is that okay?"

"That's fine," I said, managing, much less convincingly, my own willed smile. "I look forward to it."

He backed away from the car and stood there, waving. Not until we were almost around the corner did he turn to open his gate and go inside.

From Rustam's we drove to Yuri's house. It was just past five in the afternoon, the most melancholy time of day, when the shadows darken and the sky fills with loss. Inside Yuri's compound, fifteen men and women, mostly Russian, hard-looking and middle-aged, sat silently at a long picnic table. They shared two bottles of vodka and two plates of cold, unappetizing blinis. Yuri's widow, a child-sized brunette with muscular shoulders, rose to greet us before quickly reclaiming her place at the table. For the next few hours I sat alone at the table's far end and listened. Being in Uzbekistan this long had restored to my memory quite a few Russian words. Still, I could understand virtually nothing of spoken

Russian, though most of what everyone said clearly concerned Yuri. Each story was usually followed by soft group laughter that never managed to open anyone's mouth. By 7 P.M. Yuri's widow had placed a squat white candle in the middle of the table. I watched the flame's inconsistent glow illume and darken the contours of the surrounding faces. These people, even the women, were all *alpinisty,* mountain climbers. Seemingly everyone wore bits of mountain gear: windbreakers, flannel shirts, boots. Badly healed fingers, no doubt broken in some narrow handhold, wrapped familiarly around shot glasses. After the shots were swallowed, forearms bulged and beards were rubbed. Everyone kept shrugging. Forty days after their friend's death, they were still shrugging.

After a while Oleg and Yuri's widow led me from the table, across the courtyard, and into the house. I passed through rooms that appeared to have been ransacked—drawers open, boxes half-packed, clothing everywhere—before being escorted into a tiny back-house space stripped of everything but its couch. Oleg and Yuri's widow both provided long, complicated instructions that had to do with the room's light fixture, said something about flushing, or not flushing, the toilet, and mentioned I either could or could not use the outside shower in the morning. As Yuri's widow was explaining some other morning procedure, her gaze faded from mine and began to drift around the room. She stopped speaking and for a moment was still. Then her hand slapped over her mouth. She rushed away, choking back her tears. Oleg apologized and hugged me softly good night. He pulled the door shut behind him, darkness rushing across me. I sat there quietly for a while, then touched a button on my watch, which summoned up a tiny blue square. Nine P.M. I lay down on the couch in what I now realized had been Yuri Ivanovich's study.

The next morning Rustam and I installed ourselves in the aft of the school bus that Yuri's friends had chartered to take us up into Shakhimardan. Ten additional mourners had arrived sometime last night, and the bus was filling up with silent men and women carrying duffel bags filled with equipment, plastic bags stretched tight with food, and boxes, quite a few of them, stocked with vodka bottles. "You're looking at some of Uzbekistan's most famous mountain climbers," Rustam whispered.

"I thought I was looking at some of Uzbekistan's most dedicated alcoholics."

"No, dude. Seriously. Some of these guys climbed Everest for the Uzbek government."

"Yeah?"

He nodded. "And a lot of them were friends with Anatoly Bukreyev. You know him?"

I did. Bukreyev, an ethnic Russian from Kazakhstan, had been one of Central Asia's most experienced and well-regarded adventurers. He had become famous in the West thanks to Jon Krakauer's *Into Thin Air*, in which he played a significant, largely heroic part. He had been killed in a Himalayan landslide in Nepal shortly after Krakauer's book was published.

I looked at Oleg, sitting across the aisle from us, one seat up. He was asleep, his head lolled back as though his neck had been broken. "I have," I admitted, "a hard time imagining how Oleg climbed out of bed this morning, much less how he's going to make it up a mountain."

"But he does. All of these guys have the mountain sickness. That's what it's called in Ferghana. They say the mountains call your name, and you spend the rest of your life trying to figure out which one called you."

"You're not a sufferer, I take it."

"If the mountains called me," Rustam said, "I didn't hear them."

The excursion's last few members stepped up onto the bus. The first were two colonels in the Uzbek army, one of whom commandeered the bus driver's seat. Then an old Russian woman wearing multiple shawls, who Rustam guessed was Yuri's mother. Then three Uzbek men with long black hair and fancy Nike windbreakers for once, it appeared, not pirated. Then a hulking, balding Russian man with a brushy gray mustache and the tiny, penetrating eyes of an opossum. And, finally, behind him, his daughter. Seats up front were few now, most occupied by duffel bags and vodka. One of the colonels ventured back toward Rustam and me and sat across the aisle from us, behind Oleg. The young woman, right behind him, plopped down sideways in the seat ahead of us, her back pushed up against the window and her sneakers thrust out into the aisle. She looked no older than twenty. Her slept-on hair was a frizzy halo of blond-brown curls and split ends, and her pewter Russian eyes had a beautifully slight Asian cast. She wore a loose red T-shirt and, fetchingly, dog tags that read THE OFFSPRING. Her right hand was covered by a gauzy white bandage. Already her father, who had sat down with a friend near the front of the bus, glanced back at her protectively. For a moment our eyes met. I broke contact to find his daughter staring at me, then Rustam, then me, smiling in a secretive way. "I am Lena," she said in English as the bus pulled away from Yuri's.

I looked over at the colonel sitting across the aisle. An ethnic Russian in his forties, the colonel wore a black sidearm that seemed made mostly of plastic, desert-camouflage pants, and a tan tank top. On his pale, hairless bicep was a pink smear of trauma-puckered flesh. My father, Captain John C. Bissell, USMC, had a few of these scars. The colonel looked over at me and nodded. I returned his nod and, with a questioning expression, tapped the part of my arm that corresponded to his wound. "Afghanistan," he said grimly.

Rustam described our adventures to Lena. Soon he pulled out a copy of trusty *Men's Journal* to show Lena the contributor's photo of his famous American writer friend. She was much more impressed by a photo that accompanied an article about skydiving, snatching the issue away from Rustam. "I want to jump!" she said suddenly, mashing the magazine against her chest.

"Have you jumped before?" I asked.

"Many times," she said, the words coming off her tongue slowly and densely pronounced. "Thirty-six times? I do not remember." She sighed, and looked again at the photo. "Jumping. Jumping is like drug to me."

"Lena's dad is in charge of Ferghana's mountain rescue team," Rustam explained. "That gives him many . . . special benefits."

"You can have that magazine," I told Lena, "if you'd like it." It was my last copy.

She looked at me with sudden suspicion. "Yes?"

"Please."

The young *parashutistya* planted a loud kiss upon the magazine's cover and instantly turned around, head tipped forward, as she searched like an archivist through its pages for another skydiving photo. All the while she sang the Offspring's "Pretty Fly (For a White Guy)" to herself.

After thirty miles we came to Uzbekistan's border with Kyrgyzstan, a massively policed checkpoint among dusty and unvegetated mountain foothills. The border's tall chain-link fence, topped with hundreds of yards of cyclonic barbed wire, was crowded on both sides with armed soldiers and olive jeeps and pickup trucks. The gates opened for the bus without question—we did not even slow down—our colonel chauffeur saluting men on both the Uzbek and Kyrgyz sides. And, suddenly, we rumbled up the rising mountain roads of Kyrgyzstan, even though our destination was Shakhimardan, a part of Uzbekistan. This was possible due to Stalin's partitioning, which stranded several small "islands" of Uzbek territory along the southern edge of Uzbekistan's portion of the Ferghana Valley. These island enclaves, which on a map look like teardrops, were created, the Soviets claimed, to reflect their ethnic makeup. Such claims begged the question as to why, then, was Uzbek- istan given Tajik-majority cities such as Bukhara and Samarkand? And why, for that matter, was Kyrgyzstan mandated the heavily Uzbek city of Osh (the site, not unrelatedly, of horrific ethnic rioting in 1990)? For these questions the Soviets had few answers—or, at least, few to which they could admit. The answer was actually quite simple: to sow exactly this type of confusion.

Running contiguous with our road was one of the valley's many heavily bled rivers, a fast trickle skirting the bed's bigger boulders. A few old Kyrgyz men crouched along the bank, using the trickle to fill flasks and canteens. The Kyrgyz had much less Turkic blood than the region's other peoples. Many of them looked thin-faced and vaguely Chinese. In Central Asia, a large part of a man's ethnonational identity is drawn from the unlikely cistern of haberdashery. In Uzbekistan and Kazakhstan this meant the skullcap doppa. Turkmen were partial to huge wiglike things, known as *telpaks*, that strikingly resembled Julius Erving's afro from his ABA days. The Kyrgyz, far and away, sported the silliest cha- peaus in all of Central Asia—pointy black hats that fell motifwise some- where between a colonial minuteman's tricorner and a British bowler.

Poor Kyrgyzstan. One heard that quite often in Central Asia, from diplomats and aid workers and Uzbeks and knowledgeable tourists. Of the five Central Asian states, Kyrgyzstan had the freest press, the most liberal president (Askar Akayev, a former university professor), the most transparent government, and the least byzantine environment in which to conduct business. Alone among its brethren, Kyrgyzstan had made seri- ous efforts to reform its economy, privatize its land, and open itself to tourism. And where did all of this get the country? Some large early loans from the IMF, some careless Western investment (optimists briefly spoke of a "Central Asian Switzerland"), a reputation as being friendly, and now, unrest, poverty, frustration, less freedom, and an economic output that accounts for only 59 percent of its 1989 GDP. Not everyone despaired of where Kyrgyzstan's openness had left it, especially not the hundreds if not thousands of Islamic Movement of Uzbekistan guerrillas who used its hills as the launching point of assaults on the Uzbek mainland. The IMU carried out such assaults in 1999 and 2000 (during which IMU fighters came within seventy miles of Tashkent) and, I later learned, in 2001, some of the fighting occurring not too many miles away from the bus in which I now traveled. The IMU knew that the Kyrgyz army was not large or well equipped enough to hunt its drones down, and Juma Namangani himself was thought to have traveled throughout Kyrgyzstan under assumed names. This had massively destabilized Uzbek-Kyrgyz relations. After the Tashkent bombings Karimov had publicly attacked President Akayev as being weak, and later accused him of willfully harboring IMU terrorists. This, in turn, enraged Akayev. These were not Kyrgyz dissidents roaming his nation, he reminded Karimov, but Uzbek nationals Karimov had his part in creating. In this Akayev had a point. Most historians agree that the Kyrgyz cultural temperament, thanks to two thousand years of nomadism and no collective memory of Islamic glory, simply did not allow for the widespread embrace of militant Islam. The Kyrgyz came to Islam far later than the Uzbeks and, as nomads, practiced it much less. The Kyrgyz relationship to Islam was vernacular, more oral-mythological than political. A 1998 survey revealed that Uzbeks were more than twice as likely to attend mosque as the Kyrgyz.

Over the last few years Kyrgyzstan's small but reliable inflow of tourists—the nation surely ranks among the most beautiful in the world—suffered hits from which it had yet to recuperate. The first occurred in the early days of August 1999, when the IMU launched its initial offensive, taking several Kyrgyz policemen and government officials hostage in the village of Zardaly. The Kyrgyz military rushed into the country's southern mountains in response—as did the uninvited Uzbek air force, which bombed several villages and killed an undisclosed number of Kyrgyz civilians. The Kyrgyz army withdrew, claiming the IMU had been driven out of the region. They had not been. On August 22, in one of southern Kyrgyzstan's most remote areas, IMU soldiers happened across four Japanese geologists employed by the Japan International Cooperation Agency (a large provider of Kyrgyz aid) and their Kyrgyz interpreter. The geologists and their interpreter were taken hostage. A ransom of $4 million was demanded for their release. The poorly equipped Kyrgyz army surrounded the guerrillas, who numbered in the hundreds. Unfortunately, the IMU had by now taken hostage as many as five Kyrgyz villages in a narrow impregnable gorge, increasing their total number of captives to over a thousand. The standoff lasted two months and cost the Kyrgyz government the lives of a dozen soldiers and officials. The Japanese hostages were finally released in late October, reportedly after Japan's government secretly paid the IMU $3 million in ransom. Karimov, furious at the ease with which the IMU was allowed to rampage in Kyrgyzstan, put even tighter restrictions on the Kyrgyz-Uzbek border. This was to the lasting distress of Kyrgyz and Uzbek traders whose livelihood depended on their smooth and unhindered passage across the Ferghana Valley's historically open borders, and to the delight of Namangani, whose diabolical maneuvering had ensured that Uzbekistan could not act against him without first invading sovereign Kyrgyzstan. Rather than work together with Kyrgyzstan to fight the IMU, Karimov transformed Uzbekistan into an isolationist fortress. Only after the Tashkent bombings, two months later, did Uzbekistan seek outside help—not from Kyrgyzstan but from Russia, marking the first time the nations had ever cooperated on anything so sensitive.

The events that closed 1999's Rebel Season so barely stirred Western consciousness that, a year after the Japanese geologists had been seized, four American rock climbers were taken hostage by the IMU only a few miles from Shakhimardan. The rock climbers, the oldest of whom was twenty-five, had hardly glanced at State Department warnings about the situation in Kyrgyzstan, and were not cautioned at all by local travel agents, despite the IMU's published admonition that "the Islamic Movement warns tourists coming to this land that they should keep away, lest they be struck down by the Mujahedeen." An undeniably wrenching ordeal ensued for these youthful Americans: a fellow hostage, a Kyrgyz soldier, was executed practically before their eyes. The Americans' captivity ended only when a member of their party pushed one of their Uzbek keepers over the edge of a cliff. When the keeper later turned up alive, and in prison in Bishkek, the Kyrgyz capital, many wondered after the veracity of the Americans' account. While a few of the story's particulars remain foggy, the climbers, it is now clear, were telling the truth.

The American hostage crisis was a mere subdrama of the second IMU offensive. Its skirmishes featured vastly better equipped IMU guerrillas but equally superior Kyrgyz troops, whose Snow Leopard and Skorpion commando units had in the previous year trained at Fort Campbell, Kentucky. During the Kyrgyz army's attempt to rescue the American hostages, as well as the season's other, interrelated battles, several dozen Kyrgyz soldiers were slain, and the IMU retreated back into Afghanistan. Poor Kyrgyzstan.

Now it was spring 2001, Rebel Season again, though if patterns held, the IMU was simply moving and planning. The region's Islamists usually chose the fall to act, which, later that year, the world would learn did not apply only to Central Asian tactics. Juma Namangani's loyalty to bin Laden and the Taliban would, in November 2001, fatally place him beneath an American jet on a bombing run outside of Kabul, though other sources claim he was killed by the troops of ethnic Uzbek warlord Abdul Rashid Dostum in a gun battle in the Afghan city of Kunduz, a long way from Kabul. In any case, Namangani's body was spirited away by his followers, who quickly buried it to allow his legend to live on. Which it did. By March 2002 several claimed to have seen or spoken to Namangani, supposedly reorganizing for a takeover of the Ferghana Valley. His grave was then found. Of Juma Namangani, whose existence was supported by one fuzzy Soviet-era photograph, the world can take as an epitaph this report from the Russian news agency RIA Novosti: "The remains coincide with a description of the military leader—a short and fat man with short legs." Tohirjon Yuldashev, for his part, was last seen in northern Afghanistan in the Qala-i-Jangi prison fortress, located on the eradicated fringes of Mazar-i-Sharif. Qala-i-Jangi was the site of the now-famous three-day prison uprising in which the American *talib* John Walker was collared. Walker was among the very few prisoners who had not been shot, frozen, or burned to death by the Northern Alliance in the fortress's basement, where the prisoners foolishly decided to wage their last stand. In December 2001, a month after the uprising, I would visit the Qala-i-Jangi fortress. When I asked if anyone knew of Yuldashev's final fate, my translator smiled and drew a finger across his throat.

We passed out of Kyrgyzstan and into Shakhimardan with little fuss, though several Uzbek soldiers hopped aboard to hitch a ride. The mood within the now formidably armed vehicle had not lightened. Yuri's widow and his mother sat in the bus's front seat, arms around each other, the mother's small shawl-draped skull resting against her daughter-in-law's shoulder at a disconsolate angle. We had reached chillier altitudes. Jackets slipped over shoulders. Women blew into their hands. The driver went uphill gingerly. Two cows kept pace beside us. The gears shrieked and whirred. Occasionally, we rolled backward a few feet and with a harsh jolt stopped. Smooth white mounds of snow were accumulated along the road, even though the sun was shining directly on them. When I remarked on this Rustam explained it was mountain magic. Something happened up here, he said. You could drink all the vodka you wanted in the mountains and never get drunk. Sick people came to Shakhimardan and were mysteriously healed. "But," he said, "a lot of the magic disappeared three years ago."

"What happened?"

"A . . . mudslide? A huge mudslide. It washed away a whole town up here. These houses you see are all that's left."

I looked at one little house that did indeed look washed out and battered. Rustam tapped me on the shoulder. I saw out the opposite window a goat gazing down upon our bus from a nearby outcropping. One of its horns had been torn off and down its wizened gray face streamed a steady flow of dark red blood.

Lena, then, turned around and looked at me, her eyes narrowed. "Why are you here?"

"I'm a writer."

"Yes," she said. "I know this. I read your article." She pronounced "read" like *reed*.

"You did?"

"It was interesting."

This was, I had learned, code for not having understood a word of something. "I'm glad you think so."

"Why are you here?"

"I'm writing about Uzbekistan."

"You will go back to America?"

"Eventually."

"When?"

I looked at her bandaged hand. "What happened?" I asked, pointing at it.

She held out her hand to me, her face sharpening like that of a child trying to prove some ineffable conviction. I nodded. Yes, here was Lena's lovely hand. She held out her hand further. I realized she wanted me to touch it. I did, and she smiled again. The bandage was soft and fresh, like cotton. "So what happened?" I asked once more.

"Cooking," Lena said. "I burned?"

I nodded. "Cooking. It's dangerous, cooking."

She rolled her eyes wickedly. "*Very* dangerous."

The bus stopped, and we filed out to climb into smaller, more agile military troop-transport trucks someone had left for us along the dismayingly narrow mountain road. Rustam and I made for the farthest of the six queued trucks. When we climbed into the truck's roomy covered bed, I turned to see Lena following. She stuck out her tongue at me, then laughed. Her father, thank Christ, was nowhere to be seen. "Dude," Rustam whispered, "she *likes* you!" He sounded thoroughly stunned.

Lena made a show of not knowing where to sit before falling right beside me, the flank of her thigh smooshing up against mine. Her head lilted over and plunked onto my shoulder, its weight sending some galvanic charge through me. Lena sighed. She smelled slightly of scalp, sweat, her father's cigarette smoke. She was warm; I could feel her breathing. Oleg, now struggling into the truck himself, looked at us and chuckled something about "brides." Lena's head sparked off my shoulder and she teased him back in Russian. Rustam started to translate, but I cut him off: "I don't want to know."

Our driver, the colonel who had been wounded in Afghanistan, bounded into the truck and marked the commencement of our journey with a shot of vodka. We traveled even more slowly than we had in the bus. I welcomed this caution, as the road was only one or two feet wider than the truck. Rustam unzipped one of the plastic windows sewn into the bed's weatherproofed awning and thrust his head out. After a few seconds he pulled back in, his smile one of thrilled alarm. "Dude! You can't even see the road! It's like a thousand meters down!"

I looked myself. As I did, Lena pinched my waist, lightly, and with disarming intimacy. I tried to ignore this. The wind hit my face like a series of cold slaps. The drop was indeed impressive. The truck's tires nudged rocks off the road's edge, and they tumbled with silent awfulness into the perpetually shady gorge below. The bottom of the gorge was lined with huge car-sized boulders, including one blackened mass of rocks I suddenly realized was not rocks but rather the scorched remains of a truck. The truck had been the same make as this truck. I could see that from the massive Russian grille and the bed's thin broken ribbing, exposed after its awning had burned to a crisp. When I rezipped the window I asked if everyone was aware that a truck had plunged off this road.

Everyone, of course, was. It had happened five months ago, during the winter. Yuri Ivanovich himself had rappelled into the gorge to look for possible survivors. There were none. Seven people had been killed, including a baby. Lena pinched me again. I liked it, this time.

After forty minutes of our slow, patient climb up the mountain, we abandoned the troop transports. The path was too narrow to drive along anymore. Lena walked next to me. We were buffeted on the left by a crumbly scarp and on the right by howling nothingness. Her father lingered a few feet ahead of us, carrying two large duffel bags, occasionally glancing over his shoulder. The mountains did not seem so high anymore, their piedmonts invisible and their snow-thickened divides far below us. I could make out the speckled shale shining upon the mountains' shoulders and count the spurs and shelves. An occasional speck that I was told was a goat or ibex straggled across the faraway faces. The range's peaks were as jagged as badly torn cardboard, the cirrocumulus clouds that hovered above them strangely shadowless.

I watched the forward portion of our party take turns walking over a wide metal plank someone had placed across a sizable break in the path. The makeshift bridge sported no handrail, and below it rushed a fast icy river. When we came to the bridge, Oleg dug into his duffel and pulled out a stickerless bottle of home-brew vodka and the sawed-off top half of a plastic Coke bottle. After making sure the cap was screwed on tightly Oleg flipped the halved bottle over and poured into it a snifter of hooch. Lena was first. Blinking and coughing, she passed the Coke bottle to her father, which Oleg quickly refilled. Lena's father partook and passed the bottle to Rustam. "No thanks," I said once the colonel had downed his vodka and held out the bottle for me.

Oleg spoke some musical Russian homily. "It's tradition," Rustam translated. "Before you cross the bridge, you have to drink."

The dreadful vodka left my mouth awash with some mysterious sediment. I swallowed and gasped. It was as though my taste buds had been assassinated. I was deciding that I did not think I ever wanted to drink vodka again when Oleg poured me another. I protested.

"The first is tradition," Oleg said. "The second is for nerves." And, beginning with me, we all ingested another shot. Oleg gave his second a teeth-cleansing swish before swallowing and returning the vodka to his duffel bag. How was it, I wondered, that every Russian tradition, whether eating or dancing or marrying or climbing mountains or crossing a bridge, somehow managed to incorporate getting smashed? I was, at any rate, rapidly disproving Rustam's thesis that mountain air provided imperviousness to vodka. My stomach quivered as though it were filled with sea jelly. While I walked up the path, I kept a guide hand against the friable cliff wall to my left while Lena retained her hold upon my other arm.

The gorge to our right gradually filled up with bright white boulders. Once the gorge was navigable, Oleg abandoned the path and led us across it. He called this pass the Stone River. On the other side of the Stone River was a large stretch of wet, spongy grass. We were in an open, greener world now, out of the mountains' enormous shadows, and the sun seemed to encase my body in leg-weakening warmth. Up ahead I could hear various people asking Rustam, "Is the American all right?" "He's not dying, is he?" "Is he going to make it?"

Lena was still by my side. "Easy," she said, and squeezed my hand.

The final push was up an incline of loose, fragrant dirt onto a flattened hilltop that held a loose stand of pine trees. By the time we all made it atop the grassy hill, everyone's knees and elbows were filthy. I was brushing myself off again when I saw Yuri's burial marker. With the exception of Rustam, Lena, and me, our party had collected around the grave and lowered their heads: Uzbek and Russian, Muslim and Christian, every one of them bound by mountain sickness and their love of a single man. The grave rested alone below the pine trees in a clearing overlooking the valley and mountains. It was as beautiful a place to have been buried as I could imagine. The gravestone itself was a simple dark gray rectangle. A badly weathered photo of Yuri was heavily taped to its face, below this inscription: YURI IVANOVICH G——, 1951–2001. Next to the grave was a Russian Orthodox cross, which, with its characteristic three crossbars, resembled a television antenna. I sat down on the hill's edge. Rustam and Lena fell next to me. One of the longhaired Uzbeks spoke in Russian for several minutes, gesturing around at the mountains. Oleg spoke. Another Russian man spoke. Yuri's widow spoke. A cloud passed overhead, near enough to feel its cool vaporous moisture. Along the horizon were several more, darker clouds. It would rain later. The cloud floated away upon some invisible carpet of convection.

"How did Yuri die?" I asked Rustam quietly.

"Heart attack."

Lena began to touch my arm, as lightly as she had pinched me, dragging her thin fingers from the crook of my elbow to my wrist, then beginning again, as though she were petting me. "I want to stay with you here tonight," she said.

Higher up in the mountains was a small resort in which many of these climbers lived during the climbing season. Yuri had owned it. A few of us were sleeping in the resort for two nights before returning to Ferghana. I looked at Lena. "You do?"

She seemed confused, almost pained. She nodded.

Over Lena's shoulder I could see Rustam looking off into the valley below us, smiling and shaking his head.

"I ask my father if I stay here," Lena said, still touching my arm.

This young woman knew no more than two hundred words of English. She was nineteen years old. She was beyond lovely. My heart was breaking.

"I don't know if that's a good idea," I said.

"I ask my father. I don't want to go back to Ferghana. Boring in Ferghana."

Yuri's mourners were now taking their solitary turns at his grave. Some knelt before it and prayed, others placed a single flower on the topsoil. Some placed cupcakes beside the flowers, and others kissed the stone. Yuri's mother was last. She touched her fingertips to her son's photograph and with that broke down, shoulders shuddering. She began to fall over before someone rushed to her side. It was not hysterical, or undignified. It was simply loss, irrecoverable loss. In a hot watery rush tears pushed out of my ducts. I looked over at Rustam to see that he, too, was crying. "Fuck," he said, embarrassed, when he noticed me looking at him. Roughly, he ground his fists into his sockets, stood, and walked over to a nearby pine tree. He lingered there, amid its spiny bundled shadows, his back to us as Lena kept touching my arm.

Of course, Lena's father did not allow her to stay with me or anyone else. As the majority of the funeral party made its broken-spirited way back down to Ferghana, Lena kissed me on the cheek and said goodbye. Then she and her father turned and started off down the path behind the others. The nine of us who remained had to carry provisions to the resort, another kilometer up the mountain. These provisions were intended to last throughout the summer, and multiple trips were required to haul all the duffels and plastic bags and boxes of vodka. "Resort" was probably too lavish a word for the five spartan chalets set back in the pines at path's end, their red steep-pitched triangular roofs as bright as stop signs within the thick evergreen needles. Directly behind the chalets a deep river twenty yards wide rushed and splashed and filled the air with spume. In the middle of the return leg of my second trip, I blacked out or collapsed. I am not certain what happened. One moment I was walking alone, the next I was pushing myself up from the gravel, the box of vodka bottles I had been carrying upended next to me. Miraculously, only one bottle had broken. It was becoming clear that mountain sickness was in my case something more than metaphysical. Sadir, an Uzbek with long curly hair who had spoken at Yuri's funeral, rushed up the path behind me, shouting, "Tombek! Ho, Tombek!"

"I fell," I said stupidly, still struggling to get to my feet. My strength was gone, and any number of interestingly flashbulblike phenomena transpired upon my retinal field.

Sadir laughed and hoisted me up by my arm. He was a strapling of a man, as strong and ropy as a marathoner. I figured him for a rock climber. The mountains had made him ageless—he could have been twenty-five or forty. His purple Nike windbreaker flapped and popped like a sail in the suddenly vigorous wind, his long black ringlets whipping in his face. Sadirbek stopped laughing when he got a clearer look at my face. He put down his duffel bag, then held up two fingers before my eyes. *"Skolko?"* he asked. How many? I was about to answer when I turned my head and vomited.

An hour later we had a plov lunch in the one chalet equipped with a kitchen. These chalets had been put together with the little building material the surrounding mountains could provide: pinewood floors, pinewood walls, pinewood beams, pinewood bar, pinewood tables. Seated around me were seven *alpinisty* and Rustam. The topic on everyone's mind was the state of "the White American," a nickname my new pallor had earned me. If I looked white, I felt whiter. I could scarcely hold my head up. The men studied me as though I were some anesthetized zoological specimen they had been asked to anatomize. From time to time they offered advice in confident, stentorian tones that seemed directed at everyone but me.

"He needs to walk outside."

"Plov. He needs to eat his plov. He's hardly touched it."

"What he should do is swim in the river."

"He needs air. Mountain air."

Vasily, the colonel wounded in Afghanistan, forked at his food and muttered, "Give him vodka, he'll feel better."

The other colonel, Igor, quickly poured me a glass with the profligacy one might use to pour milk. "Here," he said, flecks of masticated rice popping out of his mouth. "Drink this."

"He can't," Rustam translated for me. "He says he'll throw up."

"That's right," Colonel Igor said. "That's normal."

Sadir gallantly drank the vodka, refilled the glass with cherry juice, and set it before me. "Thank you," I said.

The other two Uzbeks were named Sukhrob and Sherpa. Sherpa was not, I am fairly certain, his real name, but it was what everyone called him. Like Sadir, both wore their hair long. This was highly unusual for Uzbek men. Mountain climbing, it seemed, provided these Uzbek hippies with a countercultural layer of protection. Sukhrob, a fat-lipped man in his mid-thirties, wore thin camouflage pants as sheer as lingerie. I had never seen anything like these pants before and almost certainly never will again. Beneath the sheer camouflage pants I could see the black triangle of Sukhrob's vividly tight Speedo. Sherpa ate quietly and said little, looking sleek and expensive in his Nike and North Face mountain wear, his hair pulled back into a beautifully shiny black ponytail. This left the other ethnic Russian, Vanya. He had been Yuri's best friend and managed this resort for him. Vanya had only two teeth, an upper-deck molar and a long white incisor, and wore a T-shirt that read ALCATRAZ: PSYCHIATRIC WARD, and beneath that, in red letters, OUTPATIENT. The men toasted Yuri, and the White American, and Rustam, and the resort, which they all said would soon fare better than ever. It was obvious no one believed this. The resort had done some very good business with German, Italian, Swiss, and French climbers in the mid-to-late 1990s, but in the last few years, the IMU years, the place was nearly abandoned.

I had had enough. I thanked them for lunch and stood. Where, my friends wondered, was I going? The party was just starting! Only another shot of vodka secured the necessary goodwill for my escape. Shakily, I walked along the river to Rustam's and my chalet, and fell asleep as the first boom of low, faraway thunder spread throughout the darkening afternoon air.

When I woke up it was 7 P.M. in the T'ien Shan Mountains. Outside, it was raining. I felt somewhat restored and stepped out on the chalet's porch wrapped in a prickly blanket, my breath floating from my mouth in thick white puffs. The rain dripped from clouds no higher than ten feet above me. It was less like rain than being underwater: even beneath the eaves I was getting soaked. Over the rain and river roar I could hear a party going on in the main chalet. If I was not mistaken, they were listening to Rustam's Depeche Mode tape: "People Are People."

I had returned to bed when Rustam stormed into the chalet in the clumsy, aggressive manner of a man whose drink-blurred world had become a conspiracy of too-narrow doorways, hidden stairs, and vexingly placed furniture. After knocking over a chair on his way to my bed, he sat down, his jaw slackened, his eyes only marginally open, water dripping from his nose and earlobes. "Dude," he said. "You awry?"

"What?"

His head tipped forward, water pattering on the blanket. "You all right?"

"I'm all right. I feel a little better."

He fell asleep sitting there on the bed. Or seemed to. His eyes burst open, and he regarded me with something close to anger. "You throw up again?"

"No."

He nodded and stared hard at the bedspread. His jaw was set at a nasty prognathous angle, his temples pulsing. As suddenly as he had been roused to this unexplained anger, he faded out of it, his face relaxing. "You—you sure you don't wanna party, dude?"

"I'm fine here."

His eyes closed again. Thirty seconds later they opened. "Hey. Listen. We're cool, right?"

"We're cool."

He nodded. It took him several minutes to travel from my bed to the chalet's door. He stopped to right the tipped-over chair, then for a long time stood looking at my notebooks spread out on the room's small worktable. After this he tried to start a fire in the chalet's fireplace but stopped when he realized he had no firewood, or matches. He left. A few moments later he came back in and again sat on my bed. He had pine needles in his hair.

"Dude," he said. "Gotta tell you something. My mom's. Not sick. She not sick. I lied to you, bro. I'm sorry."

"It's okay."

"So yeah. All right. We're cool. And my dad. He's. He's not in Ferghana."

"Where is he?"

He shrugged, gazing just past my face with an intensity that unnerved me. I did not know where his mind was. One never does with drunks. You are never the person they need you to be. He leaned so close to me I could see the hair in his nostrils shiver. "Bro, he's in, like, prison. That's why I gotta. That's why I'm here. My mom's. Oh shit, dude, A fucking *problem*." With a bitter laugh he fell silent.

I looked at him. "Are *you* all right?"

In response, he sang the word "dude" to himself in a rising alto scale. "Dude, doood, doooood." He smiled at me. "Big, big problem."

"I'm sorry."

His eyes had a dull, matted shine. "I wanted you to know, bro. You're, like, my bro."

"And you're mine. I mean that."

"I know you do. I know. So that's my, uh. My problem. I don't know what to do about any of this. I'm confused about many things right now."

"Can I help?"

His head shook briskly. "Negative." He looked around the room with fresh irritation. "It's fucking *cold* in here." With that he left again and this time did not come back. I lay in bed quietly, the rain spattering upon the roof and leaking off the eaves. I listened, traveling further and further inside my head. Rustam's admission filled me with a devouring, helpless sadness, but I was not surprised. I tried to figure out what to do. My paucity of options—stay here, or go to a party with eight drunken Uzbek nationals, two of them armed—resulted in a crush of gloom as real as the blankets on top of me. Thunder again, but more distant now, a sound as strange and sorrowful as church bells in a city. Travel did many things to a person, but the one thing it did most successfully was break a person down. Admittedly, my travel experiences were not very representative. My experience with travel was Central Asia. Central Asia, then, broke a person down. It did so first by exhilaration. *Was this place real? Was I really here?* It did so next by exhaustion. Nothing was easy, and each hassle and bribe and malfunction and injustice took something of one's spirit, bent it, made it meaner. Then came the most brutal breakdown of all: the knowledge of how easily one could live within that meanness.

I counted the number of days left in this trip before I could go home. Rather than receive a dispiriting tally in the triple digits, as I had in the Peace Corps, I was left with a number in the manageably mid twenties. I had been in Uzbekistan for two weeks. But what had I done? Caused Rustam to miss an amount of school reparable only by bribes. Failed to get an impoverished woman her money. I had not even seen the Aral Sea. On the flight over I thought that it would be the first place I would visit. But now I had hesitated for too long and in that hesitation had created some strange, insuperable pretext for fear.

Upriver the music continued. The *alpinisty* were howling into the foggy night. How was it with these men? It was freezing, and raining, and every one of them was broke. They had bankrupted themselves on their provisions, even joking about it at lunch. The coming season's ledger was empty of expeditions and clients. Violent rebels roamed these peaks. And yet here they were, partying, laughing, forgetting. Mountain life seemed so elemental. Height, air, weather, gravity—these were lethal properties, not schoolhouse theoreticals. Perhaps they used the mountains to exchange the nature of their fears, to amortize their worries. If you drank a little too much, wandered a little too far, you fell off the path, and you died. Mudslides, and you died. Met the wrong person along the wrong mountain trail, and you were kidnapped, and odds were you died. But what happened to you if you were broke? Nothing. You lived.

At 11 P.M. it was still raining. Sleep was, for some reason, impossible. I got out of bed, having decided to write in my notebooks ("The most deceptive aspect of procrastination is that it, too, involves taking action; only, it is the wrong action") until the rain ceased. At midnight Rustam returned and told me how rude it seemed to the others that I would not join the party. "Look," I said. "I just don't feel like drinking." Rustam's hand floated up solemnly. He promised that, if I came with him, I would not be "pushed" to drink. I sighed, frustrated that I no longer needed to be convinced.

The main chalet had new visitors: three Kyrgyz soldiers from the Shakhimardan border and, incredibly, three Russian national soldiers who I assumed were helping the Kyrgyz army hunt for IMU guerrillas. They were friends of Colonels Igor and Vasily. All the soldiers were clad in desert camouflage and wore impressive brown belts and severe black boots. They were also carrying assault rifles and smoking Marlboros. Yet, from the looks of things, they were thankfully abstaining from drink. While Russian soldiers had been in Tajikistan since 1992, Kyrgyzstan had proved reluctant to allow its former overlords back onto Kyrgyz soil. Only in the chaos of the last two summers had this resistance been overcome. Karimov had forbidden any Russian troops from operating within Uzbekistan, his one allowance that of sharing information with Russian intelligence. These Russians, then, were in Uzbekistan illegally, though protocol was of little use in these mountains. I was not sure, as a journalist, whether interacting with the Russians was advisable. Russian soldiers in Kyrgyzstan and Tajikistan had been accused on more than one occasion of colluding with the IMU. According to the journalist Ahmed Rashid, "the fact that since 1999 the Russian army had three times helped evacuate IMU guerrillas to Afghanistan was undeniable. . . . Moscow never bothered to explain the reason for its actions nor why it was helping Namangani escape rather than arresting him." This helped make clear what I had heard from writers in Tashkent who had covered the IMU offensives. The Russian army, they said, hated journalists. (In Afghanistan the Russian military often issued weapons to Russian journalists traveling with soldiers and expected these journalists to pitch in during firefights. In his book *The Hidden War,* the Russian journalist Artyom Borovik wonders, memorably, if he will have to shoot and kill his friend, the Western journalist Peter Arnett, whom he knows to be traveling with the mujahedeen.) Why the Russians occasionally helped the IMU remained unclear, though it was likely that the double-dealing occurred only under the command of Russian soldiers who had a vested interest in IMU drug-running. Rather than embarrass itself by revealing its military's corruption, Moscow remained silent.

Despite Rustam's promise that I would not be pushed to drink, I was poured three shots of vodka the moment I walked through the door. I tipped back the first and merely held the second, stalling for time and looking around for a place to stash it. Sherpa and sloppy Colonel Igor were talking things over in the corner with two of the Kyrgyz. Near the chalet's fireplace Oleg and Vasily were singing boozy Russian songs, replacing the evening's earlier soundtrack of progressive pop. Sukhrob, now wearing only his Speedo (I did not care to know why), sat uncomfortably passed out in a chair next to them. The rest of the party lingered around the bar, upon which one of the Russian soldiers left his rifle while he impressively urinated out of the back door. I made sure to stand next to Rustam, who with Sadir was chasing vodka shots with swigs of beer and radish bites. Rustam lit me a Marlboro. When he turned away, I handed the cigarette to one of the Russian soldiers, a shrew-faced young man named Sergei. As Sergei dragged off the butt, I asked him in my pidgin Russian if he had seen any *basmachi*. Sergei chuckled, then spat on the floor. "I *kill bashmachi*," he said.

Rustam slapped me on the back. "Great party, huh, bro? I'm experiencing serious *kaif*."

Kaif was an Arabic word that had somehow achieved Russian cognatehood. It meant, basically, feeling intense pleasure. "I'm glad you're experiencing *kaif*."

He looked at me, his smile fading. "What's wrong?"

"I can't stay here another day." Only now had I made this decision. I set my shot on the bar. "I'm leaving tomorrow morning."

He learned toward me, ear first. "Say again?"

"Tomorrow morning, I'm leaving. I'm going back to Tashkent and then I'm going to Karakalpakistan."

Rustam seemed instantly sobered. He patted himself down, as though looking for a pen to alter his day planner. "All right, dude. We can—we'll leave in the morning."

I put my hand on his shoulder. "I think you need to stay in Ferghana City with your family. I'm going to Karakalpakistan alone." This decision, too, I had only now made. "Take care of what you need to take care of, Rustam, and I'll see you in Tashkent in ten days. Okay?"

He looked down at his feet. A scatter of cigarette ash dirtied the laces of one of his mountain-scarred Nikes. With the tip of his opposite Nike, Rustam nudged the ash away, leaving upon the laces a light gray smear. This only frustrated him, and his eyes returned to mine. "You're not, like, angry with me, dude, are you?"

"Impossible," I said. "We're bros, remember?"

With a forced, skeptical smile Rustam stepped away from me. Seconds later he was laughing with two of the Russian soldiers, who were reenacting for Vanya a notionally comic story about some border misunderstanding. The story required both soldiers to threaten Rustam, whom they had gamely incorporated into the retelling, with their rifles. Rustam held up his hands and pretended, or perhaps did not pretend, to be afraid. I slipped outside with a feeling of liberation. Oleg rushed into the rain after me, insisting in Russian that he walk with me back to my chalet. Twice he tripped over tree roots, each triggering a long spiel of Russian curses. His foot then slid off a riverbank stone, soaking his leg to the knee. The Russian equivalent of "Fuck me!" was all this earned. Once we reached our destination, I had to accompany Oleg back to the party. When I again slipped my wet body between the bed's refrigerated sheets, my eyes tugged down, my mouth opened, my stomach calmed, my brain dimmed. Thoughts of incrementally lessened clarity hurtled across my consciousness until my mind gave itself over to a kind of static. But suddenly, for the first time in days, I felt sure about something, something that—

And I was asleep.

"Before you go, Sherpa wants to show you the mountain," Rustam told me the next morning. "All he asks for is five dollars. His guide fee."

I had just washed my hair and face in the river, and stood in the middle of the chalet toweling myself off with the plaid button-down short-sleeve I had been wearing for the previous two days. Outside, the pine trees were still dripping dry, though the morning was sunny and warm, the mountain quiet beneath a layer of birdsong and wind. "Yeah? You want to come?"

Rustam shrugged. His face was a bloated hangover mask. He smelled like the seventeenth century. As he spoke, his mouth seemed not to move. "Do you want me to come?"

"Of course I do."

"Then I'll come," he said.

We waited for Sherpa on the porch of the main chalet. I was unsure whether to address what Rustam had told me last night, and stood beside him concocting and revising topic sentences until I gave up. Through the chalet's front door I saw countless mashed cigarette butts that someone had swept into a pile, a dozen empty vodka bottles lined up on the bar, and, on the floor in the middle of the room, a kidney-shaped puddle of whitish vomit. "That's Oleg's," Rustam explained. "There's more out back. And more in the river."

"I really wish someone had told me that before I washed my hair this morning."

"He can't handle his vodka. That's why all these guys call him Malysh. Baby."

"Everyone gets a nickname around here, don't they?"

"I think so, White American."

"So what do they call you?"

For the first time that morning, he smiled. "Handsome."

Sherpa finally appeared, looking remarkably vigorous for a man who had spent the last ten hours drinking. He looked at me and sighed, fingering the straps of my backpack in amusement.

"What?"

"Leave it," he said. "This is just a friendly walk. You don't need equipment. I'll take care of you." With a grin he pulled up his loose electric-blue Nike windbreaker to reveal a large sheathed K-Bar knife hanging off the band of his blue jeans, which a Swiss climber friend had given him as a token of his respect. I dropped my bag and we started up the mountain through a thick forest of pine. As we brushed against the branches, we reconjured the previous night's rainstorm, soaking ourselves to the skin within minutes. The trail, Sherpa guaranteed, was just a few hundred meters away. After half an hour the trail had not yet appeared. I called ahead to Rustam, "What are we going to see up here, anyway?"

"A waterfall, I think." And with that, Rustam began singing the chorus of an old TLC song, "'Don't go chasin' waterfalls' . . ."

"Excuse me," I said, drawing up beside Sherpa, "where's the trail?"

He did not look at me. "We're on the trail."

"We are?"

He nodded, knelt, and waved a short stick over some marble-sized black goat scat. "See? This is the goat trail."

"So there's no . . . people trail?"

He regarded me pathetically. "Your friend makes many jokes," Sherpa said to Rustam, still singing as he walked past us.

The trail grew more visible as we neared the upper reaches of the pass. The trees were replaced by waist-high shrubs speckled with red flowers. The air tasted Alaskan and clean. The blue atmosphere above us was swirled with wispy clouds that looked sculpted by higher, more intelligent winds. We were 10,000 feet above sea level, the sun baking the open, verdant parts of the mountain in bright golden light and dooming other lifeless stretches to huge cold shadows. I walked behind Sherpa, wheezing and wasting oxygen, the altitude having once again made quick work of shredding my bronchial machinery. But Sherpa, no matter the terrain, walked upright, his gentlemanly hands joined behind his back, his breathing as steady as a respirator. "Very close now," he told us after an hour of hiking. We walked over the remains of a landslide, its large, flat stones scattered across a slender path. The stones were round and broken in the manner of thrown-down plates and dishes. Sherpa easily picked his way over the rocks while Rustam and I balanced precariously upon their seesaws and turned our ankles and swore. Beneath our unskilled feet a few rocks slipped over the path's edge and triggered other landslides below. Once the landslide's remnants were behind us, we trudged uphill again, up the mountainside to a better path, through the scrub. Sherpa cleared much but not all of the scrub away with his K-Bar. Rustam pushed aside one of the thorn bushes Sherpa had missed and accidentally let the branch whip back. It tore open my lip as though it were a nail. I declined Rustam's horrified offer to punch him in the mouth.

We came to a windy escarpment made of hard black rock that overlooked a water-carved trench. The escarpment swept down to the trench, which was in fact a largely dry riverbed comprised mostly of smooth gray stones. With a look of satisfaction Sherpa gazed down at the riverbed, perhaps three hundred yards below us. Between our current position and the riverbed, however, was a steep, barely traversable drop strewn with sharp, nasty rock formations and massive boulders. "We have arrived," Sherpa said. "At the end of this riverbed, perhaps two kilometers, is the waterfall."

Down he went along the escarpment's nonexistent path to the riverbed. Rustam and I watched him, hoping to pick up some possible pointers on how we were going to manage this ourselves. In five minutes Sherpa was at the bottom, waving us down. We started off holding each other by the wrist, improvising belays. Twenty minutes and as many arguments later, Rustam and I were both doubled over in deoxygenated stupors at the escarpment's base. "I'm feeling *kaif* again," Rustam said. I nodded. My burning leg muscles felt as though they had been salted, and my eyes were so dry their lids were stingingly adhering to them.

Sherpa thought that perhaps we should rest for a few minutes. Each of us selected a rock and sat down. I had water in my backpack, I thought, wishing I had ignored Sherpa and taken it with me. And a Snickers bar. And Imodium. And blister bandages. "So," I asked Sherpa, still wheezing, "tell me . . . about life . . . up here." I spoke through Rustam, too wrecked even to attempt speaking Uzbek.

"It's the best life in the world," Sherpa said simply, sitting Indian-style on his stone. His mouth was piscine and lipless, his eyes narrow and far apart, his ponytail blackly sparkling in the sunlight. He looked like a mischievous boy. "The mountains make me happy."

"What . . . about . . . the coming season? Any . . . plans?"

He tsked once. "There is no business. Not until the situation improves. This makes me sad. It means I cannot see my German and Swiss friends anymore. I liked it when they came to Shakhimardan very much. You see, they understand the mountains. Not like you Americans." He smiled to show he meant no offense, then looked down at his fingers as they peeled the petals from some tiny yellow flower he had picked up somewhere. "The only clients we get anymore are students who come up from Ferghana City."

"They do that . . . often?"

"Sometimes. We like it when they come. A few years ago Malysh brought his son's class. Sadir and I were lucky. All the kids got drunk, and we fucked the two prettiest monkeys. Then we traded, and fucked them again."

"Monkeys?"

"He means girls," Rustam explained in an abruptly small voice.

I waited until my lungs had recovered and finally managed, "What form were these monkeys in?"

He shrugged. "Ninth form, I think."

Ninth form. This would have made them no older than fifteen. I looked at Rustam. His face was hard as he smacked a small rock against a larger rock. Sherpa's solitary laughter reeled into silence. "Come," he said harshly. "Resting is over."

Although the stony riverbed carried only a small payload of water, it was deep enough in a few places to fall into. We walked and occasionally leaped along the rocks until we came to the river's terminating point—a massive, shadow-cloaked cliff. Its brow was three hundred feet high and serrated with twisted, mighty pine trees. Here, at last, spilling from a break in the cliff's brow, was the waterfall. But it was still frozen, which explained the river's lack of water. Sherpa was disappointed. I was not. It looked beautiful, the waterfall's ice as smooth as marble and, in a trick of light, glowing blue from within. I pushed my hand into the waterfall's softer, snowier edges, pulling free with a handful of slush. I held it to my thorn-sliced lip and lay on a wide stone altar in the middle of the river. "I'm with you, bro," Rustam said, collapsing next to me. Sherpa sat above us, on a nearby thronelike formation of stone, using his K-Bar to whittle away at a stick.

Once my snowball had melted, I rolled over onto my stomach and watched the river quietly flow next to me. The water was so clear I could see down ten inches to the river's silty bottom and count the small stones embedded there. The water, with a kind of inanimate brilliance, found its way downriver by falling off sharp ledges, bending around larger rocks, rising in still, flat plateaus that melted magically into a faster burbling rush of foam. "I'm so thirsty," I told Rustam, "that I'm thinking of drinking this water."

"Go ahead," he said, his eyes closed. His T-shirt collar was miscentered on his neck, and beginning to fray. His jeans were filthy. "It's too cold for parasites."

"You sure about that?"

"Not at all."

I scooped up a handful and sucked it out of my palm.

"How was it?" Rustam asked.

"It's good, man. *Fucking* good. Try some." We lay on our stomachs on different sides of the stone altar, cupping water into our mouths until our stomachs were stretched as tight as wineskins. Only after we had finished did Sherpa decide to tell us that we probably should not have done that, that we would get sick. We ignored him.

"Look, dude," Rustam said in a new tone of voice, "about what I told you last night." He shook his head. "I'm sorry. That wasn't fair. You did not need to know that stuff."

"Don't worry about it. I'm glad you told me."

He sat up. "But what I'm saying is that I'm not glad I told you. It's my problem."

"Can I ask why your father is in prison?"

"Now, you see—" His cupped hands briefly covered his face, then dropped into his lap. "No, bro. You can't. Because I don't want to talk about it. That's why I'm telling you—forget what I said. Do that for me, please."

"Okay."

Rustam skipped a rock across the river. "If you want to know why he's in prison it's because he's not corrupt. There were good Communists, you know. My dad worked harder than anyone I ever met. When this joke, this privatization, started, the mafiya and everyone moved in on my father. But he wouldn't cooperate. So they framed him. Every month I bring him food, but the fucking guards at the prison steal it. I have to bribe them not to steal my dad's food." He was quiet a moment. "Isn't it weird that I have to break the law to prevent them from breaking the law?"

I sat up. "Rustam, listen to me. I have some money if you need it—"

"*Please,*" he said adamantly. "I can't ask you for that."

"You're not asking. I'm offering."

"I can't accept. You're my guest. And money does not always solve problems."

"But I'm not your guest. You're my friend, and I'm yours. Right?"

"My brain," he said softly, looking up at the sky, "doesn't work like yours. I wish it did, bro. But it doesn't." Again he was silent. Then: "You've already given me so much."

"I haven't *given* you anything. The money I've *paid* you was because you're helping me. If it weren't for you I wouldn't have been able to do anything here. I'm a gigantic pussy, remember?"

"Don't say that, Tom. You would have been fine. So, yes, I agree. You've paid me. Fine. But I can't accept any more. I know you're paying me a lot more than normal. And I appreciate that. I only accepted because of my situation. If not for my situation I would have insisted on being paid less, or fairly. Whatever."

I looked away. "You gave all the money to your mom. She's not even sick, is she?"

Again his hands covered his face. "This is why we shouldn't talk about it! I knew you'd be angry!"

"Jesus Christ. I'm not angry! How could I be angry?"

Sherpa whittled. Pale shavings, like wooden confetti, covered his boots.

"This sucks," Rustam said, as though to himself. "This sucks. I shouldn't have said anything. This sucks."

It was late. If I wanted to be back in Tashkent in time to buy a ticket to Karakalpakistan, I had to leave now. I stood. "We're going to talk about this when I get back from Karakalpakistan, okay?"

"Please tell me you're not angry."

"I'm not angry. And to prove to you that I'm not angry, I'm paying you for the next two weeks now."

"But I'm not working for you for these two weeks!"

I dug into my money belt and ripped free a handful of hundreds. I counted off $400 and held it out to him. "You need money to get back to Tashkent, right? You need money to pay off your dean."

His mouth opened.

"Your mom needs food. Give some to your sister." He stood there looking at the dollars in my hand. Sherpa, I noticed from my eye's corner, had stopped whittling. I pushed the money toward Rustam. "Just *take* it, please. You have no idea how happy this will make me. For once allow economic relativity to make me feel *better*."

But Rustam shook his head. "I can't, bro. Not if I'm not working."

"Consider it advance payment, then. Please."

He turned away. "I'm sorry."

We walked back to the resort in silence, the sun so high that our shadows were little misshapen ovals amassed around our feet. We reached the resort a little after 1 P.M. I paid Sherpa his $5. When I said goodbye to Oleg, I gave him a twenty. He accepted it dumbfoundedly. While I packed up my things in the guest chalet, I stuffed the $400 in Rustam's backpack, along with my Snickers bar, his favorite. I wrote a note—"Because you are my friend"—thought better of it, then crumpled and pocketed the scrap of paper. Colonel Vasily escorted me to the troop transports and from there drove me to Uzbekistan's border proper. For this I paid him $10 in sum. I wandered the borderland DMZ until I found a cab—another Nexia—owned by a grizzled Uzbek man who was blind in one eye. A gold-mining accident, I later learned. When I said I wanted to go to Tashkent, the one-eyed driver shook his head no. But what wondrous things money could do. For $100, he agreed. I sat in the front seat with him. I felt like a caricature of an American. The noble idiot. It was strange, feeling like a caricature. We drove through the mountains in silence. After a hundred miles and several checkpoints the one-eyed driver finally spoke. "I see you carry accreditation. What are you? A student?"

"Journalist," I said.

"Yes? You will write about Uzbekistan?"

"I will."

"Write the truth," he advised sternly.

I nodded, suddenly liking this man. *"Albatta."* Of course. Certainly. The countryside whipped past us, though I was not seeing it. I was not seeing anything.

Another hundred miles later the man's curiosity got the best of him. "What in Uzbekistan are you writing about?"

At last I could tell the truth. "The Aral Sea. Tomorrow I'm going to Karakalpakistan."

"Karakalpakistan! Oh, my friend, be careful."

"Why?"

His nose wriggled up his rough, baggy face. His hands shooed away imaginary flies. *"Yomon havo,"* he said grimly. Bad weather. And again he was silent. Inside this car, then, was a strange new energy. I could not tell if this energy was coming from him, or me, or someplace else.

"The land is our heart," the driver said. He made a sudden stabbing gesture, as though he were wielding a shiv. "And the Russians," he said, pounding on his steering wheel. "What, my friend, did Russians do to us? They cut a hole in it. They killed our heart."

Seven

Eternal Winter

This procedure and this form of execution, which you now have the opportunity of admiring, have at present no open supporters left in our colony. I am their sole defender, and at the same time the sole defender of the legacy of our former commandant. I can no longer contemplate any further development of the system; all my energy is consumed in preserving what we have.

—FRANZ KAFKA, "IN THE PENAL COLONY"

The day I landed in Nukus, 150 miles south of the Aral Sea, the sky above the city lacked clouds because the air lacked the moisture to provide them. I stood on the tarmac while, behind me, our plane's engine ticked in the sunshine, its propellers just stilled. The sky's color changed and deepened as my head tipped back, the edges a light icy blue and the dome a deep blueberry blue. Standing there calmed my stomach. The flight into windy Nukus, on an elderly Aeroflot genus known, appropriately, as the Yak-40, was all pitches and yaws, as I had been warned it would be. Foreknowledge had not helped.

I was one of only six people arriving in Nukus today. All of them were now walking toward the terminal. The scuffed wheels of the suitcase I had picked up in Tashkent jounced against the tarmac's cracks as I followed my fellow passengers. Although Nukus was the capital of Karakalpakistan, its airport seemed strangely empty. No planes drank from the nozzles of gasoline trucks. Only one plane was out on the tarmac, at its other end, and I looked at it across an emptiness as eerie as the parking lot of a midwinter theme park. This plane was a large, swollen military transport that, if I was not mistaken, was known as a Hercules. Around the Herc had gathered a half-circle of well-wishers and Nukus functionaries. They were bidding farewell to departing dignitaries or maybe businessmen. Applause floated through the air with a glassy, brooklike lucidity. As the suited leader of the visitors shook hands one last time with a woman who looked to be the leader of Nukus's delegation, a Karakalpak band, hidden behind the well-wishers, suddenly broke into music. What they played sounded grand, national-anthemic. It frustrated me that I had no idea whose national anthem I was hearing. Small waving figures walked up a platform into the plane's steel belly.

Inside the terminal: sparrows. The first seemed as freakish as a deer wandering the aisles of a suburban grocery store. But another followed it. Then three, four, as fast as MiGs. Five, six. I stopped counting. They darted across the large, spring-bright terminal and lifted toward the ceiling, vanishing between girders, muscling into fissures. No one seemed to notice them. I walked to the terminal's appropriate kiosk to register with OVIR. I had been warned by officials in Tashkent that their Karakalpak colleagues were very serious about things such as registration. The kiosk was closed.

A local young MSF staffer named Manas was supposed to pick me up at the airport. I waited alone outside the airport for ten minutes, only a little concerned, before he finally arrived. He was not late, I soon realized. Flights into Nukus were irregular and unreliable. Many were canceled because of fuel shortages. MSF headquarters was across town, and only when Manas looked up and saw my plane inarguably landing did he bother to make his way to the airport. After a quick handshake he threw my bags into the back seat of a beat-up Lada with a prominent MSF decal upon its door, and off we went.

"Busy day?" I asked, sensing that my thin new friend had better things to do than drive me around.

Manas sighed, then laughed, perhaps chagrined to have been so transparent in his emotions. "Oh," he said. "You know. Always busy. Always many things to do."

"Manas," I mused. "That's the name of the Kyrgyz epic poem, yes?"

"Yes," Manas said, "it is."

"The epic poem that's longer and bloodier than *The Iliad*. The poem no one has yet fully translated into English."

"What is an Iliad?"

"It's Greece's *Manas*."

"Ah."

"Are you Kyrgyz?"

"No," he said. "Karakalpak. You are an American?"

"Yes."

"Which state are you from?"

The state from which one hails was of abiding interest to Central Asians, who seemed to think that American states roughly corresponded to the Soviet conceptualization of its former republics. "New York State."

"Mrs. Liberty," Manas said, shifting as we passed a horse-drawn wagon. "Twin Towers. Brooklyn Bridge."

I smiled and looked out the Lada's dusty window. The flat, sand-colored buildings just beyond the airport's gate provided little sense of Nukus's size. Home to anywhere from 180,000 to 300,000 people, Nukus had the pleasant feel of a quiet country city. But the quiet had weight, expectancy, patience. If something happened, it would happen here. Once we neared the city center, the wind began to blow in earnest. We drove through large tidal currents of dust advancing down Nukus's crossword of wide, Soviet-made thoroughfares. Well-dressed women covered their mouths with handkerchiefs. Children lowered their heads. Silent, squinting young men crouched on every corner, spitting sunflower seeds. Trees lined the streets, their full green foliage shuddering in the dust-swarming wind. A photo book entitled *Karakalpakistan*, published in the Soviet Union in the very appropriate year of 1984, had this to say: "Before the Great October Socialist Revolution, [Nukus] was a sentry fortification with two gloomy barracks. . . . History has hardly ever witnessed such a swift uplift from backwardness, disasters and devastation."

"Where do you want to go?" Manas asked suddenly.

"I don't know. Why don't you just drop me off here? I'd like to walk around a bit."

"Yes? Most journalists ask to visit the hotel."

"I'm staying with the friend of a friend. I don't need the hotel. Actually, if you could take my bags to MSF's office, I'd really appreciate it. I'll pick them up later."

"You know where the office is?"

"They gave me a map in Tashkent. I'll manage."

He stuck out his hand. "All right. Have fun!"

I walked. Nukus had three kinds of buildings. One was a tall, simple structure, which was variously an apartment building or a hotel or a low-level government facility. Another was more elaborate, made of what looked like sandstone and bulgy with Soviet iconography, where the powerful of Nukus typed memos and sent crawling faxes through the city's superannuated phone lines. The last and most numerous were the gated compounds one found everywhere in Central Asia. Not all of them were homes, however. Some were restaurants, others mechanic shops, some butchers, others yet the offices of international aid organizations. One had to enter to find out. I walked into a small compound the sign of which read "Café" in Cyrillic. A middle-aged man wearing an old, weathered black suit sat staring at an empty plate, a glass of half-drunk tea before him. The café's proprietor sat at another table across the room, writing in what looked to be a ledger. Both looked up at me, then returned to their reveries. The only things for sale here were *gazli suv* and Mars bars. I selected two of each and brought them to the counter. The proprietor finally came over. He looked red-eyed with exhaustion, though he smiled as he typed up my purchase on a small calculator. I gazed out the front door, where in the streets of Nukus the sunlight and spiraling dust fought for prominence.

"Korpus Mira?" the proprietor asked me as I was stuffing the water and candy into my backpack.

"No," I said in Uzbek. "Journalist."

He spread out his arms. "Welcome to Nukus!"

As I walked deeper into Nukus, dust gathered in the gutters of my leaky eyes, spackled my throat, formed a gritty wet meridian of sweat around my neck. I could barely see the sun, though through the dusty brown-out I could discern a weak, urine-colored glow. This was not, however, a dust storm. Not a real one. What I was experiencing was a "small" storm, a phenomenon so common they were not even kept track of. "Big" dust storms were different. At least five times a year a city-sized cloud of howling sand hit Nukus, an airborne apocalypse that sentenced everyone to days of life indoors and undid, in hours, months of peasants' work digging irrigation ditches and harvesting what is left of their cotton fields. In the 1950s Nukus was struck with one storm every five years. In 1975 Soviet cosmonauts first noticed the huge, destructive dust storms that would later commonly plague Karakalpakistan, and in the late 1980s dust-storm frequency increased twofold, to more than five a year, and had not abated since. Why this was, no one was quite sure. Wind erosion, regardless, was one of the region's most taxing problems. Decades of cotton-based agriculture had stripped the region's over-irrigated soil of protective plant growth. The Siberian zephyrs that swept down into Karakalpakistan gathered up its loose, poisonous dust and, as though in some lethal travesty of Jesus' mustard seeds, cast it not only upon the Karakalpaks but thousands of miles beyond them. Some of the Aral Sea area's enterprising dust had been found along Georgia's Black Sea coastline, some along arctic Russia's northern shores.

As I walked, I chewed gum. Soon when my molars met, it was as though I had a mouthful of sugar. I spat the gritty wad into my palm, my mouth instantly drying. I wished then that I had another piece. I pushed on for an hour or so to the city's western edge to find that Nukus ended with startling abruptness. The buildings disappeared, the roads lost their paving. That was it. The wind suddenly, briefly died, releasing its particulate brown haze and liberating the flat empty desert horizon beyond Nukus's perimeter. There, stitched across the hem between land and air, I saw two more dust storms—small, blurry, ferocious.

I hailed a gypsy cab and asked the driver to take me to Nukus's city hall. The young man with whom I would be staying in Nukus lived a block away from Nukus's governmental sector. The driver and I chatted. He was always happy, he said, to meet visitors to Nukus. The Karakalpaks were the friendliest people in all of Uzbekistan! I told him that, so far, I agreed.

"I am sorry that you did not come last month," he said, "before the dust storms began. Nukus is very pretty in May and October. But the rest of the year . . ." He frowned.

He dropped me off and to my shock told me I did not need to pay him. I was a guest. I protested. "Please," he said, "tell people you were treated well here. That will be my payment." I hoped to receive as hospitable a welcome from Dmitri, the young Korean man putting me up. Dmitri answered the door with an air of having been recently and thoroughly debauched. He smelled of stale beer and staler smoke, and wore unbuttoned Levi's and a Reebok T-shirt and frat-boy flip-flops. He had obviously just woken up. Nevertheless, he welcomed me inside, saying that he had not been expecting me until later. We sat down in his living room, which had several pinups of bare-breasted women torn from British magazines tacked to the walls. I learned that Dmitri was in his late twenties and worked for an Iranian company interested in tapping

Karakalpakistan's natural-gas reserves. He spoke English and Russian and middling Farsi and knew a little German from his previous work with a Berlin-based firm looking into tapping Karakalpakistan's oil reserves. His mother and father were dead, and he lived with his grandmother, whose husband had been shipped to Karakalpakistan in the 1940s. "My work is good," Dmitri said as his grandmother poured us tea and presented us with a plate of flavorless little cookies, "but it's unreliable. Foreigners are never interested in us for very long. I need to get out of Nukus. Perhaps to Tashkent, perhaps to Korea. I have saved a lot of money." I used this mention of money to ask how much Dmitri wanted in exchange for allowing me to say here. "Oh," he said, surprised. "Well. You are a friend of David's, yes?"

"Not really, no. I'm a friend of a friend of David's."

"Then you are David's friend, and hence you are my friend."

"So," I said, "what? Fifteen dollars a day?"

Dmitri smiled. "I see you are dead set to pay." He was quiet for a moment. "Let us say . . . five dollars a day."

"Ten," I said.

"Seven," he said.

The oddest haggling I had ever conducted in Central Asia was thus settled. Dmitri brushed some cookie crumbs from his thighs. "You will have a good time here. Let me know if you wish to visit our disco. I was there very late last night with my girlfriends."

I laughed. "Girl*friends*?"

"We should always have more than one, yes? You will see that Nukus girls are very pretty." Dmitri leaned forward, gripped either by inspiration of the moment or by a sudden delicious memory of last night. "Tonight. Tonight we will disco until dawn."

"Actually, I don't know if I can. I'm mostly looking to go to Moynaq."

Dmitri's face fell in disbelief. "Why would you want to go to Moynaq?"

"It's my job," I said. "That's why I'm here."

While Dmitri stared at me, his grandmother came in from the kitchen and sat down. She spoke in Russian for several minutes, fingering her worry beads. "What is she saying?" I asked. Dmitri explained that his grandmother had been hearing rumors in the bazaars, rumors of empty warehouses and withered crops, of delivery-truck drivers suddenly unemployed without explanation. A terrible drought had already afflicted Karakalpakistan for over a year. She was telling Dmitri that they had to cure their meat now. Preserve their fruits and vegetables while they could. More drought was coming to an already dry land.

"You see?" Dmitri said, sitting back with a bleak smile. "What choice do we have? Disco until dawn."

While I was walking to MSF's office, Manas pulled up beside me, beeping. "Tom!" he cried. "I have found you!" I climbed into the car to learn that he had already made for me a very important appointment—one, he reminded me, that I had already requested in Tashkent. We would go now to this appointment. Another young Karakalpak named Kemal reached back from the front passenger seat to shake my hand. He said he would be my translator. Ten minutes later I sat before the enormous desk of Dr. Damir Babanazarov. An MSF calendar hung on the wall behind his desk, next to a portrait of Islam Karimov. Dr. Babanazarov's hands, a bundle of whitened knuckles, rested atop some open newspapers. He smiled. A good-looking man, with short straight petroleum-black hair and a combed, equally black mustache. He wore fashionable glasses, a shiny red tie. As Kemal and I prepared for the interview, I struggled through a long, elaborate salutation in Uzbek. Dr. Babanazarov looked into his lap, still smiling but clearly concentrating on navigating my error-riddled sentences. Uzbek was of mostly utilitarian use out here. Dr. Babanazarov's native language was Karakalpak, which is more similar to Kazakh than to Uzbek, while Russian was the language he spoke most comfortably. As I recited my litany of Central Asian pleasantries, my eyes journeyed disconnectedly along his desk. An upright cellular phone. A small steel Eiffel Tower statuette. Four different telephones, which would ring nonstop during our interview and which he would occasionally not answer. When I had finished speaking, Dr. Babanazarov's tightly clasped hands burst open. He thanked me in accommodatingly simple Uzbek, then lit the first of several cigarettes. As he spoke, he flitted them around and stabbed the filters into his mouth as though he were plugging them into himself. Dr. Babanazarov was Karakalpakistan's minister of health.

In the Soviet Union the Ministry of Health was, famously, a sinecure for bribe-takers. It had been reassuring to hear from people in Tashkent that Dr. Babanazarov, despite a monthly salary of $25, had a reputation for spurning bribes and was regarded as an open, intelligent man who welcomed journalists and researchers. I had expected an interesting exchange. In preparation, I had filled a dozen notebook pages with pointed questions, the compassion of which I knew would be evident. Now, flipping through my notebook, I asked Dr. Babanazarov about the future of the Aral Sea, the health of Nukus's people, the legacy of Soviet rule, the role of international organizations in alleviating the disaster. Dr. Babanazarov responded with heavy, repetitive speeches in the style of one-man Soviet discourse that in no way began to answer them. I let go his first few evasions, wrongly believing that Kemal was mistranslating my questions. Finally, I turned to Kemal. Had he put to Dr. Babanazarov the question I asked? Kemal told me that he had. I asked Kemal if he could repeat the question. He did, and Dr. Babanazarov launched into another oration that bore eerily less relevance to my question. I again turned to Kemal and again asked him if he would repeat my question. Kemal looked almost sorrowful and without shaking his head very softly informed me that while he was really very sorry he simply could not do that.

Dr. Babanazarov was not one of Orwell's fly-swatting, otiose backwater functionaries. He was not incapable of honest reflection. Two years earlier he had told a journalist, "We will be witnesses to the disappearance of the Aral Sea." He was a good man. But his job was as sensitive as it was difficult. It was commonly believed that plenipotentiaries in the Uzbek government skimmed from the top of whatever relief Karakalpakistan was fortunate to receive and routinely underfunded the region's yearly budgets. But Karakalpakistan's peculiar quasi-independent status meant that it relied on Uzbekistan for virtually everything. To an average Karakalpak, the fountainheads of aggravation this arrangement created were innumerable. Dr. Babanazarov, however, was not a civilian. The health of Karakalpakistan was entrusted to him. But the Ministry of Health was not one of the "strong," attention-getting ministries such as Finance or Defense. To what lengths did Dr. Babanazarov have to go to procure for his people the little money and medical supplies they had? His frustration could only be imagined, as I was probably the last person in Karakalpakistan with whom he would have dreamed of sharing those frustrations.

But he was not open. Openness, in former Soviet Central Asia, did not mean a willingness to share or reveal. Openness was a friendliness dammed by private stricture, an instinctively shallow cordiality that delighted tourists and drove journalists mad. The most recent official medical statistics for Karakalpakistan were at least five years old. Most were worthless. ("Statistics," Lenin said, "must be our practical assistant, and not scholastic.") A particularly grim case in point was infant mortality rates. Central Asia accounted for 22 percent of Soviet births and 40 percent of its infant deaths. At 40 deaths for every 1,000 live births, Central Asia was, in the 1980s, cursed with an infant mortality rate twice the (not low) Soviet average, putting it on a par with Guatemala or Cameroon. By 1995 the official number had sunk to 26 deaths for every 1,000 live births. But Uzbekistan had carried on the long-standing Soviet practice of counting premature, underweight babies as miscarriages rather than live births, and in some cases doctors waited for months to record a baby's death in order to avoid having it fall under the rubric of infant mortality. The actual rates of other common Karakalpak afflictions—bronchial asthma, lung disease, infant cerebral palsy, cancers of the stomach and throat, urogenital and endocrine disease—were quite simply anyone's guess. It sufficed to say that all were abnormally high and getting higher. I left Dr. Babanazarov's office, then, with appreciation and anger whirling around the same mental drain. Everyone here, whether peasants or ministers, had inherited the tics and secrecy and habits of dictatorship of a regime they neither wanted nor created—a regime so monstrous in its reach and extent that most Americans could not have tolerated living within its tentacles for one hour, much less seventy years.

We drove to MSF. Just outside the large wooden double doors of its modest two-story headquarters, foreigners and stylish-looking locals smoked amid a fleet of vehicles parked at hasty angles. One of them, Kemal pointed out to me, was Ed Negus, a tall, crew-cut twenty-eight-year-old Australian on his first MSF mission. As I approached, Negus was fielding an unexpected, uninvited French visitor who had bicycled up from the city of Urgench, a 130-mile journey through desert that could only be described as punishing. When the sweating, bearded Frenchman informed Negus of his Tour de Karakalpakistan, Negus blinked. "You *do* know there's a regular bus service, don't you, mate?" The barely daunted Frenchman asked if MSF had a guest house in which he could wash and rest up. Negus promptly gave him directions to the Hotel

Nukus. The irritated Frenchman bicycled off. "The bloody frog," Negus laughed as I sheepishly prepared to introduce myself. "What does he think this is? Médicins Sans Reservations?"

"I'm Tom Bissell," I said. "I have a place to stay already."

"Right," he said. "The journalist. Want to take a ride?"

Negus and I were soon traveling to Nukus's tuberculosis dispensary to check up on its newly installed medical-waste incinerator. This was one of his main responsibilities, along with assisting MSF-supervised medical facilities in their efforts to procure faxes, computers, medical equipment, and achieve conditions of acceptable sanitation. I had never met an Australian before and was afraid that Negus would forever spoil me for meeting another. He seemed to embody everything popularly and generically affiliated with that fine island continent: size, humor, indomitableness. His head was shaped like an artillery shell and looked to have a dense mineral hardness. When I asked Negus where he grew up, he asked, "You know Australia at all?"

"A little. My brother lived there for a summer."

"Near Perth."

"Whereabouts near Perth?"

"Oh," he said, "on a little farm about four hundred and fifty kilometers outside the city limits."

"That's near Perth?"

"In Australia," he said, "that's just around the bloody corner." Negus described for me his previous job: "I was an underground miner in Australia. I had to go into a mine, put explosives in a wall, blow the wall up, get in my little truck, go to the next wall and blow that up, and that was it." He laughed. "I also studied economics for three years, because I'd actually harbored some thought that I was going to enter Australia's diplomatic service. Then I realized that I had absolutely no diplomatic skills, so I bagged that." When I asked Negus about his thoughts concerning the people of Karakalpakistan, he grew silent, a silence that seemed funereal, decent. He stared straight ahead. "My translator had an uncle in Moynaq," Negus said finally. "Ten years ago he told him, 'Get out of Moynaq now, because it's just going to end up a hole.' And his uncle said, 'When I'm the last person left in Moynaq, then, and only then, will I leave.' This year, he's leaving." He frowned. "I'm certainly not a raving lefty or anything like that but, you know, I just don't like seeing the earth get shafted."

"What do you think is going to happen to Nukus and Moynaq and the rest of Karakalpakistan?"

He shook his head. "Like something out of a Mad Max movie. Old ghost towns, with big trucks driving through."

We parked the MSF Land Cruiser—itself a big truck—in a shade-splotched alley behind the TB dispensary. Nearby, three old Karakalpak men sat cross-legged in ovals of shade. Some Karakalpak children appeared, screamed, "Hello!," and vanished. Negus waved but otherwise paid them no mind. We were approaching the incinerator from the rear because Negus wanted to arrive unannounced. This would prevent the dispensary's hardworking but morbidly self-conscious workers and managers from prettifying its present condition. While we made our way past rusty fences and stepped over enormous mounds of bovine dung, Negus described the bureaucratic lunacy installing these incinerators often entailed. To connect the gas line to each incinerator, for instance, you needed permission from the fire department. The fire department would reliably inform you that, in fact, the gas department needed to approve the connection first. The gas department, in turn, would deflect you back to the fire department. The fire department could now be counted upon to give you a form to take back to the gas department. The gas department, upon seeing the form, would instruct you that nothing of this nature could be accomplished without the fire department. The fire department would then be forced to write a letter overruling the gas department's involvement. The gas department would finally declare that nothing could be done without its approval.

We came to the incinerator. It was a long, narrow Quonset-like concrete structure, similar to the tandoori ovens in which many Uzbek and Karakalpak families baked bread. Negus slowed down so suddenly it was as though an anesthetic had just taken effect. Quickly I realized why. Small broken glass bottles were everywhere. The pieces popped underfoot like heavily shelled insects. The dusty ground sparkled with broken and, presumably, used needles. The tall narrow pipe in which the dispensary workers were intended to dispose of needles and glass was crammed with garbage. Next to the pipe was a black, indisputably human turd. The gravelike pit in which the medical waste's ashes and solely the medical waste's ashes were to be buried was filled with solids. Much of it looked nonhospital in origin. The pit was surrounded by footprints, many smaller than my bootprint by half. These prints had toes. Barefoot children had been playing here. Negus was speechless. He had visited only weeks ago, drilling the dispensary's workers on the exact procedures needed to dispose of their medical waste, a time-consuming, sometimes dangerous operation that was absolutely vital to improving Karakalpak-istan's health standards. I could see the whirl of frustration in his eyes as he gathered himself, walked over to the incinerator, and swung open its creaky iron door.

Clear plastic bags of waste, sanitary napkins, syringes, all tumbled out—a nightmarish landfill in miniature. Proper waste disposal depended on igniting the incinerator's pilot light and allowing it to heat up for at least fifteen minutes. Then, and only then, was waste to be placed inside. This was the best way to assure that the waste would burn cleanly and thoroughly. The bricks inside the incinerator should have been clean and white—properly managed, anything placed inside would ignite almost instantly—but the bricks of this incinerator were charred, briquette-black. I held my notebook at my side, too stunned to write anything. Without looking at me, Negus said, "Don't write anything down or I'll throw your fucking notebook in the incinerator." Guilt awakened me. I stepped back and jotted some observations, starting with the human turd. Negus glanced at me but said nothing. He chuckled and returned to staring forlornly into the incinerator. "This is not my finest moment."

It may be hard to understand why the dispensary's workers could not be relied upon to dispose of this waste correctly when doing so would immeasurably improve their lot. But one must summon the Soviet war-lock and the sorcery it had worked upon the minds of all the peoples of its empire. No other industrial civilization so impartially poisoned its land, water, air, and citizens while at the same time so loudly proclaiming its efforts to improve human health and the condition of the natural world. For decades the Soviet Union was the world's leading producer of oil and steel, held a quarter of the planet's forest resources and fresh water, and was in careless possession of what was probably the most beautiful and varied assortment of landscapes on the planet. "We cannot expect charity from nature," ran one Stalinist slogan. "We must tear it from her." Trotsky was more explicit: "The present distribution of mountains and rivers, of fields, of meadows, of steppes, of forests and seashores, cannot be considered final. . . . Most likely, thickets and forests and grouse and tigers will remain, but only where man commands them to remain." (Lenin, a nature lover whose brother was a biologist, was of the alpha Bolsheviks a notable exception to this line of sentiment. Another was the Soviet ecologist V. I. Vernadsky, coiner of the terms "biosphere" and "geosphere," who warned in 1932 that the natural world has limits, and that these limits "are not imaginary and they are not theoretical.") By the time of its demise, three-fourths of the Soviet Union's surface water was hopelessly polluted. Its forests were clear-cut. Its mines were stripped of resources. Its people were some of the least healthy in the developed world.

Even a brief catalog of the former Soviet Union's ecological and health misadventures stupefied, sickened, silenced. The Soviet Union was a nation in which one could stand next to a waste-spurting pipe near the town of Chelyabinsk and absorb a lethal dose of radiation in a single hour. Where surgeons were often forced by supply shortages to perform appendectomies with straight razors rather than scalpels. Where 40 percent of its medical-school graduates could not read an electrocardiogram. Where the Hippocratic Oath was forbidden, scorned as "bourgeois," and replaced with a pledge "to conduct all my actions according to the principles of Communistic morale."

Soviet joke: What would happen if the Soviet army conquered the Sahara Desert? For fifty years, nothing. Then it would run out of sand.

The Soviet Union was a nation that placed effluent-spraying factories in residential neighborhoods as a matter of course, and once built giant ammonia storage tanks adjacent to an artillery practice range. Where, until the late 1980s, smokestacks were viewed as symbols of great beauty and progress. Where some cities, such as Magnitogorsk, were so polluted they had "prophylactic clinics" in which children were given regular "oxygen cocktails." Where factory directors guilty of willfully discharging polluted water into the drinking supply were fined fifty rubles, enough for two packs of imported cigarettes. Where people were so enthused over humankind's new technological prowess they named their daughters Elektrifikatsiya and their sons Traktor.

Soviet joke: Two doctors are examining a patient. One doctor looks at the other. "Well," he says. "What do you think? Should we treat him or let him live?"

The Soviet Union was a country whose experts maintained that radiation sickness was basically a mental problem, and called the Aral Sea "nature's error" and hoped it would "die in a beautiful manner." Whose medical personnel were sometimes instructed to wash bandages for a second use. Whose doctors, 66 percent of whom were women, took home 80 percent of the average male factory worker's salary. Whose minister of health in 1989 advised, "To live longer, you must breathe less." The Soviet Union was a country where, in 1990, remembering Nikita Khruschchev's boastful promise to overtake and surpass American standards of living, angry, abused, and exhausted protesters marched past the Kremlin carrying placards that read LET US CATCH UP WITH AND SURPASS AFRICA.

Some Americans might regard these statistics as proof of American capitalism's superiority to Soviet Communism in every imaginable way. (This is not even to mention other capitalist paragons such as Japan, its tropical logging practices, brutal whaling, and busy involvement in the international plutonium trade making it a veritable ecological criminal state.) Such citizens hexed Al Gore as a "radical environmentalist" on the basis of his sensitive and ideologically tame book *Earth in the Balance*. Their organizations have names like the Abundant Wildlife Society of North America. They have wiped from their minds a history in which Ohio's Cuyahoga River periodically burst into flames. They possess crusaderly faith in Le Chatelier's principle, which posits the tendency of the environment to restore itself in the face of destabilizing forces. But the ecocidal histories of the United States and the former Soviet Union are startlingly similar. In the years following World War Two, Americans cut down vast forests, built thousands of factories, assembled millions of atmospherically toxic automobiles, and filthied the water throughout North America. In 1970 the United States passed the Clean Air Act twenty-one years after the Soviets had decreed their own version. (Interestingly, the president we have to thank for the Clear Air Act as well as the creation of the Environmental Protection Agency is one Richard Milhouse Nixon.) Our Clean Air Act was actually more lenient toward polluters than the Soviet Union's in fixing carbon monoxide limits—not that the Soviet Union, whose environmental pledges were filled with high-minded ideals, actually bothered to obey its own laws. The Pittsburgh of the 1940s and 1950s, to name one locale of acute American environmental shame, bore a ghastly resemblance to the manufacturing urban leviathans of the Soviet Union.

In 1989, 78 percent of Uzbekistan's polluted water was left untreated. The same year, the EPA found that only 10 percent of America's rivers, lakes, and bays were significantly polluted. What achieved this level of relative cleanliness was not the intrinsic munificence of capitalism's better angels but $24.3 billion spent on water protection alone from 1972 to 1987. Without huge monetary efforts to control and ameliorate industry's impact upon the environment, parts of the United States would greatly resemble some of the former Soviet Union's most toxic dumping sites. But another, more gossamer aspect of the American character was as critical as any pure outlay of capital. From Henry David Thoreau to John Muir to Rachel Carson, there exists in American culture a tradition of reflection upon nature and stubborn activism upon its behalf. The Soviet Union had no comparable tradition. That lacuna continued to affect the minds of its former subjects—one way in which they were still *Homo sovieticus.*

Ed Negus did not wish to hear any of this at the moment. He needed no education. Here at the dispensary he was staring at failed curricula. What was at stake here but a higher form of hygiene? Manners. A simple problem whose emotional complications ruled out full assault. Negus stood next to the incinerator, hands fused to his hips, a dozen languid flies crawling upon his back. Far away, I heard Karakalpak children playing, the drubby kick of a soccer ball. The sky above us was a sickly pale blue. Someone, a young man, perhaps a patient, watched us from one of the TB dispensary's windows. With my boot I impotently gathered together a small pile of needles. I stopped when I realized there was no place to put them. Negus, at last, turned to me, his face malformed by a sun-squinty eye and the dent of a close-mouthed smile. "I think I need to have some more meetings."

Some of the newer buildings in Nukus were painted the strange manufactured blue of bathroom tile, mouthwash, shaving gel. Not color but kolor. They stood out among the surrounding sand- and concrete-colored structures with computer-generated vividness. No, I thought, as I left Nukus by car the day after Negus and I had visited the TB dispensary. This blue was water, liquid itself. Too obvious to be anything but an accident, pure subconscious longing.

I was being driven to a tuberculosis dispensary in the small town of Chimbay, about forty miles north of Nukus. With me was an MSF driver;

Taisa Zoiyava, a tall, orange-haired local doctor who had worked for MSF for three years; Maya, a nineteen-year-old translator from Nukus who wore a wristful of girlish silver bracelets; and my handler from the Ministry of Health, a short, rather round woman with frizzy black hair and large Jackie Onassis sunglasses. She was asleep.

I had a handler from the Ministry of Health because of one A. A. Gill, who had published in the July 2000 issue of London's *Sunday Times Magazine* an article about Aral entitled "The Dead Sea." In it Gill pinned the blame for the Aral Sea disaster upon Communism, a thesis not unlike shooting a goldfish in a water glass. Gill opens the piece by noting, "They don't get many strangers in [Nukus]." Actually, Nukus hosts many Western researchers, was visited by then-Senator Al Gore and by the president of the World Bank, has housed dozens of Peace Corps volunteers, and has welcomed perhaps hundreds of journalists over the years. Gill proceeds to complain about his hotel: "There's no furniture and no soap. . . . The towel is a bar mat." Here is a man visiting an ecological disaster area, the scale of which is unprecedented in human history, and he is upset about the size of his towel. Gill then mentions that the Karakalpaks have "managed to drain the Aral Sea . . . and they've done it in twenty years." Thanks to the tsars' cotton policies, the Aral Sea had actually been shrinking for some time, which was first noted by a visiting American diplomat named Eugene Schuyler in 1868. One hundred years ago the sea was so shallow that nomads could wade with their cattle to an island eight miles from shore. It was indefensible, at any rate, to hold the Karakalpak people responsible for the disaster, even if a tiny percentage of them were its willing accomplices. Once Gill escapes from his hotel, he notes: "The tea tastes like a practical joke." An old woman selling sunflower seeds and cigarettes off an upturned box— a common sight everywhere in Central Asia—"is the summit of independent Uzbek private enterprise." He has obviously never tried haggling with an Uzbek cabdriver ("Ten quid per kilometer? Off we go, then.") or delved too deeply into rococo Tashkent. When Gill visits a TB dispensary, the disease is referred to, appallingly, as Karakalpakistan's "top-of-the-pops killer." He meets a little boy whose name "sounds like Gary," since Gill cannot be bothered getting the little wog's name right. Gill also has some thoughts about democracy: "The people don't yearn for democracy. Democracy is an indecipherable foreign language. . . . This place is antidemocracy." I didn't know which Karakalpaks Gill had been talking to. Perhaps the ancient Stalinist I had seen wandering Nukus's streets, his breast a shield of medals he'd earned at Stalingrad. Or perhaps Gill's informants were the Karakalpak children he and his photographer had, according to a Nukus SNB agent I spoke to, reportedly bribed to throw stones at a surviving statue of Lenin, an action shot of which accompanies "The Dead Sea." The Uzbeks and Karakalpaks I knew would have loved democracy. To achieve it, however, they were unwilling to risk social chaos, a condition Central Asia is congenitally and forever near. Uzbeks and Karakalpaks looked to Russia, which nearly resembled a democracy for a brief time in the early 1990s, and what a nation of gangsters and basket cases it had become. The frame of reference here was shrunken by numerous political, geographical, and experiential factors. These people did not want a Russian fate and had no way of knowing that such a fate was not necessarily preordained. (Speaking of Uzbeks, Gill writes, "A word was invented for them: horde." "Horde" actually comes through French via the Turkic word *orda,* meaning the yurt where a khan held his court. It is inversely inspiring, the amount of error Gill is able to pack into a single sentence.) Finally, of Karakalpakistan's children, Gill prophesizes that they will only "grow up and give up." What Gill does not mention is that Nukus is home to the finest English-language institute in Central Asia, and that Karakalpak children are widely regarded as some of the most ambitious and hardworking in their nation. Of course they are. They have to be.

Gill's piece had been widely translated and read in Nukus. The minister of foreign affairs was known still to be furious about it. I learned now, while my handler slept, that I was one of the first journalists allowed into Karakalpakistan since Gill's piece had appeared. This explained many things to me. Even in the vestries of officialdom outside the office of friendly Dr. Babanazarov, the suspicion I felt bear down on me was as perceptible as fallout. Until reading Gill's piece the night before, I had no answer as to why the authorities did not trust me. I now had a new, equally unanswerable question: Why should they have?

Outside Nukus the land became strikingly flat. Everywhere upon the soil were large white crystallized deposits of salt. If the DDT (6,000 tons of which were sprayed on Uzbekistan *every year* between 1978 and 1988, despite the fact that the Soviet Union banned the compound in the 1960s) and other extrastrength Soviet pesticides that befouled the Aral Sea and still maligned its soil were not enough, the soil's salt content had thrust a final stake through Karakalpakistan's agricultural heart. Karakalpakistan's soil was now approximately 90 percent salinated. From the air much of the area looked covered in snow. Millions of years ago the whole of Central Asia was a vast, highly saline inland sea (Aral was its remnant), and ancient groundwater salts were stored in the soil at an unusually shallow level. To irrigate the land was to release those salts, little by little, season by season. The Aral Sea once harmlessly collected that salt. Its gradual disappearance had left the salt with nowhere to go. And so it was cooked into the soil, or blown around, or left to seep into the drinking water. The drinking water's pollution, not only by salt but by the herbicides and fertilizers sprayed all over the Aral Sea basin at the height of the cotton boom, would have been a huge problem anywhere. But Karakalpakistan was a closed-system environment without any ocean drainage, and contamination had proved especially pernicious.

The soil not ruined by salt was toast-colored. Salt accumulations drifted snowily onto the road. On these highways, it seemed anything could happen. We passed a parts-shedding bus. A horse-drawn wagon. Another aid group's Land Cruiser. A man riding a donkey. A BMW. For a while I absorbed all the strangeness this place could furnish. But my mind could not keep nourished what I saw. As the latest oddity—laughing children mushing a herd of sheep through a pasture of salt—was safely passed, everything decomposed beneath its improbability. I fell back in my seat, openmouthed, my mind neonatally self-occupied.

Conversation offered the quickest relief. I leaned forward to ask Dr. Zoiyava about her work in the region. She explained that it was mostly concerned with alleviating Karakalpakistan's TB epidemic, one of the world's worst. TB did not have a causal relationship to the Aral Sea's withdrawal, but it rode close herd on poverty, malnutrition, and poor sanitation, all of which the disaster had greatly exacerbated. The TB problem began to grow uncontrollable in the late 1980s, she explained. But too many people here waited too long to consult a doctor. This only spread the disease and further stunted Karakalpaks' faith in traditional medicine, which was never strong to begin with. I asked Dr. Zoiyava if she worried about catching TB herself. "Of course there's a risk," she said, and drifted off. MSF's doctors were checked for the disease routinely, and Dr. Zoiyava had herself tested positive for TB twice but never developed any of its symptoms. When I returned from the Peace Corps, I, too, tested positive for TB.

We arrived at the dispensary, a large three-story building that had the sad, incomplete aura of some American low-income housing. The windows were as dark as skull sockets. Behind the dispensary, TB patients sat on splintery benches, some huddled beneath blankets. It was at least 80 degrees, the day bright and dustless. One old man, from his bench, stared a fumarole into me. I smiled at him, hopelessly. His face transformed into a grin.

When we reached the dispensary door, I took Dr. Zoiyava aside to inquire if, as an ethnic Russian, she had ever thought of returning to Russia, as the vast majority of Karakalpakistan's other Slavs had done. "I was born in Moynaq," she said in sudden, hard English. "They're not waiting for Russians in Russia." We stepped through the threshold. Maya presented me with a protective pink mask to guard against TB's microscopic rod-shaped bacilli. It was shaped like a duck's bill, with a pliable metal strip to bend over the bridge of my nose. This I did, quickly sealing off any tubercular invasion. After I met with the head doctor of Chimbay's dispensary in her plant-crowded office, my tour commenced.

Some of the hospital workers wore masks, some did not. Some wore masks but left their noses uncovered. The eyes of anyone wearing a mask became doubly expressive. The shyness in the eyes of the Karakalpak nurses floating by in the hallways seemed twice as shy. The resolve in the eyes of the doctors carrying small, hand-written slips of paper twice as resolved. The doctors wore thin, white, robelike outer coats and tall cheflike white hats. Everyone worked purposefully. Very few looked at me. Of course, they knew I was coming. Of course, I wondered how much of everything was rehearsed. Of course, this did not matter. But one thing did seem to matter, at least to me. Roughly 90 percent of the dispensary's medical personnel were women. I asked why this was. "Maybe the men are interested in technology," Dr. Zoiyava said with a snort.

Word spread among the patients that an American journalist was on the premises. They crowded doorjambs as I walked past, their bodies draped in pinned-together clothing and their faces long and yellowy with sickness. (*Sarriq,* the Uzbek word for "yellow," is also the word used for jaundice.) I nodded, a hand over my heart. All nodded back, hands over hearts. On each floor was a different sort of patient. New patients, chronic patients, children. I had expected to hear coughing. I heard nothing and could not decide whether this silence was one of dignity or reticence. Covering the hallway's walls were consciousness-raising posters and slogans: TUBERCULOSIS IS AN INFECTIOUS DISEASE! The scarred wood floors were attended to by ubiquitous women who swabbed them every hour with dirty, medusal mops. I was shown labs. Most seemed empty, their windowsills lined with lonely rows of microscopes. Here I found a health-related instructional booklet with a Muslim family on its cover. Above the family it read: NESTLÉ: GOOD FOOD, GOOD LIFE. Equally empty-seeming was the dispensary's drugstore. Yet its caretaker gratefully maintained that she had everything she needed: "I have drugs, gloves, needles. Enough for a month and a half for each floor." MSF had provided all of this. I was shown shelves of pills, an X ray (the lungs black saclike pouches surrounded by blue-white ribs), and some highly antiquated medical equipment.

Soviet medicine evolved over the course of seventy years with virtually no contact with the West; Karakalpak medicine evolved over the same period of time with hardly any contact with *Soviet* medicine. These people knew that as an American I was used to a different standard of medicine. They had heard stories. They had seen bootlegged videocassettes of *ER*. And yet they wanted me to see what they had. They were proud of it. Deservedly. There is an actual Russian word (*blat*) for the unofficial, costly, and almost always illegal processes one had to endure to obtain such goods, and here they had come by them honestly. I thought of the dozens of articles I had read by aghast Western journalists who had visited Karakalpakistan's hospitals. Inevitably, they were tales of antediluvian practices and Potemkin façades. (The slobbering propaganda of *Karakalpakistan* tells us that the "overwhelming majority of the population in pre-revolutionary Karakalpakistan did not even have a vague idea of medical services. . . . Today our republic has 92 hospitals provided with the latest medical equipment.") But hospitals were not always places where PA systems soothed and summoned and gurneys and doctors torpedoed from every double-swing door. A hospital could be dark. Was this unimaginable? In a hospital one could hear typewriter bells and step over gas pipes athwart every doorjamb. In a hospital one could smell the sewage from the pit latrines out back, where patients and doctors voided alike. In a hospital one could not necessarily expect hot water. Instead, outside, in a small building, twenty yards from the hospital's back door, one could find each department's bowl of water, heated by a small stove. A hospital could be a building in need of 125 different repairs.

I was taken to a patients' room. Thick, syrupy sunlight poured over the beds. Each bedside table was covered with little knickknacks, photos. A lucky few had some bread. I stood in the doorway. Four women and two teenage girls blinked at me from their beds. These beds had frames of thin metal piping. The mattresses were flophouse-gray. The women upon them were chronic TB patients. They looked sick and poor and worried. Some of this dispensary's patients were so impoverished they had to borrow clothing from their neighbors to come to the hospital. MSF's TB program assured that these patients had free access to drugs, but I was not thinking of that at this moment. I was recoiling with horror as all four women and one of the teenage girls stood up and began to fuss with themselves and make their beds. I was a visitor and, more significantly, a man. In this culture, I commanded such respect. I had had visions of kneeling beside these patients' beds and asking them how they felt, inquiring after their treatment, learning of their hopes. The silence grew. The women were expressionless. Some stared at their bare feet. The one teenage girl who did not stand up remained supine upon her sunbathed bed. She hacked quietly, her ravaged lungs providing a sad little whistle at the end of each cough.

An older nurse pulled me aside. Her painted-on eyebrows had soft parenthetical curves and her neck was bumpy with the tiny red igloos of mosquito bites. "Please," she said. "We work very hard here. We provide company for the patients. We give injections. We do everything. And our salaries are so low." How low? About $8.50 a month. Why? Because these nurses worked with infectious disease. Poor people were most vulnerable to infectious disease, and poor people, most often, could not pay for treatment. And so the women who cared for them did not get paid either. When had she last been paid? It had been weeks. "Please," she said. "Do not write badly of us. It can affect our work. Please."

I stammered something about wanting to write about the determined, good-hearted people of Karakalpakistan.

"In that case," she said brightly, "my name is Rosa and I have worked here for twenty years."

Upon returning from Chimbay, I set off for one of Nukus's most remarkable tourist sites, aware even as I journeyed there how unlikely those words seemed. The Igor V. Savitsky Art Museum was housed within a crumbling building in a surprisingly leafy quadrant of central Nukus. (A little over a year later, the museum would move into far grander quarters.) Savitsky was an archaeologist and a painter who foresaw better than most how the coming holocaust of Soviet Communism would annihilate Russian art. Modern dictatorships inevitably spell doom for art of any kind, but dictatorships administered by men who fancy themselves artists (and the Bolsheviks were pedantic about their literary and artistic expertise—even the Georgian hillbilly Stalin wrote poetry) seem, somehow, to wound art more profoundly. As in the painterly Hitler's Reich, the poet Stalin's Union of Soviet Socialist Republics saw art glorified. Art was the germ by which its ideology spread. Nazi and Socialist art was, of course, always in perfect synchrony with the reigning dictator-dabbler's prejudices. One thinks of Isaac Babel, bullied into nonproductivity by Stalinist censors. "I have invented a new genre," Babel said before he was shot, "that of silence." Savitsky, too, invented a new genre—that of concealment. Shortly after the Bolshevik Revolution he relocated to Karakalpakistan, and between 1918 and 1935 he is thought to have saved 80,000 pieces of art from censors' razors and Soviet incinerators, helped along by artists still living in Moscow and St. Petersburg and sympathetic officers working within the Soviet regime. Savitsky preserved nothing less than the world's most comprehensive record of early Soviet art. The museum, not to mention Savitsky, survived largely because of its distance from Moscow. This was not the case for the artists themselves, most of whom perished in gulags.

The museum's director was the wife of Karakalpakistan's health minister, Damir Babanazarov, though I learned she was not in today. Where was she? Marinika Babanazarova was off on a fund-raising junket to Tashkent. This was not surprising, as her Savitsky Museum existed in a perpetual state of financial crisis. It needed more storage space, better air-conditioning (several masterpieces had been marred by melting paint), more employees, more public relations. An admirably frank sign greeted one upon entrance. SALVATION FUND, it was headed. Below that:

FINANCEMENT OF OUR MUSEUM IS IN A CRITICAL SITUATION. PLEASE, DON'T FORGET TO PAY THE ENTRANCE FEE AT LEAST. The nearby donation bulb was nearly empty. A museum worker pulled me aside and proudly showed me the Savitsky guest book. She lingered with special pride upon the slot where Albert Gore, Jr., had more than a decade ago signed in. I walked the hallways—I was the only visitor—and fell under the museum's spell, hours floating away. I went slowly, noting what seemed to me the strange inconsistencies abounding within much of this early Soviet art: Cubism and Surrealism uncomfortably attempting to accommodate the demands of Realism, Realism fooling around the gauzy shades of Impressionism. Stalin's ever-shifting obsession with what constituted "pure" Soviet art was well known, and these artists' not uninteresting confusion mirrored this. First, Stalin was against any glorification of the peasantry (this is because he was killing them); then he was against any vilification of the peasantry (this is because he had killed so many of them that Soviet birth rates had fallen to disastrous lows). First he was against Old Russia; then he was elevating Old Russia and its folkloric heroes as a chapter of almost sacred cultural import. I looked at allegorical images of old men handing off glowing orbs to young men, a phantasmagorical painting from the 1920s depicting a smooth gray satellite sweeping across the cosmos, some beautiful portraiture (S. Nikritin's *Portrait of a Girl in Red* attempted to stay true to Communism by cloaking its subject in an appropriately scarlet dress), many striking pastel-heavy paintings by Uzbek and Karakalpak artists showing us provincial Central Asian life. *Going Out for Work* gave us Uzbeks going out for work. One artist, S. Kalibanov, had an entire wall of lovingly observed still lifes of Uzbek table settings. Another painting by an Uzbek was simply a huge canvas filled with a block of hazy, almost boiled orange-red that managed to out-Rothko Rothko; its title was *Intense Heat*. A painting of Venus by a Russian addressed classical themes forbidden by the Soviets. The painting was unremarkable, though its Russian title, *Venera*, Venus's Russian name, gave me new insight into the etymology of "venereal." Finally, I came to a gallery of hard-hitting Soviet art, painting after painting of faceless men in stovepipe hats building railways, factories, roads. One was called *Excavators*. Another, almost identical painting was called *Irrigators. Fishermen. Miners.* Where, I wondered, was the error that brought them to this safe haven? Were the hats not right? Were the excavators not working hard enough? Did some small afterthought image—a cottage, say—along the paintings' horizons inappropriately glorify the bourgeoisie? No doubt a real Soviet could have found some microscopic doctrinal violation. When I had seen about half of the museum, one of its employees gently approached me and told me that I had to leave. Why? I asked. "Because," she said apologetically, "now it is time for our lunch."

I walked several miles to the Progress Center, Nukus's other notable destination. This was the English-language institute A. A. Gill had failed to mention—the finest such school, somewhat unaccountably, in all of Central Asia. Found within a former Komsomol meeting hall, the Progress Center was tucked behind a wall of trees, its outer stone façade loudly triumphalizing Young Pioneers and cosmonauts in bas-relief. A few dozen Uzbek, Russian, and Karakalpak teenagers loitered in gender cliques outside the front door, laughing and smoking and catcalling the nearest assemblage of the opposite sex. These were prototypical Cool Kids, the boys wearing sunglasses and sharp black slacks, the girls wearing platform shoes and tight T-shirts. They chewed gum. They drank Coke. Every one of them quieted down as I passed, not even looking at me, my fresh absence of youth as heavy on me as cologne. The Karakalpak boy at the front desk had gelled hair and a light sprinkling of acne. He was reading an English-language paperback of Gemingway's *The Old Man and the Sea*. As I approached him to ask for directions to the e-mail lab, he looked up from his book and said, "Hey." Not "Hi," or "Hello," but "Hey." The Progress Center's wide hallways were decorated with hundreds of hand-drawn posters of we-are-the-world sentiment, and streamers bearing the colors of the Uzbek flag sagged from the ceiling. I was thinking how unlike every other Uzbek school this place was, until I came across an outsized portrait of Islam Karimov, then another, and another. Posters advertising UNICEF, one of the Progress Center's biggest benefactors, were nearly as ubiquitous. The doors of every classroom and office I passed were stamped with a small gold plaque that read REPAIRED BY UNICEF. The only classroom to break from this pattern was 3A, the British Classroom, which was MADE POSSIBLE BY THE GENEROUS SUPPORT OF THE BRITISH EMBASSY. The hallways of the three-story school were angled around a large open central gymnasium. From the second-floor hallway I looked down into the gymnasium to see ten little Karakalpak and Russian girls learning ballet beneath a large UNICEF banner. At the other end of the gym an Uzbek gym teacher, wearing an actual whistle, taught several little boys how to dribble a basketball. The local male teachers I saw strolling the hallways seemed nearly as well dressed as the kids outside, with primary-color dress shirts and bright ties, all of them walking with students, laughing, repeatedly touching their female students on the back. The Progress Center had a café, and a library, and an Internet lab, and a separate computer lab, and a separate e-mail lab. Depending upon whom you asked, the Progress Center's director, Lily Lagazidze, a woman once profiled in the *New York Times,* was either a genius, a saint, a shrieking harridan, or a manipulative monster. I imagined that, to have put together all this, she would have had to be a little of all the above. Local opinion of Lagazidze seemed to be determined by whether those offering that opinion had once worked for her, or whether their sons or daughters had been admitted for study here. I stopped by Lagazidze's office to chat, but she, too, was out fund-raising.

I made it to the e-mail lab, a small, clean white room overseen by a courteous Uzbek student named Davron who was deeply engrossed in an issue of the *Economist.* Posted outside the lab's door was a warning issued by the Uzbek government. This reminded me that it was illegal to use these computers to access any "porno, slander, fascist propaganda, or other material intended to incite the overthrow of government." While I cleared away my Hotmail account's detritus, a tall Russian girl took a seat beside me. She was attractive in a barely legal kind of way, her long black hair impossibly thick, her pebble-sized silver nose ring sparkling. Proximity to attractiveness is always a discombobulating, motive-fumbling prospect, and after a few minutes I looked over at her screen. I saw her typing, "Dear David Mills. Thank you for your e-mail. I am a eighteen-year-old Russian girl living in Nukus. . . ." She glanced over at me. My eyes flicked back onto my screen. A beautiful girl, a student at the best English-language institute in Central Asia, and she was looking into mail-order bridery. With a tumbling heart I closed my e-mail, walked back to Dmitri's, and sitting alone in my $7-a-day bedroom drank the first of several warm Russian beers.

The next day I was sitting in an empty office within MSF's Nukus head-quarters, reading *Middlemarch* with my feet up on a desk and waiting for something to happen. A sweaty young British woman with short brown hair peeked into the office, then approached me. She had the smiling, cherubic air of someone knowingly coming to another's rescue. "I hear," she said, "that you're looking to get to Moynaq to meet Ian."

"I am," I said, removing my feet from the desk I now realized was hers.

She unrolled her shirtsleeves and sat on the desk's corner. "You know, the lot of the office is going up in a few days. It's going to be a big party."

I said I did know that. I wanted to get up sooner.

"Then let's go," she said.

Her name was Johannah Wegerdt, the *j* pronunciation of her first name ("Yohanna") explained by a German father. Wegerdt, an attractive, matronly woman of porcelain complexion and imperial poise, was a twenty-seven-year-old field research coordinator for MSF. As her job title indicated, most of her work took place outside Nukus. She knew the Aral Sea region, someone had told me, as well as her own backyard. As we packed up an MSF car, Wegerdt asked whether I minded if on the way to Moynaq we made a half-dozen other stops. I said I did not. In fact, that sounded great.

We headed for the city that, more than any other, wore the grisly diadem of the Aral Sea disaster. Moynaq seemed to me more legend than reality, enriched with catastrophe's inverse allure. Only a few miles outside Nukus, health problems grew brazenly visible. Blind men sat roadside. Old women bowlegged with rickets staggered along. Children with bulging, malnourished tummies crouched on the berm, flashing siphons to passing cars. They were selling gasoline, Wegerdt explained. This was illegal. Somewhere nearby, their gasoline cans were stashed. If a policeman happened by, they stuffed the rubber siphon down their pants. Entrepreneurialism was alive and well in Karakalpakistan.

Wegerdt's and my companions on the way to Moynaq were an uncharacteristically sullen Uzbek driver and Bahktiyor Madreimov, a twenty-one-year-old half-Russian, half-Karakalpak translator. Bahktiyor, too, had driven along these roads more times than he could count. He did not like the countryside, he said. He was a city boy, born and raised in Nukus. It felt good to be with people so young, and as we drove, we bickered amicably, mostly about my attempts to banish from Bahktiyor's astonishing English all the Britishisms I guessed he had picked up from Wegerdt. These were not only regulation U.K. terms such as "bloke" or "rubbish" but sentence-length mannerisms such as "It's hot out, I tell you." As an entrée, I taught him "Whazzup." Wegerdt despaired in the front seat. "Soon you'll sound just like a Yank," she said, shaking her head. Bahktiyor grinned at me. "Cool," he said.

Wegerdt was tracking the health of several dozen Aral Sea basin children. Environmental health was, somewhat shockingly, an area in which very little research had been conducted, perhaps because it seemed such an observational commonplace to maintain that poor environmental conditions were deleterious to human health. Wegerdt's Internet searches on "dust storms" and "human health" turned up almost nothing, for instance, and it remained unknown how exactly long-term dust-storm exposure affected one's respiratory system. Did it merely induce wheezing in asthmatic children, or did it actually cause asymptomatic children to become sick? The unprecedented nature of the Aral Sea disaster was not unlike Hiroshima after World War II, which allowed scientists a charred ground zero to study the previously unstudyable effects of widespread radiation poisoning upon human beings. Here one could find out the similarly vast aftereffects of what happened when an entire ecosystem expired in a single generation. Dust storms were but one way in which this world ended.

"Up ahead," Wegerdt told me, pointing. Before us lay the Amu Darya River. Or what was left of it. That it was once called the "river sea" should provide a sense of its former vastness. Arab geographers were in awe of the river, regarding it as one of the mightiest in the world. It took Alexander the Great's army five days to cross it on inflated tent-skins. Now, over two thousand years later, we approached the Amu Darya on a glacis, now unnecessary, and crossed on an impressive elevated bridge one kilometer in length. For the kilometer's initial nine-tenths there was nothing below but hard cracked soil furred with ashy vegetation. Near the end of the bridge I saw a powerless thirty-foot-wide braid of dirty blue water slithering along a carved flume of sand. It looked only a little bigger than the rivers I had grown up fishing in. *"Jesus,"* I said as Bahktiyor and Wegerdt stared inuredly out their windows.

After we passed over the Amu Darya—desert. It erupted panoramically, my eyes overpowered by a dull brown ache. The rest of the country may have been hampered by checkpoints and border patrols, but here in

Karakalpakistan the highways were empty. They felt large, Nebraskan, existential. Along the roads, worn little irrigation ditches linked one community to another. Groups of houses were capped with corrugated tin roofs and paired with twiggy side buildings in which hungry horses were crammed rib cage to rib cage. Desperately old women sold Fanta and Coca-Cola beside the highway. Skinny cows tramped along the gravel margin. I had not known cows could be so skinny. Huge tongue slabs dangled from their mouths and clumps of dung hung tangled in their lusterless coats. Along every irrigation ditch were rows of cattailish vegetation. Astonishingly, they were still building canals out here. Large saurian excavators stood abandoned beside half-dug trenches and massive ice-cream scoops of disinterred soil. Nowhere was the desert's simple splendor. This was a desert turned into an oasis turned into a desert again, a terraforming tug-of-war that had now been inarguably concluded. As recently as seven years ago, Bahktiyor told me, everything around us had been cotton-field green, living, verdant.

Cotton. In America the thirsty crop was human slavery's vile demiurge; here it had murdered the Aral Sea. For a season's growth, cotton typically requires thirty annual inches of rainfall. Uzbekistan receives, at most, fourteen annual inches of rainfall. Cotton had been growing in the region for generations, of course. The tsars, and then Stalin, had seen to that. In 1927 the Soviet Union imported 41 percent of its cotton; six years later it imported 3 percent. But the late 1950s marked a darkening ambition on the part of Soviet Five Year planners, and the cotton harvest was ordered to proceed apace. It was not surprising, then, that the officials during this time who decided, flat out, to drain the Aral Sea to increase cotton yields knew exactly what they were doing. ("It is obvious to everyone that evaporation of the Aral Sea is inevitable," a Soviet engineer noted in 1968.) They simply calculated the projected profits from the cotton increase against those of the fishing industry they were about to destroy. For a while it worked. Between 1965 and 1983, the Soviet cotton harvest swelled by 70 percent, making the USSR the world's leading cotton exporter. Today cotton accounted for a quarter of Uzbekistan's GDP.

Yet much of this resplendent yield turned out to be bogus. The Cotton Scandal, as it is known, was an elaborate fraud undertaken by officials at every level of the Uzbek Republic over a period of thirteen years to defraud Moscow into paying 1 billion rubles for nonexistent cotton. (One popular joke had a cotton farmer shouting, "Thank Allah for cotton!" "Allah?" scolds another farmer. "You fool. This is a Communist state. There is no Allah." "That's all right," the first farmer says. "There's no cotton either.") The inspiration behind the Cotton Scandal was said to have originated with Sharaf Rashidov. When Soviet satellites revealed hundreds of square acres of empty cotton fields and nonexistent farmland in the early 1980s, the Cotton Scandal ended with Rashidov, too. By 1983 he was dead. The subsequent Moscow response, a mid-eighties purge led first by Yuri Andropov and later by Mikhail Gorbachev, decimated the Uzbek Communist Party and aggravated Uzbeks' and Karakalpaks' sense of racial exploitation, with many citizens wondering, not unreasonably, how they could be taken to task for cheating such consummate cheaters. The four remaining Central Asian leaders, all of whom were, to some extent, in on the cotton grist, fared little better. Rashidov's colleagues in Kazakhstan, Turkmenistan, Kyrgyzstan, and Tajikistan had enjoyed two or more decades of undisputed rule. By 1986 Gorbachev had forced these supremos out of office. They did not go alone. Fifty thousand lower-level officials were also sacked. Rashidov's replacement was a forgettable Uzbek apparatchik out of touch with his poorer countrymen's needs, and he was himself pushed out of office in the late 1980s by the marginal former head of Uzbekistan's State Planning Committee, a man named Islam Karimov. Previous to this, Karimov had been head of government for the Uzbek republic's poorest province. Moscow supported Karimov's nomination for the post of first secretary of the Uzbek Communist Party largely because he was an unknown—one of the few political figures in the region not to have been a part of the Cotton Scandal. Twenty-four months later the unknown Karimov would be Uzbekistan's first president.

The sudden ascendancy of Islam Karimov was only one of the bizarrely wide-ranging ramifications of Uzbekistan's reliance on cotton. It was also one of the least directly destructive. Indeed, cotton's impact was most horrible and visible among Uzbekistan's women and children. Their tiny hands and low centers of gravity, one argument held, made it easier for them to pick cotton without skinning their fingers or ruining their backs. (Men usually procured the cotton industry's less physically demanding managerial jobs.) During the harvest season, from late summer to late fall, the schools were emptied of children. Poor women were rounded up. All were shipped to the fields and forced to toil beneath the molten Central Asian sun, sometimes without shelter or adequate drinking water. In the late 1980s Uzbek officials made several promises to stop using schoolchildren as harvesters, but every year thousands of little "volunteers" still marched out to the cotton fields. Every night, during cotton season, families still huddled around their televisions to learn of the day's harvest. Incidentally, the Russian word for cotton worker is *rabochy*, or *rab* for short. In what few Uzbeks or Karakalpaks accept as an etymological coincidence, *rab* also means "slave."

We came to School Number Twelve in Porlatau, a small village south of Moynaq that had the gray, isolated air of a lunar settlement. On our way here I had noticed that the closer we drew to the Aral Sea's former shore, the fewer road signs we had to guide us. The numerous switchbacks we used to reach Porlatau had not even been marked. I asked Bahktiyor why he supposed this was. "Many reasons," he said, then smiled. We made our way through town, a light floury dust pouring in through our vehicle's vents. We passed a playground outside a school. It was recess. A dozen boys played basketball on a sandy court. Their ball was multicolored, rather like a beach ball. Perhaps it was a beach ball. My eyes' pigment-starved circuitry locked on to what was surely the most chromatically interesting thing I had seen in days.

Wegerdt greeted these children and their teachers with genuine enthusiasm. She had added Karakalpak to the six languages she already spoke, and it was both inspiring and rather sad to see how the children bounced and smiled at her approach. She was here, after all, to see if they were sick, and they knew this. When Wegerdt noticed that one of the girls carried her schoolbooks in a plastic bag with UNICEF plastered across it, she and Bahktiyor rolled their dissimilar eyes. Apparently, whenever a nongovernmental organization such as UNICEF visited a site, it was standard operating procedure to brand with stickers whatever items it left. "Why don't they put something *useful* on the bag," Wegerdt asked indignantly. "Something like, 'Wash your hands before eating'?"

I inquired of the little girl in question what was inside her bag. "Books," she said.

"No, when you were given it."

She did not remember. When I asked if she remembered who had left it, she only shook her head. To be fair, MSF was not above this sort of thing, as every fax machine and computer I had seen in the region's hospitals sported a large MSF decal. Wegerdt herself was wearing a tight black MSF T-shirt, REBELS WITH A CAUSE written in tiny letters along the hem of her sleeve. But the toys she had brought to give the students—rulers and balloons, mostly—were admirably absent of any MSF earmark at all.

In Porlatau's homes mothers dragged out their best carpets for us to sit on while their sick children breathed into tubes that measured their lung strength. We were poured cups of tea with camel's milk. Only Karakalpaks used milk in their tea, a subject of anthropological hilarity to Uzbeks who lived outside of Karakalpakistan. Karakalpaks used milk in their tea, of course, because without it the tea would taste like boiled seawater.

I watched Wegerdt hold these children's backs straight to prevent their diaphragms from being crushed and rendering useless any reading. Most of the children she saw had some sort of respiratory disorder. It was sometimes difficult, she admitted, to come into these houses and not begin to point out all the things in clear sight that promoted respiratory illness. I looked around. Some roosters stepped about in the foyer, heads pistoning. Most of Porlatau's people, Bahktiyor added, had to walk one kilometer to reach the nearest clean water pump. Wegerdt nodded. "A lot of Karakalpak families don't wash their sheets but once a year," she said in a tone of subzero frustration. This was torture for any asthmatic child. Neglecting the laundry was all too understandable here, but in that neglect mothers were inadvertently strangling their children with dust. I was beginning to understand why Wegerdt felt so strongly about her work. She had to confront these people, week after week, month after month, and even when she had good news ("Your child is not sick") it was by any practical standard bad news ("At least, not yet"). I watched her with something like envy. I had once thought myself capable of such altruism.

"Why do you do this?" I asked her suddenly.

She looked over at me, then laughed shyly as she began to measure the lung strength of another of this family's children. "I don't know. My life's goal is be useful, I suppose. Working for MSF is a dream of mine. I remember when I was a girl seeing French doctors in Africa on the telly and thinking, 'Oh, I'd love to get out there and help.'"

"That's the difference between you and me. If I saw that as a kid, my only thought would have been an indistinct longing to see one of them get mauled by a lion."

She smirked. "Well, there *is* that, isn't there?"

We said goodbye to this Karakalpak family and drove out of Porlatau to another village, and the grim though somehow heartening procedures began again. Despite her explanation of wanting to be useful,
the more time I spent with Wegerdt, the more impenetrable to me she
seemed. I wondered if this devotion to others was not endowed with
something rather spooky and—one might as well say it—imperialistic.
In fact, I had spent several evenings in Nukus having beers with Ed
Negus and others after hours and learned that MSF's workers were not
unaware of this correlation. Many would, if asked, gladly unroll long
scrolls of misgivings and personal reservations concerning MSF's mandate. Many wondered whether their work really accomplished anything.
Why those in the field were ignored by those who were not. Why every
year some MSF desk jockey comfortably ensconced in Amsterdam saw fit
to unleash new watchwords ("sustainability" and "proximity" were both
big this year) upon the organization's heads of mission. They complained with particular bitterness about the "disaster tourists" in their
ranks, enemies within who sought to pull impossible transcendence from
the equally impossible font of a refugee camp, who longed for nothing so
much as to return to the pubs of Brussels or London, knock back a few
pints, and compose for their mates odes on a Rwandan hellhole. They
bristled, some of them, when I pointed out what they had given up. They
retorted, accurately, that they had not given up all that much. They got to
go home, for starters. Pressed further, however, they admitted how
uncomfortable they felt when they returned for visits to their native
lands, how soul-sick they became at weddings, parties, and other social
gauntlets thrown down by what they now moldily dubbed "the world."
They described how they had learned to power down their brains and
smile when concerned mothers and sisters and uncles asked them, "What
is it that you're running from?" Who were these people? MSF did not pay
very much compared to other international aid organizations, but it had
a knockabout élan, a seemingly divine commission, that other international aid groups sorely lacked. Many MSF workers pointed out to me—
at this point ensnared by the golden lariat of too many Russian
beers—that this is a business, this humanitarianism, it's a bloody *business,* one all about recruitment and profile and fund-raising. They
deplored MSF's waving about of its Nobel Prize. Of course, they were
right and, of course, they were wrong. The world is a conflicted place,
and those who attempted to sort out those places where conflict became

tragically straightforward were equally conflicted. One only had to sit down with these Dutch and Brits and Belgians and Aussies and Canadians and Nigerians and listen to them slag one another and complain about the frustrations of their work to know that they would not have it any other way. They found fulfillment in being unfulfilled. They were people most comfortable not being at home. They made giving seem cynical, and cynicism itself seem the stuff of the deepest bounty. The work they did was a kind of small, secular miracle. This was the problem. Small miracles could only suggest the later, better miracles to come.

Later that evening, Wegerdt, Bahktiyor, and I stopped for dinner at a local doctor's home in the village of Raushan. The doctor owned a large plot of land. His nearest neighbor's home was forty yards away. A spacious loose-dirt driveway divided his two broad, flat houses. Wegerdt and Bahktiyor greeted the doctor and walked inside to make sure our sleeping arrangements were in order. I stayed in the car. It had been a long day and I felt cudgeled. "What is to be done?" That was Lenin's famous question. It came from the title of Nikolai Chernyshevsky's famously bad 1863 novel of the New Man revolutionaryism would create. Lenin read the novel five times in one summer, claiming that it "completely reshaped me," stressing, as it did, "what a revolutionary *must be like*." The revolutionary question "What is to be done?" had been asked here. Around me was one answer to that question. But now "What is to be done?" had returned, this time with calamity clamped between its teeth. What, I wondered sadly, is to be done? Could it really be that I had been in Uzbekistan for weeks and had not heard anyone say anything even guardedly optimistic about the people of the Aral Sea basin? What I had heard, from people such as the World Bank's David Pearce, were words like "resettlement." People were already leaving. Roughly 50,000 Karakalpaks had left Karakalpakistan over the last ten years. Maybe 100,000. It was hard to know. Most had vanished, visaless, into Kazakhstan, as Kazakhs are linguistically and culturally closer to Karakalpaks than any other people. The rest were waiting. Moving was not simple here. To move one needed an intranational visa. Some waited for money to bribe their way into that visa, some waited for things to improve, and some waited to die. Ton Lennaerts's map appeared in my mind, impossible to furl. How many countries did this problem afflict? When the Soviet Union collapsed, paradoxically, the Aral Sea's last real hope collapsed with it. Instead of one nation's internal problem, it became overnight an international crisis, with the sea's feeder rivers running through five nascent, highly uncooperative nations and providing water for five nascent, highly differentiated economies. (Only in July 2001 did the five Central Asian states finally come to terms, however fractious, on a water-sharing agreement.) How could so many compelling factors—economic, sociological, political—ever be reconciled? One could spend ten years studying ten different disciplines to approach the disaster and "What is to be done?" would be no easier to answer.

I sat perched half in and half out of the car. The door was wide open. My chin rested upon the shelf of my hand. The sun was going down, the horizon dyed a Creamsicle orange. I watched a skinny, ravaged-looking dog sniff around various piles of refuse. A dog's life. Then it occurred to me that American dogs have no idea what a dog's life is. Suddenly, two little boys appeared from behind one of the houses and approached me. They were brothers, clearly. One was taller and certainly older. The other was small, perhaps five years old. This boy's head was pumpkin-sized, seemingly twice the circumference of his brother's, who was regarding me coldly. The younger boy smiled, his teeth cavitied and yellow, his skinny body completely naked and covered in dust. The dust was spread so evenly over his body it seemed deliberately applied. His uncircumcised penis looked like a tiny anteater nose. I smiled back at him. *"Ismingiz nimah?"* I asked. What is your name?

Before the boy could answer, his older brother inexplicably struck him from behind. The boy flopped face-first into the dust. The shove was two-handed and savage, like something out of provincial hockey. A sound, perhaps "Hey—," filled my mouth. But I did nothing. The younger brother coughed into the dust. He had landed badly, arms at his sides. Now he tried to get to his feet. His brother placed a foot upon his naked bottom and, almost tenderly, pushed him back into the dirt. He stared down, having satisfied some obscure but insatiable impulse, and then walked away. I waited for tears, the shrieks and cries of fraternal terror. But no. Nothing at all. The naked dusty child was silent. The dog trotted over and, as the boy picked himself up, he searched the ground blindly with a small pawing hand. Finally, he stood holding a triangular rock. He turned and threw it at the dog, hitting the creature full in the ribs; the dog flinched but otherwise took the blow in silence. The younger boy simply walked away. I made soft kissing sounds to summon the dog. It was understandably skittish, but I persisted. I did not know what else to do. When it slunk over, head lowered and panting, I saw a strange red spiderlike creature dug into its collarless neck. I extended my hand. The dog bit me and staggered off.

Hours later Bahktiyor and I stood beneath an extravagantly starry Karakalpak sky. Our stomachs were filled with bread and rice, our brains soaked in fermented camel milk. Everywhere around us, but for the occasional tiny peal of cowbells, was a silence as involved as thought. Bahktiyor wore an anachronistically fashionable mesh T-shirt and cool-guy sunglasses that dangled from his neck on sporty yellow string. I asked him how he learned to speak English so well. What I was actually asking was why he did not look, speak, or act like anyone else here. He told me that he received a highly competitive scholarship to study in England in 1998, an experience he said changed the whole of his life. He had seen the world. "And that," he said, "means I have seen everything. Do you know what I mean? I saw a situation, my own country, that I thought I knew very well, from another point of view. It was like looking *into* a bottle when you have spent your life seeing it only from the side."

I lied and said I knew exactly what he meant, then congratulated him, retroactively. I told him that this was fantastic news, just fantastic. I praised travel, that movable feast, shamefully aware that I was of course transparently flattering myself for being there, with him, at that moment.

Even in the darkness I could see Bahktiyor's slender, handsome face twisting. He shook his head. He had come home from England early. While on vacation back in Nukus, a gentleman from the Ministry of Education stopped by to inform him that "border problems" with Islamist insurgents 1,400 miles away from Karakalpakistan meant that fewer students would be studying abroad that year. Bahktiyor was forbidden to return to England. Later he ran into another gentleman, a young man, in Tashkent, who informed Bahktiyor that he had purchased his scholarship spot for $2,000. "He was too rich," Bahktiyor said to me.

"Too rich for what?"

"Too rich to kill."

Now I stopped breathing. Bahktiyor was told, soon after the run-in with his usurper, that he was expected to repay the government its scholarship money. He refused and wrote several letters protesting this corruption to the Uzbek government. Those letters never made it past Karakalpakistan's minister of education, who had now effectively blackballed Bahktiyor from attending college even in Nukus. Was all of this a matter of discrimination? The boy who procured Bahktiyor's scholarship was an ethnic Uzbek, and Karakalpaks have historically been on the losing end of Uzbekistan's chauvinism. Or did it concern the sense of ethics with which Bahktiyor was either blessed or cursed? I did not know whether to encourage him to fight or plead with him to apologize and bribe everyone with two hands. Or was this about a simple and irreducible corruption made more rapacious by a decade of worsening economies, fewer jobs, and disruptive privatization coupled with an equally disruptive dependence on state controls? Bahktiyor no longer cared. "My biggest worry," he said, "is that I'll just stay here, which means I'll quit everything, just like everyone else. Many people here make every effort to continue their studies in America. They try and they fail, and they start drinking, they forget everything—all their plans, all those dreams of seeing Las Vegas one day, or going to the Avenue of the Stars. That's the biggest nightmare for me, because if I get to that, it means that I lost my hope."

I looked at the ground. Everything I wanted to say had in my mouth the hollow, disappointing feel of an empty piggy bank.

Bahktiyor shook his head. "This whole country is corrupt. They are all just sitting there, collecting money. And I think that the only solution to this would be to replace all those ministers and chiefs with young people. It's absurd, I know, but it's the only answer." His head tipped back to bathe in starlight. "You know what? I wanted to be an ambassador once. To serve my country. Now? No way." He looked at me evenly. "My entire life is fucked."

The next morning I learned that one did not approach Moynaq. Moynaq appeared. It did not appear as a mirage or a vision but with the same sudden shock of a shipwreck through krill-swirling brine or an overturned truck through a blizzard. From a distance it was not unpleasant. In fact, it had the enchanted smallness of a shire or valley-nestled village. Moynaq's close arrangement was no accident. Thirty years ago the entire town was surrounded by water—not to mention populated mostly by Russians—and anyone wishing to go to Moynaq had to employ a ferry to do so. Now it was engulfed in a dust storm. But it was not so dusty that I could not make out the twenty-foot-high sign that welcomed me to Moynaq. Painted upon the sign were a large fish and a seagull.

Moynaq had enjoyed several different guises. In the 1930s it was a virtual (though not, it was said, unpleasant) gulag—one of the very few benevolent places Stalin shipped enemies for whom he had a softer than usual spot in his normally sclerotic heart. In the 1960s it came into its own as a resort community for Soviet bureaucrats on holiday, and many enjoyed its beautiful beaches and unchangingly pleasant weather. In the 1980s the growing devastation endowed it with the competetive distinction of being one of the most difficult to penetrate places in the entire Soviet Union. What was Moynaq now? I was about to find out. We parked somewhere in town. I stumbled from the car, told Wegerdt and Bahktiyor that I would meet up with them later, and walked slowly through Moynaq's deserted streets. The level of ambient strangeness was so high that when I realized the horizon was on fire several moments gathered and dissolved before it occurred to me that this was worthy of note. "Horizon," I jotted. "On fire." I looked out upon huge mile-wide black blossoms of smoke bulbed orange-red at their fuming core. They were burning brush out in the former seabed. Dump trucks filled with brush. Why? No one was nearby to ask. I simply stared.

I had standing orders from Ian Small to visit Moynaq's museum, which he and his wife had almost single-handedly reinvigorated through their benefaction. I took the long way, prowling the former seaside. The still-lingering maritime feel of the place filled me with disquiet. A pretty, thatched fence surrounded each home I passed. The sand beneath my feet was soft beach sand redolent of sunstruck water and oily backs and Sidney Sheldon novels. One could see, even now, why Moynaq was once such a popular vacation site. The city's moribund airport used to accommodate fifty flights a day during the summer and spring. Now it was home to nothing more interesting than tumbleweeds and a rusty front gate that still bore the intaglio of a Soviet hammer and sickle.

Moynaq's bazaar, too, belonged not to the developing world but to the deteriorating one. Some generic chocolates, Uzbek cola, rows of unplucked fowl, and poignantly cast-off household wares (old shoes, teacups) lined the beaten tables. A fishwife with a mouthful of gold teeth held up for me a long and horrifically dry smoked carp. Where this carp had come from I had no idea. Nor did I want one. After the Aral Sea's fishing industry died, Moscow actually authorized numerous shipments of fish from the Caspian and Baltic seas to be delivered to Moynaq's canning plants. This went on for close to a decade. One admired the sentiment even as one could not comprehend the fantastically wasteful reasoning behind it.

Farther into dusty, flat Moynaq, I attracted a retinue of children. Child shoelessness seemed pandemic. Feet were so dirty and beaten they appeared almost cloven. Nearly all of these children seemed slightly deranged. Some blew raspberries at me, some shouted, some ran around me in fixated circles and ran off gobbling. Later, I was told that severe goiter, a common Moynaq malady, can, when suffered at an early age, lead to mild retardation. I stopped walking when I came to a half-constructed building near the middle of town. It was a large concrete gray block, its tic-tac-toe of windows as yet unglassed. A woman strolling by told me it would be a college. This, I thought, was optimism.

A few blocks from the museum a smiling, healthy-looking boy advanced upon me. "Hello!" I returned his salaam. He spoke a small, confident amount of English and was delighted when my biplane Uzbek took shaky flight. He was Kazakh. His name was Saghitjan. He had buckteeth, his tiny nose was densely freckled, and his eyes were shiny in the unknowable little-boy way that promised either malice or its utter absence. Despite the heat, he wore formal black slacks and a fuzzy maroon sweater. When I told Saghitjan he spoke English well, he said, "Yes, I do." He asked if I was a tourist. I told him I was a writer. Facial fireworks from Saghitjan. Would I write him a letter? Of course I would. I asked him if he liked Moynaq. He became preposterously thoughtful. "Yes," he said, "very much, despite its problems." Saghitjan looked around eight, perhaps nine years old. But I was not certain, so I asked. Saghitjan was fourteen. The distressed effort it took to hold my smile upon receipt of this information was, to say the least, significant.

He accompanied me to the museum. It was a large, teal-walled single room filled with a cube of limpid, warm sunlight. Saghitjan looked at the high ceiling, openmouthed. I asked if he had ever been here before. "Oh, yes," he said unconvincingly. A large mural on the farthest wall depicted a blissful Karakalpak family. Behind them was the sea, boats, seagulls. A huge, hand-painted aerial map of the Aral Sea next to the mural placed Moynaq happily on the sea's edge. I did not know what either intended to suggest. Outrage? Nostalgia? Nothing at all? Whatever the case, it was disturbing in the transporting way old propaganda was disturbing. I felt complicit, pointed at, negligent in preventing from happening that which had already happened.

One of the most puzzling aspects of the Aral Sea disaster was how it was able to deteriorate so rapidly while so little attention was paid to it. But in the end, not even the Soviets could hide a vanishing sea. In the comparatively permissive year of 1987 the Uzbek writer Maruf Jalil published an eyewitness article entitled "The Sea That Is Fleeing Its Shores." A number of Central Asian celebrities, including the Kyrgyz novelist Chinghiz Aitmatov, mobilized to fund a Save the Aral committee. The outcry grew, until the Politburo in Moscow was prepared to divert two Siberian rivers, the Ob and the Irtysh, toward the Aral Sea in order to restore it. This unbelievably bad idea was well under way when Mikhail Gorbachev canceled the scheme, having bowed to sensible pressure from Russian environmental groups and what many viewed as nakedly racist pressure from Slavic supremacists. (Islam Karimov tried as recently as 1995 to resurrect this proposed solution to the Aral Sea disaster.) While Moscow did scale back its demands for Central Asian cotton, it persisted in blaming the Uzbeks and Karakalpaks for "wasting" water. By 1990 the Save the Aral committee, after reviewing its three years of work, concluded that all had been for naught. Less than naught. The Aral Sea was still shrinking, despite the fact that forty organizations were now at work on the crisis. Amazingly, this had been the zenith of hope for Karakalpakistan.

Saghitjan and I lingered near the exhibits in the room's center. Thanks to Ian Small's donations, each item was indentified and described on a little placard in Russian, Karakalpak, and English. Saghitjan proudly told me that his English teacher had provided these translations. Together we looked at twenty-five-year-old tins of fish from Moynaq's old cannery. Shriveled carp in glass tubes. Model ships. Nets and fishing hooks of notable variety and ingenuousness. Animal skins, too, as the Aral Sea basin was at one time host to a thriving, now vaporized, muskrat-fur industry. Anchors. A cracked, carbon-datable butter churn exactly like the equally ancient yet still functional churn I saw, two days before, in a home in a nearby village. I felt a tidal whelm of despondency looking at these items, all laid out with such postmortem precision. Saghitjan looked at it, too, his eyes full of sparkling, empty engagement. All of this, I realized, meant nothing to him. The sea was now just a legend, dead before he had first teethed.

On the other side of the museum was a sign: PEOPLE, SAVE THE ARAL SEA! The sign was in English. Its chipped, flaking paint suggested that it was quite old, which it would have to have been, since "saving" the Aral Sea in any real sense was now completely impossible. Restoring the Aral Sea to its original volume (disregarding any notion of water quality) would require, according to one estimate, sealing off all the canals in Central Asia for ten years and allowing the sea's feeder rivers to take their original course. All that could be done, then, was to save some small part of Aral, as Kazakhstan was attempting to do with a decapitated northern part of the sea found within its borders. This was now known as "Little Aral." Fish had even been reintroduced there, with some success.

We found a wall of black-and-white photos hung on a mid-room partition. Saghitjan and I looked at water in photo after photo. In this place it was easy to forget that water, as a bulk phenomenon, still existed. Even black-and-white water seemed exquisite, primally wet. The fishermen in these photos smilingly held aloft nets bulging with their haul. Some photos seemed almost pornographic in their abundance of fish. Slowly, the photos seemed less sad than hubristic. Overfishing the Aral Sea was a problem long before the amphetamine of Soviet industrialization arrived. The Aral Sea was not a deep body of water. It was a desert sea, fragile by definition, as disastrously susceptible to heavy fishing as the League of Nations was to global war. What had these people expected?

An older English gentleman also visiting the museum sidled alongside me. "I'm not sure I approve of all this wallowing in nostalgia," he said. "I think I should prefer revolution." That he shared this with me a few moments after drawing my attention to a mistake on one of the placards ("fishing rods" where it should have read "fishing hooks") did not make me very willing to consider his point. But his point stood. In America police officers spend Super Bowl Sunday polishing their batons to wallop celebratory revelers, and large portions of our population find rioting a reasonable response to courtroom verdicts with which they disagree. Karakalpaks, on the other hand, are victims of some of the most untrammeled abuse in post-holocaust history. Why, then, do they not revolt?

Karakalpaks form slightly less than half of Karakalpakistan's population, with the remainder made up of Uzbeks and Kazakhs. Formerly a nomadic fishing people, Karakalpaks failed miserably to adapt to the forced urbanization the Soviets insisted upon throughout their empire. One sensed in most Karakalpaks a deeply riven consciousness. Here were nomads who were going nowhere, fishermen with nothing to catch. "Karakalpak" means "black hat people," and their cultural amnesia was so stark that the Karakalpaks had to fund a research project to determine what this "black hat" business referred to. But their culture was astonishingly old. Some scholars believe that the one-breasted Amazon warriors Alexander the Great famously refused to fight were Karakalpak. Despite its history-long denial of self-determination, a moody, independent-minded streak still existed in Karakalpakistan. Karakalpaks were famous within the USSR for their failure to take seriously much of its dogma. As some of the poorest and most rural people of the former Soviet Union, Karakalpaks still possessed the reflexive recalcitrance any American familiar with Appalachia or Michigan's Upper Peninsula would recognize. One young Karakalpak man told me that the cardinal difference between Uzbeks and Karakalpaks was that when an Uzbek was ordered to do something, he did it; when a Karakalpak was ordered to do something, he pretended to do it.

Today many Karakalpaks complained bitterly of Uzbek rule. But even though their constitution granted them the theoretical right to secede from Uzbekistan, no one spoke seriously of doing so. Such a tactic might allow the Karakalpaks to throw themselves at the fickle mercies of the international aid community, but it would also make them citizens of one of the most shattered countries on earth. And the Aral Sea was not their sole problem. In Soviet times Karakalpakistan served not only as a site for testing Le Chatelier's principle but as the piñata for some of the USSR's most wicked chemical and biological bastinados. In the middle of the Aral Sea, for instance, was Vozrozhdeniya (Rebirth) Island, on which, a British explorer was told in 1840, stood an enchanted castle guarded by dragons and surrounded by flaming quicksand. The Soviet Union gave its all to make these stories metaphorically accurate, operating on Vozrozhdeniya Island one of its most secret anthrax-manufacturing plants. This was the plant that the West first learned of in 1960, when Francis Gary Powers's U-2 spy plane glided over the Aral Sea and photographed the plant in high detail. This was also the plant that had been left unguarded for a decade following the Soviet collapse. The island's soil was still heavily inundated with vaccine-resistant anthrax the Soviets had bioengineered. Cows could now walk to and from the island. Any cow unlucky enough to chance this journey was, reportedly, shot on sight. The island's desperately needed cleanup was, according to the brisk Nukus rumor mill, being handled by the U.S. Department of State, a rumor officially confirmed in October 2001, when Uzbekistan became an official ally in America's war in Afghanistan. What Karakalpakistan was rapidly becoming in its modern, Finlandized Uzbek incarnation was a huge prison colony. It was estimated that 7,000 to 15,000 people, many of them religious Muslims, were currently detained in Karakalpakistan in inhuman prison camps the existence of which the Uzbek government was increasingly powerless to deny. One of the most infamous prisons was found just outside the town of Jaslyk, a few hundred miles west of the Aral Sea. Constructed by the Uzbek government in 1998 for the explicit purpose of containing the ballooning number of Muslims convicted of illegal religious activity, the Jaslyk prison camp was widely viewed as one of the most spectacular neoplasms upon an already tumor-ridden body politic. One Jaslyk inmate told his relatives, who later spoke to Human Rights Watch, that "the first month when we got here, they beat me all the time. They beat people to death. One man died in my arms. Several men have already died. Twenty men beat us with nightsticks." Many of Jaslyk's inmates were legitimate Wahhabis, no doubt. The rest were collateral damage.

But even as the Karakalpaks' culture, economy, spirit, and ecology have completely foundered, one encountered here very little social unrest. Sociologists tell us that nomadic people the world over have resiliently different psychologies compared to those, like the Uzbeks, who have been settled agriculturists for generations. But the stubborn, indomitable Karakalpak approach to life was difficult to square against the seemingly docile resignation with which they still regarded Soviet perfidy. Again and again, when I asked Karakalpaks if they were angry with the Soviets, they merely shrugged and said that at least in Soviet times they had jobs. Perhaps, deep in their collective consciousness, they were still perplexed by the higher administrative workings of urban society. Perhaps the legacy of the gulag has made social outrage impossible. Who, at any rate, would listen? They had been abused for so long. When Jenghiz Khan passed near Karakalpakistan in the thirteenth century, he destroyed all livestock and every granary and irrigation ditch, a tactic he called, approvingly, "killing the land." Having their homeland murdered by interlopers was a recurring Karakalpak nightmare.

343

Later that night, after dinner with Ian Small and his wife in their rented home near the former seashore, I strolled across Moynaq, sensing beneath its quiet exterior colliding tectonic plates of human despair. It was not uncommon to see at all hours on Moynaq's streets teenage boys and grown men devotedly accessing vodka's properties as a spiritual disinfectant. I walked past such teenagers on my way to watch some Karakalpak children play soccer in the former seabed. I stood there watching the sun get swallowed by a haze of twilit dust above whooping, pushing, laughing boys. Their soccer field was jagged with salt accumulations, but no one seemed to get hurt. After a while I stepped over to a low fence on the former seashore and watched two Karakalpak women bake bread in a large outdoor tandoori oven. We exchanged greetings, and I asked if I could watch. They smiled demurely and nodded. It was all very neighborly, almost suburban. The near night filled with a scent both light and yeasty and black and ashy. Once they had baked the first batch, they handed over to me three warm circular loaves. I protested, suddenly knowing that, to them, my desire to watch had made this offer inevitable. They would hear none of it. "Feed your children," they told me.

I walked on, down a narrow street, night falling quickly. To make good on the kindness of the women, I ate the bread greedily. Some small, hungry children emerged from the shadowy plinths of streetside darkness and tugged on my sleeve. I tore off little pieces and felt them pulled from my hand. The children then scrambled away. A short skullcapped man wearing a heavy, long chapon wobbled up to me. His face was rodential, his beard leprous. His blinks took seconds to transpire. He spoke. His slurred Russian would have been a mystery even to someone whose command of the language was more extensive than my hundred verbs and nouns. Finally, the man spat something about Islam Karimov and loped off. I would remember the word and later learn that the man had accused the president of Uzbekistan of pederasty.

There were no manic-depressives in Moynaq. No cutters. No self-made anorexics. No ADD. No workaholics. No anxiety disorders. No Prozac or Lithium. No twelve-step programs. No sex addicts. No learning disorders. Dysfunction saw far fewer special-interest fragmentations, and biblically old dramas like wife-beating and alcoholism and child abuse were its clearest manifestations. This is not to say that the above-mentioned disorders, all of which make metastatic the American specialties of leisure and pleasure, did not exist in Moynaq. Only that no one would have thought to diagnose them. It was as though Moynaq's populace existed in order to prove how much hunger, degradation, and disease a human body could stand without parting with its last glint of life. Misery had its own diagnostic purity around the Aral Sea.

But if one were not able to quantify misery here, one could certainly catalog the many varieties of Karakalpak denial. Urbane Dmitri from Nukus, for instance, thought nothing of allowing his house's leaky spigots to run all day. People washed their cars regularly. Canals kept getting dug. Cotton still grew where it could. Poor water management was rapidly leading the region toward total, endgame drought, and average Karakalpaks would not even discuss it, waving their hands or clutching their skulls whenever the topic was broached. But to think about one's portion of responsibility in draining the Aral Sea would mean that one would have to recognize it as a problem in which one had a meaningful role. Given the problem's gigantic nature, such recognition had the potential to make existence itself unendurable. How does one live with the biggest sword in the world held over one's head? Instead, many Karakalpaks chose to believe the old Soviet saw about the Aral Sea's historical tendency to wax and wane. They told me that the sea would return, eventually, that the ecology would improve, eventually, and Moynaq and Nukus would again come alive. Could one blame them for this failure to confront reality? The people of Karakalpakistan were faced with a prisoner's dilemma so dire that I, for one, could not. They had two choices. The first was to completely restructure their cotton-based monoculture and prevent all but certain future ecological and economic collapse. The problem with this was that the resultant turmoil would open the doors to some of the worst privation any society has intentionally brought upon itself. The second was to do nothing, to carry on, and watch the same malignant doors magically open themselves.

"Rise and shine," I heard the next morning. Sunlight gushed into my room, and I rolled over to see Ian Small standing next to my bed with his invincible smile. "Can I get you anything? Coffee? Paper? The *Times,* perhaps?"

"What time is it?" I asked.

"It's early! Really quite early. Some of my colleagues are coming up from Nukus today, and I thought you might want to get a look around before it got to be a zoo around here."

"What do you have in mind?" Across the room, in sleeping bags, lay Wegerdt and Bahktiyor. They were, I noticed, still asleep.

"Get dressed and find out," he said.

The road out of Moynaq and into the nonexistent sea was, like everything, covered with thick salty dust. I bounced around in the roomy stern of a blocky white Land Cruiser. The wind had a low constancy. Sometimes, when it caught the Land Cruiser just right, the wind came howling through the tiny slots and cracks in the frame and poorly sealed windows. Outside, along Moynaq's gradually depopulated streets, the wind whipped up a dirty miasma. Thin trees bent calisthenically. Children carrying pails walked backward, hands over their eyes, their tissuey white T-shirts blown tight against their backs.

The Land Cruiser reached the outermost edge of Moynaq. With a bump and momentary plunge it exited the town proper and entered what was, in living memory, the bed of the Aral Sea. Looking out the window quickly became an exercise in dislocation. Beyond the Land Cruiser's porthole was not reality but something purely conceptual. The Scene of the Greatest Ecological Crime in History. A land made alien by betrayal. Whatever its nature now, it was threatening and hostile. No human presence to reassure one here. This was off-planet, a place of low roads and poison flora. Moynaq was gone now, surely, fallen away from the husk of this world as though it were a space shuttle's rocket. I looked out the back window. Moynaq was a hundred yards away. Possibly less. Small wrenched around in his seat and looked at me. He smiled in a way that suggested everything but a smile. The Land Cruiser, I noticed, had stopped. "Ready to go boating?" he asked.

My feet came down on hard, crunchy soil that was, by far, the most chemically transmuted I had yet encountered in Karakalpakistan. My boots left no footprints. This was interesting, but not nearly as interesting as the huge beached trawler to my left. About the size of a baleen whale, this vessel had once been part of Moynaq's considerable armada of fishing boats. At their peak the Aral Sea's fishermen provided a tenth of the entire Soviet catch. In the 1920s their heroism and resolve helped save Russia from widespread famine. In Moynaq alone 10,000 fishermen plied their trade, a number more than triple its current population. Even if the Aral Sea were not more than an hour's drive away, the most determined angler would have found it impossible to eke out a merely miserable existence. Not a single fish, not even the fish that had been reintroduced into the sea as recently as last summer, survived. I studied the boat, its strangeness tearing through successive veils of disbelief. It was sun-blistered, gutted, encased in a shell of baked, flaky rust. The rust came in six different hues, the whole spectrum of oxidation. The boat was atop a high dune, its bow pushed out over the dune's edge as though recalling the weightlessness with which it once breached the Aral Sea's crests. Mote-speckled sunlight poured through the slots of its missing ribs.

I turned to see half a dozen other boats thirty yards away. From a distance they looked like alien technology, a desert-roaming flotilla of skiffs piloted by pirate mutants. I walked toward them atop a dirty white crystallized glaze of salt. Despite the condition of the soil, life, of a sort, had carried on. Growing from the seabed were hundreds of shrubby plants and small, evil-looking trees that looked conjured up from a terrifying children's book. One walked near them at one's peril, their grayish branches covered with long white hook-tipped thorns. Revenge plants, these were, the helpless counterstrike of a devastated ecosystem. Littering the ground were the Aral Sea disaster's *objets trouvé*. Chunks of cable, bits of fiberglass, mystery metal, rusty springs, cigarette butts. When the soil gave way to a boggy patch of mud (only here could mud and desert have existed side by side), I had to walk around a half-submerged propeller as high as my chest.

Small stood near one of the boats on a dune tonsured with gray-green vegetation, his hands plugged into his pockets. I joined him on the dune. "Do you mind if I smoke?" he asked, after having already burned his way through half a cigarette. I said I did not. We looked at a boat. Half of this boat, for some reason, bore a bright, newish coat of white paint. Small explained that this was the work of a Dutch film crew who arrived in Moynaq a few years ago to make a documentary. During the shoot someone decided to slap a fresh overlay of paint on the side they were filming. I could not fathom how, precisely, these Dutch filmmakers could have found Moynaq's naval graveyard dramatically or pictorially deficient. Small tamped out his cigarette and shook his head. "They promised the people of Moynaq they'd come back and show the film," he said, "but they didn't. People are still talking about that."

This was a topic of some sensitivity in the Aral Sea area. The people here suffered from many things, but perhaps none was more acute than visitor fatigue. From the plot of this emotional exhaustion an actual folk saying had sprouted: *If every scientist and journalist who visited the Aral Sea brought with them a bucket of water, the sea would be filled again.* Experts and journalists and the nuncios of international aid had been piloting their Land Cruisers through Moynaq for over a decade, and the area the desertified former seabed now occupied was larger than Massachusetts. Last year not a single drop of water from the Amu Darya reached the Aral Sea. Two-thirds of the Aral Sea basin's population was now considered, in the simplest medical terms, "sick or unwell." The people had been pummeled into reticence, regarding with indifference the ballpoint pens and tape recorders and television cameras of those who would view and document their decay. Their own doom was of no interest to them.

"I was interviewing this former fisherman," Small said suddenly, "who lives all of two hundred meters that way, and asked him, 'Where's your ship now?' He said, 'Out there, behind the tuberculosis dispensary.' I asked, 'Do you go out to see it sometimes?' He thought that was an absolutely bizarre question. His response was, 'Why would I?'" Small smiled yet again. "To him, there isn't any kind of romantic notion to these ships. This guy was working from five in the morning till nine at night. For him, it was a tool, and now that trade is gone. He's not going to cry over his tools."

Of course, this fisherman's boat did not belong to him but to the collective farms that dominated Soviet agriculture. It was a peculiar thing to stand here in one of the most obscure corners of the former Soviet empire. Socialism was not supposed to work like this. Never had a systematic way of thinking been nobler in theory and more destructive in practice. In 1918 Lenin used an Ovid quote, of all things, to inspire the Russian masses: "The golden age is coming; people will live without laws or punishment, doing of their own free will what is good and just." Gazing around, as close to Jerusalem as I was to Moscow, I wondered, suddenly, how anyone could have believed that any other result but this was possible. It was simply infeasible for decades of central planning to have succeeded in a nation as vast as the Soviet Union. As though one Gordian gnarl of Moscow bureaucrats might have ever been able to simultaneously provide for the Yakuts of the high arctic, the *flâneurs* of St. Petersburg, the Muslim tribal elders of Merv. And they knew it. They knew it.

Everyone did. How did this happen? Why did anyone allow it? As far as I knew, no one had ever explained why the reddest sort of Communism seemed able to beguile (with the exception of Cuba) only gigantic nations of huge topographical, philosophical, and ethnic variances such as the Soviet Union or China. Perhaps it thrived on the confusion such societies created.

We decided to visit another batch of grounded ships. The Land Cruiser rumbled far beyond the naval graveyard found at town's edge upon a well-traveled road lined with hundreds of year-old telephone poles. These poles provided power for the oil rigs drilling deep in the former seabed. It seemed that the withdrawal of the Aral Sea had led to the discovery of oil. Surely, I thought aloud, this will benefit the people of Moynaq. Actually, Small explained, oil is probably the worst thing that could have happened to Moynaq. In Kazakhstan the post-Soviet discovery of vast oil fields had done nothing to improve the lives of average Kazakhs. The Kazakh president, Nursultan Nazarbayev, believed in privatization so fervently that he privatized the entire petroleum industry to himself. Barring some unprecedented outgas of executive goodwill on the part of Islam Karimov, the discovery of oil near Moynaq would bring nothing to its people but the eerily beautiful diversion of watching the oil rigs flame off at night.

The landscape surrounding this road was huge, yellow, vacant as sky. It looked somehow microwaved. The farther we got from Moynaq, the more Blakean the terrain became. A stanza from "Holy Thursday" filled my suddenly cavernous mind: "And their sun does never shine. / And their fields are bleak & bare. / And their ways are fill'd with thorns. / It is eternal winter there." After a few miles' journey, we jackknifed off the road and jumped along an uneven tire-trenched path. The ships soon appeared. Five of them lay in a careless cluster among erosion-planed dunes. Another half-dozen ships were visible in the heat-distorted distance.

There were several separate batches of ships scattered around the former seabed. This batch had the sad distinction of being the farthest from Moynaq. For years after the sea abandoned Moynaq's shoreline, some of the town's more desperate fisherman dug numerous canals out to meet it. Each morning they patiently steered their ships down the narrow, brackish passageways. "Chasing the sea," they called it. In 1986, commonly regarded as the year in which the last of the Aral Sea's native fish expired, the ships were left more or less where they lay. I found I did not want to contemplate the long, difficult walk back to town these brave, deluded men had the day they realized everything was over.

"I remember when I first came out here," Small told me as we walked toward the stranded ships. "I was about to jump on a boat. But then my immediate reaction was, No, it must be hot-wired, or booby-trapped. That's the typical MSF context. Despite the fact that this place wasn't about war but environmental disaster, I was convinced that MSF needed to be here. Anyone who ever wondered if it was an appropriate MSF site had their mind changed quickly when I hauled them out here. The Aral Sea makes a very strong case for itself. It's a place that changes you. Cynics don't last long here. Some of the most powerful conversion experiences I've ever seen have happened around these ships."

"You said you're leaving Uzbekistan at the end of the summer, right?"

He nodded, his smile now a mere spasm of musculature. "I am. I am."

"So this is the last time you might ever come out here again."

"Thanks for reminding me!"

I gestured. "I just mean . . . how do you feel?"

Before he could answer, we came to a large boat half duned-over with sand. The boat's name, *Molodyozh* (Youth), peeled from its hull. I touched the hull and watched it crumble beneath my palm. I had peeled off a few large pulverous wafers of rust before realizing I could have dismantled the entire craft with little more than my thumb and index finger. We climbed atop another one of the ships. I gingerly kicked in the door to the captain's cabin. The narrow space held an ankle-deep accumulation of sand. It felt sarcophagal, not in the least how it had been engineered to feel: elevated and sheltered, the very heart of naval omniscience. The meters and gauges were filled with half-moons of sand. The porthole window was spidery with cracks. The walls were grotty with thick, corrosive rust. I placed my hand on the speed control, but it was frozen in place. Before I departed, I found in the sand a small broken teacup fragment. After some deliberation I left it there.

Small and I made our way to another batch of ships, hundreds of lizards scrambling beneath our feet. The sound was like mice in drywall, but worse. The lizards were gray-green, their heads as sleek as fingers. When they moved, their bodies stayed battened flat, but their tails somehow aggressively lifted. Their legs were so blurry they seemed powered by cold-blooded lightning. What was once one of the most interesting and diverse desert ecosystems in the world had devolved into a massive skink preserve.

We strolled along the high edge of a dry, gouged-out canal. The seashells I did not scoop up as morbid souvenirs crunched beneath our feet. Small fumed about the Bush administration's recent hedging over and ultimate miscarriage of the Kyoto Protocol, the world's first serious multilateral attempt to decelerate the processes of global warming. Small said he found it a complete failure of any notion of humanitarian law, of international law, of the conventions of the last hundred years. He said he found it shortsighted, even criminal. The impact of that decision, he said, was astounding. And yet the United States got away with it. I said nothing. He was right.

We neared another stranded ship. Unlike its more obviously forsaken sister ships, this one was parked, purposefully, across the desiccated canal. I turned. The ships behind us, including the ship in which I had just crawled around, were sitting in what looked to have once been this canal's shallow reservoir. I was looking, in short, at a naval parking lot. This boat was as wide and flat as a pontoon, bedecked with busted searchlights and pulpits. Why was it bestride the canal? Had the contrivances of time stranded it in such a fashion, or was it used to block the other boats in? If so, why? Violence had clearly been done to this boat. It had been scavenged, its bolts and rivets stripped out and the glass in its portholes punched free. The ship's large, rusty anchor had been heaved onto the canal's declivitous bank. The anchor looked like a parody of an anchor, the barb-tipped mirror-J that was affixed upon the caps of intoxicated yachters everywhere. It sat here in the dust like some sort of deeply unfunny exercise in visual incongruity.

Everything around me had the same pleading obscurity. What had happened here? What did these ships want to tell us? Was this the world's most potent symbol or merely local scrap? It meant everything, nothing. It meant there was still hope for those societies on the edge of environmental catastrophe, and it meant that all eventually came to rust. It meant that to remain ignorant of the Aral Sea disaster was to dodge deliberately its eschatological implications, and it meant that all the knowledge and attention in the world proved unable to save the Aral Sea. Small regarded the Aral Sea as "a fable of our time," and it was that, too.

Indeed, it held a fable's multitude of dark, simple, immutable meanings. No society can consume heedlessly and expect to survive. Finite environments cannot withstand infinite economic expansion. The world could be unevenly divided between those who diet and those who starve, those who gobble antidepressants and those who die of curable diseases such as tuberculosis. American affluence was no mere bystander to that division, and while responsibility and complicity differ in both degree and intention, they are born of the same moral surrender. "Maybe," Ian Small told me, "it's time. The Aral Sea's already dead. It's all about palliative care right now. Maybe it will be a blessing when it's finally gone, and it will just become this remote postdisaster place that once had a sea."

The sea was not coming back, nothing would improve, people like Small would continue their impossible triage, many Karakalpaks would continue to sicken and die until, one day, the Aral Sea would be spoken of in the doomed, sepulchral tones of Gomorrah, Pompeii, or one of *The Tempest*'s "still-vexed Bermudas." A luckless place where angry fates and unwitting human need saw their devastating concussion. It meant there was hope, but not here.

A mile out of town, atop a small hill overlooking the cliffs of Moynaq's former seashore, stands a small war memorial honoring the dead of World War Two, which is known in the former Soviet Union as the Great Patriotic War Against Fascism. The people of the former Soviet Union take their war memorials very seriously, as they should. Uzbekistan alone sacrificed around a million soldiers to defeat the man they know as Gitler. The dead this memorial honors gave their lives to end a war that only gave rise to another, colder struggle. Discounting its half-dozen proxy conflicts, its secret agents garroted in East Berlin basements, and its handful of obliterated spy-plane pilots, the Cold War's balance of terror is commonly thought to have ensured a confrontation without casualties. But cotton was grown to outfit the Soviet army in socks and trousers and T-shirts, to perpetuate the Cold War, to *win* the Cold War. And as with Afghanistan, another of the Cold War's hidden, long-quiet casualties, the full ramifications of the Aral Sea's destruction might not be apparent for years, perhaps decades. I look out over the cliffs, past the homes of people who have little worldly stake but that of their own well-being. What once must have been a lovely vista of foam-etched sea is now an empty yellow wilderness broken only by an occasional salt marsh. But it, too, is beautiful, terribly so. The wind sounds like waves. Everyone who came here remarked on that. But it does. A few seagulls circle overhead, altogether confused. Socks, I think. *Trousers*. In a few hours a party will begin at Ian Small's rented house. In a few days I will return to Tashkent. I do not want to leave. What is to be done? Listen to the wind blow.

Glossary

A word said is a shot fired.
—UZBEK PROVERB

ADVOKAT. Lawyer (Russian and Uzbek)

AMIR. Non-Islamic title with roots in the nomadic culture of tenth-century Central Asia; the only title Timur, for instance, could rightfully take, a source of lifelong frustration.

BACTRIA. Fifth-century B.C.E. Persian satrapy that covered modern-day Uzbekistan, Tajikistan, and Afghanistan; heavily influenced by Greek Hellenism

BASMACHI. Literally "bandits," the name for the anti-Soviet Central Asian resistance of the 1920s (Russian)

BLUE TURKS. Central Asian invaders from present-day Turkey; repulsed in 751 C.E.

CHAPON. Long, traditional, brightly colored thick outer coat (Uzbek)

CHILANZOR. Working-class neighborhood of Tashkent

CHOIKHANA. Literally "tearoom" (Uzbek)

CIS. Commonwealth of Independent States, used to denote the former Soviet Republics

COLLECTIVIZATION. Brutal, compulsory, and disastrous conversion of individually owned agricultural holdings into large collective farms that occurred in the Soviet Union in the 1930s

355

COMINTERN. Internal organization of Communist parties set up by Lenin in 1919 and abolished in 1943

DAEWOO. South Korean manufacturer of appliances and automobiles and active investor in Uzbekistan

DOPPA. Traditional, often embroidered four-cornered skullcap worn by Uzbek men (Uzbek)

ELITE. Term used by Central Asians for Central Asians employed by Russians as proxy rulers

EMIRATE. Traditionally, the kingdom ruled by an emir or amir

FARSI. Indo-European language spoken in Iran; Tajik is a dialect

GAP YOQ. Literally "talk not," used as the equivalent of "no problem" (Uzbek)

GAZLI SUV. Literally "water with gas"; carbonated water (Uzbek)

GIBREEL. The Islamic variant of the angel Gabriel

GREAT TERROR. Nineteen thirties period of most intense Soviet persecution and official lawlessness under Stalin

HAJJ. Pilgrimage to Mecca

HAKIM. Literally "wise one," the equivalent of mayor (Uzbek)

-ISTAN. Literally "place of," with *i* used prepositionally

IWAN. Vaulted hall opening onto a courtyard or room; when especially monumental, called a *pishtaq*

KETDIK. Literally "we left," used to mean "let's go" (Uzbek)

KHAN. Until the eighteenth century, royal title used by direct descendents of Jenghiz Khan

KHANATE. A kingdom controlled by a khan

KARAKHANID. Dynasty in Transoxiana from 840 to 1212 C.E., related to modern-day Turkic Uygurs of western China

KOMSOMOL. Communist organization for young people in the former Soviet Union

KORPUS MIRA. Peace Corps (Russian)

LADA. Boxy, badly made car used by many in former Soviet Union

MADRASA. School for study of Islamic law and thought

MAGAZIN. Quik Stop–type shop (Russian and Uzbek)

MALHALLYA. Neighborhood tribunal (Uzbek)

MANGIT. Uzbek dynasty of the khans of Bukhara from 1785 to 1921

MILITSIYA. Uzbekistan's military police (Russian and Uzbek)

MUEZZIN. Official who calls Muslims to prayer from minaret five times a day

MUFTI. Expert on Islamic religious law

MULLAH. Muslim cleric

NEXIA. "Lexus of Uzbekistan," made by Daewoo

NGO. Nongovernmental organization

NON. Bread (Uzbek)

NOSS. Tobacco snuff used by many Central Asian men (Uzbek)

OKTYABR. October (Russian)

OVIR. Part of the Uzbek Ministry of Foreign Affairs, hungover from Soviet times, that oversees foreigners' visas and registration

PERSIA. Empire that, at its height under Darius the Great in the sixth century B.C.E., stretched from the shores of the Mediterranean to the Indus River in modern-day Tibet; became Iran in the 1930s

POLITBURO. Formerly the Presidium, the policy-making committee of the governing Communist Party in the former Soviet Union

PISHTAQ. Monumental main entrance of mosque or madrasa

RED MULLAH. Popular name for Soviet-appointed clerics in Central Asian republics

SAMANID. Iranian dynasty in Transoxiana, parts of Persia, and Afghanistan, from 819 to 999

SELJUK. Turkish dynasty in Uzbekistan, Afghanistan, Persia, Iraq, Syria, and on the Arabian peninsula from 1038 to 1157

SEXTANT. Navigational instrument used to work out position of astral bodies

SHARIA. Islamic law

SHARQ. East (Uzbek)

SHASHLIK. Shish kebob (Russian and Uzbek)

SHAYBANID. Uzbek dynasty in Transoxiana and Afghanistan from 1500 to 1599; heavily influenced by Mongols

SHIA. Muslims who consider Ali, Mohammed's son-in-law, his only legitimate successor; also known as Shi'ite

SNB. The Uzbek successor to the KGB

SOGDIA. Fifth-century B.C.E. Persian satrapy located in what is today called the Ferghana Valley; heavily influenced by Greek Hellenism

SPANDREL. Generally, the area between two arches; can also in-fill partial domes

SSR. Soviet Socialist Republic

SUM. Pronounced *soom*, the Uzbek unit of currency

SUNNI. Muslims who accept the first four caliphs as Mohammed's only legitimate successors

TABAK. Tobacco (Russian)

TATARS. Descendants of the Mongol Golden Horde (and their Slavic subjects) who today live primarily in Serbia, Russia, and the Ukraine; emigrated into Central Asia, with tsar's encouragement, in the mid-1800s

TEFL. Teaching English as a foreign language

TICO. Small, inexpensive car made by Daewoo

TOM. Unfortunately for author, roof (Uzbek)

TRANSOXIANA. Literally "across the Oxus," generally considered the borders of modern-day Uzbekistan

TYMPANUM. Segmental space above a portal

WHITEBEARD. Respectful term used for old men in Central Asia

WHITE RUSSIAN. Russian who stayed loyal to the tsar after the Bolshevik Revolution

YOUNG PIONEERS. Ultrapolitical Soviet equivalent of the Boy Scouts.

ZOROASTRIANISM. Ancient Persian religion whose principal ingredients were fire and solar worship and a belief in an ongoing cosmic contest between a good supreme spirit and an evil supreme spirit

Bibliography
(Occasionally Fortified with
Thoughts Toward Recommended Reading)

*If you have nothing to tell us but that on the banks of
the Oxus and the Jaxartes, one barbarian has been succeeded by another, in what respect do you benefit the
public?*

—VOLTAIRE

AITMATOV, CHINGHIZ. *The Day Lasts More Than a Hundred Years.*
Translated by John French. Bloomington: Indiana University Press,
1988. If any novel has better addressed the unprecedented psychosis
of a country shooting people into space while its peasants are still
tilling fields with donkeys, I, for one, would like to read it.

ALEXIEVICH, SVETLANA. *Zinky Boys: Soviet Voices from the
Afghanistan War.* Translated by Julia and Robin Whitby. New York:
W. W. Norton, 1990. A truly heartrending oral history of "the Soviet
Vietnam." Very good at illuminating, in Russian soldiers' words, the
complications faced by the USSR in battling Muslims so close to its
own Islamicized borders. Ends with a grief-stricken, homemade
inscription on a slain Soviet soldier's tombstone: "Kozlov Andrei

Ivanovich (1961–1982) / Died in Afghanistan / My only son / Mama"

ALGAR, HAMID. *Wahhabism: A Critical Essay*. Oneonta, N.Y.: Islamic Publications International, 2002.

ALLWORTH, EDWARD A. *The Modern Uzbeks: From the Fourteenth Century to the Present, A Cultural History*. Stanford, Calif.: Hoover Institution Press, 1990. A brilliant book, especially valuable for its documentation of the rise of Uzbek identity and its intimacy with Uzbek literature.

"And It Was Hell All Over Again . . .": Torture in Uzbekistan. New York: Human Rights Watch, 2000. What United States policy will ultimately hold for Islam Karimov's regime, somehow our most important regional ally in the inertial ongoing war against terrorism, is currently and distressingly unclear. Although pressure from U.S. secretary of state Colin Powell and others has at last compelled Uzbekistan, by the middle of 2002, to allow several local Uzbek human rights groups to register with the government, one Uzbek human rights activist I spoke to in New York City in November 2001 told me, with quivering frustration, "The events of September 11 could play into the hands of Mr. Karimov. What we want most is for President Bush to control tightly the aid the U.S. gives the Karimov regime to avoid financing further repression. Really the worst thing that could happen is that American reliance on Uzbekistan in the war on terror will result in legitimizing Karimov's regime and increasing even further its arrogance."

ANDREW, CHRISTOPHER, WITH VASILI MITROKHIN. *The Sword and the Shield: The Mitrokhin Archive and the Secret History of the KGB*. New York: Basic Books, 1999.

ATHANASIOU, TOM. *Divided Planet: The Ecology of Rich and Poor*. Athens: University of Georgia Press, 1998. Impressively researched and only slightly hysterical. A must for Greens and anyone else looking to argumentatively slaughter self-satisfied conservatives.

At Home in the World: The Peace Corps Story. Washington, D.C.: Peace Corps, 1996.

BAILY, F. W. *Mission to Tashkent*. London: Oxford University Press, 1992. (Reprint of 1946 edition.) Memoir of Tashkent circa 1917 by one of the last, best players of the Great Game. Contains a gruesome account of the Bolshevik "orgy of revenge" that followed the 1919 anti-Soviet uprising in Tashkent, after which the blood froze into huge red puddles in the streets. Author is the kind of man who could write of Central Asia: "Many a British subaltern would have enjoyed this isolated but sporting post." Wonderful read but very dry in the telling, which is odd in that Baily, among other things, recounts how, while in disguise, he was once hired by the Bolshevik secret police to track down *himself*. Also reveals why the intelligent spy always carries two toothbrushes.

BOHR, ANNETTE. *Uzbekistan: Politics and Foreign Policy.* London: Royal Institute of International Affairs, 1998.

BOROVIK, ARTYOM. *The Hidden War: A Russian Journalist's Account of the Soviet War in Afghanistan.* New York: Grove Press, 1990.

BURNES, ALEXANDER. *Travels into Bokhara: Being an Account of a Journey from India to Cabool, Tartary, and Persia; Also, Narrative of a Voyage on the Indus, from the Sea to Lahore, with Presents from the King of England.* 3 vols. New Delhi: Asian Educational Services, 1992. (Reprint of the 1834 edition.)

BYRON, ROBERT. *The Road to Oxiana.* New York: Oxford University Press, 1937. For this reader's money, the greatest travel book ever written. Byron: young, British, unflappable, bizarrely learned in architecture. Details his overland trip from Jerusalem to Afghanistan in the early 1930s. Mostly, he looks at old buildings. Does not matter if one finds this the most boring scenario imaginable. Is not. Contains one brilliant moment after another: "A gentleman from the Municipality called this evening to know if I was comfortable. I admitted I should be more comfortable if the windows in my room had glass in them." Byron, tragically, was killed in World War II at the age of thirty-seven.

CHILD, GREG. *Over the Edge: The True Story of Four American Mountain Climbers' Kidnap and Escape in the Mountains of Central Asia.* New York: Villard, 2002. In the final chapters, find Child's convincing arguments that the four youthful American climbers were neither lying nor exaggerating about their ordeal after being taken hostage by the Islamic Movement of Uzbekistan in August 2000. The last scene—a reunion in a Kyrgyz prison between two of the climbers and their kidnapper, whom they believed they had killed by pushing over a cliff—chills with its many ambiguities. Though it is occasionally riveting, *Over the Edge*'s simplistic analysis seems pitched at an airport readership; its climber heroes, who learned nothing about Kyrgyzstan before traveling there, are, furthermore, often shallow and difficult to like. Child's grasp of Central Asia does not always inspire trust: "Few people in Central Asia, other than those in government or security positions, had heard of the IMU before [the Tashkent bombings]." No and no. And: "[T]he stubborn resistance of the Afghan mujaheddin [in the Afghan-Soviet war] deeply affected [Juma] Namangani; and he converted to Islam." This is a little like saying that an African decided to become black. And: "Uzbekistan's Islam Karimov tilted away from Islam despite its being the predominant religion of the country—and despite his name." Child, despite his name, is an adult, though you would not know it from sentences such as this.

CONQUEST, ROBERT. *The Great Terror: A Reassessment*. New York: Oxford University Press, 1990. Often cited as the single best book available on Stalinism's horrors and almost certainly is. This edition is an update of Conquest's earlier 1968 book of the same title, much reviled by the Left of the time, which uses recently declassified Soviet files to show that Conquest's earlier estimates of the Great Terror's victims fell short by millions. Gripping, wrist-slashing reading.

COUNCIL ON FOREIGN RELATIONS. *Calming the Ferghana Valley: Development and Dialogue in the Heart of Central Asia*. New York: Century Foundation Press, 1999.

CRITCHLOW, JAMES. *Nationalism in Uzbekistan: A Soviet Republic's Road to Sovereignty*. Boulder: Westview Press, 1991. In gasping need of a new edition or update, but compact, sternly written, and massively informative.

DAVIS, PAUL K. *The Encyclopedia of Invasions and Conquests*. New York: W. W. Norton, 1998.

EASTERBROOK, GREGG. *A Moment on the Earth: The Coming Age of Environmental Optimism*. New York: Penguin, 1995. In light of the subtitle, it is significant to note that this intermittently persuasive volume contains not one mention of the Aral Sea.

ELLIOT, JASON. *An Unexpected Light: Travels in Afghanistan*. New York: Picador, 1999.

ESPOSITO, JOHN L. *The Oxford History of Islam*. New York: Oxford University Press, 2000. Readers beware: Professor Esposito has been convincingly accused of playing down violent Islamists' influence, and of being a Wahhabi apologist.

FESHBACH, MURRAY, AND ALFRED FRIENDLY, JR. *Ecocide in the USSR: Health and Nature Under Siege.* New York: Basic Books, 1992. Slowly becoming a classic. Thorough and upsetting enough to require repeated naps while reading. Said by some to be too hard on Soviet medical system, which was not, it is said, all bad. The Soviets' horrific failings in the area of general practice, it is said, were often counterbalanced by excellence in very narrow specializations. Soviet eye surgeons, for example, were regarded as some of the world's best. (It is said.)

FRITZ, MARK. *Lost on Earth: Nomads of the New World.* New York: Routledge, 2000. Not concerned with Uzbekistan or Central Asia, but contains wonderful portraits of aid workers as Fritz compassionately details the plight of some of the planet's millions of recent refugees.

GLANTZ, MICHAEL H., EDITOR. *Creeping Environmental Problems and Sustainable Development in the Aral Sea Basin.* New York: Cambridge University Press, 1999.

GOGOL, NIKOLAI. *Dead Souls.* Translated by George Reavy. New York: W. W. Norton, 1985. As a Russian once said to me, "What Americans think Dostoyevsky tells them about Russia, Gogol actually does."

GRAU, LESTER W., AND MICHAEL A. GRESS, EDITORS. *The Soviet-Afghan War: How a Superpower Fought and Lost.* Lawrence: University Press of Kansas, 2002. Useful tonic to those who believe CIA assistance, especially its shoulder-fired air defense ("Stinger") missiles, was crucial in feeding the Soviet army the grapes of mujahedeen wrath. First Reagan war chest arrived in Afghanistan in 1986, seven years after the Soviet invasion. Despite rampant surety in the West that these 900 Stingers "won" the war, the number of helicopters the Soviet Union lost failed to rise significantly after 1986. What the Stingers did, according to this book's cache of newly declassified documents, was force a revision of Soviet aerial tactics—hardly the same thing as "winning" the war. The Soviets gave infinitely more weapons to the Viet Cong, and somehow I have yet to encounter a single authority who argues this is why we lost that equally tragic, equally misguided struggle.

GROUSSET, RENÉ. *The Empire of the Steppes: A History of Central Asia*. Translated by Naomi Walford. New Brunswick: Rutgers University Press, 1970.

GUHA, RAMACHANDRA. *Environmentalism: A Global History*. New York: Longman, 2000.

HATTSTEIN, MARKUS, AND PETER DELIUS, EDITORS. *Islam: Art and Architecture*. Cologne: Könemann, 1994. Massive (verified weight: 7.5 pounds) and beautiful book essential for anyone with an interest in Islamic art. Do not drop on foot.

HESSLER, PETER. *River Town: Two Years on the Yangtze*. New York: HarperCollins, 2001. Now, this Hessler fellow. He first went to Princeton and Oxford, joining the Peace Corps in his late twenties. This is, by most accounts, a far better age to enlist than while enthusiastically flooding the engines of one's early twenties. Hessler, at any rate, not only wrote and published a fat book about his Peace Corps experience; after his service he remained in China, where he now foreign-corresponds for various magazines, including *The New Yorker*. Anyone familiar with the Peace Corps knows his sort. He is incredibly smart, sensitive, eager, helpful, kind to others, acquires languages quickly, and forges amazingly intimate relationships with his students. The Peter Hessler in my group was a guy named Bo. I liked Bo immediately. I liked Bo immensely. That is the problem with these people. A fine and admirable book.

HOFFMAN, ELIZABETH COBBS. *All You Need Is Love: The Peace Corps and the Spirit of the 1960s*. Cambridge: Harvard University Press, 1998.

HOPKIRK, PETER. *Foreign Devils on the Silk Road*. Amherst: University of Massachusetts Press, 1980.

———. *The Great Game: The Struggle for Empire in Central Asia*. New York: Kodansha, 1994. (Reprint of 1990 edition.) Contains the most nightmarishly compelling narrative of England's disastrous misadventures in Afghanistan I have come across. A ripping yarn in every sense and Hopkirk's best book. A bit vulnerable on the ethnocultural front, however: Asians who trick Europeans are often described as "wily."

———. *Setting the East Ablaze: Lenin's Dream of an Empire in Asia*. New York: Kodansha, 1995. (Reprint of 1985 edition.)

JOLLY, ADAM, EDITOR. *Doing Business in Uzbekistan*. London: Kogan Page, 1998. Text of titular self-explanation. Underwritten by British-

American Tobacco, ABN-Amro, Coopers & Lybrand, and other Western firms navigating the shoals of Central Asia's young, unpredictable economy. First lines of book: "Uzbekistan is moving its way steadily but surely [*sic*] towards economic reform [*sic*]. The political environment is stable [*sic*] with the government adapting a gradual approach [*sic*] to macroeconomic stabilization [*sic*]. . . . As reforms bed into the political and economic culture [*sic*], the opportunities for investments look set to increase [*sic*]." Many of the book's corporate underwriters have, in the five years since its publication, pulled out of or reduced their presence in Uzbekistan.

KAPLAN, ROBERT D. *Eastward to Tartary: Travels in the Balkans, the Middle East, and the Caucasus.* New York: Random House, 2000.

————. *The Ends of the Earth: A Journey to the Frontiers of Anarchy.* New York: Vintage, 1997.

Karakalpakistan. Nukus: USSR Publications, Inc., 1984. Soviet-published photo book highlighting, among other things, Karakalpakistan's economic achievements. One section, titled "Industrial Karakalpakistan," features dozens of affectionate photos of Karakalpak tractors, tillers, power plants, train yards. One two-page spread treats the reader to nothing but cranes. Why?

KHAKIMOV, KAMRAN M. *Uzbek-English, English-Uzbek Dictionary.* New York: Hipprocrene Books, 1994.

KING, DAVID. *The Commissar Vanishes: The Falsification of Photographs and Art in Stalin's Russia.* New York: Metropolitan, 1997. Chilling illustrations of how the Soviet photographic record—and, thus, its collective memory—was suppressed, censored, and otherwise altered during the Stalin era.

LANDES, DAVID. *The Wealth and Poverty of Nations: Why Some Are So Rich and Some So Poor.* New York: W. W. Norton, 1999.

LEEBAERT, DEREK. *The Fifty-Year Wound: The True Price of America's Cold War Victory.* New York: Little, Brown, 2002. A magisterial and hypnotic account. Necessary reading for those who believe that (a) the 1950s were a swell, stress-free time for America, (b) Kennedy, as hawkish on Communism as any president ever, wanted to pull us out of Vietnam, and (c) CIA accomplishments outweigh its many, many disasters: "Already in 1958, for instance, [William F.] Buckley wrote in his *National Review* of an assassination attempt on [Indonesian dictator Achmed] Sukarno that had all the earmarks of a CIA operation—everyone was blown up except Sukarno." Final chapters argue that Reagan destroyed the Soviet Union—mostly by quoting American Reagan intimates.

LEWIS, BERNARD. *The Muslim Discovery of Europe*. New York: W. W. Norton, 1982.

LIFTIN, HILARY, AND KATE MONTGOMERY. *Dear Exile: The True Story of Two Friends Separated (for a Year) by an Ocean*. New York: Vintage, 1999.

MACLEAN, FITZROY. *To the Back of Beyond*. London: Jonathan Cape, 1974. An uncategorizable Central Asian classic. After a trip earlier in his lifetime, Maclean returned to Central Asia with special permission of Premier Khrushchev. Claims in his ninety-four-word foreword that he wrote the book "more or less" for "innocent amusement": the masterpiece as fillip. One rather gigantic "however," however, must be made. This concerns MacLean's occasional, understandable, but nevertheless unforgivable apings of various Soviet lines. For instance, after "an agreeable meal" with the Grand Mufti of Uzbekistan—a man bought and paid for by the Politburo, as Maclean well knew—we arrive at the happy conclusion that Islam is cheerfully tolerated by the Soviet authorities. Worse yet, Maclean disgracefully allows that there may be "some truth" to the charge of "bourgeois nationalism" that earned Faizullah ("You cannot eat cotton") Khojaev his summary sentence of nine grams of lead.

MACLEOD, CALUM, AND BRADLEY MAYHEW. *Uzbekistan: The Golden Road to Samarkand*. Hong Kong: Odyssey Publications, 1999. The best guidebook on Uzbekistan available. Land in Tashkent without it at your peril.

MANZ, BEATRICE FORBES. *The Rise and Rule of Tamerlane*. New York: Cambridge University Press, 1989. A long parenthetical aside deleted from Chapter Two: "We have just been heaved into the unavoidable briar patch one faces when writing about Central Asia. (It is not Tartar, but *Tatar*.) In very few literary-academic arenas is spelling such intellectual bloodsport. (It is not Tadjik, nor Tadzhik, but *Tajik*.) Seemingly every book about the region carries an apologetic note arguing the merits of its particular spelling style and usage. The scholar Beatrice Forbes Manz, in her preface to *The Rise and Rule of Tamerlane*, writes that by using modern Turkic transcription she has 'assumed' something called 'vowel harmony.' (It is not Caubul, nor

Cabool, but *Kabul,* just as it is neither Affgaunistan nor Avgau-nistaun—people really have referred to it as both—but *Afghanistan.*) I, for one, fail to understand the essential nature of the debate, even as I appreciate that the colonial British 'Hindoo' is simply not acceptable. (It is not Turcomen, nor Toorkmun, but *Turkmen.* It is not Kirghiz, nor Kirgiz, nor Qirghiz, but *Kyrgyz.*) Many of the weirder renderings of unfamiliar Central Asian names are nothing more than European misjudgments in transliteration, though there are also clearly Soviet spellings, which is a different matter alto-gether. (It is not Ozbeg, nor Ozbek, and especially not Oozbuck, but *Uzbek.*) But with their hypercorrect vowel harmonies some scholars are clearly indulging in bell hooks–style politico-typographical deliv-erance. Their care seems vaguely intended to shame those who have come before them. (It is *Jenghiz Khan,* not the apple-polishing Chingghiz Xon, not Genghis, not Voltaire's Gengis, and not Gib-bon's—rather odd—Zingis.) Systems do exist for transliteration, which is part of the problem: Systems exist. In transcribing Turkic words—to say nothing of the region's Mongol words, or Persian words, or even Russian words—one can consult three separate methodologies. What those who barricade themselves within such methodologies rarely say is this: *These are transliterations from alphabets that have sounds English was never meant to accommo-date.* It seems to me that by any practical definition one 'system' can be no more correct than any other. I happily admit that I have no consistent lodestar guiding my transliteration other than a reliance upon my own inexpert sense of what sounds the most accurate and looks the least obtrusive. (I accept that Bohkoro is probably the most 'correct,' but I cannot use Bohkoro because I find it inexplicably annoying. Since I am not able to turn to Bocara and certainly not to Boghara, I must fall back upon out-of-fashion Russian-style *Bukhara.* And it is *Samarkand,* not Samarqand. Whose idea was that? Finally, I do not care what the Uzbeks want: *Tashkent,* not Toshkent.) Only English speakers would agonize over something like this. One doubts that China, for instance, has ever been rocked by debates as how best to transliterate George, Andrew, or Grover."

MEYER, KARL E., AND SHAREEN BLAIR BRYSAC. *Tournament of Shad-ows: The Great Game and the Race for Empire in Central Asia.* Washington, D.C.: Counterpoint, 1999.

NABOKOV, VLADIMIR. *Bend Sinister*. New York: Vintage, 1990. (Reprint of 1947 edition.) Nabokov's first novel written while living in America and his most overtly political. Quite possibly his most underrated. Chillingly invents own crypto-Soviet world, complete with its own philosophy, "Ekwilism," and its own movement, the Party of the Average Man. Best last two pages I have ever read.

————. *Strong Opinions*. New York: Vintage, 1990. (Reprint of 1973 edition.) Find here Nabokov's hilarious, mean-spirited mocking of Russian-language pretenders, including Edmund Wilson, who found clerky fault with Nabokov's famously literal translation of Pushkin's *Eugene Onegin*. A typical riposte: "'Why,' asks Mr. Wilson, 'should Nabokov call the word *netu* an old-fashioned and dialect form of *net*. It is in constant colloquial use and what I find one usually gets for an answer when one asks for some book in the Soviet bookstore in New York.' Mr. Wilson [N. replies] has mistaken the common colloquial *netu* which means 'there is not,' 'we do not have it,' etc., for the obsolete *netu* which he has never heard and which as I explain in my note to Three: III: 12, is a form of *net* in the sense of 'not so' (the opposite of 'yes'). . . . No wonder he did not get it." (Wilson's book, N. means.)

NEWBY, ERIC. *A Short Walk in the Hindu Kush*. Melbourne: Lonely Planet Publications, 1998. (Reprint of 1958 edition.) One of few travel books that can be said to open in the world of London fashion and conclude in northeastern Afghanistan.

OLCOTT, MARTHA BRILL. *The Kazakhs*. Stanford, Calif.: Hoover Institution Press, 1995. Like Allworth's book on the Uzbeks—also published in Hoover Press's admirable "Studies of Nationalities" series—a fascinating account of a great people by one of the true eminences of Central Asia studies.

PACKER, GEORGE. *The Village of Waiting*. New York: Farrar, Straus & Giroux, 2001. (Reprint of 1988 edition.) A Peace Corps and travel-writing classic.

PIPES, RICHARD. *The Russian Revolution*. New York: Knopf, 1990. Shattering, encyclopedic, unforgettable.

POLO, MARCO. *The Travels of Marco Polo*. Edited by Ronald Latham. New York: Penguin, 1958.

PRESS, IAN. *Learn Russian*. London: Duckworth, 2000. Or, in my case, try and fail.

Bibliography

RASHID, AHMED. *Jihad: The Rise of Militant Islam in Central Asia.* New Haven: Yale University Press, 2002.

———. *Taliban: Militant Islam, Oil, and Fundamentalism in Central Asia.* New Haven: Yale University Press, 2001. I did, incidentally, make it into Afghanistan in December 2001 and initially included an Afghanistan chapter in this book. It was cut to preserve some measure of narrative focus. Interested readers can read my dispatch at worldhum.com. (The magazine responsible for sending me to Afghanistan ultimately declined to publish my piece, for reasons too circuitous and enraging to get into here.) That said, *Taliban* provides readers with the most thorough, interesting, and intimate account of the Taliban's rise to power, which had and has, as the world now knows, massive geopolitical implications, especially for the people of the former Soviet republics. Demands to be read by anyone interested in Central Asia, though readers should be aware that Rashid has been accused, with some basis, of nursing an anti-Uzbek bias.

REMNICK, DAVID. *Lenin's Tomb: The Last Days of the Soviet Empire.* New York: Vintage, 1994.

———. *Resurrection: The Struggle for a New Russia.* New York: Vintage, 1998.

ROY, OLIVER. *The New Central Asia: The Creation of Nations.* New York: New York University Press, 2000.

SAGDEEV, ROALD, AND SUSAN EISENHOWER, EDITORS. *Islam and Central Asia: An Enduring Legacy or an Evolving Threat?* Washington, D.C.: Center for Political and Strategic Studies, 2000. An uncommonly fascinating collection of essays by Central Asian scholars, analysts, journalists, and religious figures, including Archbishop Vladimir of the Orthodox Diocese of Bishkek and All Central Asia, who writes, movingly, of Central Asia's long history of friendly Christian-Muslim relations: "During Stalin's purges, thousands of Orthodox priests, monks, and nuns were exiled or fled to Central Asia. . . . You only have to visit Botkin Cemetery in Tashkent to realize how many members of the Orthodox clergy have found everlasting peace in this kindly soil. There were many cases of Muslims hiding Russian clergymen. . . . To quote the Scriptures, the Muslims are good neighbors for they 'showed mercy' on us (Luke 10:37)." As for Central Asia's recent influx of Protestant and neo-Islamic missionaries, Father Vladimir notes: "The peoples of Central Asia have been practicing Islam for thirteen centuries, and the ancestors of our Slavic community adopted Orthodox Christianity more than a thousand years ago. . . . What are we supposed to learn from these unwelcome guests who know nothing about our customs, traditions, history, and who do not respect our religious beliefs?" Amen, Father.

SAID, EDWARD W. *Covering Islam: How the Media and the Experts Determine How We See the Rest of the World*. New York: Pantheon, 1981.

SMITH, HEDRICK. *The New Russians*. New York: Avon, 1991. Considerably about non-Russians, though, a semantic problem Smith acknowledges (not very well) on page xi. Wonderful portraits of Gorbachev and Yeltsin (who as a young man, we learn, blew off the fingers of one of his hands with a grenade he had stolen) and brilliantly anecdotal on Russian psychology.

SOLZHENITSYN, ALEKSANDR. *Cancer Ward*. Translated by Nicolas Bethell and David Burg. New York: Farrar, Straus & Giroux, 1991. (Reprint of 1974 edition.)

———. *The Gulag Archipelago: 1918–1956: An Experiment in Literary Investigation*. Volume One. Translated by Thomas P. Whitney. Boulder: Westview Press, 1998. (Reprint of 1973 edition.)

SOUCEK, SVAT. *A History of Inner Asia*. New York: Cambridge University Press, 2000.

TAYLER, JEFFREY. *Siberian Dawn: A Journey Across the New Russia*. St. Paul: Ruminator Books, 1999.

TERZANI, TIZIANO. *Goodnight, Mr. Lenin: A Journey Through the End of the Soviet Empire*. Translated by Joan Krakover Hall. Philadelphia: Trans-Atlantic Publications, 1994. Informative, if slightly irritating, account of an Italian journalist's journey through the provinces, including Central Asia, as the Soviet Union went to pieces.

THUBRON, COLIN. *The Lost Heart of Asia*. New York: HarperCollins, 1994.

VISSON, LYNN. *The Art of Uzbek Cooking*. New York: Hippocrene Books, 1999. Contains some very good plov recipes.

WHEEN, FRANCIS. *Karl Marx: A Life*. New York: W. W. Norton, 1999.

WIMMEL, KENNETH. *The Alluring Target: In Search of the Secrets of Central Asia*. Palo Alto, Calif.: Trackless Sands Press, 1996.

Index

Index

About the Author

Tom Bissell was born in 1974 in Escanaba, Michigan, and attended its Catholic and public schools. After graduating from Michigan State University he taught English in the former Soviet republic of Uzbekistan. He returned stateside and worked for several years in book publishing, first for W. W. Norton and later for Henry Holt & Company. Among his editorial endeavors were the restoration to print of Paula Fox's novels and editing her memoir *Borrowed Finery,* conceiving and editing *The Collected Stories of Richard Yates,* and conceiving *A Galaxy Not So Far Away: Writers and Artists on Twenty-five Years of* Star Wars. His criticism, fiction, and journalism have appeared in *Agni,* the *Alaska Quarterly Review,* the *Believer, BOMB,* the *Boston Review, Esquire, Harper's Magazine, McSweeney's, Men's Journal,* and *Salon.* A collection of his short stories will be published by Pantheon next year. He lives in New York City.